T0339793

WINDOWS ON JAPAN

WINDOWS ON JAPAN

A WALK THROUGH PLACE AND PERCEPTION

Bruce Roscoe

Algora Publishing
New York

© 2007 by Algora Publishing.
All Rights Reserved
www.algora.com

No portion of this book (beyond what is permitted by
Sections 107 or 108 of the United States Copyright Act of 1976)
may be reproduced by any process, stored in a retrieval system,
or transmitted in any form, or by any means, without the
express written permission of the publisher.
ISBN-13: 978-0-87586-491-4 (trade paper)
ISBN-13: 978-0-87586-492-1 (hard cover)
ISBN-13: 978-0-87586-493-8 (ebook)

Library of Congress Cataloging-in-Publication Data —

Roscoe, Bruce.
    Windows on Japan : a walk through place and perception / Bruce Roscoe.
        p. cm.
    Includes bibliographical references and index.
    ISBN 978-0-87586-491-4 (trade paper: alk. paper) — ISBN 978-0-87586-492-1 (hard
cover: alk. paper) — ISBN 978-0-87586-493-8 (ebook) 1. Japan—Description and travel. 2.
Roscoe, Bruce—Travel—Japan. I. Title.

    DS812.R67 2007
    952.04—dc22

                        2007009087

Printed in the United States

for Matthew and Owen
— may we always find home in both countries

Maps

Photographs

TABLE OF CONTENTS

PREFACE

I walked across Japan to thread old and new observations into a fabric of understanding of the past and present. Seeking a view of the interior, I chose a route that connects the ports of Niigata and Yokohama on opposite coasts of the main island of Honshū. Ports are windows and from them we can consider our perception of people and place.

This book is intended for intellectually curious travelers and those interested in Japanese culture, environment, history, language, literature, politics, and the problem of racial perception and the memory of war. It doesn't seek to introduce tourist markers and my walk was not an athletic feat.

Why not take a train or a bus, people asked. Trains reach their destinations too quickly, and the concrete-walled elevated highways used by inter-city buses deprive passengers of informing views, whereas walking allows the panorama to permeate the senses, and concentrates and clarifies thought, thus exercising the mind.

Japan treads uncertainly in the world. More troubling is the course it follows within its borders. Was it true that this once picturesque country had nearly concreted and dammed itself to death? Was it theme-parking itself? At a measured pace, I wanted to see for myself.

But I wasn't searching for a "real" or "lost" Japan, as in Alan Booth's *Looking for the Lost — Journeys Through a Vanishing Japan*, Alex Kerr's *Lost Japan*, Lesley Downer's *On the Narrow Road — Journey into a Lost Japan*, or J.D. Brown's *The Sudden Disappearance of Japan*.

Some observers decry the Gilbert and Sullivan-era imagery of fans and screens, then record their heartbreak at not finding vestiges of those symbols after conducting the most exhaustive of searches. In some cases, the searches all but consume their lives, but the same time could be spent looking for the last cowboy in Wyoming. We can't expect to find a past that Japan doesn't preserve, though it preserves the spirit of being Japanese.

Japan leaves discordant impressions. I trawled the works of writers as different as sushi and soufflé — from Jonathan Swift to Oscar Wilde, Jack Kerouac, Shirley MacLaine and Paul Theroux — to try to understand why. Their perceptions teach, stimulate, satisfy, please, and disappoint so much. I discuss their writing in chapters which I alternate with those of my travel, as we journey through perception as well as place.

I've added vignettes of recollection and contemplation, and I provide some data not as scholarship but as a springboard for more disciplined inquiry that readers may wish to make. I discuss the influence of Japan in popular song and receive advice on becoming a Japanese. The chapters on language consider how English borrowings from Japanese affect Western thinking and the danger inherent in Japanese saturating their language with English. These chapters, too, I alternate with those of physical travel, as our journey deepens.

In the chapters "The uncountable dead" and "Featherston" this book also explores war-tinged perceptions that shadowed me as I grew up. They are a part of my journey, and I couldn't rest without writing them.

At first I tried to avoid the subject of the Pacific War, seeing it as a slow-working poison, but the more I read and considered, the more I realized that it can't be skirted. Though wars define human history, the experience of that particular war still colors and controls relations with Japan. The empire that Japan attempted to create was comparable in area and audacity to that of the Mongols. Some of the killing today would be termed "ethnic cleansing." The US response of "burning the paper houses" was biblical. People are still coming to terms with this.

I could see in faces the psychological debris of that war as I walked. A war may end on a particular day in history but people who fought or were affected register a personal ending in their own time. For many that time is yet to come.

Visitors to Japan sometimes say that the people are becoming more Westernized. Youth are less tied to tradition, they add. But the opposite is more apparent — Japanese are proud and possessive of their indigenous identity. They are perhaps becoming more so, as Internet-age togetherness amplifies rather than dissipates differences. They wear tradition as tightly as a wetsuit.

There are two Japans, or three if one views Tokyo as a beginning and an end. The trading entity that reaches the ends of the earth, converses in most languages and understands most customs, and is perceptive and urbane, is one, and none appears more capable or cosmopolitan.

Yet the individuals alone seem weak and insecure. They inhabit the second country through which I walked. They take refuge in their language as a private habitat, resent intrusions, and are captured by a cultural particularism that distances if not separates them from the mores — some say morality — of others.

They still suffer — more than they realize or care to admit — from the legacy of the Tokugawa shoguns whose isolationist policies created a time warp of two centuries, with calamitous result in the 20th century. They still speak in terms of *sekai to Nihon* — "Japan and the world," as though they are apart from, not a part of, the world.

I propose no "theory of the Japanese" and accept none. The proponents of *nihonjin ron* appear to share the desk of the early ethnographic skull measurers. Unsettled that little may separate a people from themselves, they do their utmost using their "science" to prove differences that finally a child will see as imagined.

After traveling through a place and talking to a few people, I don't pretend to understand it, and "understanding" a place isn't the purpose of visiting it. After the passage of 30 years, I'm only beginning to "understand" my hometown of a few thousand people.

Travel stimulates an awareness of self that makes possible a deeper awareness of others. Seeing ourselves in the mirror others hold to us is the beginning. When they in the exchange see more deeply into their own selves, we widen and enrich our world. It's the beginning of the homecoming, because then we can turn back, more certain of who we are.

Walking down the Niigata Plain, across the mountain range that divides Honshū, then through the Kantō Plain to Tokyo and Yokohama took only a few weeks, but my journey had begun years earlier. From language student to journalist and corporate researcher, and father of two whose first language was Japanese, Japan had become the largest part of my life.

Before I set out, no one had made calls on my behalf and I carried no cards of business identification. Paths are cleared and carpeted for visitors who are received by invitation. But I would arrive on doorsteps unannounced. This was a test. Later I returned by bullet train to some of the towns on my route. I wanted to meet some people again. For all the value of first impressions, I sought second and third encounters. I still seek them.

Notes on music — that life language that requires no simultaneous interpreter, the music that Japan hears, the music that's written for meaning, and jazz, that most international of media that includes us in its conversations and which some Japanese embrace — accompany the narrative.

My fabric of understanding doesn't stretch to the future. Japan, unchanging though it is, mutates too quickly for that. I've noted every road I took so that walkers can take the same route if they wish. Though the route is far from scenic, there's much to gain from proceeding slowly. Time isn't lost but found.

A NOTE ON STYLE

Consistency and common sense aren't compatible when rendering Japanese names and proper nouns into English, and little uniformity of standard is found in Japan. I use mostly English convention.

Japanese names are presented first name followed by the surname, except in the case of historical figures who are universally known by their surnames. I italicize Japanese words for the first mention, then use Roman type. A list of Japanese words that the Concise Oxford Dictionary accepts as English, such as "shogun," precedes the bibliography. I haven't italicized any of these.

To avoid repetition I write Uono River, not Uonogawa River; Bandai Bridge, not Bandaibashi Bridge; and Mt. Kanashiro, not Mt. Kanashiroyama. But for temples, I include *ji* (temple) as part of the name.

Measurements are given in the standard of the country referenced, and metric or imperial equivalents are supplied in brackets. The yen is converted into US dollars at the rate of ¥120 per dollar. All dollar values are US dollars.

When discussing resident foreigners, Korean means those affiliated with the South or North.

I've used macrons to distinguish long vowels in translated Japanese words, including people's and place names, but not for Japanese words which have become accepted as English or for foreign loan-words written in katakana script. As with most rules, this one requires exceptions for the sake of sense, so I haven't used macrons for such universally recognizable city names as Kobe, Kyoto, Osaka, and Tokyo.

HISTORICAL PERIODS

Edo or Yedo is the old name for Tokyo. The Edo era, from 1600–1868, marks the end of the feudal age. The shogunate was the government of the shogun, and shoguns or military governors ruled for 600 or so years until the emperor was restored to power in 1868, ushering in the era of Meiji. This was followed by the eras, or imperial reigns, of Taishō (1912–1926), Shōwa (1926–1989), and Heisei (1989–).

ACKNOWLEDGEMENTS

I thank Naoko Hanaoka, Kenji Kōketsu, and Yūko Nakashima for advice, and Adrienne Alton-Lee, Noriko Murata, Donald Richie, and Charles Smith for reading and suggestions. I must own any mistakes.

CHAPTER 1. A NIGHT IN NIIGATA

The last of the snow had been cleared from the roads and summer would soon burn the heels of an early spring. The air still cool, now was the time to walk across the country I doubted and loved.

Rude east-coasters label this area west of the mountain range that divides the main island of Honshū as *ura-Nippon* — the "other side" or "back" of Japan. The division resembles the split of most Japanese towns and suburbs into "right" and "wrong" sides of the railway tracks that dissect them.

Unlike the eastern seaboard and its megalopolis of Tokyo and Yokohama that face the Pacific Ocean and the warm, fashionable Hawaii and California, Japan's other side and its largest city of Niigata look seaward to Russia and China. At latitude 37.54 degrees north and longitude 139.04 degrees east — north of the equator, east of London — Niigata lies roughly equidistant between San Francisco and Syria.

The world would be as familiar with the name Niigata as it is with Hiroshima or Nagasaki had the weather in the first week of August 1945 been different. Niigata was one of four cities selected by the US for atomic bombing. But the first clear day in August would belong to Hiroshima, and weather conditions favored Nagasaki over either Niigata or Kokura.

Niigata dates to the time of Christ. It traces its history to the first century from the study of ancient documents about legal codes. Though the beginning of the road for me, it has been the end of the road for Japanese who, having fallen from grace but whose stature precluded assassination or execution, were exiled to the island of Sado off the Niigata coast.

Emperor Juntoku (1197–1242) was banished to Sado for opposing the Kamakura shogun. So was Nichiren (1222–82), founder of the Buddhist sect of the same name, for his condemnation of different sects. This port city was the last of regular Japanese life that these nonconformists would see.

5

Niigata Station steps delivered me into a square where, taking my bearings, I sighted two young suited Western men. Their short, combed, lightly oiled hair spelled missionary, and I surmised Mormon — because they were a pair — which they turned out to be. They wore name badges. They told me that as graduates they had drawn Japan as the destination for their compulsory missionary work.

They established common ground, saying the latest edition of their magazine *Ensign* contained an article about Mormon work in New Zealand. They were excited and entranced by their surroundings. I envied them their ivory-white, unstained teeth, a tangible benefit of abstaining from tea, coffee, and tobacco. They may view individuals as potential divinities, baptize the dead, descend from polygamists, and site the Garden of Eden in Missouri, but their teeth are immaculate.

They could read road signs, and I'd overheard them conversing in Japanese at an information center near the station before I talked to them. Doors would be closed in their faces for the next two years but the rejection would strengthen them. They proselytized to reinforce their faith. After their mission, most likely they would return to the US but some missionaries stay and occupy positions in business and their church.

Police call their post outside the station "Koban," in English — not "Police" in English or *kōban* in Japanese. Perhaps they believe that the word koban has entered the English language. It hasn't, but one can imagine that one day it might.

Lightly-staffed police boxes are positioned throughout suburbs and near railway stations as a neighborly complement to central city police stations. The boxes display finely detailed residential maps and public notices. The arm of this law is long, stretching into even small neighborhoods. Such a penetrating police presence makes it hard for criminals to hide, easy for citizens to inform, and easy for police to help passersby with directions.

Critics worry that the boxes give the state a fisheye lens through which to monitor residents. They probably do, but it's a trade-off for security. I feel safer for the presence of the police and believe that their frequent interaction with residents wins trust.

Visiting foreign police officials often research the police-box system. They seem to conclude that as much as they would like to set up something similar at home, they can't for fear that such lightly-defended police boxes would be easy targets for arsonists or gangs. Instead, they barricade themselves in bulletproof garrisons downtown and talk to each other inside.

Police boxes trace their history to guard houses that neighborhoods maintained at their gates in feudal times. The community appointed guards to monitor comings and goings and enforce curfews. In Edo the curfew was 10 p.m.

Moneylenders' cynical signs — Aifuru (Aiful Corp.), Puromisu (Promise Co.), Takefuji Yen Shop (Takefuji Corp.) — glared down from soul-stripped, pencil buildings to the right of the station. Kyasshingu (Cashing) and Yuaazu (Yours) marauded nearby. If every station has a loan shark and a McDonald's, it also has a Nova English school, and Niigata's Nova menu included Chinese, French, German, Italian, and Spanish. Nova graduates perhaps could practice their pronunciation at the General Electric-owned Lake cash shop in the same building.

I wanted to meet people. Like my destination of Yokohama, Niigata as a port city would be home to jazz clubs, even on this coast, and a trio of acoustic bass, piano and drums would draw like-minded souls. A horn section would be a bonus, but unlikely. I'd put up with cigarette smoke while fighting a dormant desire to light up. It was taking years for my blood to free itself of the pull of nicotine, which seemed an everlasting cruelty of the addiction.

A young woman at the information center politely contained her smile when she heard my request for directions to a jazz club, which I had to repeat. Soon enough she found advertisements for two clubs, Jazz Mama and Paltia, in a brochure of local restaurants and bars, and photocopied the pages for me. Now I needed a place to stay.

Reservations tie you to a schedule, so I'd made none. I'd try my luck at a *minshuku* — small inns or private homes that set rooms aside for travelers and provide breakfast and dinner, or a ryokan — larger inns that also provide meals, or a *bijinesu hoteru* — "business hotels" that offer small rooms but no meals.

My edition of Lonely Planet's *Japan* guide suggested Ryokan Takeya. Rooms were described as basic and a single cost ¥4,300 ($36; this isn't Tokyo). *Lonely Planet* warned that "most Japanese-style accommodation is far from the station and reputedly unwelcoming to foreigners," but Takeya was just a few minutes' walk from the station's Bandai Exit.

Takeya's address turned out to be an empty lot but *Lonely Planet's* map was accurate enough. The ryokan had been demolished and a new hotel planned in its place, a receptionist at nearby business hotel Green told me. Green Hotel was clean, the staff pleasant, so I looked no further.

A Japanese or Western breakfast was served in the lobby dining room for a charge of ¥800 ($6.70), the receptionist said with understated, polished persuasiveness. Tired, welcomed travelers succumb to this, and so did I, feeling obligation. Ample coffee-shop breakfasts were available near the station for half the amount, but as a treat on the first morning of my walk I ordered a Japanese breakfast.

After leaving my pack in a small but adequate room — comfortable except for a single mat-shallow pillow — I set out to find jazz club Paltia. The club's number was no longer in use, a tape-recorded message said, but that may have meant that the number had changed, not necessarily that the club had moved.

I chose Paltia as the name Jazz Mama was off-putting and the brochure boasted that Miles Davis' signature was on a Paltia wall. The famed jazz trumpeter had several times performed in Tokyo and his touring schedule probably would have included Yokohama and Osaka, but surely not this outpost on the Japan Sea coast. Curiosity sparked, I would learn the truth.

To reach Paltia, I crossed Bandai Bridge over the Shinano River and located Jibun Bldg., at 8-1506 Furumachi Ave. It took 40 minutes to reach the building within the canopied Furumachi arcade but Paltia wasn't among the nameplates. I asked at a drapery and then at a sushi restaurant, but the draper didn't know and a young sushi chef, frenetically preparing for evening diners, didn't want to break the rhythm of his knife.

Along the way retail stockbroker signs jarred my senses. Two had slipped English words into their name. The "Friend" and the "Cordial" were new in Sakura Furendo (Friend) Shōken, and Nikkō Koodiaru (Cordial) Shōken. The brokers were trying to entice individuals back into a stock market that had lost three-quarters of its value in 12 years — "Trust us, we're your friend;" "You've lost your savings, but our relations are cordial," they seemed to say.

Individual investors here usually are the last on the elevator operated by stockbrokers. They are needed to buy stock from a life insurer or other favored institutional investor, who had bought and profited and was stepping off the elevator. Individuals, who often are spurred into buying stock near a peak in the price, would step into thin air, with predictable result. Individuals are lonely lagging indicators in all stock markets but here their role appears almost choreographed.

———

Paltia was nowhere to be found, so Jazz Mama didn't sound so bad. I turned back. On my map Jazz Mama looked to be no more than a 15-minute walk away, in Furumachi Bldg. — that word *furumachi* — "old town," again, but then Niigata dates to Christ — at 6-969 Higashibori Ave.

Buildings appeared unnumbered. It was dark, colder than Tokyo, and the neon was dimmer. No one answered the club's telephone, yet the club's hours were advertised as 7 p.m. to midnight and it was around 7.30 p.m. when I called. I walked most of both sides of the avenue, whose name *higashibori* translates as "east moat," feeling like an enemy that the moat was designed to keep at bay, and still couldn't spot any Jazz Mama neon or other sign, so telephoned again. This time a throaty, husky-voiced woman replied. She was probably in her mid-fifties.

"You called earlier? I'm sorry I couldn't come to the phone. I was cleaning the toilet. You can't find the club? Where are you now?"

The tone of her voice was reassuring and she kept the club clean. I looked around for a landmark to give her, and named a department store. She said I was less than five minutes' walk away. She told me to cross the street, find a narrow lane in the direction of the main road I'd followed from Bandai Bridge, and I'd see Jazz Mama at the end of that lane.

The Higashibori Ave. address was misleading. Furumachi Bldg. wasn't on the avenue. And the club wasn't at the end of the lane to which Jazz Mama — I'll call her Jazz Mama; she'd like that — had directed me. It took 15 minutes and another telephone call for me to understand that it was on a lane that ran across the lane she'd described. I found the club on the second floor of a pencil building, above a massage parlor called Salon Potato.

———

Jazz Mama wasn't in her 50s. She asked me to guess her age. Out of politeness, I offered early 60s. One cigarette in hand, others lighted in an ashtray on the bar, she said she was in her mid-seventies.

A plastic model of a trumpet and vase of plastic flowers defrauded the club's drab décor. The walls were nicotine yellow, the air smoke stale. A grand piano was unplayable in its wedged position under a staircase.

But I couldn't leave, not after the ordeal of finding the club, and doing so with Jazz Mama's help. In an empty jazz club in Niigata, it was just the two of us.

Things started to look up. The drummer arrived and busily repositioned the drum kit. A different drummer must have last used it. Tonight's trio performed irregularly.

The first customer followed some minutes later. He sat down and Jazz Mama asked him about his day as she brought him the bottle of whisky that bore his name for safekeeping behind the bar. He said he'd spent most of the day doing his laundry and washing his walls. He was a newspaper reporter on the *Nihon Nōgyō Shimbun*, an agricultural daily.

Then a trickle of customers began to arrive and in her way I could see that Jazz Mama was a mother to all of them.

Content to eavesdrop and scribble notes on the back of the photocopies the information center had given me, I avoided eye contact. The reporter's demeanor, though, suggested that we could talk without plunging into set pieces such as "When did you arrive in Japan?" or "Can you speak Japanese?" or "Can you use chopsticks?" so when he motioned me to his table I obliged.

He offered his name card. As a journalist in Tokyo I'd shared information with his newspaper's reporters. We had some things in common. We chatted about the merits of price supports for rice and the role of agriculture in preserving culture. Later he would help me trace someone special.

I stole some of Jazz Mama's time. "We don't want to become rich," she told me, speaking for herself and her husband who was out of town. "We just want to have enough to eat. We wouldn't be doing this if we wanted to become rich."

She told me the club used to own about 2,600 LP records of jazz but had to sell 2,000 of them in order to pay for medical treatment. Her husband had been hospitalized for six months and she for three months. "We don't have any health insurance," she said.

CDs? "I try not to enter CD shops."

The tall gaunt bassist wore a check beret and a wide pinstriped shirt, projecting a confused image of elite army officer and banker. But while dabbling in the music of unemployment, as Frank Zappa has described jazz, he'd sensibly kept his day job, which he told me was carpentry.

The suited pianist and drummer also wisely had remained in regular corporate employ. Each played in a busy manner as though putting their instruments through the hoops of an intermediate-level solo training book. I couldn't recognize the result. The reporter, unprompted, whispered that the pianist was "busy" and that the drummer was "busy." Still, for a cover charge of ¥1,000 ($9.10) on a Monday night in Niigata, the trio's performance was a treat.

Oil paintings of jazz vocalists adorned the walls. Billy Holiday was recognizable but I needed help with the portraits of Sarah Vaughan and Ella Fitzgerald. Jazz Mama was the artist. When she wasn't serving drinks, playing records or restraining herself from entering CD shops, she was painting.

She mentioned in passing that she'd met Bill Evans, but what could have brought a jazz pianist on the pinnacle of world acclaim to this coast? When Evans was in town, people came not so much to listen as to worship, as one critic wrote. Classical pianist Peter Pettinger, in *Bill Evans: How My Heart Sings*, described Evans' playing as possessing a "timeless quality, a feeling that the music had always been there." It was a "yearning behind the notes, a quiet passion that you could almost reach out and touch."

Though Evans had performed often in Japan in the early 1970s, I couldn't imagine him breaking free from a tight touring schedule to visit Niigata. Jazz Mama said her husband had met Evans in New York and asked him to visit them. Their club was in a different part of the city then, and Evans hadn't come to perform, just visit. Her husband had taken him to a Korean restaurant that served barbecued beef.

She sensed my skepticism — Miles Davis at the apparently defunct Paltia, and Bill Evans at Jazz Mama's. She rested another lighted cigarette on the volcano of the bar ashtray and brought me an LP record. Evans had written in thick lettering on the back of the cover, "Thanks for the Korean barbecue. Best always, Bill Evans. 74."

The name of the LP was *Waltz for Debby*.

That recording has long been a favorite. I was here for a reason. Later I'd learn what that reason was.

As I walked back to Green Hotel, I no longer doubted that Miles Davis, too, had found his way to Niigata.

O-kaeri nasai — "Welcome back," the night manager said.

When tired and disturbed I dream the same dream that has taunted me for 20 or more years. The administration office of the university tells me that I can't graduate because I haven't completed a certain course, which is no longer offered. I was tired, but not disturbed, and the dream kept its distance.

———

Niigata associates with jazz in another caring way, I later learned. Duke Ellington, the jazz composer, pianist and bandleader, performed a benefit concert in aid of Niigata earthquake victims at the end of a Japan tour in 1964. Ellington writes in *Music Is My Mistress* that he canceled a Hawaiian tour to remain in Japan to perform the concert.

"It was a big success," Ellington wrote. "The mayor of Niigata came down and was so pleased he made me an honorary citizen of the city. On a later tour, we played a concert there."

Photographs of the aftermath of the quake that struck Niigata on 16 June 1964 show the severity of the havoc wrecked upon the city. The quake destroyed around 2,000 homes, tilted multistory apartment buildings on edge, and moved bridge foundations laterally, collapsing the spans above. A tsunami obliterated the port. Miraculously only 28 lives were lost.

Musicians, actors, and other celebrities sometimes "remember" things that they want to have happened in their lives. I was wrong, though, to doubt Ellington's memory. Niigata City Office called back to answer my inquiry within a couple of days.

An official of the city's international department confirmed that Duke Ellington had indeed performed a benefit concert, on 8 July 1964 at Tokyo Kōsei Nenkin Hall, which raised ¥960,000 (then $2,650) for quake victims. To express the city's gratitude, the mayor of Niigata visited Tokyo during Ellington's next Japan tour, in May 1966, and conferred an honorary citizenship upon him at a ceremony at the US Embassy in Tokyo.

———

I'd taken a bullet train to Niigata. The nose of the train I boarded resembled more a duck's bill than a bullet, but "bullet" describes well the front of the early models of this train type. These high-speed trains are signposted in Japanese and English as Shinkansen (literally, new trunk line).

From Narimasu in the Tokyo ward of Itabashi, I took the Tōbu-Tōjō Line to Ikebukuro, where I changed to the Yamanote Line, which I left at Ueno Station. It was late morning, but I still had to stand for most of the way. It's wise to avoid taking Tokyo commuter trains between their people-packing or stacking time of 7.00–9.00 a.m.

It's also advisable to reserve bullet-train tickets as the only free seats may be smoking or in a lower deck with limited view. Some Niigata-bound bullet trains can be boarded at Ueno, the station from which this westbound service began, but most travelers now board them at Tokyo Station. I took the Asahi 12.21 from Ueno.

Travelers today don't think of "taking the 12.21 from Ueno" as though there were a choice of only two or three trains on the day. A certain romance attaches to train schedules such as "The 15.30-London to Paris," "The 16.25 from Galle," or "The Night Express from Nong Khai," as Paul Theroux titled chapters in *The Great Railway Bazaar*.

Apart from the 12.21 from Ueno, I could have taken the Asahi 6.13, MAX Asahi 6.41, Asahi 6.45, Asahi 7.30, Asahi 7.53, MAX Asahi 8.29, Asahi 9.01, MAX Asahi 9.21, Asahi 9.33 — or any of 26 later departures until the last at 21.45.

Passengers are asked to switch off their mobile phones as a courtesy to others. A jingle like the melody from a windup music box precedes announcements, which are in English, then Japanese. News items quick-march across a display panel above the automatic door at the end of the carriage.

I had glimpsed the news — the yen / US dollar exchange rate, closing prices for the NASDAQ index of US technology stocks and the Nikkei stock average, which important people were visiting the US, which important Americans were visiting Japan. Other countries seemed not to exist. In Morioka the weather would be cloudy or clear. If only we could all personally or professionally be so non-committal.

Room temperature was 26 degrees Celsius (79 degrees Fahrenheit). You read which city you're passing through, which is useful as at an average speed of about 250 kilometers (150 miles) per hour it's hard to make a positive identification from the window.

Passengers were dressed to travel, smart casual, in the way that airplane passengers used to dress 20 or more years ago. They don't seem to dress that way anymore. Glamour gone, they know their seat space approximates the per-body allocation of the slave traders, so why look nice.

It took just 100 minutes to reach Niigata Station. Feeling like an airline passenger, I made no effort to talk to the person next to me. She smiled and we exchanged pleasantries a few minutes before arriving in Niigata. No passengers within sight had conversed during the trip.

Nevertheless, it was better than driving the Kanetsu Expressway the 340 kilometers (211 miles) or so from Tokyo. This road resembles a racing circuit, replete with pit stop-like service centers. Like bullet train tracks, in most places it's raised some meters above ground, blinkering the view to the traffic in front.

GULLIVER

We now embark upon our tour of perception, beginning with the voyager Lemuel Gulliver, whom Jonathan Swift sent southward from England over 300 years ago. We ask why Japan was the only real country to which Gulliver sailed, mindful that there are firm grounds for suspicion whenever the English declare a work suitable mainly for children.

CHAPTER 2. GULLIVER UNDERSTOOD

> My stay in Japan was so short, and I was so entirely a stranger to the language, that I was not qualified to make any inquiries. — Gulliver, in Jonathan Swift's *Gulliver's Travels*

How wise is Gulliver in one sentence to decide not to form views of Japan because of his short stay and lack of language ability. Sometimes it takes a satirist to make sense.

Gulliver in Japan makes no judgments, pays tribute to the flexibility, kindness, and generosity of his hosts, understands the importance of formal introductions, and acknowledges the greatness of the country. But why in such a satirical work does Japan figure at all, and why are Swift's references to Japan clear-sighted and positive at a time when Japan was viewed in Europe as strange, conjuring, even grotesque?

Swift's purpose in *Gulliver's Travels* was to lampoon English people for their pretensions and pomposities and take shots at the competitively seafaring Dutch. Yet his account of Gulliver in Japan — the only "real" country to which Swift sends Gulliver — shows a cultural humility that some observers appear to lack today. The three centuries of technological progress in travel and communications achieved since Gulliver's time may not have fostered as much understanding or acceptance as we may think.

For all the fame of the book, the subject of Gulliver in Japan has escaped the notice of all but a few academics and sailed over even the most inquiring of minds. George Orwell, for example, cites *Gulliver's Travels* as a favorite book, one he read and reread as a child, but Japan, as though invisible, receives no mention in his essay "Politics vs. Literature: An Examination of Gulliver's Travels" in *Inside the Whale and Other Essays*. Perhaps because the country wasn't an English colony it didn't qualify for inclusion in an English view of the world, or

---

perhaps because of its perceived strangeness it was viewed as just as fictional as the other lands to which Gulliver was sent.

Swift began his book in 1720 and published it in various forms between 1726 and 1735, so he sent the fictional Lemuel Gulliver, a surgeon and seafarer, to Japan sometime in the mid 1720s. It was the third of four voyages for Gulliver, following visits from England to the fictional Lilliput, Brobdingnag, Laputa, Balnibarbi, Luggnagg, and Glubbdubdrib.

Yet Japan is on Gulliver's mind in his earlier travels. In his first voyage for example Gulliver is able to return to England on an English merchant ship that is returning from Japan. He writes of this ship being at latitude 30 degrees south, so it's rounding the Cape of Good Hope as it passes from the Indian into the Atlantic Ocean, the homeward route from Japan. In the second voyage, he suggests that European geographers are mistaken in assuming that no land lies between Japan and California.

The maps illustrating my edition of *Gulliver's Travels* were based on Swift's text references and not intended to be geographically accurate. Nonetheless, they position Swift's fictional lands all more or less on Southeast and North Asian routes plied by Dutch traders in the 1600s — around what are now Malaysia, Indonesia, and Taiwan, and the southern coast of China.

Swift must have been familiar with accounts of how the Dutch had evicted Portuguese traders from Southeast Asia to get their hands on the spice trade, which the Dutch East India Co. managed from its base in Batavia (now Jakarta). He must have read, too, that Dutch traders had, from a base on Formosa (now Taiwan) launched a China trade, and secured exclusive European trading rights with Japan.

Gulliver landed "at a small port-town" in southeast Japan. This was either Hirado, the site of English and Dutch trading posts northwest of Nagasaki, or Dejima, an artificial island built in Nagasaki Harbor for the purpose of housing and confining foreign traders. Whether Hirado or Dejima, which has since been joined to the mainland by landfill, the "small port-town" isn't southeast but southwest of Honshū.

Swift must have been looking at his world map upside down, as he positions the capital of Yedo (Edo; now Tokyo) in the northwest, whereas it is northeast. Perhaps we can expect this of a satirist, but apart from the confusion of east with west, Swift is accurate enough. He describes a "narrow strait, leading northward into a long arm of the sea, upon the North West part of which Yedo the Metropolis stands." This is Tokyo Bay, or the Inland Sea if he has confused Osaka with Edo.

Gulliver was accepting Japan at a time when Japan was rejecting the European world. In the 1630s — 90 or so years before Gulliver's arrival — the shogun had embraced a policy of isolation, in response to the political threat presented by a Christian beachhead. European missionaries were seen as harbingers of colonists. Portuguese missionaries in particular had shown more interest in gold than god, and had plundered much of Japan's supply.

The shogun proscribed Christianity, withdrew trading rights from the British and Portuguese, forbid foreigners to land on Japanese soil, and barred overseas resident Japanese from returning. Transgressors risked death from beheading, burning, crucifixion, or torture. Only Dutch and Chinese, confined like plague-carriers to Dejima, were granted trading rights, and Japan remained in this reclusive state until the 1850s.

The seafarer Swift lands in Japan therefore can't be English. He must pretend to be Dutch, as only a Dutch ship can take him to Japan. Swift is aware of this exact detail of Japanese history, as Gulliver states: "I thought it necessary to disguise my country, and call myself a Hollander; because my intentions were for Japan, and I knew the Dutch were the only Europeans permitted to enter into that kingdom."

I think Swift found the model for the character of Gulliver in Will Adams, an English shipwright and navigator who arrived in Japan in 1600 as a pilot aboard the Dutch ship *Liefde*, which became disabled in waters off Kyūshū. Adams won the confidence of shogun Tokugawa Ieyasu, who employed him as an advisor on shipbuilding and trading. He was much respected, rewarded, and remembered in Japan, where he married, assumed a Japanese name, and lived the rest of his life. Adams' letters home were among seafarers' accounts collected and published by Samuel Purchas (c. 1577–1626), an English author and clergyman, in *Hakluytus Posthumus, or Purchas His Pilgrimes: Contayning a History of the World in Sea Voyages and Lande-Travells by Englishmen & Others* (1625), a work which Swift owned.

Gulliver arrived in Japan more than 100 years after Adams, and the detail of his trip from Nagasaki to Yedo for an audience with the emperor (actually shogun; the emperor then resided in Kyoto) suggests that Swift also used the later model of Engelbert Kaempfer, the German doctor at Nagasaki with the Dutch East India Co. from 1690–92. I've taken this view from "Gulliver's Travels and Japan: A New Reading," a report published by Dōshisha University (Kyoto; January 1977, Moonlight Series No. 4).

The Dōshisha report — by two American and one Japanese scholar — intrigues also for noting examples of academics who have denied the parallel of Gulliver and Kaempfer as though they wish it untrue, as though there shouldn't be a Western model for a reasonable encounter with Japan. If the parallel today isn't denied, it also isn't acknowledged, as even in *Literature of Travel and Exploration — An Encyclopedia*, published as late as 2003, *Gulliver's Travels* is said to overstep the real into the "furthest reaches of fantasy."

This aside, the Dōshisha report introduced me to Kaempfer's seminal book *History of Japan*, which first appeared in English translation in 1727 in London. This work formed the basis of much of the English-speaking world's understanding of Japan probably until as late as the early 20th century. It's a magnificent book. It also tells a vexed tale of translation. I reference the newly translated edition by Beatrice M. Bodart-Bailey.

Kaempfer read as much as he could about Japan before his arrival, took copious notes once there, and added his own detailed sketches to his account. He may have been the first Japanologist, as none of the merchants or missionaries who had traveled to Japan from around the mid-1500s had done so with the sole purpose of writing about the country.

He was a botanist as well as doctor, and his minute observations of everyday life reflect the precision of a scientific mind. Japanese historians of the time were mostly of the higher samurai class whose members weren't inclined to dwell on ordinary people's lives. Kaempfer is also an early example of doctors making fine writers.

He appears never to have stopped asking questions, despite the danger to both him and Japanese who divulged information to him in the secretive Tokugawa era. He was known to have used European liqueurs to loosen the tongues of scholars.

Fortunately, the Japan he visited was under the rule of a shogun — Tsunayoshi, the fifth since Ieyasu — who valued scholarship and had secured positions for scholars in the castles of the regional baron-like daimyo. Such scholars were called upon to befriend Kaempfer and monitor his activities but it seems that he did the most monitoring. His accuracy later shocked some Japanese, though he was mistaken in believing that Japanese had faithfully recorded their early history, to which they added much myth.

Kaempfer lived from 1651–1716, and Swift from 1667–1745. In the Europe of that time, when churches still dominated and religious and racial tolerance weren't virtues, it wasn't acceptable to praise a "heathen" nation such as Japan. (In some circles, it still isn't.)

Kaempfer's account did praise Japan or rather didn't judge it, and his even-handedness prompted editors to rewrite parts of it according to their own prejudices, according to Bodart-Bailey. His praise was toned down and his criticisms amplified; some sentences were added, others deleted. The translator, J. G. Scheuchzer, a young Swiss who struggled with the level of English demanded by the translation, probably lost control of the project to editors. After toiling for nearly two years over what he described as an "intricate and obscure" text, Scheuchzer's health failed and he died aged only 27.

Although the history wasn't published until 1727, it's believed that sections of it circulated ten or so years earlier in manuscript form among members of the Royal Society who were Swift's friends. Voyages of discovery were among Swift's favorite reading. Literary critics who had denied that the Swift work was based on any model had neglected to read or perhaps even acknowledge the body of 17th-century travel literature on Japan.

Parallels in the two works, however, are striking. Kaempfer was a doctor, and Gulliver a surgeon. Both had studied at Leyden.

Dutch traders were asked to humor the shogun by putting on a stage performance, which showed them walking, standing still, singing, dancing, putting on and taking off cloaks, and speaking their own language and broken Japanese. Kaempfer himself twice participated in these shows. So was Gulliver required to humor people in the land of the giants where he was placed on a table and asked to walk and talk and show respect. He was exhibited often as something resembling a human who could speak and perform tricks. He used sticks to "play a jigg to the great satisfaction of both majesties."

Japan didn't value the practice of philosophy; neither did Swift. Japan's penal system of the time stressed rewards as well as punishments, and didn't use fines because they wouldn't punish the rich as much as they would the poor; Swift echoes this in Lilliput.

In tone, too, the Swift and Kaempfer accounts are similar. The satirist isn't copying the Kaempfer work. Rather, he's using the Japanese behavior it describes as a mirror, and inviting us to look at ourselves, or rather the Dutch, in contrast. We then see the Japanese behavior as reasonable.

Accounts of crucifix trampling are an example. Japanese officials required foreign traders to tread on this Catholic model of Christ — they used a crucifix about a foot long — to prove that they weren't Christian. Some Dutch traders reportedly denied that they were Christian, to save their lives. Kaempfer doubts that most did so, but instead suggests that they denied affiliation to the offending Portuguese sects while admitting to being Christian.

Gulliver confesses his Christianity to the shogun and pleads to be excused from the trampling ceremony because he had arrived in Japan only by accident and had no intention to trade. The emperor responds that Gulliver appears to be the only Dutchman who had shown any scruples in the matter, which caused him to doubt that Gulliver was Dutch. The emperor warns him not to make his religion known to the Dutch, as they would cut his throat if they found a Christian among them.

Swift shows even Japanese pirates to be reasonable compared with some Dutch people. When Gulliver is sailing toward Japan on his Third Voyage, pirates overtake and board his ship. A Dutchman is among them and he recognizes Gulliver as English. The Dutchman tries to persuade his Japanese masters that Gulliver and his fellow sailors should be tied together and thrown overboard. One of the pirate captains determines that they shouldn't die, which prompts Gulliver to say to the Dutchman that he was "sorry to find more mercy in a heathen, than in a brother Christian."

The captain reaches his merciful decision only after asking several questions. His is a considered judgment. The Dutchman then convinces the captain to send Gulliver adrift in a canoe with only four days' provisions. The captain doubles this amount to eight days, but permits no search that might have turned up more than that allowance.

This echoes the attempt by Jesuits to persuade the shogun that Adams and fellow English sailors were no more than thieves who should be executed. Adams recounted this attempt in his first letter home. The shogun's response was to say that as Adams had harmed neither himself nor his land, it was against reason and justice to put him to death.

Swift is standing many perceptions on their head, just as he is reading his world map upside down, and one can almost sense the delight of the satirist in finding a work such as Kaempfer's that provides him with rich opportunity to do so.

It wasn't Kaempfer's intention to visit Japan. A Dutch East India Co. official, who had become enchanted with Japan and who had noticed Kaempfer's substantial intellect and powers of observation, persuaded him to visit and produce an accurate description of the country.

Which Kaempfer did, but tragically he couldn't find a publisher for his work while he lived. Once published, however, it became an immediate bestseller and some 12 editions and translations appeared in the decade after its release, according to Bodart-Bailey.

The full title of Kaempfer's work is echoed in *Gulliver's Travels*. I reproduce it from Bodart-Bailey: *The History of Japan, Giving an account of the ancient and present State and Government of that Empire; of its Temples, Palaces, Castles and other Buildings; of its Metals, Minerals, Trees, Plants, Animals, Birds and Fishes; of the Chronology and Succession of the Emperors, Ecclesiastical and Secular; of The Original Descent, Religions, Customs, and Manufactures of the Natives, and of their Trade and Commerce with the Dutch and Chinese.*

Gulliver, too, is asked by his captain to record his travels, after he returns to England. He says he'll think about it, but lowers sensationalist expectations by saying that his story "could contain little besides common events, with those ornamental descriptions of strange plants, trees, birds, and other animals; or the barbarous customs and idolatry of savage people, with which most writers abound." He doesn't believe that he's been in the company of savages.

And in the early 1700s, Gulliver wasn't convinced of the value of adding to the available store of travel literature. He told his captain that he "thought we were already over-stocked with books of travel: that nothing could now pass which was not extraordinary; wherein I doubted, some authors less consulted truth than their own vanity or interest, or the diversion of ignorant readers."

Which shortly will bring us to Paul Theroux.

DISAPPEARANCES

We now make our way to Niigata Port, where the North Korean cargo-passenger ship, *Man Gyong Bong-92*, long suspected of facilitating espionage, is docked. We ask why Japanese are invisible to some people, discuss denial of personhood, and advance a motive for North Korea's plucking of Japanese nationals off the coast.

CHAPTER 3. MISSING PERSONS

A wall-mounted TV remotely controlled the sparsely scattered guests in Green Hotel's dining room. Gazes fixed to the screen god, the guests ate in slow-motion frames as though masticating and broke their gaze only in second intervals to clamp food between chopsticks with the dexterity of the blind.

I welcomed and loathed the TV this Tuesday morning as the company of the guests who hadn't come or sat near me. It wasn't personal. No one sat near anyone. The program, too, betrayed a measure of quiet desperation. Local wisdom on the dismal state of the economy seemingly exhausted, the morning program sought answers from a foreign economist.

A set breakfast was served on trays. Though the helpings were small all the nutrition in the world seemed supplied in the stir-fried carrots, beans, mushrooms, grilled salmon, rice, *miso shiru* soybean-paste soup, tub of fermented soybean paste, raw egg, strips of dried seaweed, pickles, and hot barley tea.

Coffee was served amid punditry such as "...under continued deflationary pressure..." While other governments combated inflation, Japan fought the ninja of a downward spiral in prices. The deflation in asset values and consumer prices characterized what observers were calling the lost decade, except that the phenomenon looked likely to last 20 years. But why was it bad for a family to be more able to afford a house?

Economists are also unhappy when everyone has a job. They see full employment as a sign of strong consumer demand, which is a sign of inflation, which is a sign that a central bank may raise interest rates, which is a sign that the prices of stocks, other financial assets, and land are likely to fall.

Such economists aren't concerned with the livelihoods of working people, who don't pay their salaries. They are paid from the profits made by investors who correctly judge the timing of the price inflation of financial assets. They lecture during breakfast.

19

I paid ¥5,565 ($46) for the room, bought an umbrella from hotel reception for ¥550 (that was too much; I could have found one outside for less than ¥200), and stepped out into the rain.

Umbrellas have advantages. Rather than unpack your coat each time there's a downpour, then pack it away when the rain stops, you can slip an umbrella out of the side straps of a pack and slip it back in. Motorists easily see umbrellas, making you safer. Their disadvantage, apart from a knack of disappearing from forgetful hands such as mine, is that they catch gusts of wind. But there's no comfortable way to walk in rain.

———

Before setting out for the small city of Sanjō, I wanted to see how Niigata connects to the world through ships. I made my way to Niigata West Port, which lies upstream from the mouth of the Shinano River. This port serves ferries and coastal and near-seas freighters, while container ships, chemical and oil-products tankers, and liquefied natural gas carriers call at the larger Niigata East Port, 16 kilometers (ten miles) or so north. East Port is flanked by oil storage tanks, a thermal power plant, and metals and fertilizer plants, and others are welcome to visit it.

The older, original port was one of five, along with Yokohama, Hyōgo (now Kobe), Nagasaki, and Hakodate, that Japan agreed to open to foreign shipping in 1858. As a precursor to trade issues which Japan would negotiate to resolve not over months but years, Niigata Port accommodated foreign shipping only ten years after signing the treaty. But in those years the Tokugawa shogunate was losing its grip on the country, and 1868 marked the last year of its rule before the restoration of the emperor.

Some expectation for commerce must have accompanied the opening of the port, as the US, the UK, and the Netherlands opened consulates in the city, but later closed them. Writing in 1878, Isabella Bird noted in *Unbeaten Tracks in Japan*, that Niigata was "a Treaty Port without foreign trade and almost without foreign residents. Not a foreign ship visited the port either last year or this."

Bird found she couldn't freely send her luggage from Niigata to Hakodate, the port which was "opened" in Hokkaidō. Her interpreter knew to send the luggage in his name and address it to an acquaintance. Today only Russia and South Korea maintain consulates here.

Nevertheless, the port has greatly assisted coastal shipping since 1671, Teruo Kobayashi notes in *Nihon no Minato no Rekishi* — "The History of Japanese Ports," when the government designated it as western Japan's main port. According to Kobayashi, around 3,500 ships or at least four a week were observed to call during the 16 years of the prosperous Genroku era (1688–1704), when samurai read more than fought and the arts flourished. When foreign trade was authorized, Kobayashi notes, the port was equipped to serve mainly anchoring whaling ships, and wasn't modernized until the Taishō era (1912–1926).

Niigata Port opened a trade with the Russian port of Nakhodka in 1966, Kobayashi records, mainly to cater to the Russian demand for used cars. Buyers of these cars are limited mostly to Russia and former British colonies in Southeast Asia, which drive on the left side of the road.

Japan's car-fitness certification regime charges exorbitant fees for models older than about ten years. Consumers suffer this. The political certification helps carmakers move new models out of showrooms, but the cost of disposing of an "old" but still road-worthy car in Japan can reach ¥40,000 ($330). Foreign buyers of some of the used cars pay about that much if they can buy through auctions, not dealers. So instead of paying ¥40,000 for the disposal of aged cars, Japan receives about that much for them.

If foreign buyers forsook their idiosyncrasies and formed an association that spoke with one voice, in the manner of a Japanese industry association, and offered to remove the used cars free of charge, the offered prices would tumble as the offer to take them for nothing would still represent a cost saving for Japan. But achieving that level of collusion requires much discipline.

———

I walked through a light drizzle to the port, where a police van blocked vehicular access and the entrance to the main pier was roped off. This unconvincing security — I could have entered along either side of the pier; the police presence simply asked me not to do so — was for the *Man Gyong Bong-92*, a North Korean cargo-passenger ferry which connects the eastern North Korean city of Wonsan with Niigata and provides the only passenger link between the two countries.

Niigata West Port, June 2006. Photo by Niigata Nippō.

The North Korean passenger-cargo ship, Man Gyong Bong-92, *docked at Niigata West Port, 18 October 2005. Photo by Niigata Nippō.*

The *Man Gyong Bong-92* is rumored to transport contraband from Japan such as weapons parts and machinery for weapons manufacture. North Korea withdrew the irregular service in 2003 after Tokyo declared it would make "thorough inspections." One example of "thorough" was the symbolic dispatch of 1,900 police and other inspectors to comb the ferry's insides. Small North Korean freighters call at Japanese ports for repairs and supplies but are unwelcome.

Too much is made of the Man Gyong Bong-92. Electronics components can find their way into North Korean missiles and submarines via a number of indirect routes, such as China or Asian front companies for Japanese exporters. There's no need to use a direct shipping service.

I climbed the stairs to the third floor of the Niigata Port and Harbor Office, where the administrative section is located, just as a port official was arriving at work. The official, strong coffee and stronger tobacco on his breath, viewed me with some suspicion. I told him I intended to walk from this port to the port of Yokohama, to see a cross-section of his country. He paused in thought. Then his expression told me he understood. His work connected him to foreign lands, so it could connect to me. He invited me to climb another two flights of stairs to the lookout room.

Though the official had seen what at first he must have thought was a peculiar specimen of the homeless, he had decided to be helpful. He could have said, "Would you please submit a fax to us of your questions. The fax should include your resume and contact details."

He soon joined me and from the observation floor began patiently explaining the workings of the port. Then, in the manner of a well-trained tour guide, he named and described the ships we could see, beginning with high-speed ferries, capable of 80 kilometers (50 miles) per hour, and cement carriers.

An earlier interest in ships enabled me to distinguish in Japanese among gross, deadweight and displacement tonnage, and I can recognize most ship types. We made an odd couple — a caffeined, nicotined, port official at the start of his day, and a tall disheveled foreigner in backpacker disguise — but we could communicate.

We looked down to see the Shinnihonkai Ferry that plies the rough seas between Niigata and Otaru on the northerly island of Hokkaidō, via Tsuruga and Tomokomai. Small general cargo ships bore Cambodian, Panamanian, and South Korean flags. The official led me to his floor and directed an assistant to continue the briefing.

We sat, the assistant and I, poring over the log of scheduled ship movements. She was happy that I could read the schedule. She said she was new in her job. Enthusiasm on her sleeve, she was excited to learn how ships connect her city to the world. She said there would be ten arrivals and 12 departures today.

So as not to overstay my welcome, I added myself to the departure list and walked the 2.4 kilometers along Road 113 to its intersection with Road 116, turned left toward Niigata Station, then right into Road 1, which follows the Shinano River in a southwesterly direction. It would lead me to the Shinano-ōhashi Bridge and Road 8, which I would walk to Sanjō.

Ships aside, Niigata connects by air to Khabarovsk, Vladivostok, Irkutsk, Seoul, Shanghai, Xian, Harbin, and Guam. The Korean link via Seoul is the busiest, with an average 200 arrivals or departures a day (2005 year), followed by China (160), and Russia (130).

———

As the Shinano River wends its way toward the sea, it separates a finger of land between its west bank and the coast. About half of Niigata is built on this windward side. Access is secured by one rail and five main road bridges, all over a distance of less than seven kilometers (four miles) from the river mouth. Bandai Bridge, which leads to Jazz Mama, is the busiest. As if these aren't enough, on the tongue of the river's mouth Niigata Port Tunnel links to the isthmus-like land almost at its tip.

Wherever I walked a bridge seemed to come into view. I wondered how many were built out of need and how many originated in *sode no shita* — "under-the-sleeve," cash-for-contracts, deals in that murkiest of industries — construction. Kimono sleeves, bulky in their folds, are ideal for concealing cash, though money may not change hands in that way any more than it changes hands under a table.

J. W. Robertson Scott, who arrived in Japan in 1915 and wrote *The Foundations of Japan* after traveling some 9,650 kilometers (6,000 miles) through rural areas, observed that Niigata resembled Amsterdam in that it was a "city of bridges." He thought there must be at least 200 bridges here but his survey,

I think, must have included the area around the Agano River, which meets the ocean just north of the airport.

Scott would have traveled to Niigata via Nagano on the Shinetsu Line, which was opened in 1899, as Niigata didn't link with Tokyo by rail until 1931 with the completion of the Jōetsu Line. The Jōetsu Shinkansen or bullet-train link opened in 1982. On the Shinetsu Line, train "boys" had "boy" written in English on their collar.

The *Foundations of Japan* was published in 1922. Luckily, I was able to purchase an edition which had been deleted from the Nash Library of the University of Science and Arts of Oklahoma. Return date stamps appear to justify the university's decision to make room for more popular titles. In the 53 years from 1947, the book was borrowed only 28 times, or just over once every two years. It was borrowed most during the post-World War II occupation when Japan was at the military mercy of the US and during the 1980s when the US appeared to be at the economic mercy of Japan.

Nobody can borrow it now.

———

The temperature at sea is colder than the temperature on land, and seafarers who call at Niigata seek warmth on the northeast side of the station's Bandai Exit, between the tracks and Higashi Ave., where one or two blocks are set aside for them as though the town were planned that way.

Though most port cities have an underbelly of bars and brothels, this area speaks of utility and order. It oozes sleaze but clean, neat, organized sleaze. I detoured here from Road 1. The streets were still as night workers used our day to sleep.

A massage parlor called *ai moodo* showed a penchant for punning. *Edokko* — original inhabitants of downtown Tokyo — are said to be especially skilful at such word plays. A cell phone company gives the name "i-mode" to its Internet service but *ai*, depending upon which ideograph is used, can also mean "love."

Bold stand-up signs on the pavement for Mat Max and *kogyaru paaku* — "teenage girl park," competed with ai moodo for attention."

Even seedy streets were neat, well swept, garbage unseen. Perhaps they always have been. Bird in Niigata was "reluctant to walk upon its well-swept streets in muddy boots." She observed that "every vagrant bit of straw, stick, or paper is at once pounced upon and removed, and no rubbish may stand for an instant in its streets except in a covered box or bucket."

But there's little color and neon lighting doesn't count. Homes, shop fronts and factory walls are bleak gray in a color scheme of permanent rain cloud. It would make such a difference if someone gathered a posse of painters and went to work — almost any color would do. The disinclination to add color may be an effect of living for long dark months amid snow, and this is where the snow country begins.

Air masses moving east from Siberia collect water vapor from the stretch of ocean between Japan and China and dump it as snow on the windward side of the mountains. Three to four meters of snow can accumulate. It slides down sloped roofs but householders must quickly shovel it off flat ones lest they collapse under its weight. Before the advent of snow-removing machinery, this region was isolated in winter months. My route is unsafe to walk from November through March.

––––––––––

An advertisement on the cover of The Travelers' Tales 2000 edition of Bird's book reads, "Traveling solo in 1878, a time when women did not travel alone, the courageous Isabella Bird..." Bird traveled every inch in the company of a young man who translated and negotiated on her behalf — for accommodation, food, ponies — and, though she took a personal dislike to him, wrote fully of his efforts.

Bird's publisher isn't alone in the regard of Japanese as invisible or the denial of their personhood. Still today, writers seem able to win praise merely by depicting Japanese as people and it's a greater achievement to portray them as individuals. What else would they be? Such conscious consideration may represent a subconscious reaction to wartime propaganda that dehumanized Japanese. The strangeness becomes clear if we imagine a Japanese book review beginning: "The writer wrote of the English as people, drawing out their foibles and strengths as individuals."

As though a puzzle to publishers, Donald Richie's portraits of 48 Japanese appeared first as *Geisha, Gangster, Neighbor, Nun*, then as *Different People: Pictures of Some Japanese*, then again as *Public People, Private People: Portraits of Some Japanese*. Richie told me he fought the publisher over the stereotyping in the first title — his purpose was to portray individuals — but to no avail.

Some Japanese seem not to mind being identified as a version of someone else. Compatriots called saxophonist Jirō Inagaki the "Japanese John Coltrane," E. Taylor Atkins notes in *Blue Nippon*. Akira Miyazawa was "Japan's Sonny Rollins," George Kawaguchi was "Gene Krupa," Fumio Nanri was "Satchmo" (Louis Armstrong), and Kyōsuke Kami was "Paul Whiteman."

There's a history to this. Descendants of Europeans who believed that cultural enlightenment was furled in their sails extended the denial of individual identity to a denial of national identity, or they superimposed one identity upon another to suit their likes and dislikes. Some lazily but hurtfully still label in this way when they refer to Filipinos as the "Italians of the East" or Koreans as the "Irish of the Orient."

Masao Miyoshi noted in *As We Saw Them*, an account of the envoy of officials Japan dispatched to the US in 1860, that Americans showed their approval of the Japanese as a race by saying that they were like them and by separating them from the races they despised. Thus, *Harper's Weekly* called the Japanese "the British of Asia," according to Miyoshi's research, and the *Washington Evening Star* asserted that "No nation possesses so many elements of the Anglo-Saxon mind as the Japanese." The *Daily Alta California* of San Francisco said, "The countenance of these people wore a far more intelligent look than any Chinese that we have seen."

In jazz in Japan there's more to it, Atkins explains. A consensual value attaches to conformity and the school or *iemoto* system requires artists or crafts people to create a specimen of a type, not an original type. The specimen should be as near perfect a copy as possible. This is an overlay upon centuries of cultural borrowing. Some fight it. Atkins quotes pianist Kichirō Sugino as having complained that "they're always calling some Japanese musician the "Japanese Coltrane" or the "Japanese Miles Davis." They won't let the young people who are creating original music have any credit for it."

———

Walking on Road 1, I remembered a man who sold kitchenware and hardware in the shopping street in Tokyo I'd passed through each day on my way to work. His eyes drooped with a resignation that some things can't be changed and a part of him seemed dead.

People I knew bought small items from his shop but this patronage sprung mostly out of sympathy as a broader range of the items he sold could be found at lower prices at larger stores. When they spoke his name their tone betrayed an unspoken past. Years later, I learned that one of his two daughters had disappeared in her early 20s. She may have been kidnapped, she may have been murdered. No one knew. They still don't.

Niigata is also known as the coast from which people disappear. Megumi Yokota vanished while walking home from school in 1977. She was 13. Others have vanished from different points along the Japan Sea and Kyūshū coasts. Some Japanese have long suspected that North Korea was behind the disappearances though they couldn't convincingly explain why. What could be the motive for kidnapping nondescript residents? Japan's government seemed disinterested in the subject until evidence of abductions, supplied by North Korean defectors to South Korea, began to mount.

North Korea in September 2002 admitted to kidnapping 13 Japanese of whom 8, including Yokota, had died. The five surviving victims were allowed to return to Japan but as of this writing, their families haven't been allowed to follow. Tokyo hasn't been satisfied with the reasons given for the eight deaths. Not all names on Pyongyang and Tokyo's lists matched and the true number of those kidnapped may never be known.

Those who will never return, Bradley Martin suggested in *Under the Loving Care of the Fatherly Leader — North Korea and the Kim Dynasty*, may have met a fate "even worse than the original abductions — imprisonment and death by starvation in the gulag, for example." Japan's foreign ministry, too, feared the worst, asking why a single North Korean hospital had issued certificates for the deaths that Pyongyang said had occurred in different regions.

But even if Pyongyang had kidnapped the Japanese for their identities and for use in teaching colloquial Japanese to espionage agents, why 13-year-old Megumi, whose case came to symbolize the tragedy of the disappearances and galvanized Tokyo into pushing Pyongyang for answers? Some guessed that she may have stumbled across a kidnapping in progress and herself been abducted as a result.

I believe a simpler negotiation underpinned this story, and doubt whether the kidnapped residents would have been useful as teachers. They weren't teachers. A large proportion of Japan's 625,000 or so Korean residents align themselves with North Korea, and they are native speakers of Japanese. There is, therefore, no shortage of naturally fluent Japanese speakers among Koreans. Recruiting one or two of them would be easier than going to the trouble of secreting residents off the Niigata coast and transplanting them in North Korea.

Issuing a Japanese passport to a North Korean saboteur or spy may be a simple way of getting the person into South Korea, but why steal the person when the passport is enough?

Those kidnapped may, I think, have been intended for use as bargaining chips in future negotiations, to soften Tokyo up on requests for food or money. Apart from the threat to build nuclear weapons and the provocation of firing missiles across the Sea of Japan, North Korea doesn't have much to bargain with. But it can collect Japanese nationals and store them in a cupboard. This hadn't worked as Tokyo unusually showed little interest in its lost citizens. So the bargaining chips that hadn't died would be returned.

There was a logic to the timing of North Korea's return of the surviving victims. The children of a hermit communist state's leaders can easily believe that they are invincible and can do anything in their or other worlds. They sometimes test this belief.

Kim Jong Nam, eldest son of North Korean leader Kim Jong Il, in May 2001 boarded a Japan Airlines plane in Singapore and walked off it at Narita airport with the intention of visiting Disneyland. His arrival unannounced, he was reportedly in the company of two women and a child and traveling on a forged Dominican Republic passport. He was briefly detained and allowed to return home, via China. This was the largest of negotiating chips to fall into Japan's hands, and a deal may have been struck before he was released.

The foreign minister at the time, Makiko Tanaka, a Niigata representative and daughter of former prime minister Kakuei Tanaka, was castigated for not seizing on Kim Jong Nam's illegal entry to extract the truth from North Korea over its suspected role in kidnappings. But it's likely that she or her prime minister did seize on it, and made a trade. It's not the type of trade that either would be able to discuss. The timing makes sense.

Though 30 years or so had lapsed since the first disappearances, only 18 months were now needed for the truth to come out. Kim Jong Il reportedly admitted and apologized for the kidnappings in a meeting in Pyongyang in September 2002 with Japan's then prime minister Junichirō Koizumi. It seemed likely that one purpose of this meeting was to thank Japan for the safe return of Kim's son and probable heir, a son who was known to travel incognito and without his father's permission.

Japanese investigative journalists spend much time trying to uncover the truth about the disappearances. What recurs as a theme in their work is distrust of their leaders. They believe that their government knows more than it reveals on the subject and don't believe all of what it does reveal.

Niigata has produced its share of famous children. One son, Yoshio Yamazaki, Bob Johnstone informs in *We Were Burning*, was a chemical engineer who joined watchmaker Suwa Seikō in 1965. His employer had been following the product launches of Radio Corporation of America — the world's first TV in 1939, the first color TV in 1953 and, in 1968, a flat TV screen that used liquid crystals, a new technology. The flat screen had shown only a static, black and white image.

RCA let slip at a May 1968 press conference that liquid crystals could also be used in the digital displays of electronic clocks. Earlier, Yamazaki had puzzled over his employer's interest in a chemical engineer, but now this snow country protégé knew why he'd been hired. Liquid crystals were chemicals.

Yamazaki synthesized his own crystals and after five years of development the company produced its first liquid crystal display or LCD watch, in 1973. This work was the seed of the pocket calculators that engulfed the world, and also of the LCD color TV.

Suwa Seikō had earlier patented quartz timepieces which set in train the developments that were to convert watches from mechanical to electronic products. The company, later renamed Seikō Epson, in 1964 supplied the Tokyo Olympics with a portable quartz timepiece that allowed athletic records to be measured for the first time in hundredths of a second. It built the world's first quartz watch in 1969 and the world's first wristwatch TV in 1982.

Watches, and later calculators, could be mass-produced, they could be cheap, and they could be good. The perseverance of a young son of Niigata was an agent of this change. He conducted his early research at Suwa Seikō facilities in Suwa, in the southerly neighboring prefecture of Nagano. He hailed from Tsubame just across the Nakanokuchi River from Sanjō.

THEROUX

A new book by Paul Theroux used to excite former colleagues. The American writer was brashly seeing much of the world by train, bus, and on foot. He would bounce a reader along for the ride. He used his knowledge of flowers and birds to add a soft touch. Then he would describe how people ate.

He was held in some esteem. A *Far Eastern Economic Review* editor once asked, "Do you think we can get Paul Theroux to review this?" Theroux has much to say about Japan, but I felt hollow to have enjoyed some of his work when I realized the depth of the prejudice it contained. Our journey through perception visits his books and essays.

Chapter 4. Paul about Himself

Japanese are bandy-legged, can't see without glasses, smaller than you, creaseless, wrinkle-proof, fang-toothed. They wag their heads, twitter, sniff. They're like flawed clockwork toys.

These are the descriptions of Paul Theroux, who has written some 23 works of fiction and 12 of nonfiction, mainly travel.

Theroux is knowledgeable about birds, protective of animals, fearful of dogs. He appreciates music. "Mendacious" is a favorite word. He was an activist student who opposed the Vietnam War — now a respectable credential. A typical baby boomer, perhaps. Not all bad.

Yet through much of Theroux's work runs the toxic thread of his contempt for Japanese people. How does one learn to despise and disdain in such a way? Theroux offers no explanation, and his writing on Japan has escaped critical notice. But he leaves clues, which challenge us to identify the source of the toxin.

Theroux writes in "The Old Patagonian Express" in the collection *Fresh Air Fiend*:

> A book like this — or any book I have written — is not a problem for a reader to study and annotate. It is something I wrote to give pleasure, something to enjoy. As you read it, you should be able to see the people and places, to hear them and smell them.

But Theroux himself studies and annotates — "she is named once, and mentioned eleven times in three hundred pages," he writes of the cousin who accompanied Graham Greene on his travels in Liberia, which became the subject of *Journey Without Maps* — so we are free to do the same.

Theroux inserted a singular viciousness into his observations of Japanese people in his first travel book, *The Great Railway Bazaar*, an account of his return trip, mostly by train, from London to Tokyo. In this book he launched his style of denigration and mocking that produced a perverse form of entertainment.

He was a published novelist in his early thirties when he wrote the book, after teaching English literature at the University of Singapore, working as a Peace Corps teacher in Malawi, and lecturing at Makerere University in Uganda. He was an educated man and an educator. It doesn't matter that he is a writer but it does matter that he was a teacher.

On the Lake Van Express, from Istanbul to the Iranian border, Theroux writes:

> I knew the occupants (in the third-class coaches): there was a bandy-legged gang of Japanese with bristly hair who traveled with a dwarf squaw, also Japanese, whose camera on a thong around her neck bumped her knees. Their chief was a fierce-looking young man in military sunglasses...

En route to Bombay, Theroux recounts a conversation with a manager of a Japanese-Indian joint venture. This manager "had had several run-ins with the Japanese — 'Head-on collisions — I had no choice!' I asked him how he found the Japanese. He said, 'Loyal, yes! Clean and hardworking, yes! But intelligent, not at all.' It turned out that they were getting under his skin, though he preferred them to the English."

In Laos:

> The only English film I could find in Vientiane was a pornographic one, and the somber reverence of the Japanese tourists, who watched like interns in an operating theater, filled me with despair.

In Tokyo, Theroux boards what he thinks is a bullet train to the northern prefecture of Aomori. Although he's a railway enthusiast, Theroux doesn't praise Japanese trains for their speed or efficiency. The pre-announced brief stops instead might result in "an unprepared passenger" being "mangled by the door" or missing his stop.

The train Theroux thinks he took in 1974 may have been the Hatsukari Limited Express, which name he uses as a chapter title in *The Great Railway Bazaar*, and its nose may have been pointed, but it wasn't a bullet train.

The Tōhoku Shinkansen (or bullet train) line on the route Theroux took was opened eight years later in 1982. Theroux, spellbound by trains since childhood, doesn't care to recognize Japan's most celebrated and probably the world's most advanced train. Perhaps he's uninterested because the US still has no trains running at the speed of the first bullet train, introduced in 1964 — 210 kilometers (130 miles) per hour; speeds on some bullet trains are now 300 kilometers (186 miles) per hour.

Theroux:

> The odorless Japanese trains unnerved me and produced in me a sweaty tension I had always associated with plane travel...I was traveling in a fast, dry bullet-train, among silent people who, even if they spoke, would be incomprehensible. I was trapped by the double-glazing. I could not even open the window!

People take bullet trains only for speed. They're too fast for appreciation of scenery. Few passengers talk; most sleep, blinds drawn. I shudder to think of the result had Theroux been on a bullet train and managed to open a window.

Japan designed bullet trains to compete with air travel, thus relieve pressure on crowded domestic skies. Tokyo's mainly domestic airport, Haneda, is the world's fourth busiest, with an annual passenger count of around 63 million (2005 year), more than double the number for Narita international airport (31 million). I think it's still true that no passenger has ever suffered injury — touch wood — because of bullet train malfunction or accident since the first of this train type was introduced in 1964.

In Tokyo, grilling a Japanese National Railways (now JR) representative, Theroux observes the railway office staff begin a company calisthenics program.

> The phone rang on the next desk. I wondered how they'd handle it. A head-wagging woman answered it, stopped wagging her head, muttered something, then hung up. She resumed her wagging.

A woman shakes her head. A dog wags its head. Theroux sees the workers exercising as he leaves the building, and writes:

> All over the country, instruments were commanding the Japanese to act. The Japanese had made these instruments, given them voices, and put them in charge. Now, obeying the lights and sound, the Japanese aspired to them, flexing their little muscles, kicking their little feet, wagging their little heads, like flawed clockwork toys...

This is mild compared with what is to come. In *The Happy Isles of Oceania*, Theroux interviews the Solomon Islands' housing minister, who asks why Japanese are "the only rich ones?" Theroux:

> Because it is a one-race, one-language, one-family island of desperate overachievers who have a fascist belief in their own superiority....These little people have a palpitating need to dominate the world and will do anything to sell their stuff.

And:

> It seemed to me grotesque but typical that the wrinkle-proof executives in this Japanese company were taking advantage of this poor barefoot country, robbing them of one of their few valuable commodities, fish.

The discussion moves to a fisheries venture between the Solomon Islands and Japan. "So you have not been earning any money from it," Theroux asks. "It is hard to say," the minister replies. "Their book-keeping methods are complicated. For example it is all done in Japan. We never see their records." Theroux: "Fish is expensive in Japan, and everyone eats it. I should say that they have been making a fortune. They are using you — probably cheating you."

Again to the minister:

> Don't ask questions. Threaten them, close them down, freeze their assets....Or why not demand that they allow you to send a delegation to Japan to start a business there.

Theroux uses "wrinkle-proof" to describe Japanese adults in the same way that he uses "creaseless." The inference is that adults who don't show their age are children who haven't grown up, in the same vein as Gen. Douglas MacArthur's postwar quip that likened Japan to a nation of 12-year-olds.

He visits the minister's brother on Savo Island, and wonders:

> What terrors would the Japanese have had in store for these happy indolent folk if they had won the war? At the very least there would have been a golf course here, and someone like Mapo would have been a caddy, and Rebecca would have had a job in the kitchen of the golf club, rustling up megapode omelets for the hungry Sons of Nippon.

A 74-year-old islander responds to Theroux's prodding about the war:

> The Japanese came here. One Japanese man said, "We are powerful and we are staying here — in Tulaghi. We will never leave. Go to your fields. Pick coconuts, make copra, grow bananas. Cultivate vegetables. Go fishing. We will buy everything you have to sell."

Theroux:

> Did they mention the Americans?

The islander:

> They said, "The Americans are very strong. They will come and try to fight. But we will beat them." We were frightened of them.

Theroux:

> "But why?" I said. "The Japanese are little bowlegged people who can't see without glasses. They are smaller than you. Why were you afraid?"

In Fiji Theroux expected to find a "Nipponese outpost, full of little Japanese vacationers in floppy hats snapping pictures of each other."
In the Cook Islands:

> The land was sometimes leased, but it has not left their hands. This was also the basis of an anxiety — that the Japanese would come and somehow wrest the land away from them, trick them somehow. They hated and feared the Japanese, and I saw no Japanese tourists in the Cooks. "We do not want them!" a man in Aitutaki told me. "We will send them away!"

An Easter Islander laments:

> All wood is expensive here because we have no trees. The Chileans prefer to sell their wood to the Japanese, who have more money. The Japanese are very intelligent people.

> "Do you really think that?" asks Theroux.

> "Well, not compared to you or me, but just in general."

Did the islander really answer in that way?
In the Philippines, in the essay "Palawan: Up and Down the Creek" in *Fresh Air Fiend*, Theroux recalls a local telling him "about the loggers, and how Japa-

nese ships had been moored for years just offshore to pick up the big apitong logs, and how the logging coincided with the mudslides, and how the rivers and river mouths were not deep anymore."

If Japan isn't exploitative, it's unethical. In the essay "Chinese Miracles" in *Fresh Air Fiend*, Theroux writes of the Tiananmen Square incident of 1989, in which Chinese soldiers are said to have crushed a student uprising (photographs are few and facts about this incident are disputed):

> As we know now, no businessman is likely to be deterred by a little thing like a massacre. The Japanese government did not even condemn the killings.

Theroux ends *The Happy Isles of Oceania* in Hawaii. The first chapter, "Oahu: Open Espionage in Honolulu," in the last section of this book begins:

> The two most obvious facts of Hawaii are the huge sluttish pleasures of its Nipponized beachfront hotels...

At a party on the Big Island, Theroux observes:

> Across the lawn, Japanese tycoons looking deceptively child-like were clustered around Arnold Palmer — his name was impossibly difficult for them to pronounce.

Arnold Palmer as "arunorudo paruma" isn't difficult for a Japanese tongue nor the sound in English so different that an unsympathetic ear couldn't recognize the name. Theroux's Japanese — the children who don't grow up — deceive by their appearance.

Of a Japanese family that were taken to their luxury bungalow by limousine:

> But they were soon back in the bungalow garden, sniffing flowers and thrashing in the pool.

This family doesn't "smell" but "sniffs" flowers. An animal sniffs. They don't bathe or swim but "thrash" in the pool. A shark thrashes, the word connoting violence. Earlier, Theroux observed at a nightclub that "overdressed Japanese men screamed songs" into a karaoke mike in front of a TV set.

Even in South America, Japan is on Theroux's mind. From *The Old Patagonian Express*:

> Traveling on your own can be terribly lonely (and it is not understood by Japanese who, coming across you smiling wistfully at an acre of Mexican buttercups, tend to say things like Where is the rest of your team?).

At a swimming pool in Barranquilla, Colombia, Theroux singles out Japanese for their sunbathing:

> ...the Germans, the British, the Lebanese, the Americans, the sun-bathing Japanese — all the communities that live in Barranquilla, all members of the Cabana Club, were observing the curfew from the swimming pool and patio of the Prado Hotel.

In *The Pillars of Hercules*, an account of his Mediterranean coastal travels, he continues to stereotype. In Spain:

On the way to Figueres a little sorority of Japanese girls twittered among themselves. They lacked the characteristic Nipponese submissiveness...

When Theroux needs to rest, he tells us how much others hate Japan. In *The Kingdom by the Sea*, he discusses Channel Tunnel plans with a retired air force officer.

I was going to say that the Japanese had just this year dug a thirty-six-mile tunnel under the Tsugaru Straits, from Honshu to Hokkaido. But...he would have replied, "Nips!" The English hated the Japanese for being rich over-achievers, for being guiltless racialists, for eating raw fish, for working like dogs, and for torturing their prisoners during the war.

Similarly, in "Down the Yangtze" in *Fresh Air Fiend*, he relates that a fellow traveler "despised the Japanese" because a Tokyo hotel had allocated her an unnecessarily expensive room.

Theroux trawls the memories of his Chinese hosts in an attempt to draw out residual bitterness or prejudice, after supplying the prompts. To an elderly Chinese musician:

"Didn't you write songs about the Japanese as evil little fiends?"

"Oh, yes," Mr. Zhang said. "In the songs we called them all sorts of names. Ghosts, robbers, rapists. Because they were robbing and raping. If you say 'rapist' most people will know immediately that you are talking about a Japanese, even now."

In conversation with a former civil servant:

"Don't your experiences make you hate the Japanese?"

"No," he said, "it is only the generals we hate."

More than once, the answer is wiser than the question.

Waiting for the Peking Express at Canton Station, Theroux observes a "middle-aged Japanese couple, looking wrinkle-proof but anxious." In Harbin, here and there was "a Japanese roof or a Chinese ministry or statue — mostly monstrosities." The city of Qingdao is "actually overrun with Japanese businessmen."

In novels in which there isn't reason for Japan to warrant much of a mention, Theroux infects his characters with anti-Japanese sentiment. In *The Mosquito Coast*, Allie Fox, the father who takes his family to the Honduran jungle, visits a hardware store to buy a rubber seal. He's shown a Japanese product, and responds:

"What are you, working for the Japanese?"

"If you don't want it, just say so."

"I just said so, Jack. It's made in Japan. I don't want my hard-earned bucks turned into foreign exchange for the sons of Nippon. I don't want to bankroll another generation of kamikazis (sic)."

The same character says of people in Central America:

> "No TV where they come from. No Nipponese videocrapola."

Later, Allie Fox got "Jerry to tell the story of how American camping equipment was made by slave children in China and Japan."

In the companion novel *Millroy the Magician*, the cultist chef asks:

> "Ever wonder about the Japanese? They eat tons of fish. If you take a good look you'll see that they've gotten to look like fish."

The protagonist of the novel *Picture Palace*, an elderly photographer, dines with a fictionalized Graham Greene at a London restaurant. She narrates:

> I saw eight Japanese gentlemen gliding noiselessly in. They wore dark suits, they were small and they had that deft, precisely tuned, transistorized movement...They were Greene's own magic trick, eight creaseless Japanese conjured from this air and seated muttering their gum-chewing language.

And:

> Greene's face animated with laughter...creating light; and in the background, just visible, his triumph, the circle of Japanese, their tiny heads and neatly plastered hair.

Greene, who wrote the story *The Invisible Japanese Gentlemen*, never wrote like that.

Most references to Japanese people in *Hotel Honolulu* are sexual. Women are cheapened as submissive; prostitutes seek men as easy quarry. The treatment is more tedious than titillating. In the chapter "The Limping Waiters," one waiter had been

> waiting on a young Japanese woman. You noticed their big floppy hats, which, with their skinny stemlike bodies, gave them the aspect of decorative flowers.

The woman lures one of the waiters to her room for sex.

> Her body said: For the sake of my modesty, I must pretend that it is rape, but do not be fooled — look closely and you will see that it is rapture.

Her body was "full of chicken bones." She "infected" the waiter with "regret, a humiliation, a casual demon."

Theroux kills the one figure who offers the best opportunity to develop character, in the chapter "Christmas Cards." The narrator manages the Hotel Honolulu. His counterpart managing the hotel next door is a Japanese — Hideo Takahashi, who works himself almost to death through personally inscribing "at least a thousand Christmas cards" before he commits suicide. The narrator:

> At their palest, the indoor Japanese are chalky, whiter than any haole, and Takahashi looked dusty and translucent — sleepless, skinny, fading to gray...There was hardly any life left in him, just the insignificant scrap that fluttered like a rag within him as he hurled himself off the balcony.

Buddy, the Hotel Honolulu owner, says, in the chapter "Human Remains":

> You get these rich Japanese who kill themselves by slamming the door of their Mercedes on their silk Hermes tie and strangling by the side of the road.

In Theroux's short novels, too, Japan is unappealing. Says the character Hoyt in *Bottom Feeders*:

> Hey, I was asked to give a business talk in Tokyo. I turned it down.

In his essay "Rudyard Kipling: The White Man's Burden," in *Fresh Air Fiend*, Theroux notes that several of Kipling's stories and poems show his hatred for certain races or groups of people. Perhaps Theroux feels that he's in good company but his disdain of the personal extends even to the products.

He mocks Japanese products for being Japanese, and for their small or large size. In the story "Neighbors," in *Collected Stories*:

> His motorcycle was a Kawasaki — Japanese of course.

Who doesn't associate the word "Kawasaki" with Japanese machinery or motorbikes? Who writes, "IBM — American of course"?

And:

> I had one of those huge Japanese cameras that can do anything. They're absolutely idiot-proof and fiendishly expensive.

If the product isn't too big, it's too small. In *Picture Palace*, a Japanese camera is a "capsule, the size of a tranquilizer, with a tiny pinhole eye." The photographer "brushes these trinkets aside."

In *The Old Patagonian Express*, Theroux describes the bullet train as an "overpriced roller-coaster." A Mitsubishi Motors "Gallant" car in *Riding the Iron Rooster* is a "ridiculous little Nipponese car" that "looked like a Dodgem car."

Japan's subway fare structure is "run by computers which spit tickets at you and then belch out your change," Theroux writes in "Subterranean Gothic" in *Sunrise with Seamonsters*.

In *The Old Patagonian Express* Japanese pipes "look as if they're for blowing soap bubbles" and cameras are "ridiculously complicated." In the novel *Kowloon Tong* the character Bunt boasts that his radio isn't Japanese.

Theroux gave the writer V.S. Naipaul a "wholly unsuitable red-leafed Japanese maple, a dwarf tree, as a housewarming present," he tells us in *Sir Vidia's Shadow*. He must know that bonsai is as English a word as samurai or sushi, but he uses the word "dwarf" to exaggerate the smallness. He says that ikebana demonstrates a "Japanese passion for dead branches, in "The Past Recaptured" in *Sunrise with Seamonsters*, though the word means "flowers with life."

The language, like the products, is one to mock. In the London-based novel *The Family Arsenal*, two characters, Hood and McGravy, compare their skill at imitating foreign accents.

> Try something hard. Can you do a Japanese?

"Hai!" said McGravy, sneezing the word, Japanese-fashion.

Theroux calls Japan "Nippon," not "Nihon." Japanese use both, "Nippon" more when in proud mood, such as occasioned by a sports win. He constructs variations such as "Nipponized," and the phrase "sons of Nippon" appears in both his travel writing and fiction. This, from "Hawaii" in *Fresh Air Fiend*, is typical: "Local Chinese seldom speak Chinese; local Japanese tend not to be Nipponized."

Theroux's "kamikazis" should read *kamikaze*; his "arrigato" should read *arigatō* — a mistake he repeats in his books. The demon-haunted mountain he calls "Osorayama" is *Osoreyama* or *Osorezan*. In Tokyo he saw a Nichigeki Music Hall skit called "Onna Harakiri" and explained that "Onna is the name of the girl stripping off her kimono and unsheathing a sword and holding it to her stomach." *Onna* means "woman." Unaware of the irony, he curses himself for not buying a Russian phrase book in Tokyo, as preparation for his trip home via Russia.

Midway through my Theroux reading, I wondered whether he could fairly be described as "racist." According to the *Concise Oxford Dictionary*, racism is

> 1 (a) the belief in the superiority of a particular race; prejudice based on this. (b) antagonism toward other races, especially as a result of this. 2 the theory that human abilities etc. are determined by race.

Though Theroux is contemptuous of Japanese people, nothing in his writing suggests that this contempt stems from a belief in his superiority. It isn't racist to dislike or even despise a people.

Perhaps this is too generous, considering Theroux's liberal use of the words "racist" and "racism." In *The Pillars of Hercules*, after hearing a policeman in France assert that Arabs "are the cause of all trouble," Theroux states:

> In such circumstances, talking to someone who was generalizing in such a racist way, I had a choice of challenging his logic, scolding him for uttering such offensive things...

He later notes:

> The French are entirely frank in expressing their racism. I wondered whether this lack of delicacy, indeed stupidity, was an absence of inhibition or simply arrogance.

He ponders the "relationship between racism and xenophobia" and among Turks on a cruise ship, remarks:

> It was relaxing to travel among people with so few prejudices.

In Theroux's essays and literary reviews, fairness and racism are much on his mind. In reviewing William Least Heat-Moon's *PrairyErth*, in *Fresh Air Fiend*, he writes:

> Heat-Moon does not make much of the xenophobia he encounters, nor does he explore the racism — the anti-black and anti-Hispanic sentiments

— he hears. He takes people as he finds them, and they put up with his note-taking.

In the same book, writing on William Simpson, "the first war artist" and "indestructible Scot" Theroux asks:

> ...who is more welcome as a friend and fellow traveler than a person of tact and discretion?

Theroux's appreciation of Simpson's work belies a Jekyll and Hyde condition, or is it the Strange Case of Mr. Hyde and Mr. Hyde? How can the person who wrote *The Happy Isles of Oceania* also write:

> Travel also vindicated Simpson's fair-mindedness. He believed he held "exceptional" views on the subject of national character — in a word, he was not racist, and he felt strongly that it was politicians who whipped up feelings of nationalism and xenophobia...His 1876 album Picturesque People depicts individuals, not stereotypes... the absence of cant and bigotry in his nature made him a brilliant observer.

Theroux's case may present an inverse of racism. Confronted with Japan's metamorphosis from postwar ashes to wealthy modern nation, the racist writer's first response is to deny the achievement. When the denial isn't persuasive, the racist defames the reputation. Japan fills racists with doubt about the central tenet of their racism, which is their superiority. Thus, Japan upsets Theroux because it makes clear that he needs to reconsider much about himself.

Japan upset European thinking about what was acceptable in the world. It exemplified the first case of a successful non-Christian capitalist country. Japan in that way upset Theroux's sense of what is right by being Asian and successful — Christians right, pagans wrong.

Japan's land and stock-price appreciation in the 1980s — when Theroux was producing some of his most vitriolic work — produced an ugly arrogance. The market value of all stocks listed on the Tokyo Stock Exchange briefly exceeded the market capitalization of the New York Stock Exchange. Some Japanese believed that the value of the Imperial Palace land in Tokyo exceeded the value of the state of California.

Japanese realtors collateralized over-valued land to raise low-cost loans to purchase American trophy properties such as the Rockefeller Center in Manhattan. Developers bought Hawaiian hotel and golf club properties, in a flamboyant, boastful way.

It all became too much when landmark cultural properties passed into Japanese ownership — Columbia Pictures to Sony Corp. and Universal Studios to Matsushita Electric Industrial Co., in 1989 and 1990, were the most spectacular examples. Ezra Vogel had published *Japan as No. 1 — Lessons for America*, ten years earlier, and there was a deeply felt anxiety that Vogel may be correct. Popular writers such as Tom Clancy (*Debt of Honor*) and Michael Crichton (*Rising Sun*) struck back. Theroux is of their ilk.

In the US and throughout much of the Pacific, Japan's asset purchases were triggered by the steep revaluation of the yen which the US engineered through the

Plaza Accord of 1985. This agreement was designed to slow the pace of mainly Japanese exports to the US and give US manufacturers breathing space in order to regain competitiveness.

Central bankers coordinated their intervention in currency markets to push up the value of the yen against the US dollar by 88 percent in the three years following the accord. US goods thus became cheaper for foreign buyers, but the country itself seemed for sale. The more enduring result was that Japanese firms became even more competitive. They pared fat from manufacturing processes at home and relocated factories offshore, directly into the US and into Asian countries that linked their currencies to the US dollar.

Populist writers show little interest in this history, or in the fact that Japanese buyers were notoriously overcharged — "mugged in Hollywood," as Bill Emmott noted in *Japanophobia — The Myth of the Invincible Japanese* — for much of what they bought, particularly in the United States.

TOMBSTONES AND KARAOKE

There is more to say about Theroux's Japan, but we break from him now, and leave the city of Niigata, though we remain in the prefecture of the same name. We consider the boost to confidence brought about by soccer and the honesty of odometer readings. Walking southward down the Niigata Plain, we pass tombstone sellers and karaoke cabins for late-night lovers. Young women extend an invitation and a kind tobacconist offers a place to stay.

CHAPTER 5. SOUTH INTO SANJŌ

Cold drizzle fell as I passed the monolithic Niigata prefectural government buildings on Road 1.

A soccer player in neon kicked a ball above the prefectural building entrance. The sign counted down the days to the World Cup soccer kick-off. There were 52. This competition truly embraces the globe, more so than the United Nations if we compare membership strength. Around 204 national soccer associations belong to the Federation International de Football, or FIFA, compared with a UN roster of around 191.

I thought that most large nations had belonged to the UN since its inception, but they haven't. The then two Germanys joined as late as 1973, and Switzerland only in 2002. Though the global world is still in its infancy, the forces of soccer, other sports, and religion work on a mind-numbing scale to collapse borders. I remembered the Mormon missionaries, and recall having read that they number 60,000 — or just over 300 for each UN member country.

Soccer ignited a new self-confidence in Japanese. With a fervor not witnessed probably since the Tokyo Olympics nearly 40 years earlier, it was all right again to wear and wave the national flag. And the sport forced a wholesale if not whole-hearted cooperative effort with South Korea, to which FIFA awarded co-hosting rights. Korean-language signs were put up at main stations and, contrary to some expectations — including mine — they haven't since been removed.

Sport is supposed to teach that it's all right to lose as long as we play our best — does anyone believe that? — but in this case it taught Japan and South Korea that they must accept a draw. As both sides had seemed to fear, their preparations for the co-hosting were showing that they had much in common.

The event would catapult some players to stardom. Hidetoshi Nakata and Shinji Ōno, both of whom play or have played for European teams, would become household names across the soccer-playing world. American and English sporting heroes in golf or soccer had always been recognizable, but Japan's popular heroes, in sports as in movies or music, had rarely been celebrated outside Japan.

In the nearly ten years since Japan's first professional football league was formed, fans of J. League teams had become as fanatical as their English counterparts. Now their energy would channel nationally and they would wave the Japanese flag without fear of censure, from left-leaning schoolteachers or anyone else. And Koreans, who were more accustomed to burning Japanese flags, would watch their own and Japan's share the same sky.

Sebastian Moffett, in *Japanese Rules — Why the Japanese Needed Football and How They Got It*, notes the envy of a J-League player at the "easy patriotism" enjoyed by footballers in England, where the Union Jack was flown and "God Save the Queen" sung at every opportunity. Japan's defeat in World War II had produced feelings of national inadequacy and patriotism had been a divisive issue, but soccer allowed Japanese to express national pride and feel that it was all right to be Japanese.

Though leaving the city of Niigata, I was still in the prefecture of the same name. It's one of 47 such regions which resemble US states but without the freedom to legislate separately from the national government. Some 2.4 million people live in the prefecture (2005 year), making it the 14th most populous. It records economic production value of around ¥9.8 trillion ($82 billion; year to March 2005), putting the prefectural economy ahead of that of smaller Organization for Economic Cooperation and Development (OECD) member countries such as Czech Republic or New Zealand.

Among Niigata's chief boasts are cookies and cut flowers. It produces rice confectionery to a value of around ¥128 billion ($1.1 billion) and sends about 25 million tulips to market (year to March 2005). It also fetes the arrival in January of white swans, which migrate south from Siberia on the East Asian Flyway. Swan arrivals in January 2006 were recorded at 12,769, down from 16,006 in January 2003, perhaps reflecting the loss of wetlands.

Around 13,800 foreigners reside in the prefecture (2005 year), double the number of ten years earlier. Chinese account for the largest proportion (34%), followed by Filipinos (16%; compared with a 10% share on a national basis), Koreans (17%), and Brazilians (mostly of Japanese descent; 10%).

Many of the Chinese and Filipinas are brides to farmers whose lives don't attract modern Japanese women. Apart from Koreans, who likely spread across several walks of Japanese life, and the typical scattering of missionaries and English teachers, most of the other foreigners are likely to be factory workers from Indonesia, among other Southeast Asian countries. Only about a quarter of the foreign contingent lives in Niigata City, the majority camping in most towns of size in the prefecture.

It was 1.45 p.m. by the time I saw urban Niigata give way in patches to rice paddies. A phalanx of luxury European-model used cars — BMWs, Mercedes

Benzes, Volvos, and Audis — confronted me on Road 8 a kilometer or so before the patchwork surrendered to blazes of emerald seedlings. The cars' statement of fashion and wealth contrasted with the bleak industrial urban landscape on Roads 1 and 8. Perhaps the owners had sold because they could afford a later model but in the lost decade more likely the expense of running a foreign car had become prohibitive. No life stirred in the yard.

Most of the cars were priced from ¥2 million to ¥3 million ($16,700–$25,000) but I was more interested in their advertised odometer readings — 49,000 kilometers (30,500 miles) for one of the BMWs, 42,000 kilometers (26,100 miles) for a Volvo, and 36,000 kilometers (22,400 miles) for an Audi. Were they believable?

How easy is it to "wind back the clock"? If half the rumors are true, still little is believable. And Niigata residents, with fewer trains and buses to board, would drive more than Tokyo or Osaka people, so the incentive for dealers to tamper with odometers would be greater. I wasn't going to ask, but I did ask once.

A year earlier, while waiting for an auto accessory shop to open in western Yokohama, I kicked tires at a nearby used-car dealership. I didn't want to inflate unfairly the sales-commission hopes of staff, so I told the operator I was killing time, which he appreciated. The operator, a fluent, articulate English speaker, said he had a master degree in business administration from a US university.

I believed him. Could I believe the advertising detail for his cars?

He told me that mostly they were honest but that almost any odometer, on any car, could be wound back. His yard often received unsolicited faxes from technicians who made a business out of this deceit. A recent fax, he said, was from a technician offering to wind back the digital odometers on late-model Mercedes Benzes for a fee of ¥100,000 ($830) per car.

I didn't ask this MBA holder and fine English speaker what he did before selling cars. That would have been an intrusion, the undercurrent cruel, but he seemed to suspect that the question was on my mind.

———

Rows of tombstones broke the air a short distance from a used-car yard. Travelers can expect to see car yards and fast-food joints as they enter and leave cities, but not this. Buddhist altars of all sizes stood amid other accessories of death on shelves inside the tombstone seller's liquor store-like shop.

One of the shop's billboards advised: "Children become parents, and parents become grandparents." That was all the sign said, but it was a subtle advertisement. What do grandparents become? Grandparents die, and in their death become customers for this shop's products.

The tombstones recall the dark side to the snow country. Out of the range-finder of the east coast, some people here have been able to hide what they do, like the oil tankers which, far from the view from land, lose oil to the ocean less through accident than through operations.

Leaving the troublesome elderly deep in the mountains to die is an example. Folklore has it that the elderly who no longer wished to burden their family walked into the mountains and selflessly lay down to sleep, knowing they wouldn't awake. For some time I believed that such deaths were suicide, but now I don't. The elderly I've come to know have the will of a teenager to live. The terminally ill may have chosen to freeze, but not the merely frail. And the term *ubasuteyama* — "the mountain where we discard an old woman," is precise.

And there were the *goze*, the blind women of Niigata and Nagaoka who used to walk through the snow with shamisen in hand to play and sing for food and lodging. These women were all but condemned to a wandering and celibate life for the sin of their sightlessness. The condemnation was for their looks as well, as the condition of their blindness was seen as ugliness. The partially sighted among them were chosen to lead the small troupes from door to door.

Goze instilled fear in some who believed that in their blindness they could see what the well sighted could not. Japanese romanticize them now and regions in the snow country seem to compete to produce accounts of the "last goze." Haru Kobayashi, who passed away in April 2005, aged 104, was, according to Nippon Television, the country's last such itinerant entertainer. Haru said in an interview before her death that her mother had told her at a young age that she was ugly. She had at times wondered whether this person was her birth mother.

Haru Kobayashi, one of the last goze, performing outside Kahōji Temple, Agano City, Niigata Prefecture, on 27 May, 1973. Photo by Niigata Nippō.

A forlorn, deserted park of rent-by-the-hour cabins, ostensibly for karaoke singing, appeared on the right of the road. Late-night low-budget lovers would take some comfort here, in boxes scattered across an area the size of a soccer field, and sing in their own way.

The park was as vacant as the *kara* of "karaoke" — meaning "empty" and *oke* a contraction of "orchestra." Customers pay ¥200 ($1.70) per hour for a cabin between 1 p.m. and 7 p.m., and ¥600 per hour from 7 p.m.

"We protect youth from gangs," warned a sign on the park office door. I looked through the office window to see a cleaning woman. I thought to ask her some questions about cabin users, mindful that cleaners from the trash they collect sometimes know more than managers. I knocked on the office door but to no reply, and when I looked through the window she had frozen like a frightened doe and stood bent-backed in a corner, the side of her face against the wall.

The door sign, which carried the insignia of the Niigata Prefectural Police as well as the "Prefectural Karaoke Society for the Prevention of Crime," warned that the cabin park "would not succumb to gangster groups." Such signs were taped also to the windows of pinball-like pachinko parlors in Niigata, and I wondered whether they could have any effect in foiling extortion attempts by *yakuza* or lesser gangsters. More likely, regular payoffs already in train to an established gang, the signs served as a warning to others not to muscle in on the action.

I've never understood the fun that karaoke enthusiasts seem to get by singing to instrumental versions of popular songs played on audio equipment in small smoky bars or smaller rooms. A CD or DVD player, microphone, echo box, stereo amplifier, and speakers manufacture their entertainment. Flat-panel screens have replaced lyric books.

The mixing of the voice makes a poor singer a passable one, the good singer becomes even better, and friends and colleagues applaud. Everyone can be a star, and for a few minutes of a drink-sodden evening, that is the delusive, narcissistic appeal. No wonder this pastime spread quickly around much of the world. Andy Warhol was correct, though he couldn't have imagined that some people would achieve their 15 minutes of fame in this closeted, electromechanical way.

But karaoke will outlive me. As Bill Emmott observed in *Japanophobia*, the equipment has carried a Japanese identity abroad, unlike consumer-electronics products such as Walkman which are named in English. More than that, the product "evokes something personal and sympathetic rather than inscrutable or frighteningly efficient: people enjoying themselves, shedding inhibitions..."

———

I was lost on a straight road, though I'd made a point of studying my map before I set out so that I would be more or less aware of the villages and towns on my route. But the town through which I now walked appeared nameless.

A Mister Donut announced itself on Road 8 like a clown's nose. Inside it was clear that if Japan had not changed in its fascination with American fad and fast food, it had changed the food. The donuts were small, fluffy, feathery, and I was sure feather-light as well. They contained no food.

I treated myself to coffee. I wasn't alone in my observation of what passes fraudulently for food at some retail outlets. Friends tell me that they pick up the snack foods sold in convenience stores not so much to look closely at the items as to weigh them in their hands, before deciding to buy.

Where was the dough-less Mister Donut? I asked at the counter. Two young women were attending. One spoke but failed to communicate.

"We don't know."

"Are you sure you don't know the name of this town?"

"We don't know the name."

"Let me put it another way. Do you know where you are?"

"We don't know where we are."

This existential encounter showed how some Japanese look instead of listen. Despite what their ears hear, they are so secure in their language that they can't come to terms with a non-Japanese speaking it. Some friends intentionally make mistakes in their spoken Japanese to put their hosts at ease.

This works, as foreigners are expected to make mistakes. I should say "Westerner" rather than foreigner, as Japanese expectations of foreigners conform to a fixed view of rank and what is right in the world. Some Japanese make little or no allowance for mistakes in their language when Chinese or Koreans speak it.

"We don't know where we are."

The unknown city was Shirone. It features Buddhist altar roadside sales outlets, car graveyards, and karaoke cabins. Perhaps the women were right not to know where they were.

On Shirone's edge, where Road 8 intersects Road 460, was the Suzuki Butsudan sales outlet for Buddhist altars and tombstones, and a similar business fronted the other side of the street. Traveling north or south, you could purchase your altar without crossing the road.

Offerings — fresh fruit, water, sake, cigarettes, or some food the deceased loved — are placed on the *butsudan* or altar for the spirits of ancestors. Most homes I know have one. I associate altar with sacrifice but none is made at these tables before gods.

I was too early to see the June kite battles. Shirone and Sanjō residents build hexagonal kites, of several square meters and weighing up to 30 kilograms (65 pounds), which they pitch into battle in mid air. Clashes wreck some kites, which can cost several thousand dollars to build. Some Japanese cite a tenth-century dictionary reference to a "paper hawk" as likely evidence that Japan invented kites.

Beyond the altars and tombstones a karaoke cabin park called Anchor had plunged to some sad industrial depth by combining its business with scrap metal which lay crushed in a high heap in front of the cabins.

———

A small car pulled up in front of me. Two young women sat inside munching burgers and fries, McDonald's wrapping on their laps.

The passenger opened her window and offered me a ride. She said they were going to Sanjō, and could take me part or all of the way. This seemed brave or foolish of them. In their youthful enthusiasm they faithfully projected the illusion of partners in the fantasies of men traveling solo. *Tabi no haji wa kakisute* — "We can do shameful things on a trip" is a saying for these men but I hear women use it just the same.

This was a test of my resolve not to accept rides. Damp from walking at a brisk pace through intermittent drizzle, I wouldn't be good company in a small car. Where would my pack fit? Why was I asking myself the question? This was an invitation designed for decline.

Aruki desu — "I'm walking," I replied, and thanked them for their kindness.

The women, I guessed, were in their early 20s. People who offered to help were usually aged under 25, or over 60, and the most sympathetic were woman over 70 — our mothers, grandmothers, guardians of us all. Those in between were on an escalator, climbing, blinkered like racehorses, disinclined to take risk, unwilling to lose a minute. If you are traveling alone here and need help, find a student or grandmother.

There is a deeper significance, though, in the receptiveness of grandmothers. They don't see in me a person who is from England, Europe, Canada, Australia, or New Zealand. No such distinction occurs to them, and neither does it occur to a child. I am, to them, an American and a victor.

Grandmothers understand, more than their children, that the Pacific War could have ended differently. Some are grateful that it ended the way it did — their homeland was neither invaded nor divided. An invasion would almost certainly have resulted in Russia, whose help the US had sought in driving Japanese troops out of Manchuria, laying claim to Hokkaidō.

Had fate coursed differently, Japan may have been divided into zones as politically antagonistic as east and west Germany and north and south Korea. "We were lucky it was the Americans," a friend's mother had said in Tokyo. As it was, Russia declared war on Japan on 8 August 1945 — six days before the surrender — claimed the Kuril Islands off Hokkaidō's elbow, and after the passage of more than 60 years, a peace treaty still eludes these uneasy neighbors.

Long flaps protected the neck of a woman growing tomatoes at roadside. She was wearing the type of pantaloons that woman wore in postwar occupation years. By squaring the female shape, their design was intended to make the body unattractive to Allied soldiers.

She seemed embarrassed that I might think her an impoverished peasant. "Farmers here sell to markets. They don't like to sell to neighbors," she said. "But vegetables in the supermarket have no flavor, so I like to grow my own." She leased the small plot.

She told me her son was in his third year at Tokyo University, a public college that carries the prestige of a Harvard or Yale. "That's the only boast I have," she said. "But I've told him not to come back here. I want him to enter a good company in Tokyo after he graduates."

Light was almost lost when the Welcome to Sanjō sign greeted me on Road 8 shortly before the road again meets the Shinano River. I would turn west onto Road 289 which would take me toward Higashisanjō and Sanjō stations, and my best chance of finding a place to stay would be to look around them.

Sanjō marks the northern boundary of the electoral district of a former prime minister, Kakuei Tanaka. Niigata Third District elected Tanaka to the Diet for 16 consecutive terms over 43 years, unmoved by his double conviction for bribery, two prison sentences and maintenance of a mistress whose name he used on dubious property transactions.

———

More signs gave directions and distances to Horiai Industrial Park, Metal Industrial Park, Ōjima Industrial Park, and Hardware Wholesale Grounds. "Industrial park" seemed oxymoronic. I felt sad at the prospect of visiting a park not for its trees and lakes and children's amusements but for the industrial plant located there.

Within an hour I'd reached the inner streets of Sanjō and found a high street of drab, unpainted shops, their metal fittings rusted. Though it was only around 8 p.m., most shops were shut, a ryokan was shuttered, no minshuku in sight. Ghosts had made the town their own. Japanese call such a street *shattaa dōri* — "shutter avenue," and they are common in depopulating rural cities and towns.

A bullet-train stop called Tsubame-Sanjō on the perimeter of the city had attracted a satellite of service businesses, which explained the hollowing out of the old town center in a manner Route 66 residents would recognize.

There was little shop light by which I could read my map, and it was getting colder. I couldn't tell which lane off the high street led to Sanjō Station. A baker gave me directions and the corner on which the bakery stood fortuitously was the corner of the road that led to the station. A dwindling trickle of commuters walked toward me, none with me. No inns were in sight near the station. I inquired at a tobacconist.

"Are there any business hotels in this area?"

"No. There are no business hotels here."

"Are there any minshuku or ryokan?"

"This is a minshuku."

The shopkeeper was a stout, weatherworn woman whose lined face betrayed harder times. She may have farmed. We were, I guessed, of similar age. That helped. We quickly cleared the standard hurdles, put minds at rest. Yes, no shoes inside; yes, I'm familiar with Japanese bathing; yes, I can sleep on a futon; yes, Japanese food is fine.

The relief I felt was like the weightlessness a climber feels after removing a heavy pack. It would have been easy for the shopkeeper to say, "We have no rooms available." But her expression showed that she knew that hers was the only available lodging. Luck is a lady, I thought tonight.

Why do some people say that something is a "lady"? An American friend describes San Francisco as a lady. Neil Davis, an Australian TV cameraman who was killed by tank ammunition shrapnel while covering a Thai coup in 1985, and whose dropped, running camera filmed his death, had said while filming in Vietnam that death was a lady. He also said that he must always keep his camera running.

The tobacconist's minshuku was called Minatoya. It was hidden behind the shop façade and accessed from a narrow side lane. I removed my pack and stepped into a world of dark-stained wooden beams and frames, sliding paper doors, and narrow, angular staircases. Tatami mats scented the air.

Nothing quite compares with the aroma of fresh mats, which older males liken to women in the saying *Tatami to nyōbo wa atarashii hō ga ii* — "Tatami mats and wives are both better new."

A young maid led me to a ten-mat room. This was extravagant, as student lives are spent in rooms of four and a half mats or even three. The mat size, too, was large, probably the Nagoya area size of 1.8 by 0.9 meters (six by three feet). Kyoto area mats are larger, but Tokyo ones much smaller, and within the Tokyo size there is an apartment size as well, which is smaller still.

After I'd settled in, the maid brought a pot of green tea and soybean paste cookies. She asked whether I'd prefer to take a bath before or after dinner, and without waiting for a reply tactfully suggested that it should be before.

Lodgers dined in a curtained section of the restaurant. Miso shiru soup, an omelet in a syrupy sauce, two small grilled fish, cubes of deep-fried tofu, pickles, and a wooden pot of steamed rice were served for dinner. Destination reached and snug under roof, I added a small bottle of beer to this feast.

Two lodgers, uniformed as construction workers, entered the restaurant, loudly proclaiming *tadaima* — "We're back!"

Kyō gambatta na — "We've done a hard day's work!" one declared.

Gokurō sama deshita — "You have worked hard!" the shopkeeper said, in the appreciative tone of a mother.

The workers watched baseball on a wall-mounted TV while they ate, barely noticing me.

While I was dining, the maid had been busy. I retired to a perfectly prepared room — warmed by a gas heater, futon bedding laid out across the middle mats, an electric paper lantern beside the pillow switched on. She visited some minutes later to ask if I was comfortable. What could I say?

We chatted. I asked if foreigners ever came here. She said that once or twice a Thai or a Filipino had stayed, adding that immigrant workers such as these usually stayed in company dormitories. She left.

Sleep came in an instant.

————

Walking is good exercise, physical and mental. You can think about a lot of things and order your thoughts when you are putting one foot in front of the other on rural and city roads for several hours a day. Soon, the repertoire of songs you hum or sing to yourself wanes and you are, again, thinking. But the mind is not racing. The mind, too, walks. Thought itself becomes an exercise. It invigorates and refreshes.

Pedestrian touring won followers in England in the later half of the 17th century, as the Revolutionary and Napoleonic wars made travel too dangerous in Europe. Romantics such as Samuel Taylor Coleridge and John Keats recorded their walks in notes and poems and connected the freedom of their movement to the freedom of the mind to wander, as did William Hazlitt. Some decades before they did, a young organist set out on foot for a different and desperate purpose.

J.S. Bach was so determined to hear the famous organist Dieterich Buxtehude at St. Mary's Church in Lubeck, northeast of Hamburg, that he walked the 403 kilometers (250 miles) or so from Arnstadt, southwest of Leipzig, Christopher Wolff records in *Johann Sebastian Bach — The Learned Musician*. Bach left on this walk in mid- or late-November 1705, and arrived some time before 2 December. At the least, then, he walked around 29 kilometers (18 miles) a day. Though at age 20 Bach had youth on his side, he still must have been remarkably fit to reach Lubeck in the time that he did.

Curiously Bach's father, J.A. Bach, is wearing a kimono in a portrait of him painted around 1685. Wolff uses the portrait as an illustration in his book and in the caption describes the elder Bach as "a well-to-do citizen and home owner, dressed in a fashionable Japanese kimono."

I say "curiously" because 45 years before this portrait was painted Japan closed itself to Europe, forbid the return of Japanese who had left the country, and barred the entry of foreigners. Japan granted rights of commerce to only Dutch and Chinese traders. Kimonos must have made their way to Europe as the cargo of these traders, as luxury apparel in small quantities and at high prices affordable to wealthy homeowners.

Enemies and Women

We now complete our tour of Paul Theroux's perceptions and conclude that he can't forgive a former enemy. But rejection by women also appears to feed his prejudice.

CHAPTER 6. LETTERS TO THE PAST

The more I read Theroux, the more I felt compelled to study him. He became more interesting than the places and people he belittled. Part of him seemed to say, "You think you've been on an interesting trip? Hey, take a look at me!" Yet he wanted to rise above his books being about him. He wrote in the introduction to *The Old Patagonian Express*:

> One of the popular notions about travel books is that they are usually about the traveler. I wanted to get beyond this petty egotism and to try to understand the places I was passing through.

Or perhaps he strove, after all, to connect himself to each word. In *The Pillars of Hercules*, he wrote that one of the "virtues of a good travel book is the chance to see a traveler's mind, however childish, ticking away," and, in the essay "William Simpson: Artist and Traveler," in *Fresh Air Fiend*, that "nothing is more revealing of character than the experience of travel."

Theroux doesn't explain his contempt of Japanese people and things, beyond telling a Chinese salesman that he finds "the Japanese can be very irritating," in *Riding the Iron Rooster*. But "irritating" is an important word. Donald Richie, an authority on Japanese culture and film, used the same word in his book *The Honorable Visitors* in the chapter on Rudyard Kipling, who was

> aware of the irritated mood Japan sometimes fosters in the foreigner. Of a curio shop he (Kipling) wrote, "I tried to console myself with the thought that I could kick the place to pieces; but this only made me feel large and coarse and dirty — a most unfavorable mood for bargaining."

But Kipling, Richie noted, saw "the people. This was something few other foreign observers of Japan had done. They saw 'natives,' or objects of study, but not people. The first sight mentioned from the boat was 'an indigo-blue boy with an old ivory face,' and the first off it was his rickshaw-puller, 'a beautiful apple-cheeked young man with a Basque face.'"

I sought out Richie in Tokyo after reading the following passage in *The Honorable Visitors*:

> Living out of suitcases for months, having to worry about boat departures and train schedules, coping with "natives" whose language one does not know, concerned lest one be cheated, the traveler soon becomes weary of travel and consequently fails to do justice to the places traveled through.

> This occurs regularly to travel writers. Paul Theroux, for example, usually begins with equanimity and ends with something else. His first railway book finds him at the end so weary (as well he may have been after the Trans-Siberian trip) that he fails to do any kind of justice to the celebrated Bullet Train and the country through which it courses.

Richie was approachable and accommodating, and as alert and articulate as I imagined him to have been in his thirties. Over iced tea at the Foreign Correspondents' Club of Japan, I asked him what he thought about Theroux's Japan.

"Japan upsets puritan moralists," Richie said. "It upsets those who believe in black and white, in a wrong way and a right way."

He elaborated, taking the example of the philosophy of St. Thomas Aquinas, a Dominican theologian born in Italy in 1224, who believed that Christian revelation and human knowledge are facets of a single truth, which flies in the face of Japanese notions of acceptable ambiguity and the reality of appearances.

Richie had just returned to Tokyo from a book tour in the US to promote *A Hundred Years of Japanese Film*. "People would ask me the same questions I was asked in Berlin 40 years ago," he said. "'The Japanese live in paper houses. What do they do when it rains?' This wasn't in New York, though. I think it was in Ohio."

The Honorable Visitors provides accounts of the visits to Japan of Isabella Bird, Henry Adams, Aldous Huxley, William Faulkner, Truman Capote, Angela Carter, and Marguerite Yourcenar, among others. None were as disaffected as Theroux, but as Theroux would tell us, their Japan belonged to them; his Japan, to him.

"You either love Japan or you loathe it," Richie wrote in his essay "I Like Myself Here," reprinted in *The Donald Richie Reader — 50 Years of Writing on Japan*.

> Like Lafcadio Hearn, you grasp and press it to your heart, for a time at any rate, or else, like Bernard Shaw, the place rubs you so wrong that you even forget your manners, refuse to take off your shoes while treading tatami mats. Writers like Somerset Maugham or James Michener like it: writers such as Aldous Huxley and Christopher Isherwood do not care for it.

In the introduction to *The Old Patagonian Express*, Theroux states:

> Not speaking Hindi, Japanese, Farsi, or Urdu (among others) had made my first book somewhat facetious, I thought. It was so easy to mock. I did not want to be that ignorant again. So I learned Spanish. I went to night

school in South London and I listened to language tapes. I wanted to understand what was going on.

This seems disingenuous. Before *The Great Railway Bazaar*, Theroux could speak at least some French, German, Italian and, among other African languages, Swahili. The already well-read educated man was saying later in life that he knew he should have learned to read.

In caricaturing Japanese people, Theroux can't bring himself to give them character. Not people, they must be something else. Models are available in war movies and comics, so he borrows the stereotype that he believes his public will recognize and buy.

John W. Dower noted in *War Without Mercy*, that the

> Western perception of the Japanese as "little men" or "lesser men" meshed easily with images of the enemy as primitive, childish, moronic, or emotionally disturbed.

Theroux constantly belittles Japanese people for their stature, regards them as children, and doubts their intelligence. And he views them as a separate species in his description of Hangzhou in *Riding the Iron Rooster* as the "haunt of tourists and…little Japanese."

Looking at TV sets on display in a department store in Tokyo, in *The Great Railway Bazaar*, Theroux sees "forty-eight images of a little Japanese politician." But the TV screen has projected a pattern image, not a dimension. The smallness is in the mind.

In his novel *Kowloon Tong*, a Chinese mama-san in a girlie bar says to protagonist Bunt, "The Japanese are tough, even the Chinese too sometimes." Bunt's reply: "Can't be all that tough."

Contrast this with a British cartoon, reproduced in *War Without Mercy*, which was published in 1943 and titled: "How Tough Are the Japanese." The cartoon, in smaller print, answers the question: "They are not tougher than other soldiers… but brutality is a part of their fighting equipment." Theroux is bull's-eye accurate, but is he the ventriloquist for Bunt or the mama-san? Or is the target a mirror?

In the fictional vignette "The Sexual Life of Savages" in *Hotel Honolulu*, characters blend Theroux's preoccupations of women and war, when Sanford reminisces that Japan was the best place to be after the war:

> They were defeated, humiliated, their currency was in the toilet. The country was practically destroyed…You could get a Japanese woman to do anything. It was normal for them to be submissive, but after the war they were willing to be slaves.

And in the story "Clapham Junction" in *The Collected Stories*: "I was in Malaya during the war," Cox said. "It was long before your time. But I stayed on. I rather enjoyed the Japanese surrender. It was a terrible shambles."

Theroux pins a war image on Japanese products when he describes a jet ski in his essay "The Moving Target" contained in *Fresh Air Fiend*:

They sideswipe, they strafe, and they leave you in no doubt that these machines ("personal watercraft") are just the latest in a long line of technological atrocities unleashed on a peaceable world by Japanese manufacturers.

World War II is never far from Theroux's mind, in his travel writing and fiction. In *Riding The Iron Rooster*, Theroux attempts to coax anti-Japanese sentiment out of his Chinese hosts at most bends in the track. "By now we were all drunk enough to talk about war and friendship," Theroux recalls of his conversation with officials in Xinjian. Then:

> I mentioned the Japanese and said I thought they were planning to take over the world by dominating the world economy because they had failed to do so by military means. And how did it feel as a Chinese to be occupied again by a nation that had been driven out in the 1940s?

The Chinese railway official more sagely responds:

> We have a saying in China. You can't attack everyone, so you have to be careful of everyone.

On a train to Beijing, Theroux is in the company of two salesmen. One declares that he wished to visit Japan for his first overseas trip. Theroux is "surprised" at the choice. Then, "The Americans dropped an atomic bomb on them," one salesman says. Theroux: "That was too bad, but they started the war by bombing Pearl Harbor, didn't they, comrade?"

Theroux meets a Japanese who was walking down memory lane in Harbin where he had been a student in the 1930s and recalling it was "like a Europe to us" as it had "strippers, nightclubs, Paris fashions, the latest styles — books, songs, everything."

Theroux's reaction, customarily jingoistic:

> That seemed a very unusual way of describing a refrigerator, but of course he was talking about Manchukuo, Land of the Manchus, owned and operated by the Sons of Nippon.

In *The Happy Isles of Oceania*, Theroux imagines his enemy as he travels among islands that Japan attacked or invaded. In Vanuatu, he writes of the airfield that was named after Harold Bauer, a US fighter pilot who in 1942 shot down Japanese planes and was killed in Guadalcanal. A Japanese-Vanuatu joint venture was expanding the airfield, and Theroux wondered whether a Japanese construction company would "hide, lose, or hang" a plaque honoring Bauer in a new terminal.

In Palawan, Theroux observes a marker reading "A Grim Reminder of the Realities of War" which recorded that in December 1944 "soldiers of the Japanese Imperial Army forced 154 American prisoners of war into a tunnel, poured gasoline on them, and set them alight — 143 died, 11 escaped. The survivors' names and hometowns were listed on the plaque."

The Happy Isles of Oceania ends in Hawaii. "Fifty years later," Theroux writes, "I went to the Arizona Memorial in Pearl Harbor to pay my respects." A park service guide tells him that not many Japanese come to the memorial, but those who do sometimes "laugh and snap pictures of each other. I do not think they realize how important this place is to us."

In *Hotel Honolulu*, in the chapter "Nevermann the Searcher," the guest from Florida "was not a war buff, and all he said of Pearl Harbor was, 'We trusted the Japanese!' and that he had no intention of visiting the Arizona memorial: 'It's too sad.'"

I've visited the USS Arizona Memorial and walked through the tunnel-bridge with transparent flooring that's built directly above the sunken hull of the battleship where the remains of 1,117 crewmen are interred. To stand above the watery burial ground, the air heavy and cold, is a harrowing experience. The Japanese visitors I saw seemed as moved as I found myself. But Theroux's account of his conversation with the park guide is believable, so ignorant are young Japanese of recent history.

Theroux recounts the history of Takeo Yoshikawa, a Japanese spy who surveyed Hawaii for eight months in 1941:

> He was still on the job the day the planes were strafing and the bombs were falling and ships sinking, and the first of the 2,403 people were dying from Japanese bombs.

In his essay "Letter from Hong Kong," in *Fresh Air Fiend*, Theroux informs:

> The Peninsular's guests are mainly Japanese, who stay for the nostalgic reason that the Japanese commandant was quartered there after the siege, rape, and occupation of Hong Kong, which began the day Pearl Harbor was attacked.

This sounds contrived. Japanese can't travel to a history they don't know.
In the essay "Chinese Miracles," Theroux asks:

> These days everyone speaks of the Chinese miracle, but when has the world taken much notice of Chinese catastrophes, of which the Japanese rape and plunder of China before and during World War II and the earthquake…that instantly killed a quarter of a million Chinese in 1976 are but two instances?

The US oil embargo and other measures in response to Japan's designs on China triggered the war between Japan and the United States. How can an educated and traveled American ask the question: "When has the world taken much notice?" when the answer lies in Pearl Harbor and Hiroshima and Nagasaki?

Did Theroux grow up among people who hated "the Japanese"? Did he lose a relative — a favorite uncle — in battle against Japan, a loss that parents recounted at the dinner table? The only hint of a relative's Japanese war experience is contained in Theroux's partly autobiographical *My Other Life* in which "Uncle Hal" shows neighborhood children his Japanese sword, which he must have taken as a battle souvenir, as soldiers did.

In *The Pillars of Hercules*, Theroux says that his uncle, Cpl. Arthur Theroux of Stoneham, Massachusetts, was in Spain during World War II running a blood bank as a medic at the Thirty-third Station Hospital. Is Arthur the same man as

Hal, and did he serve also in the Pacific? The names on the radio news Hal hears are "Fidel Castro, Joe DiMaggio, the Emperor of Japan." (It's unlikely that the US ran such a facility in neutral Spain; perhaps Theroux has confused Spain with Saipan, as the Thirty-third Surgical Hospital did operate in the Pacific and may have operated in Saipan.)

What else could so upset Theroux about Japan? The use of drift nets by Japanese fishing boats in the Pacific would have angered him in same way he was disturbed by bullfights in Spain. Yet he has also noted the more than 100 cases of documented illegal Italian drift-net fishing in the early 1990s, in *The Pillars of Hercules*. Is it different because his great grandfather is Italian?

As a Peace Corps teacher in Malawi and Uganda, Theroux would have hated the white South African government for its apartheid policies. He taught and socialized with Africans while earlier writers such as Hemingway had treated the continent as an elephant-shooting ground. He would have seen Japan as abetting those policies through its willingness to trade, and hated it for accepting that country's reclassification of Japan as "white" to facilitate trade.

From the essay "Memory and Creation" in *Fresh Air Fiend*:

> Every industrialized country continued to trade with South Africa, and the apartheid regime officially declared the Japanese as white — and Japan gladly accepted the reclassification in its eagerness to trade.

In *The Great Railway Bazaar*:

> Fruit is also expensive since Japan buys cut-price oranges, apples, and tangerines from the South Africans, who are so grateful to get radios in return, they have officially declared the Japanese to be white.

And in *The Happy Isles of Oceania*:

> In the nineteen-seventies when the rest of the world refused to trade with South Africa because the whites there were treating Africans like scum the Japanese were so eager to do business they had themselves reclassified as whites and made billions.

What? "Every industrialized country continued to trade..." and "the rest of the world refused to trade." Theroux is speed-writing. Meaning isn't on his mind.

Foreign oil majors — US and European — supplied South Africa with about two-thirds of its oil needs in the 1970s and 1980s. The US declared a number of minerals such as chromium and manganese as "strategic" and exempted them from its trade ban. As for South Africa's classification of Japanese as "honorary white," this dates to 1930, to enable Japanese wool buyers to enter the country.

Women?

At least twice Japanese women, who are supposed to be submissive but who evidently don't find the libidinous writer attractive, spurn Theroux.

In *Riding the Iron Rooster*, Theroux appears envious of the former US Marine who had

> met a young Japanese woman in Canton — had just passed by the open door to her hotel room, started shooting the breeze and ended up in bed with

her. Kicker was 67 years old and had the face of a rapist. But his features softened as he recalled the encounter...

Earlier, in *The Great Railway Bazaar*, after giving a lecture on American literature in Tokyo, Theroux asks a "pretty Japanese girl in the hallway" to stay and have a drink, but she declines on the pretext that she is "shy." Theroux's interpretation:

> My offer was given impromptu and it had to be turned down for that reason. It was the wrong time: the Japanese have a sense of occasion...

In an Osaka bar, he is accosted by drunken Japanese men. One suggests Theroux should take the girl behind the counter home. Theroux: "I smiled at the girl. She winced." He flees after being kissed by a drunken Japanese man.

Perhaps mellowing with age, in Corsica in *The Pillars of Hercules* Theroux is the caring elder. Sensing that Corsican soldiers may have designs on a young Japanese woman, he asks if she is aware of the dangers of traveling alone, and accompanies her in a protective way. The conversation convinced him that "she was a good person, and she followed me back into town...I realized that by being disinterested I had won her confidence, and she clung for a while, until I sent her on her way."

Theroux is contemptuous of Japanese literature. *Snow Country*, which did most to earn Yasunari Kawabata the Nobel Prize for Literature, "seemed more and more to me like a version of Chekhov's *The Lady With the Little Dog*," he wrote in *The Great Railway Bazaar*. After reading both I doubted that he had read either. And a novelist might mention that the first example of his craft — *The Tale of Genji* — was produced in Japan.

It isn't true to say that Theroux never finds a good thing to say about Japan. In *The Old Patagonian Express*, he notices how trains accurately represent the culture of a country:

> the seedy distressed country has seedy distressed railway trains, the proud efficient nation is similarly reflected in its rolling stock, as Japan is.

In *The Great Railway Bazaar* he notes of Tokyo:

> Everything works: the place spins with polite invention.

Not once, however, does he try to explain how or why things work, so what is the point of the travel?

Perhaps the truth isn't reasoned.

In a promotional "conversation" on the website of his main publisher, Houghton Mifflin, Theroux is asked whether he can shed light on what the narrator in *Hotel Honolulu* means when he says, "The things we write are letters to the dead."

Theroux: "I'm not sure I can shed light on it, but it always seems that a serious writer in his or her work is addressing the past — issues long buried, our own pasts, our younger selves."

Can we ask him to tell us? It isn't enough for him to ask, even rhetorically, as he does in *The Pillars of Hercules*: "If you were happy and normal why would you ever want to write a book?"

I wondered whether I'd been too Therouxian about Theroux. I decided that I had, so should now admit to liking his *The Consul's File*, which appeared four years before the first of his travelogues. It's a favorite book, least so for the sympathetic portrait of a Japanese it contains. Its measured tone, bell-true conjuring of the atmosphere of the life of displaced expatriates, and intelligent exposition of a quiet love story has made the book one to keep.

Still I wondered who the intended audience for the travel books was. Not travelers, I was sure. Or people who live in the countries of which Theroux wrote. Then who?

I think I found the answer in "Traveling Home: High School Reunion [1979]" in *Sunrise with Seamonsters*. He had written for his peers — a policeman, a franchisee of Dunkin Donuts, a Toyota dealer, a trucking business owner, supermarket and newspaper chain owners, a deceased school bully and murderer, a deputy mayor, and teachers. This traveler sprung from Medford High's Class of '59 had written for those who had stayed at home.

LANGUAGE AND PRINCIPLE

We now proceed to the castle town of Nagaoka. Along the way, we consider the politics of rice, questions of language and principle, the identity of resident Koreans, and those whom the gods destroy.

CHAPTER 7. 100 SACKS OF RICE

A healthful set meal of rice, soup, fish, and salad was served for breakfast this Wednesday morning. As I was settling my bill for ¥6,480 ($54), one of the construction workers was paying for his group. He asked the innkeeper to adjust the receipt so that it showed each employee had spent the same amount. She did.

Leaving my pack at Minatoya, I walked to Sanjō Shiryōkan, a small museum on the south side of Kitasanjō Station and near Sanjō Municipal Library.

Gaikoku no kata ga miete imasu — "A foreign gentleman has appeared," an elderly attendant of Sanjō Shiryōkan announced in mild voice. There were no poorly concealed snickers or other awkward but contrived embarrassment. I felt I could relax, look at the exhibits at my own pace, and I'd make a point of buying something at the gift shop. A foreign gentleman has appeared. If only all retailers understood that we tend to spend where we are well received; but it's to our benefit that they don't.

This appeared less a museum than a shrine at which believers worship the god of industry. Crowbars, hammers, saws, nails, pliers, scissors, measuring instruments, and all in numerous sizes of minute fractional variation, impressed as examples of a dedication to precision.

It was hard to believe that so many types of carpentry and blacksmithing hardware were in use or even existed. The fineness of the exhibits produced an effect almost of novelty, and I found it hard to lift my eyes from them. This field of manufacture had almost certainly been assigned to the city by the national government. The town next door concentrates on cutlery.

Nails occupy a suspiciously lucrative place in Japan's history. Large shipments of them were needed for the rebuilding of neighborhoods destroyed by fire. The use of light woods, paper and straw in house-building, and of charcoal briquette burners and hearth fires for heating and cooking, put houses at great fire risk. Fire hurdled neighborhoods as flames jumped from one closely spaced house to the next.

Before the advent of fire engines, fire fighters destroyed rows of houses in order to create a firebreak, a practice which was continued during the US fire-bombing of Tokyo in 1945.

The demand for nails may have been artificially inflated by zestful *tobishoku* who were hired to tear down the houses, as these same people were also hired as carpenters to rebuild them, a likely conflict of interest Elizabeth Kiritani pointed out in *Vanishing Japan*.

Owners of buildings on old sites often remark, "There have been fires here. This building has been rebuilt three or four times." Fire risk became even greater after gas was piped into neighborhoods, as invariably some people would be using flame to cook or heat bath water when the pipes were ruptured in a quake.

None of the exhibits at Sanjō Shiryōkan was modeled from plastic or new materials. All testified to their age, authenticity, and utility, and that's what fascinated. A framed photo of a blackened blacksmith couple, shaping hot iron over an anvil in a six-mat room, which was probably in their house, brought life to the exhibits.

It's rare to sense history at large "museums." Rather, visitors are smothered in the newness of artificial recreations. The exhibits are expertly constructed, to be sure, but wasn't the purpose of a museum to display genuine artifacts of the past? A friend who studied museum management told me that the role of museums here is more to preserve such artifacts in sealed storage than to display them.

I left Sanjō Shiryōkan after buying postcards illustrated by a local artist, then pressed on to the Sanjō City Office, on Road 289. Here, too, was a shrine to manufacturing. Chisels, saw blades, pliers, carving knives, scissors, and wood-working planes were prominently displayed in glass cases in the lobby and bore testimony to Sanjō's pride in what it makes.

Newly planted and the size of a school swimming pool, a rice paddy was sandwiched between a gasoline station and car park, showing how every thumb-nail of land is used.

A church stood a short distance from the city office. Churches and temples tell you things. I stepped inside. It wasn't dimly lit as churches are but bright, the light filtered through blue, green, red, and yellow stained-glass windows. A bell hung awkwardly from the ceiling near the entrance. The floor was white marble. Electric candles on the walls and in chandeliers lit the aisles. Piped choral music mocked the pipe organ, which was built into the wall behind the altar.

Planter boxes of white lilies lined both sides of the steps leading to the pews. On the ledge protruding from the back of the pews, where hymnbooks might rest, were song pamphlets titled Humming Plaza VIP. A teddy bear bride and groom sat hand in hand on a low glass-topped table between one row of pews and the wall. This was a stage for the theater of white weddings. Framed portraits of couples hung from the walls. The product mix included "weekday weddings," "summer weddings," and "twilight weddings."

The Garden Chapel, I learned from a receptionist in an adjacent banquet building, is a link in the Washington Hotel chain. It supplies wedding dresses, arranges parties, receptions, photographs.

I returned to Minatoya to collect my pack, and retraced my steps west to Road 8. It was 11 a.m.

Some road signs carry the number of a road ahead, not the road you are on, without displaying a directional arrow. You may think that you are walking on Road 8, for example, when you are walking only toward Road 8. Sometimes different roads carry the same number. Sanjō quaintly supplies both confusions.

I chose the smaller Road 8. I'd follow it to the small city of Mitsuke, then take Road 216 to its junction with Road 498, which leads to the city of Nagaoka, my next stop. I was leaving a post town for a castle town, the home of a daimyo in feudal times.

Post towns, spaced 10–17 kilometers (three to ten miles) apart, were officially regulated settlements that catered to travelers along major roads. Until their deregulation in 1870, these towns were required to supply horses and porters, and must have provided similar services after that date, as Isabella Bird mentions them as a source of her horses in *Unbeaten Tracks*.

I was also leaving the birthplace of Haru Kobayashi. She had become a goze at age nine and walked and sang for her super as far afield as the neighboring prefectures of Fukushima and Yamagata. She was born to a farming family in the village of Asahi in what is now Sangan district, to the west of my route and near Higashisanjō Station.

Kobayashi may have been the last goze but she isn't the last impoverished female itinerant traveler who entertains for a living in rural Japan. They travel less but Filipinas in some ways have taken their place.

I'd thought that news media here no longer used such terms as *rōjo* — "old woman," but an NTV program preview of 2001 described Kobayashi as a 101-year-old old woman, whereas a man of that age would be described as a 101-year-old man. Several words containing the ideograph for "woman" in this language are derogatory or discriminatory. *Kan* — "wicked" and *shutome* — "mother-in-law" come to mind.

Captain Stag's billboard said in English, "Be Natural in Nature / Outside Gear / Go Outside Enjoy Life." Sakura Jutaku's sign said, "It is a Dream of a House." The composers of these signs may believe that their wording will persuade some to choose a Captain Stag tent or their dream home from the Sakura housing company. But it seems they strive more for the visual effect of English as a fashion accessory.

Banks of soft drink, snack food, and cigarette vending machines lined the roadside at seemingly fixed intervals. Yet this was the countryside. Such machines would be looted for cash at night or even in broad daylight in my country but I saw no sign of vandalism here.

"Was I Russian?" a man who had stopped at a bank of vending machines asked, after I told him I'd walked from Niigata, whose transport links to Russia probably had prompted his question. He bought a soft drink for me and insisted

I accept it. He'd been treated in this way when he once walked to neighboring Fukushima Prefecture, he said, and wanted to repeat the kindness.

The day was clear and warm. Rice paddies and dark wooden farm buildings boarded the lane I walked. Farmers were transplanting seedlings to paddies. A woman was cutting the tops off some vegetables with a scythe, against a backdrop of the light emerald of the seedlings. A farmer stood on a ladder set against a stack of sheaves of dried barley, his wife and son handing up to him more sheaves for the pile. Barley is harvested in cold weather, probably late winter here, so this farm was rotating the two crops. A dog was at ease at the foot of the ladder. Birds glided overhead.

Unlike factory-workers who wear the tired world on their face, these farmers looked at peace and contented, as I am when I bury my hands in a garden. But their backs are bent, cruelly by the makers of farm implements who attach short handles to every tool. These manufacturers seem to assume that a bent back is a correct posture for a farmer and that all crops must be tended from the low height at which rice seedlings are planted.

A man stopped his car near me at a fork in the road on the edge of Mitsuke. He told me to take Road 216 to the right of the fork, if Nagaoka was my destination. He'd seen me consulting my map. I couldn't identify the main road from among the four leading from the fork. He assured me again of the road I should choose, and I decided to trust him. It was a considered decision. His sureness suggested he was of the area and he seemed to be around my age.

Some Japanese take private delight in misdirecting lost foreigners. Or out of some misplaced sense of duty or attempt at kindness, they give directions without themselves knowing the way. Motivation aside, the result is predictable. I knew to consult my map closely several times rather than trust the directions of passersby, ill- or well-intentioned alike.

After several bad choices — maps in crowded English translation, road maps designed for cars — I latched onto a Japanese-language guide for motorcycle touring. It details country lanes and even paths through rice paddies, and provides travel notes of as much interest to walkers as to motorcyclists. As nothing is heavier than paper I jettisoned all other maps for this valuable guide.

When entering and leaving towns I found myself referring to this guide several times, so easy is it to confuse a narrow road with a narrow main road. I wore a vest of the type an angler or laborer wears, for the deep inside pockets which easily hold books or maps. It would have been a mistake to pack the guide away, thinking I'd need it only at the beginning or end of the day.

Further along Road 216, a large billboard showed a farming family enjoying bowls of rice. *Ima mo mukashi mo kawaranu aji o motomete imasu* — "We desire the never-changing flavor of rice, past and present," the billboard said. *Gambatte imasu* — "We're working hard."

The words "Never changing flavor of rice" lie deep in the channel of centuries-old policies of protectionism. The billboard's sponsor was the then Ministry of Agriculture, Forestry and Fisheries, which had designated this part of Niigata Prefecture as a "Uruguay Round countermeasure assistance region."

"Uruguay Round" refers to the 1986–1994 trade negotiations that the 108 or so signatories to the General Agreement on Tariffs and Trade begun in Uruguay and ended in Morocco. GATT members agreed to reduce trade barriers and create the World Trade Organization. Under the Uruguay Round's agreement on agriculture, Japan would allow rice imports first under a quota and later a tariff system.

This billboard told rice growers that they would never need to consume foreign rice, that they would be compensated for any harm that resulted from the trade agreement, that they would be secure in their vocation of producing rice, and that their toil in the fields was acknowledged. The flavor of their rice would never change.

Japan recycles some of its imported rice as food aid to Indonesia, Philippines, and North Korea. It keeps other imported volumes in government warehouses, the bales tagged, "emergency use only." Agricultural officials appear to have kept the implied promise of the Road 216 billboard.

Every country protects its farmers. Try exporting cheese to France or potatoes to the United States. Some of the protection must be sensible. Rural dwellers are culture carriers. Let them die and much else will, too. This, however, is the selfish argument that rich countries make.

On the subject of trade and language, why do governments, when they negotiate a "free" trade agreement, use the word "free" when they mean its opposite, "restricted" or "managed"? There's nothing to negotiate in the case of free trade, as all a government needs to do to trade freely is dismantle barriers such as tariffs and quotas. When it has finished doing that, it's a free trader.

But representative governments behave differently. They argue for exemptions for commodities which are produced by important constituents. So negotiators meet and weigh concessions and in the end produce a managed trade agreement.

Some people protest free trade agreements. I protest their use of the word "free." The ruled shouldn't permit their rulers to subvert this word. Its wrong use in trade may seem innocuous enough, but the misuse can spread.

———

At around 4 p.m. I entered the outskirts of Nagaoka, along an interminable road of used-car yards, gas stations, and noodle and fast-food joints. Music, broadcast from speakers attached to lampposts, lessened the pain of the monotony. An instrumental version of The Beatles' "If I Fell" followed "The Never-Ending Story" and both disquieted me in their suggestion of professional and personal possibilities.

I'd earlier heard Beatles' songs played at a post office in suburban Yokohama whose staff told me that the selection was part of a piped program to which the post office subscribed. But this wasn't the eastern seaboard replete with pop pretensions. It was a town of chemical and machinery industries and a pig and beef slaughterhouse, and the closer I drew to the center, the less interested I became in it. It lacked color, and there was a ramshackle quality to the buildings.

Hotel New Green Plaza, a small business hotel which adjoins Nagaoka Station, looked clean, and the single room rate was reasonable at ¥5,900 ($49). This was a lazy choice, but at least I was a stone's throw from history as Nagaoka castle, which was built in 1617, occupied the site where the station now stands.

No model of the castle has been built and I'm happier to imagine its wooden splendor than gaze at plastic. It was the residence of daimyo Naoyori Hori (1577–1639), who is credited with having used tax-breaks to attract farmers and merchants to the region. The central government should perhaps revisit his methods to stop the gravitation of people from areas such as this to Tokyo.

Travelers shouldn't keep to themselves, but sometimes one's own company is enough. Tonight I would and wouldn't eat out.

I felt an uneasy obligation to eavesdrop on local diners, write down what they said. Choose a restaurant that serves salmon, perhaps. Bokushi Suzuki, writing in the early 1800s in *Hokuetsu Seppu* (translated as *Snow Country Tales*), reported that the "best salmon are caught in the rivers of Kawaguchi and Nagaoka — their flavor is ten times more exquisite than any others!" Fish that had fought hard currents in their long, strenuous journey up the rivers from the northern sea always have a sweeter, more delicate taste, Suzuki explained.

Snow Country Tales contains a treasury of folklore, and Suzuki is down-to-earth. Men walking through the snow country, he noted, separately wrapped their testicles in wadded cotton cloth, "otherwise they are the first part to freeze, and a man's vital energies are lost."

But he was fastidious to a degree that drove his several wives round the bend. He seems to have applied the writer's tenet of "every word in its place" to each item in his house. He wouldn't retire at night until all was spotless and every possession, no matter how small, perfectly positioned. Four of his six wives left, one died at age 48 during their marriage and the other outlived him.

Snow Country Tales unconscionably is out of print, though *Hokkuetsu Seppu* is available in at least two Japanese editions. I found a "used" English edition online and received a copy as crisp as a new bank note. It must have been unsold publisher's stock. It's sad that unsold books become "used" without being read, but they're better orphaned than burned or buried.

Snow Country Tales is remarkable also for the experience of one of its two translators, Rose Lesser, who endured life in the snow country in the 1930s and through the war years. After traveling the back roads of Japan's four main islands for three years, she met her future husband, a Japanese botanist, in 1932 on the Tsugaru Strait ferry between Hokkaidō and Honshū, she relates in her preface to the translated edition.

The couple settled in Niigata Prefecture — Lesser doesn't say in which village or town — where people dug long narrow walking tunnels through the snow.

It was a time when women still blackened their teeth to show that they were married.

After war broke out, there were "endless military drills at a moment's notice" and Lesser had to stand in for her husband when he was ill. But in translating *Hokuetsu Seppu* she found herself reliving the hardship of snow country dwellers, and in doing so became able to forget her own. She must have outlived her husband, who died in 1947, by at least 20 years. She found work as a language teacher at Hōsei University, Tokyo, and said that it took 12 years after the war for life to normalize for her and her daughter.

Neglectful of Suzuki's advice, I ordered a beer at an *izakaya* bar and later would eat what I wanted to eat. Identical twins ran the bar I found on a side street near the station. They didn't stare at me because, I surmised, they'd been stared at enough themselves.

Two farmers seated at a corner table were behaving like robbers discussing the odds of pulling off their next heist. Their speech animated but circumspect and audible enough, they were plotting to label their rice as organically grown. In their subdued excitement they hadn't noticed me.

One said that organically grown rice could fetch a retail price of ¥1,000 ($8.30) per kilogram, double the price of rice grown in chemically fertilized fields. He estimated they would receive ¥40,000 ($330) per *pyō* or 60 kilogram bag of rice, or two-thirds the retail price. The other suggested that the label would look more authentic if it included a photograph and name of a farmer.

At a convenience store I bought yogurt, orange juice and cold milk coffee. Feeling foreign, I decided to spend my night in Nagaoka watching TV. Though tonight my laziness was rewarded, one doesn't expect to benefit educationally from such a pastime, given the mindlessness of the stream of low-budget quiz and talent shows where the words "quiz" and "talent" mean something else.

Worse, barrel-bottom foreign programs appear selected for the curious or perverse light in which they show the US and other countries. Even if it's true that you can buy a first rate Hollywood movie only in a package with "B" and lesser grade movies, private TV channels here seem to delight in showing the poorer grade films.

In local fare actors and interviewers seem to overact and shout. Nothing appears natural. Without acting or presentations skills, perhaps shouting is the only way to attract attention. Why people submit to this visual and audio assault may puzzle future generations of psychiatrists more than it seems to puzzle us.

———

This Wednesday evening NHK's Channel 1 was airing a docudrama on *tokkō tai in* — "special attack brigade." The program didn't use the words kamikaze — "divine wind," or *jisatsu* — "suicide," to describe the planes or the fate of their pilots.

Ravel's "Pavane for a Dead Princess" bathed in melancholy the program's beginning, which showed the end, in Tokyo in 1989. Emperor Hirohito had died. I can't say why *gagaku* court music wasn't chosen to solemnize the occasion of the end of an imperial era. Such traditional music would more befit the theme of transition in an imperial line that extends from the sixth century and mythically for several hundred years earlier. But the creators of the program may have seen a parallel between the sacrificial pilots and French impressionist or late romantic music of the 20th century that laments the death of a princess.

Then, to war years. A pilot is dining at a soldiers' mess. He divulges a secret to the waitresses, who know that they'll not see him again. He tells them that he's not a Japanese. He's a Korean. He goes outside. Waitresses follow. They ask him to sing "Arirang," a Korean folk song. He bashfully declines, then gives in — "Walking over the peak at Arirang / the sorrows in my heart / are as many as the stars in the sky."

"Why throw your life away so foolishly?" the soldier's father asks, pleadingly.

The son's reply — "There's nothing to do but leave things to fate" — is the device that places his birth and upbringing in Japan. This, I think, was the program's point — that Japanese must accept Koreans born and raised in Japan as their own, because they not only speak and act but even die as Japanese do.

In a preview of a program of similar theme, a young Korean man confides to a Japanese friend that he is really a Korean who, like his parents and grandparents, was born in Japan. His parents had told him this when he was young, but admonished him never to forget that he was Korean.

"I think my parents are really Japanese," he added, reflecting the wisdom of the young.

"I've learned Japanese history, adopted Japan's customs, I know only Japan," he said. "But some parents won't come to our weddings if we marry a Japanese. They soften only years later when we take our children, their grandchildren, to see them."

And: "When you set out on a journey, it's important to know the point from which you started." The man was training to be an action movie star.

"Am I Korean? Am I Japanese? I am me!"

Many Japanese still look down on Koreans, and Koreans harbor both inferiority and superiority complexes toward them, similar to the conflicting complexes Japanese hold toward Westerners. A tense confusion results when these complexes clash — feelings of admiration, detestation, respect, and contempt all swirl in a gumbo.

Japan has invaded or occupied Korea intermittently since the fourth century. It annexed the country in 1910 and tried to solve a wartime labor shortage by putting perhaps as many as two million Koreans to work in coalmines and factories. In a way, it reinstated Korea's centuries-old tradition of slavery. Many labor conscripts were repatriated after World War II, but still around 625,000 reside in Japan today. Most are Japan-born, second- and third-generation Koreans. Little distinguishes them from Japanese.

Stereotypically, they'll not dress as well, live in poorer areas, be more likely to work in a bar or a pachinko parlor than a regular company, and evade taxes. Actually, they dress as smartly as most Japanese, live according to their means in rich or poor suburbs, are as educated as most Japanese, and work side by side in most fields of endeavor.

Although Japan withdrew colonial citizenship from Koreans in 1952, most who have wanted permanent resident status have been granted it since 1982 and are eligible for national health and other benefits. Most Korean applications for Japanese nationality are accepted. In the five years to December 2005, 51,981 Koreans became Japanese nationals — or about 200 a week.

Japan will assimilate rather than integrate its new nationals, but nonetheless in Tokyo one feels a warmth in the sea wind between the two countries. Half or more of Japan's post middle-aged females are besotted with handsome, gentle, ever-polite Korean movie stars who presumably are the antithesis of their own neglectful, coarse men. These graying groupies have sparked a sales boom in Korean food, movies, travel, and language lessons.

In stages since 1998 South Korea has relaxed the postwar ban it imposed on Japanese pop music, TV, theater, radio, magazines and books. But the country's embrace of the Internet had already enfeebled the ban as young Koreans downloaded pretty much what they wanted from Japan. In daily life Koreans are said still to suffer both subtle and direct discrimination, but the tone and content of the NHK docudrama suggested the forming of fairer attitudes.

Korea owes some debt to Japan, which provided the model for its shipbuilding, steel, car, and electronics industries. The two countries' accounting standards are similar and they use even similar formats for the presentation of statistics in industry publications — I've observed this in shipping, shipbuilding, and heavy industries.

Compare education or living standards or rates of crime in Korea with the same measures for the Philippines, which was colonized by Spain and the US, and it's fair to conclude that Korea was more fortunate, though a northern, colder clime and Confucian and Buddhist influences surely have contributed much to the conditions for social cohesion and prosperity.

Yet during World War II Western powers would to say to their colonies, "You'll have a better chance with us than with the Japanese." Orwell said that in his BBC broadcasts to India. The choice he presented was between masters.

What state would India be in if Tokyo had ruled it for the years Westminster did? Its wealth may have been more evenly distributed and education more a universal right than a privilege of the rich. Shackling India with a language as cumbersome as Japanese, though, would have robbed people of the facility they now have to interact with ease with much of the world.

Then again, none of this may have happened. The older civilization may have subsumed the younger and absorbed the Japanese language into one or more of its own, and thus spread India.

————

My appreciation of the NHK docudrama about kamikaze pilots didn't induce any guilt for not having paid NHK fees in a long time. When a student and barely able to afford the fees, I did pay. Later, when I could afford to pay, I didn't.

In the interim I'd read that an opposition politician had publicly questioned the legal basis for the fees. The basis was weak, it transpired, but NHK had always invoiced residents, assuming they all owned TV sets, and residents paid the invoices as they would an electricity bill.

Collection agents fan out through the suburbs each month to collect from non-payers. I told the agent who visited me that I'd pay if he could produce a copy of the law mandating the payments. Some weeks later I found in my letterbox an NHK brochure, in Japanese and English. It contained phrases such as *gensoku to shite* — "In principle (residents shall...)."

Japanese should, I think, ask their representatives to purge the word *gensoku* from laws and official documents. There is or isn't a law, is or isn't a requirement. People can enjoy acceptable ambiguity in literature but shouldn't allow it in the way they're governed.

A bewilderingly uncaring use of the word *gensoku* is in the expression *hikaku sangensoku* — "three non-nuclear principles." These are not to make, own, or introduce nuclear weapons. They are rules, not laws, and words for "policy" such as *hōsaku* or *seisaku* aren't used. The larger question is why the issue isn't debated. Even by the only country to have suffered nuclear attacks, the ambiguity is accepted.

If the principles were policy or the rules law, US warships would offload nuclear warheads at a point offshore before entering naval bases in Japan, and collect them after leaving port. Otherwise it would have "introduced" nuclear weapons. But no one believes that the US would do that, and Tokyo maintains the fiction of adherence to non-nuclear "principles."

Over dishonesty of a different kind — the reported embezzlement of programming expenses by NHK staff — many Japanese now decline to pay NHK's fees. What began as a protest by a few has grown into a revolt, the number of non-payers reaching nearly a half million as of this writing. The revolt has produced an atmosphere conducive to the scrutiny of NHK practices, such as notifying politicians before politically sensitive material is aired, which sometimes results in censorship.

NHK collected around ¥650 billion ($5.4 billion) in fees in the year to March 2005, and the shortfall from non-payers was estimated at ¥6 billion to ¥7 billion ($50–$58 million).

———

Nagaoka took the losing side of the shogunate in the Boshin War against the Satsuma and Chōshū clans from Kyūshū and southwestern Honshū, and the clans succeeded in restoring imperial rule in 1868. That experience bore the saying *kome hyappyō* — "100 sacks of rice."

Amid a food shortage after the civil war, a neighboring province sent 100 sacks of rice to Nagaoka. Most city officials argued that the rice should be distributed among the hungry but one official, Torasaburō Kobayashi, vigorously countered that it should be sold and the funds used to rebuild schools. Kobayashi's wishes prevailed, and kome hyappyō has come to mean sacrificing short-term needs for longer term goals.

Some politicians expediently invoke the saying to divert their constituents' attention from current conditions but nonetheless it seems also to embody a genuine gratitude to earlier generations for their sacrifices. Nagaoka makes Kome Hyappyō awards, recently to people who have helped fund schools in Cambodia, Laos, Thailand, and Ghana, and declares 15 June Kome Hyappyō day.

Within the memory of parents, war visited again. Nagaoka was razed on the evening of 1 August 1945, starting at 10.26 p.m., according to city records. For one hour and 40 minutes, 126 B-29 bombers firebombed the city, killing around 1,460 people and destroying some 60,000 homes.

I don't write in this way to elicit sympathy for Japan or to judge its punishment. It's just that I've mulled that bombing date over and over. What could have been the point of destroying any city, let alone a small one, just five days before the nuclear bombing of Hiroshima and eight days before that of Nagasaki?

Surely destroying the industrially less consequential city first is akin to blowing up a footpath at a time when a decision has already been made to obliterate the highway. Yet the only targets US pilots had been instructed not to firebomb were the four pre-selected nuclear targets. If nuclear bombs were used out of the certainty that they would convince Japan to admit defeat, why then attack any other target? A friend commented that British bombing of small, non-strategic German cities in the closing days of the war raises the same question.

A Japanese friend's mother, now in her late 70s, accepts the argument that those who died in Hiroshima and Nagasaki were sacrificed to save the many more Japanese who would have been killed if the Allies had decided to invade Japan. This is a compelling argument.

But in the climate of the time it's conceivable that an overriding purpose in using atomic bombs was to seize an opportunity — which all at the command level knew would be short-lived, because they knew that Japan was already prostrate — to test them on a people whom propaganda had portrayed as subhuman and whose annihilation was therefore permissible. If Britain had had atomic bombs at the time, I wonder whether it could have brought itself to use them on Germany.

Nagaoka links as a sister with Fort Worth, Texas, and as a friend with the German city of Trier, near Luxembourg. The cities swap students during the summer months. Some people put down sister cities as excuses for city officials to junket. They may be that in some cases, but the large number of student, sport, cultural, and business exchanges that sister ties facilitate must be mutually beneficial. The link between my hometown of Christchurch, New Zealand and Kurashiki in Okayama Prefecture has created associations and friendships that will span generations. Tragically it seems that war is a prerequisite.

The US led the sister-cities movement as part of its battle for hearts and minds in Europe and Asia in the aftermath of World War II. Today, around 35 percent of its sister links are in Europe, 27 percent in Asia and, tellingly, only 2 percent in the Middle East. Perhaps that percentage will increase after the Iraq war.

Nagaoka, in 1946, designated 1 August as a day to commemorate the rebirth of the city, and named it Nagaoka Festival Day in 1951. On 2–3 August, one of Japan's largest fireworks displays is held along the banks of the Shinano River in memory of those killed in the air raid. The Obon festival for the dead, which marks the return of ancestral spirits to their hometowns or villages, follows a few days later. The spirits are sent back to their world on paper lanterns floated out to sea.

Do the people who saw their towns firebombed later think to remember the pyrotechnics of the inferno by lighting up the sky with fireworks? Some pyrotechnical designs seem to strive for breadth in an effort to create a continuous falling wall of flame — for example, chrysanthemums across 650 meters (710 yards) or waterfalls 800 meters wide. I mentioned the possibility of this association to a friend, who didn't understand; then she did and became upset.

Dresden, which Britain and the US firebombed at the close of World War II, adds a fireworks display to its summer classical and jazz music festivals. Tokyo stages spectacular fireworks over the Sumida River in summer, but this tradition dates to 1733.

The US began firebombing Japanese cities in March 1945 — first Tokyo, then and continuously Osaka, Yokohama, Kobe, and Nagoya. By war's end, fire bombs had accounted for two-thirds of the tonnage of bombs dropped on 66 Japanese cities. The death toll from this bombing is estimated at 183,000, compared with a combined Hiroshima and Nagasaki toll of 210,000 from atomic-bombing, according to John W. Dower.

(The common estimate of 668,000 dead from fire- and conventional bombing, such as appears in *World War II Almanac 1931–1945*, is based on a mistranslation of the Japanese word for casualties [*shishō*], which includes the wounded, Dower notes.)

The firebombing wasn't a response to the attack on Pearl Harbor, as planning had begun the month before. Gen. George C. Marshall had instructed his aides in November 1941 to develop contingency plans for "general incendiary attacks to burn up the wood and paper structures of the densely populated Japanese cities," according to historian John Costello, as quoted by Dower. Some Tokyo residents reported that they saw the gasoline-filled bombs being dropped concentrically to ensure that all inside burned.

The notion of burning Japanese wasn't new. Eighty years earlier, in the course of negotiations between Britain and the hostile Chōshū clan of Kyūshū for access to Shimonoseki, an English admiral warned a Japanese official at Shimonoseki that if a "single European were hurt, the whole town should be burnt to the ground," Sir Ernest Satow recounted in *A Diplomat in Japan*.

Burning people seems part of Western culture, with biblical precedent. Witch incinerating aside, Judges 20:48 records: "The Israelites then turned back to deal with the Benjamites, and put to the sword the people in the towns and the cattle, every creature that they found; they also set fire to every town within their reach."

And as Kurt Singer wrote in *Mirror, Sword and Jewel*, "religious or racial wars...tend to extinguish the male population, or at least to terrorize it into subjection by every method available."

Japanese, too, practiced the setting of flame to flesh. Japan's earliest history, *Nihongi*, records several cases of death by burning for crimes small and large. Japan, too, targeted civilians in China, as part of a tactic within a strategy to demoralize and weaken resistance — it isn't enough to say that the imperial army ran amok. Japan began bombing Chinese cities in 1937, which practice Britain and the US deplored, then copied.

There are no precise figures for the number of Chinese civilian dead at the hand of Japan's army in its eight-year war with China, but estimates range from three million to 20 million, in addition to 3.1 million uniformed Chinese killed.

As Dower noted, the Pacific War began and ended with the bombing of civilians. Thus continued a centuries-old tradition, embraced by the Peloponnesians in their war and, to prove that being a foreigner isn't a factor, by US union troops in theirs.

Nagaoka occasionally advises the US on the finer points of fireworks. City records detail assistance lent by Nagaoka pyrotechnists to the Louisiana World Exposition, New Orleans, 1984; the Los Angeles Olympic Games, also 1984; in Fort Worth, to celebrate Independence Day, in 1994; and to mark the 150th anniversary of the foundation of Fort Worth, in 1999.

Do we worship the gods that destroy us, erect monuments to them, celebrate them in moving, colored light? We may not, but we recognize such gods. The Greek tragedian Euripides (480? BCE–406 BCE) is credited with having said, "Those whom the gods wish to destroy, they first make mad." Some do worship these gods, and in firebombing, the bombers and the bombed are deprived of their senses.

SHIRLEY MACLAINE

The actress Shirley MacLaine called Japan a second home. We next visit her thoughts.

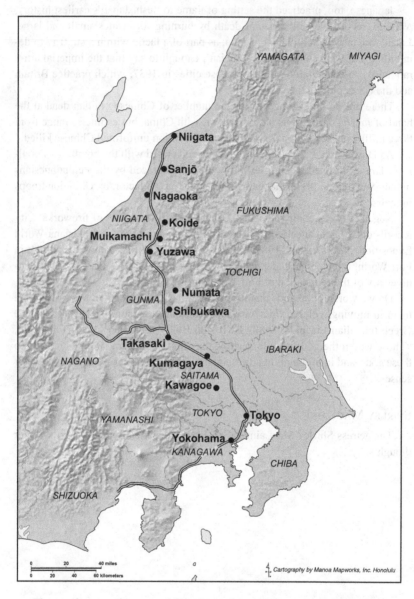

The northern prefectures of Honshū and my walking route from Niigata to Yokohama.

CHAPTER 8. SHIRLEY'S CLOAK

It was easy to get my hands on actress Shirley MacLaine's *Don't Fall off the Mountain*, which is part autobiography and part fantasy but illuminating and heartfelt on the subject of her encounter with Japan.

It's the type of book mothers recommend. Mine recommended it to me. My local bookseller and librarian both recognized it as soon as I prompted, "The title begins with Don't Fall..."

"*Don't Fall Off the Mountain*," they said. "Yes, I've read that."

MacLaine has appeared in about 54 movies, nearly one a year since her debut in Alfred Hitchcock's *The Trouble With Harry* in 1955. They include *My Geisha* (1962), *Terms of Endearment* (1983), and *Steel Magnolias* (1989). She's nothing if not hardworking.

To those who say that she is Warren Beatty's sister, others would say that Warren Beatty is her brother.

Like Theroux, MacLaine doesn't tie herself too tightly to facts. But she doesn't believe that she can supply answers or even that she understands questions. She packs an open mind in her suitcase, shows a willingness to learn, and appears always more quick to inquire than condemn.

Travel "opened up" and "expanded" her life. It enabled her to see people as people and disinherit her father's racist outlook. As a child in a white Southern Baptist family, she admits to never having seen African Americans as individuals, only as "a mass."

Her early misconceptions about race were the "most jarring, and the most personally offensive...because the truth as I learned it was so directly in conflict with the 'truth' I had been taught as a child, mainly by my father," a man who "adored philosophy, art, and music," and was a school principal, but who "referred to anyone with dark skin as a 'nigger.'"

73

MacLaine "developed a passion for the Japanese theater. It took me outside myself." The kabuki theatre was like a "giant, tragic fairy tale. Life was interpreted with vast brushstrokes on a magnificent stage, yet in exquisite detail."

She does sometimes seem to be "outside" herself, but her experiences in Japan, where she lived on and off for several years, are no less real. She lived in her Japan.

She writes much of the Japan ties of her late husband and show-business entrepreneur Steve Parker. They met in San Francisco in 1952 and married in 1954, when she was around 20. He was around 32. She wanted to "understand Japan — try to be a part of it — not only because of the challenge of Japan itself, but because it was a large part of the man I married."

She recounts that Parker first sailed to Japan on a cargo ship on which his father worked, became more Asian than Occidental, learned his schoolwork in Japanese in Yokohama, and by the age of 12 could "speak, read, and write several other Asian languages as well."

As a paratrooper, Parker had fought hand-to-hand with "people he had actually gone to school with." He'd been separated from his outfit during a mission in the jungles of New Guinea, where he'd survived by "making friends with headhunters."

In Tokyo, MacLaine observed people:

> How influenced (Japan) was by our world, and yet how different...The traditional Japanese man watched in silent confusion, seeming unable to cope with the transition. His customary robes seemed pompous and out of place when he saw himself reflected in shop windows, and yet the Western suit he had made did not fit him properly...Too fast, he seemed to be thinking. It was all too fast, this meeting with the West...

MacLaine saw Japan as a "children's paradise" where children "roamed free and unattended in the crowded maze of shoppers, without fear, without harm." It takes a good mother to pick up on this — travel writers, Isabella Bird excepted, seem not to.

She appears to have confused the name of her daughter, whom she refers to as both Sachie and Sachiko. But it's possible she had chosen a name — Sachie — which can be English or Japanese, then added a Japanese version of it, to make it even easier for her daughter to mix with Japanese children. (Her daughter has shortened both names and blossomed into the actress Sachi Parker.)

Foreign residents will share her observation that "Japanese see only what they want to see" nearly 50 years after her first visit. But sometimes she swallows a Japanese version of Japan:

> In Japan there is no sharp delineation between right and wrong. Everything is approached from all sides at once. If disputes occur, a mediator is called in who does not necessarily allow the "right" to win, but rather arranges a compromise. No one must suffer the degradation of losing face, and to cause it is the most serious of all offenses, and "right" is sometimes sacrificed. "Right" is not necessarily relevant anyway, but people and their feelings are.

Social etiquette may disguise conflict as interaction but Japanese appear to rationalize in terms as black and white as soot and sugar, as English people do, unless obfuscation serves some preconceived purpose. Everyone seems to use the form and expressions of compromise to pacify losers.

MacLaine wrote that Japan "never attempted" to conquer nature and that Japanese didn't "harness water, tame the wilderness, and conquer space. They blended with the elements, and created a balance to nourish life by bowing to a greater force." Japan does all the things she says it doesn't, and with reckless abandon. Or did Japan appear that way in the 1950s and 1960s?

I don't believe that MacLaine's late ex-husband at the age of 12 could read or write several Asian languages, because Chinese and Japanese students at that age can't read or write their own languages well.

I don't believe that he "fell over a rice-paddy wall and nicked his nose on his own bayonet," because rice paddies don't have walls. She writes that this nose nicking won him a purple heart. I believe that if he won a purple heart, he won it for something else.

I don't believe that her husband recognized in a Tokyo bar a pinstripe-suited man as the soldier he'd confronted at night in a rice paddy in Leyte, Philippines, in 1944. In the bar, "suddenly their arms flew around each other and tears came to their eyes."

I don't believe that during a meeting with a Japanese magazine owner the owner left for 45 minutes to kneel and meditate before a floral arrangement so that he could feel at peace, then returned to the meeting.

I don't believe that she smoked a Peace cigarette, not right through. One or two puffs on this impossibly strong concoction, maybe. I don't believe that she bathed communally with Japanese men who "lounged around stark naked, discussing their day's business."

She said she climbed 14,000 feet in Bhutan in one day, to reach a monastery. She's forgetting that she was several thousand feet above sea level when she started the climb.

MacLaine writes of Japan as though she visited during the Meiji or Taishō eras, though she was there in postwar Shōwa. Tokyo prohibited unisex bathing in 1869 — at least 80 years before she arrived on the scene — and reinforced the ban, which at first mustn't have been much respected, with further prohibition in 1870 and 1872, Edward Seidensticker recorded in *Low City, High City*. And the Japanese man who puts his kimono aside for a Western suit more likely belongs to the 1920s than 1960s.

MacLaine, like Theroux, mistakenly transliterates Japanese words. Her "shitaganigani" should read *shikata ga nai* — "it can't be helped;" "Caburenjo" should read *kabu renjo*, which isn't a geisha training school but a dance theater; the Japanese couple in Bhutan used the greeting *irrashaimase* not "irashaimas;" "Oksan" should read *okusan* — "wife;" and "mushi mushi" should be *moshi moshi* — "hello," for telephone conversations (the repetition was necessary in the early days of the telephone when lines weren't clear).

These aren't capital offenses, and one or two mistakes will creep in — oversight by the writer, the editor, the proofreader. But unlike Theroux, MacLaine's primary profession isn't the written word. Something other than carelessness — contempt? — underlies a pattern of such errors by writers who only write.

A critic said, "Because MacLaine lives in a kind of fantasy world it's hard to critique her work for veracity. She doesn't draw lines between the real and spiritual worlds. What's problematic is one's view of reality. Perhaps everyone does encounter a genuinely different Japan."

I didn't look to MacLaine as a source of information or insight. An actress is a practiced illusionist — a polished confusion of the real and staged worlds is her profession. Like her enthusiasm, such confusion is bound to enter her writing, but she conveys feelings and the gist of meanings with the sincerity in her sinews.

MacLaine may have been time-warped in romanticizing a Japan of some decades earlier. But she never stopped trying to understand the place she said she'd be happy to claim as second home. As an American she faced the same former enemy Theroux faced, but with an interval from war to peace of only ten years, compared with 30 for Theroux. Yet she allowed herself to view her hosts as people and become close to them.

Masks fascinate Theroux. So do they MacLaine, though her mask is a cloak. She learns, pleasantly, that travel is self-discovery:

> My curiosity of others and their ways of life was endless. The more I learned about others, the more I learned about myself. I was beginning to understand why I had become an actress. To wear and understand the cloak of another person had been a motivating force in me all my life. The world was so rich in characters, so rich in varying points of view…I loved trying to understand anything different because I always found something different in myself…

I'd like to read her next book.

INTO THE MOUNTAINS

We now turn west into the mountains, where the handiwork of an extraordinary prime minister appears underfoot.

CHAPTER 9. FEUDAL FACSIMILE

> All streams run into the sea, yet the sea never overflows; back to the place from which the streams ran they return to run again. — Ecclesiastes 1:7

Buoyed by a breakfast of yogurt and cold barley tea, I set out at 8 a.m. this Thursday for the small mountain town of Koide, a walk of about 37 kilometers (23 miles).

I'd take Road 498 from Nagaoka Station, then Road 17, which is an extension of Road 8 from Niigata, all the way to Koide. Before Road 17 connected Niigata and Gunma prefectures in 1959, rail provided the only — and irregular, as snow often stopped the trains — link between the west and east coasts of Honshū.

Fort Worth Nagaoka Stockyards, named for the sister-city tie, was signposted on the outskirts of Nagaoka and explained the beef-slaughterhouse smell I'd noticed upon entering the city. It's a sweet, zephyr-light pungent, hoof-and-hide smell that seems to radiate for miles from the epicenter of cattle death. Chicago residents may recognize it.

Road 17 follows the Shinano River on its left side until the town of Kawaguchi, where it begins to parallel the Uono River, a tributary of the Shinano.

My dog's hind leg is straighter than Road 17, and the background to the bends tells us much about Niigata's most famous son and former prime minister, Kakuei Tanaka, and much about Japan. But the bends in the roads, which impress a walker by the distance they add, are only a small part of the legacy of this progenitor of the construction state.

Under the slogan of "remodeling the archipelago," Tanaka brought the bullet train and expressways to his prefecture, and much else besides. It's a measure of a politician's prestige if he can stop a bullet train in his electoral district, for the construction work and status it brings to the area. The trains first represent the business of concrete, as the tracks are set in a bed of shingle within a low-walled concrete canal supported by concrete towers. The external structure thus resembles a never-ending concrete road bridge.

The Jōetsu bullet train between Tokyo and Niigata has eight stops. Tanaka located four of these in his electorate of Niigata Third District — Echigo-Yuzawa, Urasa, Nagaoka, and Tsubame-Sanjō. The ski town of Echigo-Yuzawa and city of Nagaoka are defendable choices, less so the small town of Urasa and Tsubame-Sanjō, which is a short commute from Niigata.

Tanaka won hearts first by raising funds to electrify the Nagaoka Railroad, which enabled farmers to deliver produce to markets after coal price increases made steam trains unviable. He took over management of the railroad, added buses and taxis, and also a gravel division which he sited in Koide. Vast volumes of gravel were needed for the several dams of the Tadami River project and the linkage of the Tadami and Shinano rivers.

On just one page of my Niigata map I counted ten black bars across the blues of rivers. The dams are built at close intervals, each spawning an artificial lake that rises and forks into mountain valleys.

———

Later along stretches where Road 17 follows a river, large signs warned that the "river is flowing." What else would a river do? Then I realized that the river level would rise and the river flow as a dam lake was lowered. Nobody can play on the banks of these rivers.

Japan has built 2,202 dams since the modernizing Meiji era began in 1868 — an average of 16 a year or one every three weeks. A further 241 constructions are planned, counting scheduled completions from April 2005. These data, sourced from the Japan Dam Association, exclude dams of less than 15 meters (50 feet) in height, which are classified as *en* — "dike" or "weir." Though no dams have been scrapped, opponents have halted some 94 projects. Most dams supply water for city drinking, rice-farming, and factory use.

Japan may have imported its penchant for dams from the US, which last century built around 75,000 of them, or one a day since declaring independence from Britain. They block some 600,000 miles (965,000 kilometers) of what were once free flowing rivers. They were built for electricity, irrigation, drinking water, and flood control.

Some of the dams were viewed as monuments, an answer to the pyramids. The US "gloried in the construction of dams across America's rivers," a US interior secretary has said. People believed that fresh water flowing to the sea was "wasted." But from the 1970s it began to dawn that the dams had come at a terrible price. Rivers had been deformed or killed and two-thirds of all fish species — salmon, shad, striped bass, herring and sturgeon — had become endangered or lost.

Japan has "disrupted the cycling of materials by rivers and damaged their ecosystems" and "many rivers have been turned into cold, uninteresting ditches detached from our lives," according to Dr. Takashi Okuma, a professor of civil engineering at Niigata University.

Japanese once knew how to coexist with rivers. They created forest belts along riverbanks to act as a buffer zone and directed overflows to areas where damage would be minimal, Dr. Okuma wrote in his report, "Japanese Flood Control." They built houses with raised floors. Farmers welcomed the occasional flood as the sediments it left enriched their fields. But the import of modern civil engineering techniques in the late 1880s enabled Japan to adopt an attitude of zero-tolerance toward flooding.

Dr. Okuma noted that an industrial culture evolved that demanded regular, scheduled commuting and production regardless of the changes wrought by nature. This culture has borne a social attitude of intolerance of even small-scale floods. He believes that in order to restore the lost functions of rivers, people must accept that they're part of nature and be willing to tolerate floods to a certain extent.

While walking I heard only one political campaigner speak out against dams. She drove a small sound truck and unconvincingly broadcast a one-sentence "no dam" message.

———

Road 17 turns crooked — really crooked — shortly after the town of Horinouchi a few kilometers before Koide. There are suspicious bends before this point, but after Horinouchi the road forms a wide horseshoe to encompass the village of Hirogami, the town of Koide, the village of Yunotani, and the town of Yamato.

I crossed the Uono River and a tributary back and forth over five bridges. I crossed it at Kawaguchi, then crossed it again after Echigo-Horinouchi Station, then crossed a tributary of it above Koide, then crossed it again to reach Koide Station, then crossed it back again to rejoin Road 17, then crossed it again after Yairo Station in Yamato. I can't say whether all five bridges were necessary.

Each of the heads of villages or towns through which Road 17 winds belonged to *Etsuzankai*, Tanaka's electoral support group. *Etsuzan* means "crossing the mountains," and *kai*, "group" or "organization." Etsuzankai sent Tanaka, its candidate and star son, across the mountains to Tokyo.

It was said that it was hard for a company to prosper in the Third District unless it networked within Etsuzankai, which spread its chapter tentacles throughout the district. It logged the birthdays and wedding anniversaries of those who mattered, sent gifts of money, took donations from companies, and mobilized voters.

The impetus behind the weaving of Road 17 may have come from the town head of Koide, where Nagaoka Railway's gravel business was based. Tokyo had planned to build the road in a more or less straight line from Ojiya to Muikamachi, bypassing the five villages and towns which it now connects, but the Koide town boss learned of this plan and lobbied for its demise.

———

It doesn't seem such a crime that Road 17 was diverted to link a number of villages and towns. Isn't it more interesting when roads take us to where people live? Wouldn't this new infrastructure help slow the population drift from rural areas to cities? Is saving 50 or so minutes of a driver's time by building a straight road that important? Save-a-second drivers can take the Kanetsu Expressway.

Other roads in this corner of the prefecture seem wasteful. Road 502, for example, on paper adequately connects the hamlets to the east of Urasa with Road 17, yet Road 291 and the Shiroyama Tunnel have been built to do the same. Perhaps it's not a matter for visitors unfamiliar with local snow conditions to judge, but the location of the Shinwa concrete factory between Roads 17 and 232 prompts the question.

I had admired Tanaka. At first with little money and from the wrong side of the tracks, he took on Tokyo's educated bureaucratic elite, moneyed political elite, and shadowy power-broking underworld, and won. He was born in a rural hamlet in 1918. The 1930s' depression cut short his education and he found work as a railcar pusher with a building firm, Steven Hunziker and Ikuro Kamimura noted in *Kakuei Tanaka — A Political Biography of Modern Japan.*

He took the initiative to train as a draftsman and his choice of a career in construction was fortuitous for reasons he couldn't have understood at the time. Japan would need rebuilding after its defeat in World War II and, later in politics, as long as he continued to bring construction projects to his electorate, voters would keep sending him to Tokyo.

Tanaka was first elected to the Diet in 1947 at age 28, and rose through party ranks like a seagull in an updraft. Appointed a vice minister of justice at age 30, minister of posts and telecommunications at 39, minister of finance at 44, secretary general of the Liberal Democratic Party at 47, minister of international trade and industry at 53, and prime minister at 54, then Japan's youngest postwar prime minister, he impressed with vigor, power and an uncanny ability to raise and redistribute money.

His political skills were compared to those of US president Lyndon Johnson. Like Johnson, Tanaka was said to be able to calculate at any one time the strength of his support. He was rarely wrong in this arithmetic, and could quickly identify individuals whom he had to sway to achieve a political goal.

Tanaka seemed, too, to walk under the umbrella of providence. He was conscripted into the army — as was most farm youth in the 1930s — but luckily discharged from duties in Manchuria for ill health before the tide of war turned against Japan. Later, after making his way to Tokyo to seek his fortune as a young draftsman, he married into a position as head of a construction company.

———

A young man who lived with words believed he could persuade a girl to like him. Not taking "No" for an answer, he wrote love letters, telling her he would win her heart by writing 1,000 pages of them. When, two years later, he'd produced almost that many, he met with her to reassess his chances, but his pen hadn't produced the desired result. He stopped short of writing the thousandth page and reacquainted himself with unrequited love. His literary confidence shattered, he descended into the depths of Tokyo's night-hawk ward of Shinjuku and ran a bar. That explains the 1971–72 year gap in the resume of journalist Takashi Tachibana, who recounts this experience in the preface to his book *Tanaka Kakuei Kenkyū* — "Study of Tanaka Kakuei."

When Tachibana next began writing the first few of a thousand pages on a single subject, he brought down a prime minister. The respected monthly magazine *Bungei Shunjū* launched his investigative articles about Tanaka's use of public office for private gain in its November 1974 edition in a series that, like the love letters, ran for two years. By the end of the month, Tanaka had resigned. In the interim, the beleaguered prime minister had held a press conference, the contents of which Tachibana described as "800 lies."

Tachibana wrote that when he was later congratulated on the day of Tanaka's arrest, he felt an emptiness, a second failure. Though the impact of his first article had been great, he said, it was little more than the "last straw on the back of an overloaded mule."

The *Bungei Shunjū* articles taught much about divisions of responsibility among Japanese journalists. Magazines were expected to run exposes. Mass-circulation daily newspapers — more than ten million copies, including evening editions — such as *Yomiuri* or *Asahi*, weren't. Reporters on these establishment dailies may have champed at the bit to write follow-ups. Or they may have wanted to report what they knew but had withheld. But editors had no need to tighten their reins as they would continue to censor themselves.

What changed that protocol was the detailed reporting of the *Bungei Shunjū* article that appeared in US newspapers. This foreign coverage licensed the dailies to disclose what they knew. The issue of responsibility for initiative had been erased, and the reporting of what foreigners had reported conformed to a pattern of permitted tasks within approved roles.

The first *Bungei Shunjū* article prompted a government audit committee to investigate, but Tanaka resigned on the day — 26 November 1974 — the committee was scheduled to meet. A woman treasurer of Etsuzankai had been summoned to testify. Tanaka spared her that agony and probably the agony also of taking her own life, as in his world of blood-thick loyalties she may have coolly reasoned that the testimony of the deceased can't be used in court.

I heard Tanaka speak in Tokyo shortly after this time. "Look at what the magazines are writing about me!" he exclaimed. Then loudly: "But there are still people who listen to what I say! Isn't that so!" There were, and they would queue at his residence to see him, and without this consultation the machinery of government would slow. He was ruling as a shadow shogun.

Some foreign news media later reported that Tanaka had resigned as prime minister for taking a $2 million bribe from Lockheed Corp. in return for persuading All Nippon Airways to buy Lockheed TriStar jets. But the Lockheed revelations came two years later, in Senate hearings in the US in 1976, when Tanaka was still a Diet member representing Niigata Third District, but as an independent.

Tokyo prosecutors pursued Tanaka, and the Tokyo District Court convicted him of bribery in 1983. He was given a suspended four-year prison sentence and fined ¥500 million (then $2.1 million). The Tokyo High Court upheld the verdict in 1987. The Supreme Court hadn't ruled on a further appeal at the time of his death in 1993. Tanaka's defense team, which included former judges and prosecutors, played for time. This had worked for him, but the snail-paced judicial process penalizes many others who seek redress through the courts.

Tanaka had suffered a debilitating stroke some months before the high court ruling, but even that wasn't enough to stop the Third District from re-electing him. Etsuzankai didn't advance his candidacy for the 1990 election and for the last three years of his life he wasn't a Diet member.

He brought into sharp relief the stain of money on politics. Businesses customarily pay large amounts of money for access to political decision-making. It's an ingrained system of money politics. In Tanaka's company in accepting Lockheed bribes were, among others, the All Nippon Airways president, the ministers for international trade and industry and construction, and the secretary general of the Liberal Democratic Party.

Many Japanese came to resent Tanaka less for his methods than for the transparency and scale of them. He was scorned, too, for his foolishness and treachery in accepting foreign money, because he had shown for all to see that foreigners knew precisely how to get things done in Tokyo. They knew who and how much to pay. In the case of Lockheed, the "how much" amounted to around 3 percent of the $430 million sales value for 21 TriStar jets, Chalmers Johnson noted in *Japan: Who Governs?* Johnson found informally in Tokyo that a commission of 3 percent of the value of a project was a usual amount that Japanese paid to the Tanaka machine to persuade the bureaucracy to act, for example to get a building permit out of the construction ministry.

Tanaka was more a feudal facsimile than an original. As E.H. Norman wrote in *Origins of the Modern Japanese State*, "The Tokugawa bureaucracy was among the most corrupt and avaricious to be found anywhere. The forms of bribery, exaction and political blackmail were Protean; the line between a gift and a bribe became blurred."

"Bribe" translates severally into expressions of different shade and nuance, reflecting the scope of the act. Tokugawa times aren't so far removed, for bribery remains a facet of the art of the gift. Cash is commonly gifted to nurses and schoolteachers to ensure kind treatment of patients and pupils. Culturally, cash itself is an acceptable gift. It's gifted at weddings and funerals, for example, in ceremonial envelopes and in amounts that are understood to be appropriate to the status of the giver.

I praised Lonely Planet's Japan guidebook (seventh edition) for its detail but it errs in saying that you can fly to Niigata from Tokyo. You can't, as of this writing. If Tanaka had financed an airline, perhaps you could. But he didn't. He put in roads and rail, so you can drive or take a bullet train. Niigata does connect by air to most other major Japanese cities — Osaka, Nagoya, Hiroshima, Fukuoka, Sapporo.

Tanaka's daughter Makiko, a short-lived foreign minister in the government of Junichirō Koizumi, also intrigues. Her downfall was brought about ostensibly by revelations that she had channeled salaries for her secretarial staff through a family company which had pocketed some of this money and paid the secretaries less than their entitlement.

But sharper daggers had earlier been drawn. The salary siphoning appeared amoral but equally as though it were something most Japanese politicians did. Friends told me that young secretaries — male or female — would work for a cabinet minister almost for free, as the position greatly enhances their marriage eligibility and opens up later career avenues. Makiko wanted to run her ministry but locked horns with its senior bureaucrats often and publicly.

I remember her most for her observation that there was no international clock in the foreign minister's office.

———

Tanaka's predecessor Eisaku Satō, who held office for seven years, was anathema to Beijing, in part for his snugness to Washington. A Japanese cartoonist once lampooned him by writing his name EisakU SAto. But Tanaka impressed as being his own man. China thus allowed relations between the two countries to be "normalized" — ending, in effect, a state of war which had persisted for 40 years — under Tanaka's watch.

It's odd how China's radar picks up such pragmatists and decides that it can do business with them. Tanaka was in the company of US president Richard Nixon, who spearheaded the US recognition of China, and of Tung Chee-hwa, whom China handpicked to run Hong Kong after the departure of the last British governor.

Whatever elections were held in Hong Kong for the post of chief executive, Beijing had followed Tung's career, in which he transformed a small family-owned company into the giant of Orient Overseas Shipping, from an early stage. It didn't count against him that his family had fled Shanghai to escape from a communist government. Shipping fortunes are built on the buying and selling of ships, not the transport of cargo, and Tung was a ship trader who had shown that he could read the world.

Japanese banks lent Tung much finance for the ships he ordered in Japan, understanding that he had Beijing's support years before this had dawned on political pundits. True, shipbuilders' guarantees attached to this finance, but Tung was bankable even when his company floundered in the wake of a collapse in tanker prices.

Tung resigned as chief executive of Hong Kong in 2005. Some observers speculated that he had fallen from Beijing's favor, though he had said that his health was failing. They believe that, in the examples of Nixon, Tanaka, and Tung, Beijing's knack was more for choosing the wrong people.

———

GRACE

What magic is at work in the writing of Jack Kerouac? Grace lies lightly. We visit briefly.

Chapter 10. Jack's Epic

Jack Kerouac, remembered most for his book *On The Road*, died at age 47 in 1969. *On The Road* impresses less as a travel book than a celebration of life, of the years Kerouac had, years which his older sister and brother did not, as theirs were cut shorter than his.

Kerouac wrote of his wayward car trip through New York, California, Colorado, and Mexico in *On The Road*, which took three years to finish and six more to publish. He's alive every second of the journey. Sentences such as "Every muscle twitched to go," "He could hardly get a word out, he was so excited with life," and "Oh, man, I'm high on this air!" underscore the book's obsession with the thrill of life. It's less an ode than an epic to joy. That may explain more than anything else why it's still read.

When Kerouac was working in 1949 at a wholesale fruit market in Denver, he found himself alongside some "Japanese kids" doing the heavy work of ratcheting a boxcar along a stretch of railroad track. He doesn't characterize them as a subspecies in Paul Theroux's manner, but an unembellished "Japanese kids." They were the children of people to him, though World War II and its Pacific theater were on the doorstep of his life. He lost his best and several good high school friends to fighting in Europe. He joined the Merchant Marine in 1942 and the Navy in 1943, but was later discharged on psychiatric grounds for refusing to handle a gun.

Theroux wrote in *The Old Patagonian Express* that he had read that Kerouac "at the age of fifty" had decided to repeat some of his youthful travels, and hitchhike from New York to California. Kerouac was "fatter now and felt defeated, but he was convinced he could repeat his cross-country epic," Theroux wrote, adding, "His menacing features were ineradicable, and times had changed." In this account, Kerouac had given up and taken a bus home from New Jersey after standing for hours in the rain and failing to get a ride.

I can't say how much of Theroux's account is fictional or the punctured product of speedwriting and faulty memory — certainly Kerouac was never 50 — but it typifies his tendency to mock and belittle. Kerouac may have been "fatter" and his features may have been "menacing" and times may have changed when he tried later in life to get a ride in the New Jersey rain, but his style would still have been to praise and uplift.

JUST SAY "NO"

We next explore the meaning behind a rural sign announcing the "Japan That Can Say No" and face rejection by a hostile chef in an orderly town.

CHAPTER 11. AN ORDERLY TOWN

After passing a string of forgettable installations such as a manure plant, used-car yard, and tombstone sales outlet, by 9.30 a.m. I'd found farmland in dollops between inert businesses.

Cherry blossoms bloomed behind a camera shop whose sign reading Art Studio from a distance had raised hopes of an exhibit. Two dogs were tethered and asleep on the concrete floor inside. Dogs in the countryside were just as confined as those in the cities. Farms are separated more by irrigation channels than fences, so owners tie up their dogs, which lie on concrete or dirt for the term of their life.

Kondō Shōten, a seller of used household items, stood unbowed, unlike its early Tokyo brethren. Such shops have proliferated in the last decade as consumers shed their wasteful habit of discarding good items that were a few years old, only to replace them with new models of the same thing.

Operators of such stores initially were apologetic, worrying that they were viewed as a blight on the neighborhood. Cash-strapped shoppers would enter stealthily, lest they be seen at a place their neighbors wouldn't differentiate from a pawnbroker. Then the image began to change. Recycle shops lost their stigma as people welcomed a secondary market for used items. Women treated them as a valuable trading exchange for used but good clothes. Shops in Tokyo districts such as Shibuya began to draw young buyers in search of a fashionable retro look.

A rusted tin sign on a farm building bleated *No to Ieru Nihon* — "The Japan That Can Say No." The sign showed a painted scene of the US in the form of a devil aiming a spear at Japanese farmers. A Star-Spangled Banner flag was furled over the spear tip. A woman was clutching a bundle of rice, standing firm. The US, which cyclically blasts Japan for its agricultural protectionism, symbolized foreign demands for access to the rice market.

The sign bore the signature of the youth division of Nōkyō, the national agricultural cooperative, which is now Japan Agriculture. Car and truck wrecks littered the ground. Farm buildings stood empty. Youth had already said "No," but more to a life farming here than to the United States.

Japanese wartime propaganda similarly depicts the US president or British prime minister as tailed, horned demonic foe and US propaganda portrays Japanese soldiers as vermin or monkeys, as John W. Dower showed in *War Without Mercy*. But the call to "say no," or stand up to the US, is more recent. It's taken from the 1989 book *No to Ieru Nihon — Shinnichibei Kankei no Hōsaku —* "The Japan That Can Say No — Policy for a New Japan-US Relationship," co-authored by Shintarō Ishihara, a novelist and politician, and Akio Morita, the late co-founder of Sony Corp.

As I write, Ishihara, born in 1932, is governor of Tokyo. But it was the publication of his first and prize-winning novel *Taiyō no Kisetsu —* "Seasons of the Sun," that made his name a household word. His younger, late brother Yujirō made his cinematic debut in the movie version of the novel and became a star. Yujirō was, some said, the "Japanese Elvis Presley."

Some Japanese welcome Ishihara as a breath of fresh air amid political malodor. He speaks his mind, at times eloquently, at times offhandedly. He's managed to offend almost everyone at some time. I don't believe he means everything he says. Upset that his compatriots don't speak out or stand up for themselves, he deliberately speaks in a way calculated to incite them to think about issues. He has worked with words for a long time and is good at this.

Residents enjoy his "Tokyo That Can Say No" slogan, which he uses in challenges to the central government on taxation, among other issues. He has extended his challenge to the US by campaigning for the return of the air base at Yokota, which he wants Tokyo to use as a civilian airport. This effort struck a chord in particular among those who long for independence and leadership.

Ishihara declares himself a nationalist but behaves more as rightwing populist. If others at intervals along the political spectrum could charm and debate with his confidence, he wouldn't attract so much attention. But few can, so he raises alarm.

Though he has said he doesn't have ethnocentric ideas that everything Japanese is better, he appears xenophobic. He's unhappy that a large number of Asians now live in Japan. When he said that Japan should be ready to defend itself against rioting foreigners in case of a natural disaster, he used the word *sangokujin*, a derogatory prewar term for Japan's colonial Chinese, Taiwanese, and Korean populations. The translation "third-country nationals" is misleading or doesn't say enough. These are countries that because of their colonial status could neither win nor lose a war. Not in that first or second position, they were in a stateless, dependent third.

Confronted with novels written in Japanese by non-Japanese, Ishihara is observed to have said that foreigners couldn't write such Japanese. He took offence when *The Japan That Can Say No* appeared in unauthorized English translation. He's the type of Japanese who wishes for two worlds — one for the exclusive habitation by Japanese, and a separate, sanitized, authorized world where Japan can control its interaction with non-Japanese. He has much in common with the Tokugawa shoguns.

The Japan That Can Say No as a title struck a chord elsewhere and spawned similar articles and books. A group of Chinese writers pooled their efforts to write the weighty tome *China Can Say No* (1996) which, apart from its tirades against the US, castigates Japan as a defector from Asia which has copied the West in culture and much else. Future works such as *The Korea That Can Say No*, *The Taiwan That Can Say No*, *The Philippines That Can Say No* and so on, around the globe, are easy to imagine.

———

Beyond a car graveyard, I found the Shinano River again, at Koshino-ōhashi Bridge, and didn't see the point of this bridge as it leads to a short bypass which bypasses nothing, and rejoins Road 17 about two and a half kilometers further along after looping back across the same river via Ojiya-ōhashi Bridge. The loop and two apparently pointless bridges are the first segment of the Ojiya Bypass, which skirts Ojiya Station. Road 17 could have split then rejoined itself to create the same bypass. But this is Niigata Third District.

Gibraltar Life Insurance, signposted near Ojiya Station, bespoke histories in its symbolism. The company is a resurrection of Kyōei Life Insurance Co. under the capital participation of Prudential Financial, Inc. of the United States.

Why Gibraltar? The reborn Kyōei was a haven for savings as safe as the impregnable fortress of the Rock of Gibraltar. Before responsibility for Gibraltar was transferred to the British Colonial Office from the War Office in 1830, it was called the "town and garrison of Gibraltar in the Kingdom of Spain." Kyōei employees clung to an American financial rock, and the colonial imagery still seems appropriate.

Gibraltar Life in promotional material said it planned to "aggressively increase its sales force." How do you "aggressively" increase anything? Why do so many businesses — American, European — use the adverb "aggressively" in media dross?

The *Concise Oxford Dictionary* defines "aggression" first as "the act or practice of attacking without provocation." A secondary meaning is "self-assertiveness" or "forcefulness." In the case of Gibraltar Life, the word is probably a translator's choice for *sekkyoku teki*. But "aggression" seems to have become an acceptable synonym for enthusiasm. It's a terrible word, yet businesses throughout the English-speaking world select it for their promotions and translators store it at the top of their quiver.

Other signs contorted the English language but the more you think about some names or expressions the less sense they make.

Mosquitoes and dragonflies followed me into Ojiya.

I was too early for Ojiya's sumo wrestling-style bullfights, which are held from May through November. It seems wrong to encourage animals to fight for our viewing pleasure but I haven't seen these fights so I can't judge them. At least the objective, as in sumo, is to compare strength and skill, not bash body or brains. Gamblers are kept out of the bullfights by the admirable practice of declaring every match a draw and the government has designated the sport as an "intangible cultural asset." There are said to be 140 fighting bulls in and around Ojiya.

Fish were bred in elaborate concrete tanks at roadside. Bokushi Suzuki described Ojiya as a major market town of Echigo, the old name for this region. It developed as a river port and boasts a long history in the weaving of *chijimi* or crepe fabrics, in linen or silk. Suzuki also described the town — now a city — as *jigokudani* — "Hell Valley," probably in reference to the vaporous nature of the area's natural gas deposits. I should have explored more.

———

Road 17 climbed as it led into Kawaguchi and snow-flecked mountains cut the sky. A sign cautioned that the road would be closed if 180 milliliters of rain fell continuously, as though motorists were equipped with measuring instruments of Sanjō manufacture.

The shed-like Hotel Rainbow Kawaguchi crouched low as a frog in reeds, the pastel glisten of its neon unblushing. In a parallel to the long straw hats worn by visitors to the Yoshiwara pleasure quarters in Edo, the hotel car park was covered. The cars were thus as incognito as their owners and rural busybodies were denied their chance at mischief. The room charge was advertised as ¥3,200 ($27) for two people and — which still makes me wonder — ¥6,500 ($54) for four.

It was 259 kilometers (161 miles) to Tokyo from Kawaguchi. Camp Kawaguchi Holiday Park for Families advertised a ryokan, cottage-style accommodation, camping ground, meeting rooms, a hot spring, indoor gateball — a type of croquet, gym, tennis court, baseball, and golf. Children would want to swim most but there was no pool. I feared the place would have a youth-hostel feel to it, rules posted on walls, routines in place, communal tasks assigned. I thought of detouring the few kilometers to test my suspicions but in spring before the Golden Week holidays the park would be empty.

Road 17 entered a tunnel about 300 meters (330 yards) ahead, a sign said. This was the first of several tunnels that would cut through the mountains that separated me from the Kantō Plain and Tokyo. The sign also noted that three radio frequencies could be heard inside — NHK 774 kHz, NHK 837 kHz, and Niigata Hōsō 1026 kHz. Drivers can tune into these channels for emergency broadcasts if trapped in a tunnel accident or fire.

Japan's worst tunnel disaster occurred in 1979 when seven people died and 173 vehicles were destroyed in a collision involving four trucks and two cars in the Nihonzaka Tunnel, Shizuoka Prefecture. Considering the narrowness of some road tunnels, accidents are surprisingly few.

There are seldom footpaths inside the tunnels and trucks can barely pass from opposing directions without scraping sides. A walker inside could easily be killed or cause a fatal accident. Disinclined — and not fit enough — to scamper over mountains to find the other side of tunnels, I'd prepared a sign which read, *ton-*

neru ga nukeru made nosette kudasai — "Please give me a ride through the tunnel." Drivers would understand that my request was for their sake as much as mine.

So I stood holding my sign. Fifteen minutes later I was still standing after dozens of cars and six or so trucks had passed, among them a roomy, double-cab road-servicing truck which of all vehicles I'd expected to stop. I'd given vehicles enough distance — 100 meters or so — to see me and stop before the tunnel. I decided to walk it and, hugging the damp spidery concrete wall inside, felt saved to see dim light after a distance only 100 meters or so. I was wearing my sun hat, and realized that no one had stopped because no one could see my face.

"You can take your hat off," a popular lyric advises, and that's what I resolved to do when I next raised my sign.

The cars that passed were mostly small — many of an engine capacity less than 700 c.c. — and the trucks light. These are the fuel-efficient vehicles of sensible rural dwellers. I saw few large four-wheel-drive, or so-called sport utility, vehicles, though these tank-like behemoths are common enough in Tokyo where they appeal to urban cowboys and the insecure rich. Cars seem designed to suit drivers, not roads.

Most people who drive from Tokyo, Saitama, or Gunma to Niigata these days won't take Road 17. They'll take the Kanetsu Expressway, which was completed in 1985. Its elevated concrete platform resembles that for bullet trains and, from a distance, it's hard to tell one from the other.

It was dusk when I walked into Koide.

At Koide Station a disturbed man was role-playing an old-fashioned station master. He loudly announced the arrival of each passenger train. Then he commanded all around him to board. He was out of his mind but he bothered no one and no one tried to remove him. Earlier in Tokyo, I saw a youth gyrating spasmodically and singing percussively inside a CD shop. His presence, too, appeared strangely tolerated and no one tried to evict him.

My presence embarrassed the innkeeper at the first ryokan I tried, which was on the main street. She didn't tell me that her inn was fully booked. She said that not a single room was available. I didn't believe her but you can't argue with someone who's decided to reject you.

I trekked back to the station, across Koide Bridge over the Uono River, and at the entrance to the Kawazen Ryokan struck up a lengthy conversation with a Labrador retriever named Lab. This effort was rewarded with the warmest of welcomes, and I remembered evenings walking my dog in Yokohama. Then as now, I could converse with a Japanese on almost any topic if that person, too, was walking a dog. But take away the dogs and our communication would become the guarded exchange of strangers.

An elderly lady led me to my room, laid out a futon, and told me that she'd call when dinner was served. Students and grandparents will help us. I took green tea in my six-mat room, the curtains smoke-stiff and walls nicotine-yellow. This was a skier's room. As with other fresh-air fiends such as yachtsmen, skiers seem always to be among the heaviest smokers.

My feet were fine, this time. Once, in hastily chosen heavy plastic-molded "walking shoes," they heated, blistered badly and shed their skin like a lizard. That painful experience taught me to choose strong light sneakers over heavy walking shoes — the lighter, the better.

Unless you're a seasoned long-distance walker, you can expect your feet to swell and remain slightly swollen for the duration of your walk. To accommodate the swelling, I chose a shoe size one-half larger than my own. I shopped for the shoes on a weekday when shop assistants weren't run off their feet and had time to spend with me. I took at least an hour to try on as many pairs as would fit before making a choice.

There's another important item. If you aren't fit when you start out, you may chafe in areas where you can expect to chafe, and each stride will become unpleasant. I used baby powder.

————

After a dinner of miso shiru soup, fish, pickled vegetables and rice, I set out to survey the town.

On and off the main street shops and houses had been finished in building materials of high quality. Usually in rural towns buildings are flimsy prefabricated structures made of light compound materials that are designed to disintegrate after seven or eight years. Gluttonous renovators are thus able to feed on a predictable market. Construction companies have taken a leaf from the book of compatriot car and consumer electronics manufacturers for whom built-in obsolescence has graduated from second language to mother tongue. But Koide has been built to last, and much business has been brought here. Skiers added pastry to the pie.

The red lantern of a *yakitoriya* grilled-chicken bar glowed down a side street. Only one of the several tables was occupied. I stood in the doorway and politely greeted the chef.

Wakaru tokoro ni itte iro — "Go where you'll be understood," the chef ordered in coarse Japanese, after a stony silence.

"You should put up a 'Japanese Only' sign outside your shop," I said, still in his entrance.

I've kept a photo of such a sign which an earlier employer had posted on a dining room door in a Jeddah work camp, where I lived as an honorary Japanese. But I'd taken my Yemeni driver into the dining room when it suited. The Japanese cook would later reprimand me for this, but I'd combatively argue the matter on the spot and my transgression was tolerated.

From a company bus window at the gate of the Jeddah Oil Refinery I once saw a laborer of North African origin whose leg was badly gashed for most of its length. I think he'd been caught under some construction machinery. Sitting next to a Japanese engineer, I asked whether we should order our driver to stop and rush this wounded worker to hospital. I could tell that the engineer was considering the same question, that the sight of deeply torn, dark-blood-red flesh tore at him as it did at me.

The laborers would have their own medical facilities and health insurance, care would be in place for them, the engineer told me. We couldn't take him to the hospital we used, he said. Our bus went through the gate. We both knew he was right and wrong at the same time and, looking back, I wonder whether that stricken laborer can walk, whether he is still alive.

This Thursday night in Koide, the yakitoriya chef's two diners lowered their shoulders and, like timid turtles, pulled their heads in.

Every word I spoke was understood. But I'd have to retreat. This wasn't a situation that could be resolved by discussion. The chef was working with flame and with knives and I sensed danger.

"Go where you'll be understood." As the chef spoke those words his eyes fixed not on me but the dishes he was preparing. Apart from a cursory glance when I first entered, he never looked at me again.

There was nothing to do but leave. I put the xenophobic chef in his early forties. Perhaps he had lost someone dear to war or a foreigner had married then deserted his sister. Or he was being himself.

But this wasn't the ski season, when one or two ski-packaged foreigners might be expected for two or three days. No Japanese guides or acquaintances accompanied me. I was alone in a mountain town at night, asking questions and expecting to be accepted. I was pushing my luck.

Not a scrap of litter lay on Koide's streets or shopping mall lanes. Wastepaper baskets were attached to street posts at short intervals. Pavements were swept. Everything seemed to fit, be in place. I didn't fit, was out of place. Koide, surrounded by mountains, was insular, cold.

I imagined it was like the small Austrian town a traveler once described to me. He had nowhere to stay and every place of lodging in this town turned him down. An English-speaking Austrian had noticed his predicament and tried to help, but still no inns would accept him. They were Austrian, he wasn't.

That town and Koide share traits with the village elders in Shirley Jackson's story *The Lottery* who perpetuate an old custom of ordering the head of each household to draw lots in order to single out a villager. The fate of this winner — I won't spoil the story — is the same each time the lottery is held. Koide folk would also enjoy Jackson's *We Have Always Lived in the Castle*.

Breakfast was similar to dinner except that it included fermented soybeans and an egg. I paid ¥5,800 ($48) for the lodging and two meals and walked into a cool spring morning. I retraced my steps to the yakitoriya as though returning to the scene of a crime. In broad daylight I would collect evidence.

The restaurant was called Toritei. There was a deep gash across the aluminum front door, as though someone had taken an ax to it. Or perhaps a delivery vehicle had backed into it. I, too, would respond, but not with an ax.

I made my way to the town office. A restaurant directory placed Toritei at 595 Oji Koidejima, Koide-chō, Kitauonuma-gun, Niigata-ken. It's operated by Sadao Takizawa. Telephone 02579-2-6594 to reserve a table.

I intended to use the foot-in-the-door technique to see the town head. By walking directly into a Japanese office, without appointment, you force your unwilling host either to be directly rude or accommodating for the sake of avoiding confrontation. Most will go out of their way to avoid a scene. I'd walk into the town head's office, ask him which century he thought his town was in and, to his face, repeat the words of the Toritei chef.

"I've just dropped by to ask the name of the town head," I said to the town head's secretary.

He told me.

"I'd like to send him a copy of my book when it comes out," I explained.

He thanked me.

Like most rehearsals that sound convincing when you make them to yourself, my earlier rehearsal of the protest didn't and couldn't come out.

Feeling foolish, I left, but not before collecting some brochures to see how Koide promotes itself.

One brochure introduced the Koide General Visitor Center, which boasted a restaurant, information center, product display area, tourism information desk, and tatami-mat rooms. A young couple with child — the dream of the mountain town — were the only people captured in the brochure photos. Businessmen would meet quietly at night in the private rooms of discreet restaurants, not showcase themselves here. Koide would host formal events at the center, while what mattered would take place elsewhere. The center exemplifies the plethora of such facilities that Japan built across its islands during the money-centered 1980s. No sense of community attaches to them. Children can't use them.

A photo in a Koide tourism pamphlet shows boys and girls no older than six or seven straddling a long thick brown wooden phallus as though it were a playground toy, as part of a festival in the name of the goddess Benzaiten.

Rural fertility festivals often enjoined children to phalli but Koide may be alone in promoting such a scene in glossy color — and more than 100 years after much of the rest of the country was encouraged to leave like custom behind. W. G. Aston, in notes to his translation of *Nihon Shoki*, remarked that in the late 1800s, the Japanese government was doing its "best to suppress this very gross form of nature worship" which still existed in "out of the way places."

A rust-dark sign read: *Iesu wa watashitachi no tsumi wo jūjika de aganatta* — "Jesus paid for our sins on the cross." A second sign: *Iesu wa eien no inochi no minamoto de aru* — "Jesus is the source of eternal life." The signs were nailed to farm shed and shop walls on Road 17 a few kilometers out of Koide toward Muikamachi.

The signs were only in Japanese, and carried no church address or telephone number. Had foreign Christian missionaries or Japanese Christians put them up? What use were they without addresses or telephone numbers? Jesus paid for our sins. What should passersby do after reading them? Our sins.

We were innately, originally sinful. We were born bad. I've never accepted this. I believe that I was born good. Since being born good, I've made wrong choices from time to time, but I made those choices after I was born. They didn't result from badness within me at birth.

I was born good.

THE USES OF REJECTION

The Koide chef's hostility recalled an earlier rejection by a golf club in Kanagawa Prefecture. Then, rejection saved me, or rather my savings. And now it had stimulated thoughts of an historical association that may be new.

CHAPTER 12. GOLF AND TULIPS

Before Koide's Toritei chef decided not to serve me, a golf club in Kanagawa Prefecture decided to reject me as a member, saying that membership was restricted to Japanese.

It didn't help that I spoke Japanese or held a residence permit. Or to explain that when I'd last played golf regularly my handicap was 17 — not great, but evidence enough that I could play and should know course etiquette.

Rather than argue with the club manager, I let things sit for a week or two. I then telephoned him and suggested that he couldn't be serious in rejecting me as a member, pointing out that Japanese belong to golf clubs all over the world. I live here, I told him. We're talking to each other, so there's no language problem, I argued.

I'd expected the manager to serve up a platter of clichés about foreigners, perhaps referring to their butter-smelling body odor, which could put other players off their putts, or that the strength of their drives off the tee might send balls over the netting fence and through house windows, or that their ungainly sight on the course might discourage regular members from playing.

He said none of this. He opened up like a clam that knew it needed to disgorge impurities. The ban on foreigners was aimed at Korean residents, he said, but the club couldn't spell out that it didn't admit Koreans. So it banned foreigners. This policy had worked, he said, because Koreans usually were the only foreigners who wanted to join. American and other foreign executives in Tokyo sought membership at more prestigious clubs, which had a history of admitting them.

Golf club memberships enable people to network at the highest levels of business and politics. But courses ritualized the playing experience. They injected extraneous rules and extracted fun. The memberships became marketable securities, traded by dealers and sold by brokers in the same way as stocks or bonds. Banks accepted some memberships as collateral for loans.

The *Nihon Keizai Shimbun* newspaper averaged the membership prices for around 500 golf clubs in 1982, indexed the average, and began publishing what was to become a novel wealth barometer, and lagging indicator for the economy as a whole.

I'd wanted to enjoy a game of golf once or twice a week and own an investment that perhaps would return some capital gain. I'd skip the compulsory banquet lunches and caddy hire. But my prohibition prevented me from making an investment less wise even than purchasing a Dutch tulip bulb in the early 1600s.

Dutch traders converted their East Indies voyage profits into magnificent residences surrounded by flower gardens, Mike Dash relates in *Tulipmania, the Story of the World's Most Coveted Flower*. Tulips, then incomparable in their brightness and beauty, assured their own scarcity by taking seven years to grow from seed. Speculators mortgaged assets to buy rare bulbs. So did Japanese mortgage houses to buy golf club memberships.

The golf club membership index soared to 933 from 100 in eight years, then collapsed to its starting level, then halved from that. The last time I looked it was at 45.5, down 95 percent from its peak. As for tulip mania, the price of bulbs peaked in 1636–37 at around 6,000 florins and collapsed to 500 florins, a fall of 92 percent, Charles Mackay notes in *Extraordinary Popular Delusions and the Madness of Crowds*.

Tokugawa shoguns may have precipitated the crash in tulip bulb prices. They began disconnecting from Europe around 1630, in response to the greed of missionary and trader alike. Fewer — and more regulated — voyages would have slashed voyage profits, so reducing the cash available for speculative purchases of rare bulbs. Dutch traders, who were allowed to remain at Dejima as agents, would likely have anticipated this outcome and wrote of their fears, but their letters would have taken a year or more to reach Europe. And it would have reasonably taken four to five years for the impact of the shoguns' policy to climax in the Netherlands.

Historians may not dwell on such coincidence, as trading in tulip bulbs — and golf-club memberships — existed only on the unregulated fringe of commerce. But the connectedness of the world is sometimes self-revealing.

THE CONSTRUCTION STATE

We resume our journey in the snow country, where we stumble upon a priceless collection of Western art, learn that Japan is pouring more concrete than even China, and relax to the balm of jazz in an unusual coffee shop.

CHAPTER 13. THE SCENE CHANGES

A convoy of thundering trucks shook the road. They were laden with earth, some road or dam construction site beckoning.

A young woman drove one of the trucks. I'd seen uniformed women at road construction sites near Sanjō, but none driving trucks. Still, the picture-book image of truck driver as a burly, thick-skinned man who loads his own truck belonged to the past.

The trucks have changed, too. Those that sped past me were driven as sports cars. The interior of their cabs would resemble more an airplane cockpit than dashboard — the controls electronic, the lighting galactic.

A dog sat straight-backed and stately in another trucker's passenger seat, surveying all from his window.

Itsukamachi, or five-day town, presented itself, but appeared unremarkable except in name. Daimyo permitted this town to open its markets to visitors and trade with other towns only on the fifth day of the month. This regulation protected the commerce of the larger castle towns during the Edo era. Such trade barriers were erected locally long before hurdles were placed in front of foreign sellers.

Market towns today remain by name only. Consumers visited them less and less as food and dry goods distributors used new rail and road links to penetrate villages and towns.

Twenty or so kilometers (12 miles) to the west along Road 258 is Tōkamachi, or tenth-day town, one of several so-named throughout the country. It's a center of kimono making, and a short ride on the Hokuhoku Line from Muikamachi or sixth-day town.

It was a cool spring afternoon, but Muikamachi warmed me. You feel a sense of belonging as you enter some towns. Others isolate you in their coldness. I felt that I could settle here.

It was mid afternoon by the time I reached the main shopping street after a walk of 21.6 kilometers (13.4 miles). I walked to the station, where an elderly woman was using arm-length tweezers to pick up cigarette butts from the pavement, and discovered a collection of Japanese and foreign art works that borders on the priceless. Energy to spare, I surveyed some of the town and discovered a collection of Japanese and foreign art works that border on the priceless.

Gallery Muikamachi occupies one room in the station building but has space for only about 100 exhibits out of a collection of 380. I bought a catalog of the collection from the adjacent travel office. A woman there told me that until the gallery finds larger premises the bulk of the collection will remain in storage.

Works by Picasso, Chagall, Vlaminck, and Buffet are among the 82 foreign paintings in the collection. French Impressionists are most represented, but there are surprises. A Warhol silkscreen of Marilyn Monroe is here, as are works by Polish (Kisling), American (Francis) and Armenian (Jansen) artists. Prints by Hokusai, Yoshida, and Munakata are part of the Japanese collection.

Most of the collection's 16 Picassos are sketches or etchings dated 1904–5 but there's also the 1962 linocut titled "Woman's Face." There are three Vlamincks, nine Chagalls, and sixteen Buffets. Although these works were cataloged, none were exhibited. It seemed unfair that residents couldn't enjoy most of the art works. The space explanation wasn't convincing. Possibly the paintings were still in private hands for private enjoyment after ownership had been transferred to the town.

———

Family members who inherit land, works of art, or other valuable assets often must sell much of the bequest to pay inheritance taxes. Some wealthy Japanese gift assets to nonprofit organizations or temples in the way that wealthy American families use foundations to own their assets.

As I write, Japan's top inheritance tax rate is 50 percent (or 70 percent if the inheritor is not a family member), levied on bequests whose value exceeds ¥2 billion ($16.7 million). Most inheritors of such assets will need to sell 50 percent of them, by value, in order to pay the tax, unless millions of dollars are on hand or other assets worth millions of dollars can be sold. When inheritors aren't that rich, large tracts of land are broken up into smaller lots and sold and art works go under the auctioneer's hammer, which scatters the collections. The tax, designed to thwart the generational transfer of wealth, spawns elaborate avoidance schemes.

I didn't suggest to the travel office that the gallery was a tax dodge. The woman had been helpful and her attitude would have soured. I may also have been wrong. Her boss was away. She chatted happily. But when I visited again the next day, she acted as though we had never met. She dutifully relayed my questions to her manager and relayed his answers and comments to me. But still the office was warm, and her manager rose to greet me and offered his name card.

Some Japanese companies speculated in foreign art works as though they were real estate in the late 1980s, but paid little attention to the ownership history of the works. As many as 10,000 such paintings are believed to be held by banks as collateral for loans, but as much as two-thirds of this cache reportedly lacks provenance.

Unlike real estate or shares, sales of art don't need to be recorded, and valuations don't conform to any transparent standard. Paintings are like a currency with a sliding value. Borrowers or lenders can adjust this value to suit when using them as collateral for loans. Or buyers or sellers can generate paper losses for tax avoidance or gains when profits need to be shown. Art can be bought and sold in untraceable ways that benefit power brokers.

Some celebrated and, in about equal measure, scorned art purchases — Van Gogh's "Portrait of Dr. Gachet" for $86.5 million and Renoir's "Le Moulin de la Galette" for $71.8 million, both in 1990, by Ryōhei Saitō, a paper company baron; Picasso's "Les Noces de Pierrette," for $52 million, in 1989, by Nippon Autopolis, the racetrack business of Tomonori Tsurumaki; Picasso's "Acrobat and Young Harlequin" for $37.6 million, in 1988, by Mitsukoshi Department Store; and a Van Gogh "sunflowers" for $39.9 million by Yasuda Fire and Marine Insurance, in 1987. Before the "sunflowers" purchase, no painting was believed to have ever sold for more than $13 million.

The buyers were scorned for their seemingly artificial ramping of prices, but those who have wanted Japan to trade fairly can't complain when the market mechanism of auction determines prices. The scorn appeared to feed on something else, too. It was the notion that such icons of Western culture don't belong in Japanese hands, in the way that John Lennon as an icon of popular culture didn't belong in Japanese arms.

Japanese ownership of works by Van Gogh, Picasso or Chagall isn't remarkable in itself. I once spotted a collection of early Cezannes in a Japanese catalog, and saw at an exhibit in Yokohama a Rembrandt of a skull on a dining table, which was from a private Japanese collection.

Japanese collectors may recognize a value that foreign collectors don't. Similarly, much precious Japanese art is in foreign hands. Foreign collectors, such as architect Frank Lloyd Wright, understood the value of *ukiyo-e* woodblock prints while most Japanese collectors were blinded by French impressionists. Wright began collecting and dealing in the prints in the early 1900s, a business that supported him during his fledgling years as an architect. He's reported to have bought as many as 20,000 of them and credited with introducing the prints of Hiroshige to the US, at an exhibition in Chicago in 1906.

Alex Kerr related in *Lost Japan* how he unsuccessfully tried to interest Japanese buyers in a scroll of the celebrated kabuki play *Chūshingura*, about samurai loyalty and suicide. Kerr believes that the large scroll, which illustrates each of the 11 acts of the play, was probably used in the mid-1800s by a traveling kabuki troupe. He'd not seen the like of it in any Japanese museum, but not even a temple dedicated to the memory of the fallen samurai showed the slightest interest in acquiring the work. He sold the scroll to an American living in North Dakota.

The Muikamachi gallery was holding an exhibition of prints and drawings by Shikō Munakata (1903–75). It has about 90 of them, and they make up a large part of the gallery's collection. Munakata wanted to be "Japan's Van Gogh," the catalog said. His work is loud and emotional, his women alive, not ornamental or passive. The obsession with Van Gogh has infused his work with a jarring spontaneity, as though freeing him from the prison of conditioned expectation that Japanese art should suggest its themes only subtly.

"From the Munakata of Japan to the Munakata of the World," the exhibition's title declared, showing how recent is Japan's isolationist past. You have to view yourself as apart from the world to think of that title.

From the Warhol of America to the Warhol of the World?

American or English or Chinese people wouldn't title an exhibition in that way. They wouldn't necessarily view the step into an outer world as progress, unless the purpose was to replicate their own habitat. Centuries of seclusion may have catapulted Japan into the future.

Some of the collection's 12 woodblock prints by Hiroshi Yoshida are here. "Mt. Fuji in the Morning," made in 1923, is stunningly restful. Perhaps Yoshida could capture Japan so well because he took such a large interest in foreign countries. He visited the US three times, and made trips also to Europe, Africa, India, China, and Korea. He died in 1950, leaving unfinished a series whose working title was *One Hundred Views of the World*. Today he may have been ahead of his time.

Henry Miller observed in *The Air-Conditioned Nightmare* that in the US you can "ride for thousands of miles and be utterly unaware of the existence of the world of art. You will learn all about beer, condensed milk, rubber goods...but you will never see or hear anything concerning the masterpieces of art." Miller was writing in the 1940s and perhaps spent little time in Manhattan or Boston and I can't say how much has changed in his country since then. But in many Japanese villages and towns you can easily find an art gallery which possesses a handsome store of native and foreign work.

A young woman at a travel center near the station recommended Hotel Uotoshi. I suggested a less expensive ryokan, but she said most wouldn't be prepared for guests without reservations as the ski season was coming to an end. She was a saleswoman and I fell for her pitch.

She called the hotel. The guest was traveling alone and would stay for one night, she said. She confirmed the price and said the guest would arrive within the hour. Only when each of these details was understood and the reservation accepted did she mention that I was a foreigner, almost as an afterthought. I silently applauded. The hotel wasn't given the opportunity to decline the reservation. My otherness was the last thing she mentioned, not the first. I had to pay the center a deposit on the reservation, which was its commission, but the center had earned it.

As I walked toward Uotoshi, a ryokan called Echizenya appeared along a shopping street running between Road 17 and the Uono River. It would cost half as much as the hotel, but canceling the hotel reservation would result in losing the deposit and putting to waste the effort of the tourist center, which I was still applauding. So I decided to stay a second night in Muikamachi.

Echizenya's innkeeper appeared in the entrance after I called out *gomen kudasai*. Eyes round and warm in a moon face, she looked like a schoolgirl's favorite aunt. Yes, she said, this was a ryokan. She knew I knew it was, but I needed to make some conversation before making any request. Rooms were available, she said, making a small boast or apology that the inn was the oldest in the town. She added that it had been razed by fire and rebuilt several times over the years, a common refrain of the owners of wooden buildings. It was arranged that I would stay the following night.

At Hotel Uotoshi, rooms were named after fish. Mine was *iwana* — "char," an extravagantly large 14-mat room. Others were *kawamasu* — "river trout" and *sawara* — "mackerel."

From my window I could see a sign saying *happyaku meetoru saki kōji chū* — the Ka River was "under construction" 800 meters ahead. How can a river be "under construction"? The sides of the river were being concreted. The river was being turned into a canal.

Kerr discusses the concreting of Japan in *Lost Japan* and also in *Dogs and Demons*. So does Robert Neff in *Japan's Hidden Hot Springs*. Kerr compared Japan's volume of cement production with that of the US and concluded that Japan pours about 30 times more concrete per square foot. He used figures for 1994 (97.4 million tonnes), a high year for Japanese cement production, and appears to have understated US, and overstated Japan's, cement usage by not adjusting for US imports or Japan's exports of the commodity.

But it doesn't matter if Kerr's calculation is approximate. His is the type of comparison that an astute and caring foreign observer makes and a Japanese critic may not.

I updated Kerr's comparison, using figures for 2005. US cement consumption (production plus imports; exports are negligible) was 130 million tonnes, compared with 64 million tonnes for Japan (production less exports; imports: negligible), or 33 million tonnes less than the figure Kerr used.

The comparison nonetheless indicates that Japan is pouring 12 times more concrete than the US on a same-area basis, and still points to environmental mayhem.

But how much concrete is this? A local cement company told me that in the case of structural-use concrete for commercial buildings, a reasonable rule-of-thumb is that it takes about 350 kilograms of cement to make a cubic meter of concrete.

Japan, then, is pouring about 490 cubic meters of concrete per square kilometer, compared with 40 cubic meters in the United States. The more interesting comparison is perhaps with China. Japan is pouring 1.6 times more concrete than China's approximate 310 cubic meters per square kilometer, and China's is a high-growth economy.

Japan pours such volumes every year. Kerr notes that apart from cementing wetlands, rivers and mountains it has also cemented 60 percent of its coastline.

Some people contest that figure, saying that reclaimed land, which serves as the foundation for Tokyo Disneyland and Kansai International Airport, for example, can't be counted as cemented coastline. They add that much Japanese cement is used for *kiban kairyō* — "foundation improvement," specifically the piling of marshy ground.

Neff observes that Japan has "rapidly yielded to rampant concrete, vinyl, vending machines and loudspeakers." He asks, "Whatever happened to the 'real Japan'?" And, "Is Japan's once-vaunted serenity, subtlety, and affinity for the sublime gone forever?" The answer, according to Neff, is yes, but he nonetheless manages to locate a number of hot springs in areas still unspoiled. His book shows you where.

Dinner served in my room this Friday evening comprised no fewer than 13 dishes — a clear soup, an egg custard, vinegary vegetables, sashimi, tempura, slices of boiled pork, tofu, pickled vegetables, rice, horse radish sauce, meat sauce, soy sauce, a desert of sweet bean paste wrapped in a leaf. A pot of rice and another of green tea were placed on a tray at the base of the low table. Alone I ate this meal which should have been shared among family or friends for a special occasion.

Yet Japanese expect such elaborate meals when they stay at good hotels or inns, as sampling regional culinary delights is an important pleasure of travel. Taste seems as important as sight, which attests to the strength and depth of the food culture. Rural towns and even villages go to great lengths to promote their indigenous dishes. "Your country should promote regional cuisine," a friend told me. "Japanese will travel to eat."

A man came to put down my futon bedding. Perhaps I wasn't trusted with female hotel staff. Later reception called to ask if I'd like bread added to the breakfast menu. That was a nice touch.

Because I'd decided to stay two nights in Muikamachi, I'd take a long, after-dinner bath at Uotoshi, stay inside, and explore some of the town the next night. A TV guide advertised an exorcism and I wanted to watch it.

A Buddhist priest began performing this rite on a young, delirious woman who was speaking uncontrollably. Family members sat behind her, the priest sat in front, his eyes fixed on hers.

The priest said he thought that several spirits possessed this woman. He questioned them through her and learned that one was a deceased uncle, one a student friend who had died in a traffic accident, one a woman who had been buried on the site where the house stood. I felt cold when I heard the priest recount the story of the next spirit. It was of a boyfriend who had died in a motorcycle accident on his way to visit her. He said that he was still on his way to visit her. The last spirit wouldn't identify itself.

Inattentive relatives upset the priest, who felt that they were not concentrating on the task at hand, and implored them to pray for the afflicted woman. "Pray for her! Pray for her!" he commanded them as he tried to draw out and rest the spirits.

It didn't seem likely that the program had been scripted or that the priest or young woman were so accomplished as actors, though it was possible that they were playing a little to the TV camera. But the woman remained deeply troubled and the priest wasn't satisfied that he had rid her of the spirits. That is how the program ended, which is reason to think that the attempted exorcism was real. It hadn't worked.

Exorcism exists in Christianity, too. The Bible notes several instances of Jesus performing this rite. In Mark 1:25–27,

> "Be silent," he said, and the unclean spirit threw the man into convulsions and with a loud cry left him."

In Luke 4:35,

> "Be silent," he said, "and come out of him." Then the devil, after throwing the man down in front of the people, left him without doing him any injury.

Devils can occupy animals, too, we learn in Matthew 8:30–32. After curing a leper and calming a storm, Jesus drove devils from two violent men.—

> In the distance a large herd of pigs was feeding; and the devils begged him: "If you drive us out, send us into that herd of pigs." "Be gone," he said. Then they came out and went into the pigs; the whole herd rushed over the edge into the lake, and perished in the water.

The pigs had done nothing to deserve this fate. They lost their lives because evil had chosen them. Perhaps they were born bad.

Breakfast was served in a large tatami-mat hall. Guests — nearly all couples — sat or knelt at low breakfast tables positioned at body-length intervals.

My bill for ¥11,312 ($94) included a ¥120 tax for "hot-spring entrance." The bathwater tax, I was told, was levied by the town and contributed to the maintenance of the source of the spring.

I set out to stroll the town.

Muikamachi has its share of quaintly named businesses — a bed shop called Bo Peep, a cosmetics shop called Life Box. Gibraltar Life is here, too. The dress shop Voir International advertises a "powerful bohemian look" and the Pic Guitar School teaches classical, folk, jazz, or rock guitar at *mai peesu* — "your own pace." Custom Joy Box specializes in camping and custom-built vehicles.

The smell of stationery and books drew me to a small shop, where I was the only customer and soon understood why. I was charged ¥300 ($2.50) for five envelopes and 10 sheets of paper. The homely stationer told me that business was poor these days. She said young people didn't buy much stationery, so reliant had they become on cell phones.

I was reminded of a high school graduate who had posted a letter in Yokohama without attaching a stamp. Raised on e-mail and text messages, this young man had never had occasion to buy stamps or post a letter. It seems these days that students can finish high school without learning the practice of letter writing or manage the task of posting one.

Poor Meal No.1 appeared to be the only coffee shop in town — there are actually around 11, though they must be well hidden. It opened in 1904, a sign says, but the building it occupies looked less than 30 years old. I ordered a toasted cheese sandwich and coffee.

Poor Meal piped an instrumental version of The Supremes' "You Keep Me Hanging On." No one entered the coffee shop while — because? — I was there. But I was sitting upstairs, out of view of the entrance. The food was passable, so perhaps discerning residents don't think much of adulterated Supremes. What is in the mind of a person who calls a coffee shop "Poor Meal No. 1"?

A pet shop advertised a Welsh fox terrier male puppy for ¥98,000 ($817) and a Pomeranian male puppy for ¥90,000 ($750). Puppies should be adopted, not retailed in this way. But at least no puppies had grown large and old inside the cages, a case of which I'd seen in Tokyo.

Toa Butsuzō was marking down the prices of Buddhist altars in a spring sale. Altar prices ranged from ¥290,000 ($2,400) to ¥12 million ($100,000), with most priced at around ¥600,000 ($5,000). The discounting of altars unsettled me and I wondered whether Christians discounted crucifixes.

Jazz Dance Studio was signposted on a short street leading to the station and, before the station, on a street to the right, I noticed a jazz coffee shop called Schi Heil — "Ski Hooray!" What passed for jazz in this mountain town? An outside staircase led to the second floor of a small apartment-like building. Inside, the manager was circumspect, the waitress cold. Music could be turned down or off, but what to do with me?

Most Schi Heil menu items cost more than ¥500 ($4.20). I ordered the least expensive coffee. Barriers began to break as I talked about jazz musicians — I'm just a listener who devours jazz biographies and histories. The manager invited me to choose a record or two from among the shop's collection of some 3,000 LPs and CDs. This was a test.

I took out Bud Powell's *The Scene Changes* and Wes Montgomery's *Full House*. It was the Powell choice that changed everything. As the manager took *The Scene Changes* out of its sleeve and lovingly placed it on the turntable as though he were handling a fragile, rare artifact, I felt I'd always be welcome here. Powell was a large influence on Toshiko Akiyoshi, whom history may record as Japan's greatest jazz pianist. He lost his mind, but recovered it enough to record *The Scene Changes*.

At the heart of the stereo equipment were valve power- and pre-amplifiers, which appeared custom-built, a Denon turntable and JBL speakers. A magazine rack was amply stacked with back copies of *Swing Journal* and *Jazz Life*. This was somebody's life.

TRADING TERMS

We next briefly tour topics of language. Japanese words have entered the English language in ways dictionaries don't grasp, and may change the way English speakers think. We also discuss "lifetime employment" as the creative concept of a translator.

CHAPTER 14. TRADING TERMS

Muikamachi — the town that daimyo allowed to trade only on the sixth day of the month — was named from the vocabulary of trade regulation. English borrows business vocabulary from Japanese without, it seems, so much as a second thought.

"Trade friction" is an example. It's a translation of *bōeki masatsu*, a term that came into vogue during trade disputes between Japan and the US in the 1980s. A disagreement between traders is a dispute, not friction, and the difference is direct, not subtle. Disputes can be resolved after blame has been apportioned, wholly to one or in different shares to both sides.

But friction is blameless. It results naturally and only from two sides coming into contact, from a mutual interaction. It isn't an English or Western concept but it now frequently appears in English-language media reports about arguments over trade.

A second example is "orderly marketing" or "orderly exports." This is the selling or exporting of products in a way that doesn't upset apple carts, but the expression, though it is in English, is surely not English. It's a translation of *chitsujo teki na yushutsu*, is Japanese to the core, and gained currency in the English language also during the 1980s.

It isn't in the nature of American or European business people to sell products in an "orderly" way. They sell as much as they can in as short a time as possible. They tend to take a five- to ten-month view of the potential of the foreign markets they target, not a five- to ten-year view. They use words such as "strategic" or "aggressive" to describe their methods of market penetration. "Orderly" isn't a word that would occur first or even at all. I think the English term is "managed trade" but even that expression may not have come into use without interaction with Japan.

Taking a leaf from Japan's book, the US entered into "orderly export" agreements, which allowed a predetermined volume of semiconductors or other products to be sold at prices set within a certain band in order to secure a certain share of Japan's market. Such agreements would reduce "trade friction."

Such behavior isn't characteristic of competitors but the word "competition" evidently found no equivalent in Japanese until the late 1800s, when educator Yukichi Fukuzawa translated it from an English economics text. He combined the ideographs for "race" and "fight" to produce the word *kyōsō*, he explained in his autobiography. A Japanese official at the time protested the "race-fight" word because of its violent tone.

Fukuzawa countered that all merchants "race and fight" and in this way "monetary values are fixed." Japan didn't lack the behavior, only the science of economics to explain it. This Fukuzawa introduced, along with much other Western thought, through his voluminous translations. He didn't win acceptance for "race-fight" from the censorious official, and deleted it from his translation. But it later became accepted, and today "competition" is most often translated as kyōsō.

The term "industrial policy" also may not be English. It may have entered English as a translation of *kōgyō seisaku*. Western governments and their central banks set fiscal policy and monetary policy as part of economic policy. The Japanese government and central bank do these things too, but through kōgyō seisaku or industrial policy, the government also has been midwife, shepherd, and undertaker to some industries. Some of the policies succeed — steel, machine tools, cars; others fail — aerospace, fifth-generation computers, pharmaceuticals.

There's more of Japan in the English language than samurai and shogun. The borrowings may not be insidious but over time they must change the way English speakers think about some things.

Language aside, Japan had reason to be watchful over the trading activity of Europeans, whom it straitjacketed after discovering that Portuguese missionaries in the 1600s were looting the country of gold. "Everyone did his best to fleece the Japanese of their money, primarily with worthless European curios and foreign medicines," Engelbert Kaempfer noted in his landmark study.

Foreign traders were confined "like plague carriers" to Dejima, the artificial island off Nagasaki, where Kaempfer and Dutch East India Co. colleagues were based. The governors of Nagasaki had "used their brains to throttle foreign trade to the advantage of the citizens and disadvantage of the foreigners to the point where the latter still just consider it advantageous to remain in the country."

They did this "to the great pleasure of the shogun."

Most cities had two governors, but a third was appointed to Nagasaki in 1688 to "permit closer attention to the arrival of foreigners."

———

Without James Abegglen's 1958 book *The Japanese Factory*, the term *shūshin koyō* — "lifetime employment," might never have entered the Japanese language.

Abegglen used the term "lifetime commitment," which, in the first Japanese edition of his book, was translated as shūshin koyō, literally employment till the end of one's life.

This new term gained currency in journalistic explanation of the perceived superiority of Japanese over mainly US business practices — US companies coldly fired at will; paternalistic Japanese companies looked after everyone till the end of their days. Drawing on some of this Japanese-language work, foreign journalists translated shūshin koyō as "lifetime employment."

Hence mythology was born. Some observers still praise what they believe is a superior Japanese corporate custom but instead it's the creative concept of a translator. There may be other explanations as to how shūshin koyō entered the Japanese language but this account seems the most persuasive.

Abegglen wrote that the Japanese worker "commits himself on entrance to the company for the remainder of his working career...This rule of a lifetime commitment is truly proved by its rare exceptions, and the permanent relationship between employee and firm imposes obligations and responsibilities on both the factory and the worker."

The author was referring, I think, mainly to large manufacturers in growth industries. For at least 40 years from the 1950s in most major Japanese electronics or automotive companies, for example, there was hardly any need to fire except in cases of extreme wrongdoing, because demand from within and outside Japan for the finely made products was so strong.

But cyclical industries don't enjoy secular demand growth. In some heavy industries — shipbuilding, for example — I'd studied, large numbers of people were hired or effectively fired as demand for their companies' products rose or fell, as elsewhere. When companies in these industries fell on hard times, they turned some business divisions into subsidiary companies. When the parent could no longer direct a sufficient volume of business to the subsidiary, bankruptcy was declared. No one had been fired but they all lost their jobs.

When I showed this chapter to Abegglen, he said that he'd been "quite aware that when companies go to the wall, employment commitments smash as well, in 1955 as well as 2005. Nothing new." But he insisted that I "allow the conclusion that the employment system — representing Japanese social values as it does — has essentially remained unchanged. And notably, Japan's most successful companies are its strongest upholders. The Japanese employment system was built on Japanese values, was not a crude copy of the West, and that fact goes far to explain Japan's success in industrialization."

The Japanese Factory, in depressing conformity with other authoritative works on Japan, is no longer in print in English. The work was, however, reprinted in revised Japanese translation as *Nihon no Keiei* by Nihon Keizai Shimbunsha in 2004 as a companion volume to Abegglen's new work *Shin Nihon no Keiei — 21st Century Japanese Management, New Systems, Lasting Values*.

UNTOAN

We next meet a Zen priest who ponders the meaning of a Biblical parable, pronounces on culture and politics, and dreams of making a pilgrimage to England to celebrate the life of a novelist.

Chapter 15. Amid the Tall Cedars

Untoan Temple is nestled amid a grove of towering cedar trees at the foot of Mt. Kanashiro, about three kilometers (two miles) southeast of Muikamachi on the outskirts of the neighboring town of Shiozawa. It's a Zen temple of the Sōtōshu sect.

Bokushi Suzuki described Untoan as the "most important temple in Echigo" which keeps "many old documents, books and treasures."

Echizenya's innkeeper offered to drive me. I told her I was happy to walk. Just south of the station on Road 17 there's a bridge across the Uono River to Road 434, which you follow until you turn right onto Road 28. Untoan is well signposted.

Emperor Juntoku (1197–1242) is said to have spent time at this temple in the 13th century on his way to exile on Sado Island as punishment for arguing with the Kamakura shogunate, which represented the first of the military governors that relegated the emperors to ceremonial roles and ruled Japan until 1868.

Water gurgled in rice paddy ditches and cacophonous frogs conferenced in the submerged paddies. Birdsong filled the spring air and cherry trees bloomed along the way. Road crews were using construction machinery to widen some of the lanes.

Soaring cedars, which cool the air in their shade, dwarf the tall wooden fence that surrounds the temple like the wall of a fort. A woman as silent as a prisoner sits in a sentry box at one corner of the fence and dispenses admission tickets at ¥300 ($2.50) each.

Markings for buses in the car park show that tour companies include Untoan on their itineraries, but this isn't a tourist-track temple. Nothing is brightly painted or gaudily gilded. The buildings are of old, oiled wood. Tourists take nothing away. They should come here.

Beds of daffodils bloomed in a pure yellow outside and inside the temple precinct. The inner garden was still, blanketed in crisp snow.

"We grew up being told Niigata was nothing but rice paddies but it has a wonderful temple such as this," I overhead a middle-aged woman say to her two friends. "We should come here and see it in autumn. Look at those maple trees!"

Tombstones stood in clusters in the hills beyond the temple's back perimeter but within the precinct were two tombstones of army officers.

Crows perched menacingly in the trees.

The temple traces its history to the 700s — so it must later have been absorbed by the Sōtōshu sect, which traces its beginning to 1227 — but without knowing that one can feel here the passage of hundreds of years.

Temple names usually end in *ji*, the ideograph for temple. The *an* of Untoan translates as "hermitage" or "retreat." Friends told me they think of a thatched cottage and smallness when they hear the word. The temple may have originated as a nunnery — it records that a granddaughter of the patriarch of the Fujiwara clan, a powerful family of the Heian era (794–1185), was its sponsor.

Apart from the temple, three other buildings are sited within the precinct — a two-storied side building, a two-storied residence, and a box-like structure that houses the temple bell. A head priest — *jūshoku*, a priest — *o-bōsan*, and an elderly woman who administers the temple office, occupy the residence. Untoan isn't an abbey or monastery; the priests aren't abbots or monks.

In the side building, a ground-floor room of around 20 mats opens to a view of the front garden. The upstairs room is furnished with old, soft leather sofas for visitors. I sank into one and was sedated by quiet and peace.

Statues of bodhisattvas — those who can reach nirvana but out of compassion stay behind to help us — line the entrance path and also the corridors around the main hall of the temple. One and five yen coins fill plates at the base of the statues.

Inside the temple sit as many as 100 figures of the bodhisattva Avalokitesvara or *kannon*, who personifies compassion. The Dalai Lama is regarded as an incarnation of Avalokitesvara, but in China and Japan this bodhisattva has become female. Here she appears as *senjū kannon* — the bodhisattva of 1,000 hands. She has several heads, too. Her multiple hands and heads enable her to help large numbers of people who face difficulty or are suffering.

I don't understand why some army officers' tombstones are placed within the precinct, but I'll ask. It may relate to the pre-eminent social position samurai held in feudal Japan. Honjōji Temple in Sanjō connects historically with the army in some way, too.

When Suzuki visited Untoan he noted that the tombstone of a certain general had collapsed and had it restored and placed upright. This general had served a warlord who ruled Echigo in the 16th century, according to *Snow Country Tales*.

The warlord noted is probably of the Uesugi family, whose members served as hereditary deputies of the shogun from the 1300s. The family first dominated in the Kantō region, which includes Tokyo, but later extended its grip to regions to the west and north, including the present-day prefectures of Niigata, Yamagata, and Akita, until the mid 1860s when the Edo era drew to a close.

———

The life of Uesugi Kenshin (1530–78), the family member who is omnipresent in the folklore of the snow country, shows how flexible Japanese can be in their family relations, a state which continues to the present.

People aren't always who we think they are. Families sometimes adopt the children of relatives. A husband sometimes assumes his bride's surname when marrying into a strong family which has only daughters. Uesugi Kenshin was neither Uesugi nor Kenshin. He was Nagao Masatora.

He ruled in Echigo, now Niigata, and became head of his household at age 16, daimyo at 19, and died at around age 48. His older brother, Harukage, wasn't cut out to be a ruler, so he adopted Kenshin as his son in order to create the appearance of orderly succession.

Both Kenshin and his brother were born into the Nagao family. They were rewarded with the Uesugi name after extending protection to a member of that family who had fled to their region. Kenshin's first name was Masatora. He used the name Kenshin in his role as a lay Buddhist priest.

Suzuki relates that the general whose tombstone he restored had been ordered to kill a rival general. Some say the general sent salt to this foe before doing away with him, so that he would be in good health for the fight, from which was borne the expression, "send salt to the enemy," as a show of fairness.

The general drowned his rival and himself in a death embrace after capsizing their boat on a lake. This end recalls the tale of the frog or turtle that agrees to carry a scorpion across a river, with predictable result. But is it really in the nature of the scorpion — or any other creature — to be suicidal?

These thoughts in train, I wondered, do suicide bombers look to the example of kamikaze pilots? Is the past the present? The flying of planes into the World Trade Center towers in New York in September 2001 seemed kamikaze copycat.

———

Water at Untoan Temple is said to prolong life — that was from a temple brochure, and sounded like an unnecessary play for tourists. Like nearly all large temples, Untoan sells souvenirs such as pens embossed with the temple's name, ceramic teacups, and amulets. Most items are priced from ¥700 to ¥2,000 ($5.80–$16.70).

I approached a priest who was walking toward the temple office.

"This is a Zen temple," he said.

"Nothingness must be difficult to understand," I offered as a prompt.

"It's not difficult. It's easy. It's the release from all that you believe," the priest said.

"Zen is a fight against your will."

He didn't champion *za-zen*, which requires painfully kneeling in the same position for long periods. The pain never goes away. One simply learns to endure

———

113

it. "Za-zen is a demonstration," he said. "It's more suited to Olympic athletes than it is to me."

He said he wanted to make a pilgrimage to the grave of Charlotte Bronte, whose novel *Jane Eyre* has deeply affected him.

What drew this priest to the story of Jane?

Jane is an orphan who, as governess, falls in love with her employer but leaves him after learning that he is married. Later he is blinded in a fire that destroys his house and kills his first wife, who is believed mad. Jane rejects a Christian minister's offer of marriage to return to the man she loves. They marry, his sight partially recovers, they have a child.

Jane Eyre is a love story laced with cruelty, insanity, destruction, and death — all book-ended by misfortune and fortune.

The priest said he had read much English literature. He thought it first asked the question "Who am I?" then tried to answer it. This may explain his fascination with Jane Eyre, who was starved of identity in childhood and only after much anguish, torment and guilt and through love came to understand who she was.

He believed that the influence of English literature in Japan in the Meiji era contributed much to the quality of written Japanese. Through reading it in translation, Japanese became aware of new possibilities and precision for their own language, he said.

I wondered whether this man who officiates at a Zen temple yet admits to not practicing Zen is truly enamored with the life of Jane Eyre. If Zen is the "release from all that you believe," then the question "Who am I?" is one his religion doesn't ask but denies.

And why are personages from English literature appearing in the most unlikely Japanese settings? In Donald Richie's *The Inland Sea*, a prostitute he meets in Onomichi is obsessed with Elizabeth Barrett Browning, whom the young woman has appointed as an alter ego. Unaware that Elizabeth was happily married to Robert, she has convinced herself that the poetess was forced into a vocation similar to hers and that she wrote poetry to console herself. She can recite only one Browning poem. She is a pitiable and ridiculous character.

But Bronte isn't known for writing bad poetry. Moreover, the priest has been sent away and, in a sense, adopted, and there may be some parallel in aspects of Jane's story. But his interest in Bronte stems more, I think, from the precision of the language the translator would have had to use to render Bronte's elegant sentences into Japanese.

He was single. "We can marry, but it's better if we don't," he said.

"Will you ever leave Japan?" I asked.

"It doesn't matter where I am," he replied.

He moved to a room behind the temple office and invited me to join him. We sat on the tatami-mat floor. A town resident soon joined us. He and the priest began discussing the latest goings-on within the ever-ruling Liberal Democratic Party. Their tone was one of scorn and distrust.

The woman who helps in the office brought green tea and *manju* bean-paste sweets. "Do not shame yourself in front of the gods by bringing food or drink into the temple," said a notice in the priest's calligraphic hand at the entrance foyer, but this was intended to keep drink bottles and fast-food wrappers out.

Unable to follow a monologue on Zoroastrianism — the priest will take detail from the distant past and apply it as a lesson to the present, but he made no allowance for Japanese not being my native tongue — I picked up one of my two sweets and couldn't restrain myself. The second soon followed. Nothing is more delicious that a manju sweet with hot green tea.

The priest is a raconteur who enjoys an audience but after each few sentences he paused, and waited for either his other guest or me to contribute. If we did, he would engage us on our observation, then return to this thread. Such are his skills as a conversationalist.

———

He said he was the disciple of an earlier *waga mama* priest who had passed away. It seemed odd to describe a selfless priest as selfish, but their relationship would have resembled that of officer and cadet. He speaks to the elderly current head priest (who regarded us suspiciously as we talked on the path outside the residence) when spoken to, and said days pass without a word exchanged.

Untoan has been staffed by about only 20 priests since the 11th century, the priest said. He meant head priests, as at most times one or two priests would have been in training here. It was hard to believe that anyone could live here for 50 years unless he were wholly preoccupied with intellectual or spiritual pursuits. The priest said that in time he too would need to search for a disciple and successor.

He described Japanese culture as one without purpose — *mokuteki no nai bunka*. Culture accretes, I thought, and can't purposefully be built. This declaration nonetheless impressed as outrageous and significant. Japan was either rudderless or its rudder directed it pointlessly.

Politics could be described as the efforts of the rural poor to obtain a share of the wealth of the city rich, the priest said. Did the US have a political party similar to the Liberal Democratic Party? Was President George W. Bush, who the priest noted hailed from Texas, redistributing the wealth of New York City?

His words were of the US but his mind, I think, was at home where, despite its environmental failings, the government has done much through tax policy to redistribute prewar fortunes — private and corporate — more evenly among the populace. He remarked how deeply religious a country the US appeared to have become.

He pondered the Biblical advice, in Luke 18:25, that it's easier for a camel to go through the eye of a needle than for a rich man to enter the Kingdom of God.

"Why doesn't the Bible say that it's impossible for a rich man to go to heaven? Why doesn't the Bible use the word 'impossible'? Isn't the Bible saying that it's just extremely difficult?"

I asked him if he had seen the TV program on exorcism the night before.

"Yes," he said.

"Was that real?"

"Yes."

He regarded Paul as the most impressive of the Biblical apostles. I should have asked why, but his confident pronouncement on an aspect of Christianity unbalanced me. Without Paul, some scholars say, Christianity may have remained a small sect within Judaism. The roads to Damascus are long. I'll ask when I visit again.

A corridor leads from the side of the temple office within the main building to a museum room built at basement level to the right of the largest figure of *senjū kannon*. I visited it before I left.

Exhibits include a vest said to be 1,300 years old, a saddle and stirrups said to date to 1510, examples of calligraphy from the Muromachi (1333–1568), Sengoku (1467–1568), and Edo (1600–1868) eras, and a Ming dynasty (1368–1644) vase. One could spend not days but months studying Japan in this room. How different this is to city museums whose exhibits are new copies of old artifacts.

Suzuki describes one of the temple's possessions as a "hell-wagon repelling surplice," which I glimpsed in the museum. This garment is said to have been worn by the priest Hokkō who lived at Untoan in the late 1500s as its tenth priest.

The story is told that Hokkō was walking in a village funeral procession during a snowstorm when a fireball fell from the sky and hovered over the coffin. A hell-cat sprung from the fireball and tried to tear the coffin open. Hokkō cracked its skull with his staff, and the gushing blood stained his surplice. The hell-cat vanished, the storm cleared, and the villagers continued their funeral.

In some Buddhist mythology, demons drive a sinner from deathbed to hell in a hell-wagon but over time hell-cat came to replace hell-wagon, *Snow Country Tales* explains.

Carp streamers, tied to a pole atop a new house amid rice paddies, blew in the spring breeze as I walked back to Echizenya. Infant children were playing with their father in a field behind their house. Traditionally the streamers signal that boys live here but now they fairly advise the approach of Children's Day.

Mechanized diggers cultivated a rice paddy on the other side of the road.

Iesu no chi wa tsumi o torinozoku — "Jesus' blood takes away sin." This sign was affixed to the wall of a concrete farm building on the road back from the temple. I paused at a newspaper delivery office and bought Monday's and Tuesday's papers. Then I read: *Kami wa Iesu no hoka wa nai* — "There is no other God but Jesus."

Konditorei Confiserie Matsumoto Seit 1958 defined elegance. Finely turned and stained wooden café chairs and tables awaited customers who wanted to take tea or coffee with thumb-sized but exquisitely presented cakes. The shop had originally sold Japanese sweets and was a third-generation business, the woman at the counter told me. The German name and style dated only seven years.

In Tokyo you have to search out the once-ubiquitous common and boutique Japanese-style coffee shops, which have lost their customers to fast-food or café chains such as McDonald's and Starbucks. There, taste and fashion are so fickle that it's hard to imagine that a cafe could be family-run for even one generation, though there may still be some generational family ownership of retail outlets in the *shitamachi* or old downtown suburbs in the eastern quarter.

At Echizenya dinner was served with a politeness so calm it appeared measured. Only one other guest was dining, a young man whom a TV weather forecast had hypnotized. He kept repeating to himself that he wouldn't go if it rains. People appear ill when they repeat things incessantly. He was unsettled and unsettling, and oblivious to me.

It had been a full day and I'd had a hearty dinner. But I'd promised myself that in return for watching TV the previous evening I would venture out tonight for a Japanese experience. I already knew the way, and once at Schi Heil coffee shop, browsed the record and CD selection, chose Bill Evans' "Waltz for Debby," and ordered a glass of red wine.

The wine was barely drinkable but the cold waitress started to warm. She held a spare power-amplifier valve up to my eye. They now cost ¥25,000 ($210) each, she said, but at one time had risen to ¥100,000 ($830) when it appeared that fully transistorized amplifiers would replace the valve type for good. (They haven't, and some audiophiles have returned to valve amplifiers for a softer, more spacious sound.) She said the valves were now made in China or Russia under an American brand.

Later she came to my table, smiled, and shook dried shellfish into the peanuts.

Among Schi Heil's records were Japan pressings that aren't in current CD catalogs and are probably rare. One, *Hello Japan*, was of a live concert the clarinetist Benny Goodman had performed in 1937. Goodman can be heard making a good effort to speak Japanese. Another was of a 1974 recording of clarinetists Shōji Suzuki and Peanuts Hucko, who played with Louis Armstrong.

Someone hijacked the turntable and put on a Japanese balladeer. "I'm crying, but there's sake for two," a crooner sings in a smoky velvet voice — a couple have parted but say, "We can still have a drink."

At Echizenya later that night I marveled over a TV news item pictorially addressing nothing more than tulips in bloom — what needed to be said? — and wondered where else I could see Picasso works, talk to a Buddhist priest about Jane Eyre, and listen to Bill Evans' records all in one day, if not in a small Japanese mountain town. California, perhaps; and Japan is about the same size.

There are other reasons to like Muikamachi. It's near Bokushi Suzuki's birthplace. It recently opened an office for passport applications, which suggests that it wants to make it easier for residents to travel abroad. You can use your seaman's identity card when you apply for a passport — so towns such as this supply sailors.

I'm going to visit Untoan again. The peace there may come from the mountains. It may come from the tall cedars, which have staked their claim for 300 years. It may come from something else. When I do, I expect that the priest will still be there, critiquing English literature, contemplating conundrums.

I'll give him directions to Haworth Parish Church, West Yorkshire, England. Charlotte Bronte has rested there since early April 1855, just three weeks before her 39th birthday. The priest hasn't left Japan before, but I'll do my best to persuade him to make this trip to England.

WHERE IS THE WILDLIFE?

I'd seen few animals and learned why they don't call Japan home.

CHAPTER 16. ONCE WERE ANIMALS

In the shade of these mountains in Shiozawa I'd expected to glimpse some wildlife. Disturbingly, I'd seen only confined dogs and hardly any birds, though I'd walked lanes as well as roads. Neither had I seen any traces of run-over animals.

Engelbert Kaempfer, who lived in Japan from 1690–92, wrote: "Wild and tame four-legged animals aren't found in great numbers in this country. The former find few uninhabited locations where, timid as they are, they can hide and breed." Kaempfer observed that farm animals were raised for work, not for their meat, and that Japanese knew how to use their limited space "more profitably than for raising animals."

Japanese were stricter Buddhists then. They didn't eat meat or animal by-products. Horses were used for show, riding, carrying, and plowing; cows and oxen for plowing and pulling, never for producing milk or butter. Europeans had introduced sheep and Chinese had brought pigs, but only for their own consumption.

J. W. Robertson Scott recorded that he had the "delight of seeing during my country house visiting many ancient pictures of country-life and of animals and birds." He saw pictures. Farmers even then may have been memorializing the wildlife that they could no longer see. The only animals Scott notes with any frequency are unwanted cats and dogs.

Yet I'd been warned: "Watch out for snakes!" and "Beware of mountain bears!" I'd seen neither.

Japan has two species of bear — the brown bear, which lives on Hokkaidō, and the Asiatic black bear, which inhabits wooded and mountainous areas in Honshū and the southerly islands of Shikoku and Kyūshū. So black bears should be here.

Untoan's priest told me that bears do come down to search the temple precinct for food but only in the early hours. Emperor Meiji (1852–1912) opposed the killing of bears, he said, adding that monkeys, squirrels, and deer still inhabit the mountains behind the temple. But except for monkeys, who have learned that some humans will feed them, animals sensibly give people a wide berth.

Bokushi Suzuki described bears as "lord of all the beasts in Japan. He is brave and virtuous. He lives on nuts and berries, tree bark, and insects, and never eats animal flesh. The bear will not ravage farmers' fields: when, rarely, that does happen, it's only because he can find no other food."

The eight or so species of bear left in the world are all endangered. They're jailed in small cages for life in China for the extraction of their bile for medicinal uses, killed in Cambodia for soup, and killed in the US for what? Manhood rights? They've been savagely trapped in Japan, too, and the few survivors must be threatened by shrinkage of their environment.

Foxes in the snow country met a cruel end, Suzuki wrote. Cylindrical holes the length of a fox's body were dug straight down, and baited at the bottom. A fox would enter head first but couldn't back out of the hole. On winter nights hunters poured water into the holes, and in the morning pulled the frozen foxes up by their tail like radishes.

Japan has lost its two species of wolf. The Japanese wolf, a subspecies of the common wolf, which inhabited Honshū, Shikoku and Kyūshū, died out in the late 1800s. The larger Hokkaidō or Yezo wolf was hunted to extinction.

Suzuki wrote that wolves were the "most hated of animals." He noted malignant meanings in examples of compound words that contain the ideograph for wolf: *rōsei* — a "wolf's voice;" *sairō no kokoro* — "a wolf's heart;" *rōrō* — "wolf-wolf" for chaos of the worst sort. He commended wolves, though, for acting like wolves, whereas men who act like wolves hide their wolfishness.

Dogs descend from wolves, with whom humans are understood to share some several thousand genes, which may explain the bonding we are capable of with dogs and also the occurrence of wolves in our literature. But we can never feel safe when wolves howl at night. They are harbingers of something — but we can't tell what.

Some say wolves' bad rap can be traced to their scavenging among battlefield corpses, in the way that stray dogs fed off corpses at execution grounds outside Edo in the early 1700s. But wolves and dogs didn't do the killing.

REFUGES OF A LEADER AND LOVERS

We now descend deeper into the snow country, where we visit a temple in which a Burmese leader hid at the end of the Pacific War, then trace the life of immortalized lovers.

CHAPTER 17. MATSUE'S LIFE

I quietly breakfasted in Echizenya's dinning room, not wishing to disturb the one other guest, whose senses had been stolen by a US golf tournament on TV.

Saying it wasn't much, Echizenya's innkeeper this Sunday morning gave me a small cloth coin purse. She apologized for giving me something that had been given to her and said she had no use for it. I've kept it.

I settled my ¥7,995 ($67) bill for one night's lodging and two meals, which I paid in cash. I carried the cash I needed for my trip, and would have been easy pickings for thieves but I never once felt unsafe, except on sections of road that were too narrow to walk.

Elfin Hair Studio — we live in the mountains, but we're well groomed — and Amusement You, a game or pleasure parlor (I didn't inquire), and other of this charming town's establishments were behind me by 9.30 a.m. as I strode toward Yuzawa, the town most symbolic of the snow country.

I would return to Muikamachi, but not for its advertised attractions. I would return for something else. Others can visit the "fishing park" that smelt of organization — you'd have to pay to get in; it would have a "restaurant" and a "souvenir shop" and the fish may have been caught elsewhere and let go upstream or put into a pond so that they could easily be caught again. The facility west of Muikamachi Station off Road 291 is something like that and a similar entertainment in neighboring Yuzawa is exactly like that.

Or visit the Saguri Dam, which some Japanese profile as a tourist sight — watch speed boats race across it, they suggest. What type of voyeurism is it that draws some to ogle the damage wreaked upon nature and the tourist markers staked into the ground?

I recall a primary-school field trip to the Benmore Dam across New Zealand's Waitaki River. The scale of the civil engineering work impressed and shocked — so large a wall, so much concrete amassed in one place, such a sheer drop from lake to river below. It taught, too, a physics lesson in the generating of electricity. But thinking about dams has changed since then.

I left Road 17 and tramped village lanes to find Yakushōji Temple, which appealed as a diversion when I noticed it on my map. Yakushōji stands at the foot of hills between Muikamachi and the neighboring town of Shiozawa. Temples are usually so located to make it easier for spirits to enter the mountains. When I arrived black-suited guests were observing the first anniversary of a death.

The temple is part place of worship, part museum, part art gallery. Tibetan bowls, a model of a temple, jewel-inlaid daggers, jade Buddha statuettes, and Chinese Ming dynasty ceramics incongruously share exhibit space with Papua New Guinean headdresses. A large image of the Buddha Dainichi Nyorai surveyed all below from its place high on a wall adjacent the reception.

In the gallery hung an oil painting titled "Roses" by Camille Pissarro (1830–1903), a West Indian-born painter of the French Impressionist school, "Girl at Prayer," an oil by Hocedi Ribera (1588–1652; the *Oxford Companion to Art* doesn't mention this painter, but the year of death is the same as that noted for Spanish painter Jusepe de Ribera, born 1591), and an unnamed oil by Vevelio Tiziano (1490–1576), an Italian painter of the Venetian school.

One painting in a collection of Japanese oils depicts two soldiers, one with sword in hand, the other holding a bayoneted rifle. They are crouched on the outskirts of a jungle, visible only in the light of exploding bombs. It was painted in 1942 by Tsuguharu Fujita (1886–1968), a long-term resident of Paris who was honored by the French Government and whose work is viewed as Impressionist.

The book *Kubikarizoku no Sekai* — "The World of Headhunters," sits on a ledge at the base of a display case off the main corridor. Three heads, seemingly crafted from leather, caught my eye in their vacant state, as though seeking answers to impossible questions. Strings of beads are threaded through the lips. But the modeling was too expert. The shriveled, shrunken heads had once attached to necks in a region of the Amazon, and now they sit on a shelf in this temple.

Above the heads are four skulls, string tied through their eye sockets, another string looped through the nose. They are from Papua New Guinea. Near them are five ceramic models of heads, three of which are from Vanuatu.

Did Buddhism condone the display of severed heads in a temple? I quizzed acquaintances. A friend's friend in Tokyo was appalled. Not in a temple, not a head, she exclaimed. A journalist lectured me on differences between Buddhism and Christianity — Buddhism can view all of life, the good, the bad, he said, whereas Christianity would show only what was considered good. This was unconvincing, but it was a start.

My thoughts turned to customs at Narita airport. How does one declare a head?

———

A small inner room in Yakushōji contains a capsule of Pacific War history. In the months after Japan's defeat, this room hid Ba Maw, the Burmese leader of

Japanese appointment, and now it serves as his shrine. I took time to observe the memorabilia in this room and later read about the life of this remarkable man.

Ba Maw was born in Maubin in 1893, and educated at Rangoon College and the universities of Calcutta, Cambridge, and Bordeaux, where he received a doctorate in 1924. He also qualified in England as a barrister. Like his father, U Kye, who had opposed the establishment of British colonial rule in 1886, Ba Maw was a nationalist who agitated against the British imperial presence. He was the first Burmese to be appointed to the faculty of British-run Rangoon College, in 1917. He became education minister in 1934 and, when Burma was separated from India in 1937, the colony's first premier.

After losing his position as premier in 1939 — he was outvoted by a British-led bloc — Ba Maw opposed Burma's siding with the Allies in World War II. The British response was to charge him with sedition and imprison him. Japan released him after capturing Burma in 1942, and upon declaring the country "independent" in August 1943, appointed him as head of state and prime minister.

Earlier, Burmese political elders had reasoned that the outbreak of war in Europe would weaken Britain's hold on their country. They seized the moment clandestinely to court Japanese support for a campaign of independence. Chinese support had earlier been sought by student leaders, who wanted arms, but to no avail.

U Maung Maung, in *Burmese Nationalist Movements 1940–1948*, records that Burmese independence fighters had trained in Japan from around 1941, though approaches to Japan had been made as early as 1935. In December 1941 the pro-Japan Burma Independence Army marched into Burma from Thailand, where it had received Japanese military training, and cleared the way for Japanese forces which arrived the following month.

After Japan's defeat, Ba Maw was secreted into Japan — the British would have imprisoned him again as they reoccupied Burma — and brought to this temple. His room of refuge contains a life-sized bronze statue and is thick with his presence. Tributes, some handwritten in Japanese and moving, are pinned to the wall. There's a photo of his son, Uzali Maw, who visited in 1997, sitting beside the statue.

Ba Maw had won hearts and minds. I thought about the lazy use of the term "puppet" to those of enemy appointment. Burma was a Japanese satellite but Tokyo's control of its government wasn't complete. As U Maung Maung has noted, Ba Maw made the Japanese military administration in Burma aware of the depth of Burma's will for independence. He ignored as impractical, for example, a military directive to use Japanese as the language of administration. Some in the imperial army, unimpressed with his recalcitrance, had wanted to do away with him.

He didn't administer the construction of the Burma-Thailand railroad, which the imperial army forced prisoners of war to build from October 1942 to November 1943. But when more laborers were demanded for the railway, he supplied what he called the fourth or "sweat" army. Burma, he said, needed four armies to rebuild itself — the civil service, the civil defense force, the defense army, and the sweat army.

Malnutrition, maltreatment, and disease claimed the lives of an estimated 60,000 Asian laborers (mainly Javanese, Tamil, Malayan, Burmese, and Chinese) and 16,000 Allied POWs (mainly Dutch, British, Australian and Indian) who worked on the railroad, or about 114 lives per mile of track. The purpose of the railroad was to create a military supply route into India, which Japan had planned to invade. Estimates of "death railway" casualties vary considerably according to source. I take mine from John W. Dower.

This railroad is an enduring symbol among mainly Australian, British, and Dutch people of "what the Japanese did to us." The memories of those who suffered on that railroad belong to them. But the collective, still open wound is, I think, psychological and racial. It's a European lament for the loss of empire. If the loss had been to a white power, it may not have been felt so keenly nor lingered over for so long.

In the three months following Japan's attack on Pearl Harbor in December 1941, Hong Kong, Malaya, Singapore, the former Netherlands East Indies (now Indonesia), and Burma were in Japanese hands — the Philippines and much of the rest of Southeast Asia would soon follow — and the boundary of a new Asian empire on a scale comparable in size and audacity to that of the Mongols under Genghis Khan was drawn. Those months were, in the words of historian Barbara Tuchman, the "three most humiliating months of Western history in relation to the East."

Churchill described Japan's war machine as possessing a "hideous efficiency," Tuchman notes in *Stilwell and the American Experience in China 1911–45*, which may be the genesis of the later "efficiency" tagging — more a resentment than compliment — of Japanese manufacturers.

Ba Maw hid in this temple for about five months before his whereabouts became known to the Occupation forces. Soldiers came to capture him and he was imprisoned in Japan from December 1945 to July 1946. He was allowed to return to Burma, made an unsuccessful attempt to reenter politics, and died in Yangon (then Rangoon) in 1977.

His youthful hopes of Japan as a benign liberator and partner were dashed when Tokyo reneged on its promise to grant Burma independence by the end of 1943. Japan had wanted Burma for its oil and to cut off the roads into China which British and US forces were using to send supplies for the war effort against occupying Japanese troops.

Years later and safely in his homeland, Ba Maw was to write: "The brutality, arrogance, and racial pretensions of the Japanese militarists in Burma remain among the deepest Burmese memories of the war years; for a great many people these are all they remember of the war."

I wondered why Yakushōji had been selected as Ba Maw's sanctuary. There are six main Buddhist sects in Japan — Pure Land, Zen, Shingon, Nichiren, Tendai, and Nara, in that order if we measure size by the number of temples. These split into various factions. Yakushōji belongs to the Chizanha faction of the Shingon sect. This faction, founded in Kyoto in 1598, is relatively new. Most other sects' factions were established between the sixth and 14th centuries.

As newer establishments, temples of the Chizanha faction may have been more pliable in relation to demands on their facilities made by the military. Cemeteries flank many Buddhist temples but some temples accommodate the tombstones of ranking army officers within their precinct. There may be a connection between providing such protection in life as well as in death.

The Shingon sect is a branch of Mahayana Buddhism. It differs from other sects about the source of basic sutras. Among Japanese sects it's said to maintain the closest affinity with Hinduism and with the Lamaist Buddhism of Tibet. Perhaps Ba Maw chose Yakushōji for religious reasons. I'd like to understand the background to the choice. Possibly Uzali Maw will know. Until I know I'll guess that amid postwar confusion and in the dead of night an army officer telephoned a priest he knew and asked for a special favor.

———

Some women were discussing the suitability of items at the temple's souvenir counter. They settled on towels sporting the animal signs used in the 12-year Chinese calendar — rat, ox, tiger, rabbit, dragon, snake, horse, sheep, monkey, rooster, dog, boar. One woman was distressed that she'd been born in the year of the monkey. As the same animal sign occurs every 12 years, you can guess someone's birth year, which is a nosy convenience of a cyclical calendar. The woman looked too young to have been born in 1944, too old to have been born in 1968. So 1956 it was. She was 46.

Another woman in the group was giving advice. "You fold the towel until only the animal sign is showing, put it inside your pillowcase, and sleep on it," she said.

The receptionist told me she'd just returned from Hawaii but admitted to not putting even a hand in the ocean. She'd preferred to shop, and the climate eased her shoulder and back pains, which the rainy season aggravated. She was the priest's wife. I asked her about her sect. "We marry, we have children, we eat fish, we eat meat," she said. She brought me coffee.

Who in the temple had heads on the brain?

The priest's wife told me that the late Ryūhei Imaizumi, a former Shiozawa mayor, had donated the heads from his private collection of some 6,000 mainly Papua New Guinean and South Pacific island artifacts. She said Imaizumi Municipal Museum held most of the collection.

I found this museum nearby on Road 17 in the type of building a light manufacturing business would occupy and looking as out of place on farmland as do shriveled heads in a house of worship. It was closed on Sundays. Posters in the entrance suggested a focus on dolls and masks and both may associate with heads.

Later in life Imaizumi moved to Saitama Prefecture, bordering Tokyo, to raise cattle. More of his collection reportedly is in the Saitama city of Tsurugashima, in empty classrooms at a primary school. The collection isn't critically acclaimed as Imaizumi apparently didn't always distinguish between authentic artifacts and replicas made for tourists.

I'd viewed original Italian Venetian and French Impressionist paintings, shriveled heads and skulls, the refuge of a Burmese leader of World War II, and become privy to the holidaying habits of a priest's wife, all in a snow country temple which I'd noticed because I was on foot. Buses and trains wouldn't have brought me here.

Later, in a moment of weakness watching TV at home, a travel documentary on Ireland noted that the decapitated head of St. Oliver Plunket is displayed inside Drogheda Cathedral, north of Dublin. I thought of the heads at Yakushōji which, though exhibited, weren't promoted as an attraction, and reached for the notepad I keep near the TV. "Drogheda Cathedral, gaze in awe at the preserved head of St. Oliver Plunket (executed 1681)," I later read in a tour wholesaler's itinerary.

The past had been allowed to stand along this stretch of road toward Yuzawa. The derelict Ishiuchi Hills Hotel looked like a headquarters for the homeless and the flimsily built Ai Di Da, a motel of sorts — none paid by the night — blighted the lower mountainside. Weeds grew through the broken windows of Fuji Lodge, a disused ski field was visible higher up, and gravestones jutted out from the top of a pass.

Outstanding debts may have prevented the redevelopment of these sites. Perhaps the land was held as collateral but couldn't be sold for an amount that would cover the outstanding loan. This made sense, as some Japanese investors notoriously hold rather than cut losses. I may have witnessed a mountain miniature of the troubled banking industry. But no post mortem was needed. The gigantic Shiuchi Twin Tower, replete with customary convention center and restaurants, had been built at a higher level, depriving these lesser tourist take-ins of light and life.

The Yuzawa Road Station impressed with its provision of vending machines, toilets, and bulletin board which posted advice on snow chains. This facility could be staffed in an emergency to life-saving effect. Further along, I lost the footpath from beneath my feet and was again sharing a mountain road with thundering, diesel-exhaust belching trucks.

Diesel soot combined with dust and hovered low in a carpet cloud above the road. Emission standards were being flouted with imperial confidence. Diesel defenders say the fuel pollutes little if truck engines are regularly tuned but truck owners think differently about what "regular" means. The manager of the mobile asset seems always able to operate on the fringe of the law. The stationary offender is easily apprehended, but errant trucks or ships must be chased to be caught.

The Mikuni Pass loomed ahead in low cloud. It cuts through the Mikuni Mountains on the border of Niigata and Gunma prefectures. Before rail, this was the only route connecting the west coast with Edo, and this section of Road 17 is called Mikuni Kaidō or highway.

An unnamed tunnel appeared a few kilometers before Yuzawa. I stood about 100 meters in front of the entrance to give drivers time to consider my sign and stop, took my hat off, outstretched my sign, and faced the traffic.

The seventh or eighth car stopped. The driver said he owned his own business and looked every bit the entrepreneur — too alert to fashion for a regular company employee and wearing his leather-upholstered left hand-drive Mercedes like an Italian suit. Thus cocooned he would reach Yokohama later in the day. There wasn't much to say for the minute or so we were in the tunnel but so relieved was I to get this ride that I left my hat inside his car. I would need to buy another or risk being burned by bright light reflecting off snow.

Snow-flecked mountains corralled the road as I walked into Yuzawa. Their beauty would double in winter, so too their danger. In these warming days snow soon would cap only the peaks. Die-hard straggler skiers dotted the upper slopes.

My map upside down, I confused left with right and missed the turnoff to Takahan Hotel, where a snow country geisha called Matsue had worked in the 1930s. I was learning about her life, and this was the one hotel reservation I'd permitted myself to make. A travel office gave me directions, and after retracing my steps for 20 minutes, I reached the hotel to find my name written in katakana script on a rice-paper plaque above the door of a pre-assigned room. Reciting or writing a guest's name is simple but effective. We want to hear or read our names.

Matsue had worked in the original wooden hotel on this site. She was born in Sanjō in 1915, the eldest of ten children, to a blacksmith couple. Her parents sold her to a geisha house in Nagaoka at the age of seven. Impoverished rural parents used to raise cash in that way.

Geisha house discipline was severe. Food might be withdrawn as punishment for poor singing or dancing; a missed shamisen note might result in a child being ordered to sit outside in the snow. But Matsue had to endure. She was a chattel and she was bonded.

To get her back, her parents would have had to reimburse the geisha house the cost of her board and training for the years she was in residence. Little chance of that. She would work as a geisha into middle or later years. But if she was attractive and learned her craft well, a suitor might secure her release by reimbursing the geisha house for her costs. He might also have to compensate the house for loss of income after her departure.

At about the time Matsue was born, J. W. Robertson Scott wrote that Niigata had a "dark reputation for exporting farmers' daughters to other parts of Japan." Brought up in a region blanketed in snow for much of the year, Niigata geisha were known as more patient and hardworking than other indentured entertainers.

Matsue was 14 or 15 when work was found for her here. She was 19 when called upon to attend novelist Yasunari Kawabata; he 35. That was in 1934. Matsue was her working name. Her real name was Kiku.

Novelist Yasunari Kawabata at home in Kamakura, June 1966. Photo by Kyodo

Photos and Graphics.

*Matsue, the geisha and companion of Yasunari Kawabata, circa 1940. Photo by Nii-
gata Nippō.*

So that he could have Matsue to himself, Kawabata made a point of staying at
Takahan in off-season months. During his stays, he began the novel *Snow Country*, in which he gave Matsue the fictional name Komako. He said the story wasn't
about their relationship. She said it was.

Though it's said that two myths surround geisha — that they sleep with their
guests, and that they don't — there's no ambiguity about Kawabata's relationship
with Matsue. He'd asked for a geisha and one was sent; and, as Edward Seiden-

sticker noted in the introduction to his translation of *Snow Country*, men never took their wives or family to these resorts.

In the novel, Kawabata finely depicted the character of the young snow country geisha whom he, as the fictional Shimamura, a wealthy dilettante from Tokyo, had made unhappy. Worlds change in one word. When she's called a good woman after being called a good girl, she realizes that she's been more used than loved.

The novel, along with *The Sound of the Mountain* and *Thousand Cranes*, earned Kawabata the Nobel Prize for Literature in 1968. Donald Keene opined in *Dawn to the West — Japanese Literature of the Modern Era* that Komako was his most successfully drawn female character. If Kawabata had written no other work, Keene wrote, his portrait of Komako "would still have earned him the reputation of a master of feminine psychology."

As sensitively as Kawabata creates his characters, he seems aloof from them — in the way that a smocked scientist is detached from the specimens under his microscope. There's an undercurrent of morbidity and fatalism, too. None of Kawabata's characters has any fun nor do they look forward to any event.

Kawabata can't be blamed for this. His father died when he was two, his mother some months later, his grandmother when he was seven, his sister when he was nine. He then was alone in the word with his aging, ailing grandfather. He was called a master of funerals, so practiced was he at attending them.

Takahan has kept intact the tatami-mat room in which Kawabata wrote and slept. The floor area is eight mats or about four square meters and the room sparsely furnished. Judging from the wooden walls and door and window fittings, it must have been bitingly cold in winter. A kotatsu foot-warmer table placed in the middle of the room appears to be the only heat source. Perhaps a kerosene heater was used in winter.

Kawabata memorabilia is exhibited in an adjoining, carpeted room in a long display cabinet. There are first editions of *The Sound of the Mountain*, *The Izu Dancer*, and *Thousand Cranes*, translated editions of *Snow Country* in Korean, Indonesian, and German, and copies of magazine and newspaper articles which serialized his novels. Bokushi Suzuki's *Snow Country Tales* is among the exhibits.

There's a manuscript of *Snow Country* beautifully written in thick calligraphic ink. Kawabata used hiragana script to write *tonneru* for "tunnel" in the novel's first, famous sentence — "The train came out of the long tunnel into the snow country." Language teachers will say that tonneru should be written in katakana, which is for foreign or new words. Kawabata may have viewed the use of katakana in his first sentence as un-Japanese. Perhaps unversed in the original, Japanese media seem mostly to use katakana when quoting the sentence.

Or he may have used hiragana to skirt the ban on foreign words in the militarist Japan of the 1930s. Then, even musical instruments had to be named in Japanese, no matter how clumsy the rendition. So *toronbon* for trombone, for example, became *kinzokusei magari shakuhachi* — "bent flute made of metal." The style of writing in which much is subtly suggested and little directly stated also may owe much to prewar censorship and therefore be more modern than "traditional" or "Japanese."

Takahan Hotel preserves the room where novelist Yasunari Kawabata wrote Snow Country. *December, 1992. Photo by Niigata Nippō.*

Kawabata in one display photo is dining with foreign guests, among them Seidensticker. Another foreigner, I think, is from the publishing company Alfred A. Knopf, which took a deep interest in Japan and published much of the best Japanese literature in translation. Kawabata gives the appearance of a nonchalant Bohemian — a bottle of wine is closest to his table setting; bottles of beer to those of the others.

A note to the photo says that Kawabata was visiting the hotel for the filming of the movie *Snow Country* but doesn't name the guests. The photo would have been taken in the mid-1950s, as the movie was made in 1957. There were later screen adaptations, but the first film, which is regarded as the best, must have occasioned this gathering.

Takahan clan members stand in front of the hotel in another photo, taken in 1905. The building was then a three-storied wooden structure. The present eight-floor, steel-concrete reincarnation is replete with vending machines and souvenir shop. Birdsong is broadcast at low volume. An unsightly escalator occupies the center of the lobby but at least it starts only when stepped on.

In the lobby a poster depicts a fairy-tale starry night over the snow country but in the exhibit room a notice laments that since Yuzawa has become a resort, the beautiful stars that Kawabata described can no longer be seen. What hides them isn't stated but I'd guess that smog from diesel fumes is mostly to blame.

There's a photo of Matsue, aged 18, and a photocopy of a *Mainichi Shimbun* newspaper article, dated 21 February 1999, about her life. The article maintains that she felt the novel drew heavily on her relationship with Kawabata. They did make the visit to the shrine — it's called Ski Shrine now; Kawabata doesn't say what it was called then — that the novel describes and events in the inn did happen as he recorded them. She's understood to have burned the letters from Kawabata and other hotel guests at that shrine.

Kiku was released from her work in 1940. She returned to her hometown of Sanjō, where she married Hisao Otaka, a tailor of traditional clothes, in 1942, when she was around 27. The marriage lasted more than 50 years. She died aged 83 in January 1999 after being hospitalized with cancer the previous year.

Later I would visit Sanjō and learn more, thanks to the good will of the reporter I'd met at Jazz Mama. These lives have been the subject of a recurring fascination since a friend gave me *Japan, the Beautiful and Myself*, which contains Kawabata's Nobel Prize acceptance speech and Seidensticker's translation of it, for my 21st birthday.

Snow Country was often prescribed reading for students of Japanese literature in the 1970s. Kawabata's suicide in 1972 perversely seemed to add some urgency to the study. Some who were close to the novelist maintained then, and still do now, that he didn't kill himself. They say he had used a gas pipe for support and may have pulled it off its nozzle and succumbed before being able to fix it. But at the time he was ill, not writing, and not sleeping — three reasons to hasten his end.

———

A rake-thin man came to lay out the futon bedding, signaling that times had changed at Takahan. I knew they had, and years before.

I returned from the hotel's bathhouse to find a sumptuous dinner of 16 dishes presented on a low table in my room. Apart from standard fare of rice and miso shiru soup, there were dishes of steamed crab, salmon, mountain vegetables, sashimi cut from shrimp and tuna, grilled snails and fish, tempura, noodles, pickles, several sauces, and two slices of orange. Like dinner at Uotoshi, this feast was made to be shared.

———

After a rich, lonely breakfast I paid the Takahan bill of ¥12,860 ($107), which included the equally rich, lonely dinner and a bath tax of ¥150. I decided I'd stay another night in Yuzawa, but not here. I'd look for somewhere down market, and ask questions about Matsue along the way.

After a half hour's walk, the town office building announced its dreary grey self. Inside, I caught the wary glances of clerks but none was confident enough to query my purpose as I pushed elevator buttons with the confidence of a resident.

I announced myself at the counter of the department for tourism. The departmental head stood up and ushered me inside. We sat in chairs at a low steel table in the middle of the room, surrounded by mute clerks at grey steel desks. The head explained that tourism was Yuzawa's largest industry and much coordination was required at local government level.

Matsue?

He said he didn't know of anyone who could recall this geisha, adding that as *Snow Country* had been set in the Yuzawa of the 1930s, such people would be in their 90s. But he believed that Kiku's husband was still living in Sanjō. I would return, but not now.

I wanted to ask the retired geisha's husband a question. I wanted to ask him whether he had loved his wife. It was a delicate matter, and I didn't expect him to welcome more voyeurism into his life, journalistic or academic. He would already have put up with 50 years of that. Then again, he may have become accustomed to some celebrity.

The *Mainichi Shimbun* article reproduces a photo of Kiku, her husband, niece, and an unnamed "fan" of Kawabata's work, enjoying dinner at Takahan Hotel. The article labeled the occasion, in October 1977, a *"Snow Country* reunion." And Kiku was known to be generous in sharing her time with literature students and researchers. She was known to meet them off the train at Sanjō and reminisce in coffee shops.

I walked back to Echigo-Yuzawa Station and through its west exit onto a skier-row street lined with lodges — both ryokan and minshuku. Inside the station, 88 square meters of office space on the second floor of the station building were advertised for lease. It was unthinkable 15 or 20 years ago that such space wouldn't be taken up. A coffee shop piped the Mamas and the Papas' "California Dreaming."

"We're airing our futons. The ski season is over. We don't serve Western meals. Try some of the other inns," said the innkeeper at Kabasawa Minshuku. That sounded reasonable. She didn't want to break the rhythm of her cleaning, or perhaps hadn't bought groceries for guests, as no reservations had been received for the day. At least she gave reasons for her rejection and credited me with the ability to understand them. It's the feebly excused refusal or blank stare that upsets.

Shimamura Lodge — various visitor attractions in Yuzawa take their names from Kawabata's work — had locked its front door. The distinction between a minshuku and a ryokan appeared to have baffled Minshuku-Sakurai-Ryokan, whose sensible solution to this naming dilemma I rather admired.

Ryokan Minoriya was welcoming and reasonably priced at ¥7,000 ($58), dinner and breakfast included. An elderly lady was at reception — I needed the presence of a grandmother — and I think it was her daughter who came to the entrance to greet me. I would spend my second night in Yuzawa here.

After entering a ryokan such as Minoriya, I've found it's best not to speak for a few seconds, as silence serves to cushion the shock of the presence of an outsider. I greeted the small school-uniformed boy in the entrance as he was about to leave but this frightened him and his response was barely audible.

Some travelers avoid museums because they think their exhibits are collected for the benefit of tourists. But I was glad I visited the small museum Rekishi Minzoku Shiryōkan. It's located across the road from Minoriya, but closer to the station. The exhibits powerfully convey how snow can isolate a community but also secure its livelihood.

Ski lesson groups formed in Yuzawa in 1919, a ski club in 1924, a ski resort opened in 1932, and now about 19 ski fields operate in the area. In 1922 a power-generating plant was built. Electric lights were turned on in 1925, the same year steam trains broke through on the new Jōetsu North Line and construction work began on the Shimizu Tunnel. Road 17 was completed in 1961 and bullet trains arrived in 1982.

The town now attracts around 3.6 million visitors a year, mostly skiers. Snow falls for around 140 days a year and about 2.5 meters (eight feet) accumulates. For most of February and March, three meters of snow accumulates, and in 1945 a record 4.6 meters accumulated. Photos from that year show people surreally looking down on rooftops as they walk above on snow.

Yuzawa records its history from AD 918 when Uonuma Shrine is said to have been built, according to a museum chart. Stone implements, ceramics, and other artifacts excavated from the area evidence that Japan's earliest inhabitants, Jōmon people, lived here. A vibraphone instrumental version of Eric Clapton's "Tears in Heaven" followed by Paul McCartney's "My Love" interrupted my note-taking.

The museum displayed the same *Mainichi* article on the life of Kiku Otaka and showed a short documentary, which commented that Kawabata wrote about beauty while other writers addressed the promise of the future. I think his theme is decay, but only the time of witness differentiates the two states.

On my way back to Takahan Hotel to take more notes and collect my pack, two women asked me to take their photo with a point-and-click camera, and I obliged. It's a happy feeling to help.

Tiredness overcame me after dinner and a bath at Minoriya. In the morning I realized that the daughter and mother who had welcomed me the day before had smuggled a small tub of yogurt onto my breakfast tray and slipped a fried egg onto my plate amid standard Japanese fare. I cast a glance at the plates on other tables and none had these.

Puppetry

How easy it is to view a whole people as suicidal. But no one can ever have wanted to cut his stomach open. We briefly visit to this subject.

Chapter 18. Puppets Feel no Pain

Dwelling on Kawabata's suicide prompted thoughts about the portrayal in mainly Western media of Japanese as a suicidal people. But are they?

Japan's rate of suicide is 10th highest among 60 countries but highest among developed nations, according to World Health Organization data current as of 2004. Several former Soviet republics and Hungary recorded higher rates than Japan's. Australia's incidence of suicide is comparable to Japan's, but few would regard Australians as a suicidal people, no matter the sheep thief's end in the country's unofficial anthem, "Waltzing Matilda."

Ritual suicide invites morbid fascination, but how could anyone believe that samurai ever wanted to cut their stomach open before being beheaded? It's only when people are viewed as puppets that such notions can be entertained, and spread. No person can ever want to die like that. It was because of their social status as samurai that they were permitted to take their own lives, rather than suffer the humiliation of being executed publicly.

I didn't understand this until I read E. H. Norman's *Origins of the Modern Japanese State*. George Bernard Shaw understood it in his essay *Treatise On Parents And Children*, in which he took English schools to task for their sadism. He recounted the case of the schoolmaster who had wanted to publicly flog a pupil for smoking. This man, Shaw wrote, in Japan "would hardly have been allowed the privilege of committing suicide."

Perhaps Japanese writers in taking their own lives reinforced the notion that suicide was a national trait. There were enough examples — Mishima, Akutagawa, Arishima, Daizai, among others, in the last century. But so were there with writers working in English — Hemingway, Plath, Sexton, Woolfe.

Norman, whose work taught me about ritual suicide, became ensnared in the "communist" traps of Senator Joseph McCarthy in the 1950s, and evidently for no more than a limited use of the jargon of the left. Washington-aligned Japan scholars such as Edwin Reischauer couldn't accommodate Marxist leanings — real or imagined — in interpretations of Japanese history. They did nothing to defend the Canadian diplomat and historian, a failing which Patrick Smith explains in *Japan — A Reinterpretation.*

Norman's work, particularly on feudalism, has stimulated me more than any other Western historian's on Japan. Leaving a note which said his life was without hope, he walked off a building to his death in Cairo in 1957. I feel an affinity to him, not least because he was stationed in New Zealand when I was born.

Japan's incidence of suicide has risen sharply in the last few years. From 1978–97, the number of suicides each year ranged from 20,788 to 25,202. But in 1998, it rose to 32,863, then remained in the low 30,000s annually through 2005, the last year in my data series. As a rate it is higher, too, as the population has been static at 126–127 million from 2000–05. I looked behind the data, at age segments.

By age group, those over 60 accounted for the largest proportion of suicides, at 33 percent in 2005. But from 1998–03, the biggest increase in suicides by age group — 27 percent — occurred in the 30–39 bracket. We'd expect these people to be facing the most challenging but exciting period in their careers. They may have been lost to the pain of the lost decade.

CLOSED AND OPEN DOORS

We now course through a prefecture which produces prime ministers. Wanted posters for members of a murderous cult recall the Tokyo subway gas attack. Doors close and open in a village and we hear tribute to the individual whose vision led to the production of a remarkable car.

CHAPTER 19. TRAVELERS ARE STRANGERS

Today I faced the third longest stretch of my walk — 37.5 kilometers (23.3 miles), along the edge of winding mountain road and through the treacherous Shibahara, Futai and Mikuni tunnels, to a place called Sarugakyō, which time may remember but I'll forget.

Only locals have reason to use this stretch of road now. Motorists crossing Honshū will take the Kanetsu Expressway, which lies just a few kilometers to the left of Road 17, and dispenses with decorum and burrows in a straight line for around 11 kilometers (seven miles), to form the Kanetsu Tunnel, which is Japan's and one of the world's longest road tunnels.

Sarugakyō is a district within the village of Niiharu which, like other villages, resembles more a large town than rural enclave. *Buraku* or hamlets are more akin to villages in the English spirit of the word. But *mura* — "village," *machi* — "town," and *shi* — "city" refer to administrative areas, and villages here aren't centered on a temple in the way that English villages center on a parish church.

The *saru* in Sarugakyō means "monkey" and *kyō*, capital. Friends wouldn't agree that the place-name translates as "monkey capital" and I haven't learned of any auspicious event that occurred here on the day, month, or year of the monkey of the Chinese zodiacal calendar, which superstitious Japanese use alongside their imperial and Gregorian calendars.

Though well prepared for tunnels, I hadn't anticipated the danger of snow roofs. These are overhangs built out from the mountainside to keep snow off the road, and were unmarked on my map. Their support structure leaves no room at the edge of the road for a walker, so I kept as close to the edge of the structures as possible.

A truck blasted me on one stretch of road under a snow roof, in the manner of a merchant ship sounding a five-blast "pay attention!" warning, and I managed to climb up the side of the structure in time. This was dangerous. A false step could be fatal. Not only would no one find me, no one would look, as no one expected me in any town at any time, and my home answer phone was already full of un-heard messages.

Beyond the snow roof stood a derelict bus, precariously perched on a shingle mound on the edge of a steep bank. One push would be enough to send the rusted hulk tumbling down the mountainside. A couple had left their four-wheel-drive vehicle to collect *fukinoto* and other mountain vegetables in the cool shade. They taste bitter but go well with tempura, the woman said.

Trucks took me through the first two tunnels. The first driver regarded me strangely but seemed to understand that I was a danger not only to myself but also to trucks. The second driver, who took me through the Futai Tunnel, said he was going to Tochigi Prefecture through Maebashi. He wore the weathered face of a kind grandfather.

"This truck is going to Maebashi," he declared.

I told him I needed a ride only through the tunnel.

"This truck can take you through all the tunnels to Maebashi," he offered.

"This truck can..." His truck was an institution. "This truck" was the first person. He seemed disappointed when I affirmed I was walking.

Futai was a post station town which supplied horses and accommodation to Edo-bound daimyo, though nothing remains to suggest that history now. An in-door hot-spring bathhouse, Shukuba-no-Yu, competes for bone-weary skiers who are the new patrons of this route.

As I walked toward Tokyo in a southeasterly direction the snow thinned and soon I would leave the snow country behind. People think of it as dark but the re-gion holds no monopoly over the shadowy nature of humans. The whole country can be eclipsed by that, I was reminded in the ski town of Naeba, which vacantly greeted me along a stretch of Road 17, also mapped as Road 353.

Noodle joints, ski gear rental shops, ski lodges — all still as though part of a procession stopped in time — were closing down or already shuttered. They seemed to combine into a low, artificial edifice, sheltering ghosts.

Posters of Aum Shinrikyō cultists, wanted in connection with the Tokyo sub-way gas attack of 20 March 1995 which killed 12 commuters and made around 5,500 ill, were posted outside Naeba police station.

Five cultists were still at large seven years after the attack, betraying the boast that no one can hide in this tightly policed country for long. They could be in Rus-sia, where the cult is active. They could be here.

A "mole on the left side of the neck" and "a mole beneath the right eye" were noted as distinguishing features of two of the wanted men. Ages and heights were noted, but two very different portrait photos of each suspect, which only plastic surgery could explain, convinced me that people who knew one face wouldn't recognize the other.

———

Two women aimed telephoto lenses at monkeys scampering in trees. A man nearby threw stones in the same direction. If only all animals were as wise as these monkeys, which knew to keep a safe distance. Only one vehicle was parked, so the man and one of the women probably were a couple. Their crossed-purpose seemed starkly to illustrate a condition of marriage — capturing and expelling, preserving and destroying the same object of longing.

Those who fight like cats and dogs in English fight like dogs and monkeys in Japanese, according to the saying *ken-en no naka* — "at loggerheads like a dog and a monkey." Cats tease dogs — they really wind them up — but I've never seen them fight. The dog would want to play, but the monkey, like the cat, would tease it. There'd be no reason for them to fight.

A light truck took me through the Mikuni Tunnel, thus into the neighboring prefecture of Gunma. A sign on the Tokyo side asked visitors not to feed the monkeys. The old Mikuni Kaidō turned up into neatly terraced hillside and I followed it till the trail thinned into brush and became untraceable. Cherry trees were in flower and banks of blooming daffodils brightened the roadside before giving way to a stretch of amputated trees.

Gunma occupies the center of the archipelago. With economic production of ¥7.9 trillion ($66 billion; year to March 2005), its economy is comparable to that of Greece. Around two million people live in the prefecture, making it the 19th most populous. It's said that lightning doesn't strike twice in the same place, but it struck three times in the Bronte family and politically it has struck three times here. The prefecture, a conservative stronghold of the Liberal Democrats, has produced three prime ministers since the mid-1970s — Takeo Fukuda, Yasuhiro Nakasone, and Keizō Obuchi.

I can't say why Gunma bore these prime ministers — neither can the Japanese I asked; one mentioned cabbages from Tsumagoi — but the lightning is low voltage. Prime ministers aren't as powerful as their title suggests. Japan, as of this writing, has seen 23 of them come and go since it regained independence from the US in 1952, compared with ten presidents in the United States. Post occupation, Japan three times has had two prime ministers in the same year, which surely proves that they don't run the country.

Tanaka was an exception, but only for 18 months, though his rule as power broker lasted much longer. As for the Gunma three, Fukuda lasted only two years and Obuchi, 21 months. Nakasone, who inherited Tanaka's political faction, clung to the post for five years, his ability and flare supported by factional strength.

Conservative politicians align themselves personally to the leader of a faction, not to the policies of a party. The purpose of the factions of the Liberal Democrats is to raise money, and the faction that raises the most money attracts the most members. By contrast, factions within the Japan socialist and communist parties form around policy differences.

Politics is in the family of the Gunma three — Obuchi's father was a parliamentarian, as are or have been offspring of Fukuda and Nakasone. This is less remarkable than the dynastic Kennedy and Bush families of the United States. The *Asahi Shimbun* reported that 118 of 480 or 25 percent of those elected to the House of Representatives of the Diet in September 2005 were the progeny of Diet members, past or present. That weighting was the highest of any category of candidate, such as from business, the bureaucracy, or lower levels of public service. And 82 percent of all "family" candidates were elected, which was the highest success rate.

———

Fukuda, in his 1995 autobiography *Kaiko Kyūjūnen* — "Memoirs of 90 Years," pays no tribute to Gunma for any prime ministerial grooming skills it may have imparted and mentions as if in passing only that he and his wife were born there. After I skimmed his book for such references, it pulled me into its pages a second time. Fukuda had been a young tax and finance official in the 1930s. He saw the war budget increase threefold in 1936–37, from ¥1.1 billion to ¥3.3 billion, or from 47 percent of the nation's spending to 69 percent.

Then only in his mid-30s, Fukuda was a finance ministry chief accountant charged with liaising with the army ministry, whose budget requests, he said, "knew no ceiling." The army ministry, Fukuda observed, wrote these requests on paper as thin as toilet tissue. Despite this thinness, he witnessed a single pile of the requests for 1937 tower above his own height. In that year the army, he recalled, had launched a five-year plan to more than quadruple the number of its squadrons from 18 to 128 and increase its fleet of warplanes more than six fold from 180 to 1,200.

The climate for the war footing was set in the early hours of 26 February 1936 by army officers who assassinated the finance minister, Korekiyo Takahashi, among others they saw as dovish, and tried to kill the prime minister. Fukuda recalled receiving a telephone call shortly before 6 a.m. on that day from the home ministry informing him that the finance minister had been murdered. Telephones and radios were few and the enormity of the incident wasn't immediately understood outside inner government circles.

In August the year before, Fukuda wrote, a divisional head of the army ministry who had the "politeness of an English gentleman," had asked to be excused during a telephone call over work matters. Some minutes later he called Fukuda back to say that the director of his department, in the office next door, had just been cut down. The murderer was an army officer of the pro-war *kōdōha* or Imperial faction, which rivaled the *tōseiha* or control faction.

Fukuda doesn't say that he feared for his life in Tokyo during this troubled time but earlier, in 1931, when a finance attaché in London, he does admit to wondering whether he would be permitted to leave the house of a Rothschild financier alive. After a convivial dinner, Fukuda's superior had advised that Japan would repay a French franc bond at par value, making no adjustment to compensate for rampant inflation of the franc, which position met with furious response.

Although Fukuda, who died in 1995, later held three cabinet posts (finance, foreign affairs, and economic planning) before becoming prime minister, he probably exercised more power in senior administrative positions within those ministries. As cabinet ministers are brief guests of their ministries, so the prime minister is the guest of all ministries. E.H. Norman wrote, "The key to understanding Japanese political life is given to whoever appreciates fully the historical role and actual position of the bureaucracy."

Yet news media still seem to write about politicians as though they are powerful. Reporting instead may better focus on how power shifts within and among ministries affect policy that does bear on people's lives. A news report about a cabinet minister, I think, calls for ten about the administrative vice minister, who is the effective legislator.

————

An old bus at roadside had been converted into a noodle stall, long since closed. Bare trees, car and truck cab wrecks, and a broken windmill, on top of which was positioned a working model of a windmill, formed a surreal backdrop to a landscape of sunken hope. Weeds rushed up from the cracks in a car park of a shuttered restaurant advertising grilled meat. Rusted Coca Cola signs looked in place.

I was about only three kilometers (two miles) from Sarugakyō and the sights along the road would match the spirit of this cold corner of the village of Niiharu.

Three Sarugakyō minshuku — the Hashiba, Nakanoya and Hatagoya Maruichi, and two ryokan — the Kurayashiki and Mikawaya, turned me away. We're full, empty places said. We take reservations only for groups, others said when they saw me alone.

A woman at the Nakanoya wanted to oblige but an older man inside objected. My response to the tone of the man's voice may in future be to arrange to have made to this minshuku a telephone booking from Tokyo for a party of 12 — that should be large enough a group — but I won't be able to say later whether anyone made the trip.

One innkeeper said: "We're busy. There's been a festival at the shrine today." After these rejections I resolved not to spend one yen here.

There had been a festival, I was traveling alone, I hadn't made a reservation. But the inns were open, rooms were available, their business was lodging.

I was a stranger, but so are all travelers who seek accommodation in small towns far from home. I couldn't believe that in other countries accommodation providers with available rooms would turn down a Japanese or other traveler. Their business instincts would override whatever dislikes or prejudices they nursed. They would take the money. That's what also hurt — not even the money I carried was acceptable.

In all but obviously ominous cases cash would be accepted or a credit card swiped. But the privacy of a motel or hotel room isn't a feature of traditional accommodation, and Japanese travelers belong to a group outside and inside lodgings. Obviously ominous. Perhaps this description had fit.

A time warp or two may also have been at work. Japan hurried from the medieval to the modern, with no pause for European-like ages of Enlightenment — words such as *risei* for reason and *jiyū* for liberty entered the language in the

1800s as translations from the English. Or Romanticism, to which the walker for pleasure or thought belongs.

I felt cast in a medieval shadow that darkens the walker as poor, perhaps even criminal, on foot because he can't afford a horse. Or now a motorbike, car, or train or bus fare. Neither was I eligible for the accommodation offered the care-free young who need no excuses for their explorations. As the Frisian Islander Konrad tells Patrick Leigh Fermor in *A Time of Gifts* in 1930s' Vienna: "I am of ripe years already! I would always be frightening them! You, so tender, will melt hearts." And so he did.

No matter the year, there's something innately sinister in the presence of a middle-aged man walking and alone. Unlike Fermor, I wasn't offering portrait sketches for cash, and my time wasn't one of chivalry or gifts. I wonder, or rather I don't, what reception Fermor would have received had he walked through Europe at my age.

After walking 27.5 kilometers (23.3 miles), much of it uphill, I spent another hour and a half searching for a place that would let me stay. It was 7 p.m. before I found one, just as I was beginning to think that I might have to rough it somewhere such as a school outbuilding or shrine. I should have found a temple, asked for advice, for calls to be made on my behalf. A temple may even have put me up, in the way that temples accommodated European visitors in the mid-1800s.

But I found the parent of a parent at a small minshuku called Hanasakuya on the old Mikuni Kaidō, off the main thoroughfare. The presence of two women talking — one elderly, one middle-aged — encouraged me. It would be hard for the middle-aged woman to turn me down in the presence of the elderly woman.

I greeted them and explained that I'd walked from Yuzawa and that several places had turned me down. When the innkeeper, who was the younger of two, asked whether I'd mind the noise of some other guests, I knew that I could stay. She hurriedly took in futons from outside where they had been airing and began to prepare my room, wondering aloud whether I'd need a kotatsu.

The other guests were a lively troupe of builders. They'd come to erect a small theater, suitably so as they projected the demeanor of itinerant entertainers. One sported an elaborate tattoo of a geisha on his back, I noticed at bath time.

The grass at Saitama Stadium may not be strong enough for a World Cup soccer match, just 45 days before kickoff, TV news said. Dining rooms seem always hostage to conversation-killing TV sets. The Emperor, Empress, and Crown Prince and Princess had held a reception at the Imperial Palace for athletes who had recently returned from the winter Olympic games. Several hundred counterfeit ¥1,000 and ¥10,000 yen notes had surfaced, their design intended to cheat vending machines. Over 400 varieties of flowers were in bloom — flowers made news by blooming.

Word had spread that some places had turned me away. I overheard one of the workers talking to the innkeeper's mother, who was helping in the kitchen.

"Five places here turned him away."

"They should've taken him in. He speaks well. We'd need a place to stay if we visited foreign countries."

142

The early rejections of the day now dissolved. I was dining alongside travelers and workers. I could appreciate them and they me.

This worker spoke in sentences. You notice when someone doesn't speak in spurts of a few words. He must have been well read to speak in that way. There was a seriousness tinged with sadness in his well-spoken manner that revealed lost opportunity. Perhaps he hadn't been able to afford to live in Tokyo as a university student. The education of family was on his mind. Over dinner he said that his daughter recently had failed entrance exams for a certain high school. She would have to get a job after leaving middle school. He left unsaid that she may have to live his life.

The workers made their way to the bathroom. They spat with such vigor as to appear determined to clear not just throat or lungs but their abdominal cavity.

One of the workers tapped on my door.

"Come and share a bath with us," he said.

But we found the bath too small for more than two people, so he and his colleagues went first. One of the group later came to tell me that the bath was free.

The workers were free of pretense and prejudice and I felt that higher education sometimes strengthens both weaknesses.

I returned to my room to find the futon bedding laid out. I usually enjoy a magazine or a book at this time in the evening but in a tatami-mat room you either sit in a legless chair at the kotatsu, which doesn't support a comfortable reading posture, or stand up or lie down. Some expensive ryokan rooms are adjoined by an *engawa* or corridor furnished with two easy chairs and a small table, where guests can read or enjoy a view over a garden.

But the bare state of most rooms such as this at Hanasakuya — and nearly everywhere else — hasn't changed in 100 or more years. J. W. Robertson Scott noted that the "drawback which the Western man experiences is the lack of any means of resting his back but by lying down and the inability to read for long while resting an elbow on an arm rest which is too low for him."

Door heights at Hanasakuya were too low for me and also for many Japanese who, along with other peoples, have grown in height in the past few decades. Once outside, I had to fix my vision at my height or risk walking cat-backed. Japanese are served poorly by their house-building industry which keeps as standard the kitchen bench and door heights of an earlier generation.

Cherry trees lined the sides of the old highway, and their pink blossoms were eerily illuminated by electric lanterns when I took an after-dinner stroll.

One of several izakaya was ablaze — people laughing, singing, eating, drinking. It would be so unfair of me to go in. It would break up the party, and they were having such a good time. Revelers would turn and look, become self-conscious, watch their tongue, feel obliged to converse. Put more sake in front of me than I could drink. If I could sing *enka* or ballads in the way that Alan Booth reputedly could, it would be different, but even then I'd feel as though I were putting on a freak show. Bears must exercise discretion in their choice of bicycle.

Hardly a squeak emanated from other eateries and bars along the same strip. Some establishments seem able to create an atmosphere that pulls people in; others do what keeps people at bay.

I returned to Hanasakuya and watched an NHK documentary which paid tribute to a supposedly rare Japanese type — the individual. Though much TV has become imbecilic, NHK continues to produce documentaries to a high standard.

When I wrote to TVNZ to complain about the undemanding quality of political coverage (a correspondent, reporting on a congressional election, had said that "influence counts for a lot in US politics"), the producer e-mailed back to say that I was probably the type of person who sourced news from the Internet. He had calculatingly dumbed down.

But he was right. As a journalist I expected that I would always subscribe to a newspaper and one or two magazines, but I haven't done so for a long time. I receive online a *Reuters* news summary and an edition of the *New York Times*, subscribe to one magazine — *The Atlantic Monthly* — and for a newspaper read only the giveaway area advertiser which, for its attention to local lives and neighborhood goings-on, at times is the most interesting of all. But even in a digitalized multimedia world, TV documentaries still seem to hold a strong position.

Tonight's documentary featured the contributions to industry made by "unknown" individuals. I hadn't witnessed such homage before, so put my feet up, or rather stretched them out. There's no place in a minshuku to put them up.

Even the name of the series — "Project X" — suggested that Japanese individuals must move in mysterious ways to achieve their goals. Tonight's episode featured Yoshihiko Matsuo, who designed the *Fairlady Z*, the Nissan sports car that has won a cult-like following among sports car aficionados the world over.

Matsuo had been singled out as a troublemaker early in his career for criticizing the Italian car designs Nissan had commissioned. Nissan sent him to its version of Coventry — a job at a subsidiary designing sewage pump trucks and amusement park rides. He retaliated by building such a successful dodgem car for the park that he won his place back as a car designer.

He said the US-resident manager for North American sales, Yutaka Katayama, was the only Nissan executive ever to encourage him.

Katayama had seen in Matsuo's ideas the chance to make inroads into the US, where only the rich seemed able to afford sports cars of makes such as Jaguar or Ferrari. Matsuo wanted to design an everyman's sports car, priced much less than the Jaguar E-type model, and Katayama believed he could sell it.

Japan's early record of selling cars into the US hadn't been enviable. The first models it exported were designed more for short distances on bumpy Japanese roads, not long distances on smoother US highways. They were trouble-prone, too. Among other early faults, bonnets would unlatch and hit the windscreen.

The test model of Matsuo's sports car had car shake because of a rear axle adjustment that designers made to accommodate a large fuel tank. The size of the fuel tank had to be reduced. Engineers shrunk it but needed to lighten the car body at the same time to maintain fuel efficiency. So they punched holes in both sides of the body.

A highway patrol officer had stopped Matsuo during a test-drive from Memphis to Canada, a distance of some 20,000 miles (32,000 kilometers). Matsuo said he had expected to be arrested and jailed, but the officer had just asked, "Where can I buy one of those?"

The first model, named Datsun 240Z, went on sale in Los Angeles in March 1970. Every US dealer was allocated two of the cars to start with. The sleek, lightweight sports car was renamed *Fairlady Z*. Thirty years later, 1.4 million models had sold.

The "Z" has a line through it. I was pleased to learn what it meant. Matsuo said, "That line means a lot of water went under the bridge for us to get this far."

MASS MURDER

In Naeba we paused in front of wanted posters for Aum Shinrikyō cultists. We now pause to reflect on their gas attack on the Tokyo subway system.

CHAPTER 20. A MURDEROUS CULT

The case of Aum Shinrikyō rattled Japanese to the bone. Tokyo trains associated with death only in their *jinshin jiko* — "human life accident" — announcement of jumpers. But that was death between the platform and the tracks. Inside the carriages life was as cosseted as it was in the city itself, and the trains were a large part of almost everyone's life. They'd been a large part of mine.

The cultists' gas of choice was sarin, which was developed in Nazi Germany. It's many times more deadly than cyanide. A pinhead-size drop of this gas is sufficient to kill one person, I read in the translator's note to Haruki Murakami's *Underground*, which carries interviews of 60 victims.

Plastic bags containing sarin had been punctured aboard trains of the Chiyoda, Hibiya and Marunouchi lines. This choice suggested that the cult had targeted the state head-on as these lines run through the district of Kasumigaseki, which is home to most government ministries and the national and Tokyo metropolitan police headquarters.

Police and hospitals froze like kangaroos caught in headlights. Trains didn't or couldn't talk to each other. One of the affected Marunouchi Line trains was still running one hour and 40 minutes later. But expectations of efficient Tokyo probably were impossibly high and the question of how cities can respond to indiscriminate attacks upon thousands of people is one that appears set to recur in the new century.

There was never a time when friends or colleagues worried that Tokyo overhead or underground trains were unsafe. The worst we had to put up with were the unwanted affections of drunks who, inhibitions absorbed by alcohol, would put an arm around us and try to speak English.

Or the persistence of Japanese who were studying English and viewed us as walking dictionaries or free lessons and starting practicing to our faces. It was hard to take when you were tired, but the effort had to be admired and usually you realized that you were a guest and tried to oblige.

It was also hard to lose things on the trains. Three times one Tokyo winter I left the same pair of lambskin gloves on one of the trains, and three times I reclaimed those gloves from the railway lost property center.

The cult was money centered. As a registered religion, its revenues were tax-free and new members were quickly stripped of their cash. They were required to buy ten cassette tapes of "teachings" at a cost of ¥300,000, or $250 a cassette. A "donation" of ¥1.2 million ($10,000) bought the status of a renunciant.

Cult leaders knew that converts would be flush with cash after selling their possessions, quitting their jobs — retirement benefits in hand for some — and leaving home. That's what renouncing their world required, so that nothing would burden them in their bare life on cult premises.

The more money a renunciant donated, the more "teachings" he would be entitled to receive. Participation in cult seminars cost hundreds of thousands of yen. Most converts appear to have been recruited in Tokyo, where salaries are usually highest, then moved to lodgings in rural locations, such as in Yamanashi Prefecture, where costs are lowest.

In other ways the cult mirrored the society it purported to reject — it promoted pretty women ahead of those less attractive, it fast-tracked graduates of Tokyo University ahead of those from less prestigious universities. Its structure was "extremely hierarchic and elitist," Ian Reader noted in *Religious Violence in Contemporary Japan*. It sorted its renunciants, for example, into as many as ten ranks.

But cultists didn't all appear as misfits who had rejected the world on the basis that the world had rejected them. They included lawyers and doctors — a doctor was among the five cult members who released gas on the trains — and other professionals.

What shocked more than the shattering of the sense of public safety was the realization that the nation's prosperous soul must be fractured for such a cult to take root. How could the progeny of a homogenous, harmonious society succumb to the teachings of a doomsday cult? Didn't Japan have all that Japanese needed?

Evidently not, for "new religions" rolled like a wave into the Japan of the latter half of the last decade, collecting mainly the educated young who rejected the spiritual vacuity of cog-in-the-wheel corporate life and who, it would seem, lacked the patience demanded of long-established Buddhist sects. Aum Shinrikyō's leader, Shōkō Asahara, had been a member of one such new religion, Agonshū, before he founded his cult in 1987.

New religions in the Meiji and Taishō eras had also offered solace in spiritualism and occultism, but those entering the 1990s faced the foreboding of the millennium. Asahara overlaid apocalyptic teachings on meditative elements of Buddhism and Hinduism and drew from the Bible's Book of Revelation of St. John.

The momentum of murderous or suicidal doomsday cults gained as the millennium approached — there were, among others, Heaven's Gate (US), the Movement for the Restoration of the Ten Commandments of God (Uganda), and the Order of the Solar Temple (Canada and Switzerland). Earlier, in 1978 — I remember this because I'll never forget *The Economist* cover headline: "Is Satan Dead?" — there was Jim Jones' People's Temple, which ended with the murder and suicide of more than 900 people in Guyana.

Some researchers distinguish between cults that murder and induce suicide among their own members and those that direct murder against members of the public. By this analysis, Aum Shinrikyō fits the latter category, and shares it with Charles Manson's The Family.

Murakami's interviews of gas attack victims reveal how the experience forced some to change their jobs and others to learn how not to work, because they no longer could. It prompted some to reconsider what it meant to be Japanese, brought one couple closer together, and sealed the separation of another. It lifted a veil on some peculiar personal habits. Strands of two victims' stories revisit me. Their real names aren't used.

Mitsuteru Izutsu, then 38, was a merchant seaman until a shipping recession forced him to switch to shrimp importing. On the morning of the attack he had gone to work early to catch up after having just returned from a business trip. The last of three trains he took to work from his home in Yokohama was the fateful Chiyoda Line.

His office appeared dark, his head ached, his pupils had contracted, he couldn't focus, but still he worked until 5.30 p.m. He learned of his condition not from a hospital visit that morning — he was sent back to work — but from watching TV news in his office. He called his wife to explain his symptoms. Her reaction of indifference confirmed the reservations he had felt about his marriage during his business trip. That night, he asked for a divorce.

Keiichi Ishikura, then 65, rises at 3.30 a.m., cleans his house from top to bottom, takes a bath, then goes to work. He had descended into one of the affected subway stations after seeing passengers collapse on the pavement at the top of the steps. He had wanted to help.

Within Ishikura's world is a history that seldom registers in the Western memory of the Pacific War. It isn't a death march or a death railway. It is about his brother, who came home, and was one of an estimated 1.6 million Japanese soldiers and civilians who surrendered to Russia in Manchuria and northern Korea at the end of August 1945. He managed to return to Japan eight years later. Many did not.

After Russia's return of some hundreds of thousands of Japanese and notification of the burial in Siberia of others, it became clear to US and Japanese authorities, according to research by John W. Dower, that some 300,000 had vanished. It's thought they died laboring — Russia was desperately short of manpower in the postwar years — or were killed.

Asahara was sentenced to death in February 2004. He will be hanged. Eleven other cultists have died or will die the same way. The public — including the family of the condemned — will learn of the hangings only after the event.

There were more deaths for the court to consider than the subway 12. There was the slaying of anti-Aum lawyer Tsutsumi Sakamoto, who had battled the cult, and his wife and child. Some trouble-making cultists, too, had been killed. There was the separate charge of ordering the gas attack on Matsumoto City, Nagano Prefecture, in July 1994 in which seven people died and around 500 made ill. Prosecutors counted 27 people dead at cult hands.

It transpired from the Matsumoto attack that the Central Intelligence Agency of the US, which had been investigating Aum Shinrikyō for its attempts to source uranium, had informed Tokyo that it believed the cult was involved. Nevertheless, Matsumoto police had their man — the same man, in fact, who had reported the gassing to them — and newspapers all but convicted that suspect. The CIA viewed the Matsumoto and Tokyo attacks as instances of terrorist use of chemical agents.

The cult has changed its name to Aleph. It says it's now a benign religious group. It has set up new headquarters in the affluent Tokyo ward of Setagaya. Membership is believed to number some 1,700 — down from an estimated peak of 15,000 — in Japan and a few hundred in Russia.

The London newspaper *The Independent* described Murakami's book as "Not just an impressive essay in witness literature, but also a unique sounding of the quotidian Japanese mind." Why "Japanese mind"? No one talked about American, Ugandan, Canadian, or Swiss minds in the cases of the other murderous cults. The assumption subconsciously loitering in the journalist's English mind is, I think, that Japanese are a separate species.

GOODBYE TO SARUGAKYŌ

We now leave the goblins of Sarugakyō behind and set out for the castle town of Numata. A replica of a checkpoint recalls the travel restrictions of the Edo era. We consider the works of a shogun who loved dogs and observe how loan sharks prey on youth.

CHAPTER 21. WAKE-UP CALL

A village chime woke me at 6 a.m. this Wednesday morning. The Niiharu village office was telling everyone to rise. An hour later, Niiharu made some announcement through its public address system of small megaphone-type speakers attached to power poles. Sleepy, I couldn't catch the gist of the message and neither could the innkeeper.

Wake-up calls are common throughout rural Japan and civic authorities don't hesitate to broadcast service messages. The tradition of the calls is centuries old. In Edo a bell was rung twice a day from the castle, at 6 a.m. and 6 p.m. Later, the bell was rung to mark intervals of about two hours and thus became a people's clock. The bell was moved to Nihonbashi when it became too noisy for the shogun, Akira Naitō and Kazuo Hozumi relate in *Edo, the City That Became Tokyo*.

Japan wasn't any quieter in the late 1600s. Engelbert Kaempfer noted "constant noise," which during the day had come from "wandering salesmen, advertising their edible and other wares, from day laborers, cheering themselves up with certain sounds when lifting and carrying, and from the oarsmen in the harbor, who measure their progress by the beat of certain noises and songs. At night the sound of the watchmen beating two pieces of wood against each other comes at short intervals from the guard boats in the harbor and the streets of the city as they proclaim their watchfulness and the hours of the night with this loud, annoying clatter."

Japanese seem unable to defeat the temptation to occupy airwaves. Quietude is like empty space to them. They are loath to leave vacuums unfilled or nature untouched. Like raw materials, a natural state is something that requires alteration or processing.

The broadcasting of messages strikes some as intrusive and more befitting a centrally planned, socialist state that believes its management of society is benign. It wouldn't be tolerated in New Zealand — "Brainwashing!" "Big Brother!" people would protest — but I've never heard complaint against the practice here.

It was time to leave though it hadn't ever been time to arrive. I set out toward Numata, a half day's walk of 19.5 kilometers (12.1 miles) along stretches of Road 17 more downhill than up.

I paused outside a replica of an historical checkpoint, or *sekisho*, at the main intersection in the village. The wooden structure resembles a small but cavernous castle. Its size suggests that it must have been the most significant building in the village. Along with toll-collectors, police and *metsuke* monitors of the shogunate were stationed here to inspect and report on travelers taking the Mikuni Kaidō to Edo.

In feudal times, papers amounting to a passport were needed to travel, as were letters of introduction and explanation from the sponsor of the traveler. Checkpoint inspectors would take a close interest in women, who were thought to have no reason to travel alone.

I'm required at all times to carry my alien registration card — the size of a credit card, it carries a photo and usual personal details — but so far on this walk no police officer has asked me to produce it. That much has changed. Twenty years earlier, I'd been asked to show the card on most days I left my apartment to go anywhere in Tokyo, even to the public bathhouse.

Carp streamers bellowed in the breeze as I walked beside Lake Akaya, filled by the Aimata Dam across a western tributary of the Tone River. I was glad to leave, and to have kept a promise to myself. After the previous day's rejections, I'd resolved not to spend one yen here. Hanasakuya's lodging charge aside, I didn't.

Sarugakyō was an artificial town above an artificial lake. *Kappa Kōen* — "Water Goblin Park," looks down on it. Some Japanese believe in these goblins, which are said to be good at sumo wrestling. They pull losers into the water.

Numata would be a kinder place.

Elderly people played gateball in a car park. They didn't stop when it started to rain. Their van was the only vehicle in sight. Pylons pockmarked the sky. A lodge stood derelict, its death knell sounded by the Kanetsu Expressway.

———

Pachinko Parlor Daiei 21 raised its barren profile as I entered Numata, a northern Gunma city of around 47,500 people. The opening of the Jōetsu Line brought this small city to life in 1924 as a distribution center for raw silk, farm produce and tobacco.

A pachinko parlor sign said, "Welcome New Machine," the owner either welcoming customers to try new machines, or Pink Floyd's "Welcome to the Machine" inhabiting his head. Volunteers had planted pansies in long wide strips at roadside, and the color made a difference.

A bouquet of flowers at roadside was plastic, not withered fresh, but wouldn't the dead prefer none to plastic? Two timber mills were sited near the Tone River a few kilometers to the north of the city. Sprinklers watered down logs, perhaps illicitly if prices are based on weight. Logs are usually priced volumetrically, but what reason could there be to water logs in spring?

Rivers border Numata on three sides — the Tone to the west, and its tributaries, the Usune and Katashina, to the north and south. The knowledge that comes from living alongside them must have assisted the city in its successful opposition to a Tokyo dam project in the 1960s. The central government had planned to dam the Tone on an urban edge for drinking water supply.

Some 3,000 families, whose houses would have been submerged, fought back. They and the city won in a reasoned resistance that took ten years. It was an astonishing victory considering the high-growth climate of the time when large-scale projects such as Narita airport and the Tōmei Expressway were proceeding apace.

I asked at a police box by the station for accommodation advice. A young officer, pointing to the map board outside his station, directed me up a steep hill to Miharashi Kan, but a shocked woman there told me that her silent ryokan was full.

Summits — even lowly hilltops — pull up those on their slopes. The road tapered into steps and wound upward. A cat on a roof panned its knowing gaze across my path. An upper level of the city plateaued out at football field-height above the lower.

A short distance from the top of the hill I found Hotel Aoike, a boutique western-style establishment, clean, refined. It wasn't hidden but after the rejection of Miharashi Kan it was Shangri-La to me. The hotel's name translates as green or blue pond — many Japanese see these colors as one — and perhaps such a pond was once here. The manageress fussed over me and allocated a twin room at the price of a single and my map and papers later settled onto a bed of their own.

It was mid-afternoon and time to explore. I would sit down first, consult my map over coffee, gather thoughts. But coffee shops are more a big-city refuge for the idle and I could find none here. Banks of vending machines maintained a pollutant presence and I succumbed to a canned offering then felt cheated by the thimble volume. Water bottles may be wise but I'd jettisoned mine, along with secondary maps, to lose weight.

Six red-bibbed Buddhist *jizō* statuettes lined the path to a temple, flowers in vases at their feet. Their purpose is to save the children who are piling stones at a riverbank in hell as punishment for the sin of having died before their parents. Devils destroy the piles, which the children must rebuild in perpetuity.

Snack Black Cats, the Korean pub Cho Ayo, Pub Blue Marine, Pub Mediterranean, and an izakaya bar congregated collusively at the opposite end of the road to the temple as though presenting a choice between virtue and vice. A forklift truck stabbed the air in front of a tombstone seller's yard. An "Italian" restaurant was selling puffed cream cakes.

Youths congregated around a McDonald's, as they did in Sanjō. Couples seemed younger here, infants at their side. The smaller the place, the younger parents seem to be.

I'd visit the site of an old castle — Numata had flourished as a castle town in the 16th century — in Numata Park, then retire to my comfortable room, watch a game of soccer between Japan and Costa Rica.

Beds of tulips bathed the park in warm yellow. Inside a park building I found an elaborate 1/200th scale model of all five stories of the castle. The complex system of inner and outer moats and their bridges and gates must have been designed to repel the most doggedly determined of assassins. It was good not to be entertained by a theme park-like replica of the castle built from modern materials. When I'd earlier visited Odawara Castle in Kanagawa Prefecture, which is such a replica, I was told that no feudal castles have survived intact.

A small old wooden church in the northwest corner of the park houses Sekiguchi Koh Kirie Art Museum. *Kirie* is the art of paper cutouts. Sekiguchi is a master of these. His adult characters are cartoon-like yet oddly real and his children are alive in emotion. I bought postcards of his work and later learned that the cards had impressed friends.

Some people of displaced literary mind disdain postcards as the thoughtless souvenirs of tourists who can't be bothered writing a letter, but as a child I felt special to receive a postcard from a traveling relative. A postcard gave me my first glimpse of London and most inspired me to travel. I've kept the cards I received. Apart from the thought behind them, they are valuable also for providing fledgling artists and photographers with an outlet for marvelous work — kirie paper cutouts, for example.

The kitchen was busily preparing dinner when I returned to Hotel Aoike. But in the small dining room I'd risk involvement in the obligatory exchange of set conversational pieces. Or I'd eat in embarrassed silence. Or I'd enjoy a hearty meal but lacking confidence in this last of possible outcomes I retired to my room.

I'd taken for granted that good sports commentators do their homework — practice pronouncing the players' names, research their strengths and weaknesses, familiarize themselves with both teams' recent performances. The more hardworking may note some personal details about the players to enliven their commentary.

But in the soccer game I'd settled down to watch, the commentators failed to mention the name of a single Costa Rican player in the game's first half. They commentated not on the game but exclusively on the home side, in the way that in wartime each troop movement of your own is propagandized to maximum effect, the enemy's face collective and anonymous.

I felt embarrassed — and let down — for the commentators, so transparent was their myopia. Cosmopolitan Japanese, too, would surely be embarrassed to watch this. Notepad in hand, I wondered whether the second half could be as bad as the first. It almost was, as only in the last minutes of the match was the name of a Costa Rican player mentioned.

I ventured out for a night stroll in the park. Red lanterns were strung spookily around the perimeter. The air was muggy but tense, thick with the history of spilled blood.

Nine dogs had died after eating poisoned scraps of food in Iwatsuki Park, Saitama Prefecture — the next prefecture I would enter before Tokyo — and earlier crows had died suspiciously in the same park, late-night TV news said. In a different time the heads of the purveyors of this poison would have been separated from their necks.

The fifth Tokugawa shogun, Tsunayoshi (1646–1709), who was born in the year of the dog and derogatorily nicknamed Dog Shogun, forbade the killing of all living things, especially dogs. His "Laws of Compassion" also protected the unborn child. He hailed from Kozuke Province, then a region within this prefecture, where he was a daimyo before becoming shogun.

Although some accounts suggest that Tsunayoshi wasn't always taken seriously — he did such strange things as set up a registry of dogs and build and staff kennels for them; the type of things local governments try to do today — his importance in hastening the country's transformation from a warrior to civil society is now acknowledged. He built institutes for the study of painting, poetry and the stars. The observatory built under his watch enabled Japan to correct its calendar.

TV showed a scene of a teenager waddling down a wharf in flippers, diving mask, and snorkel. Friends in wetsuits were waiting in a boat at the end of the wharf. "You too can go scuba diving!" This was a loan shark's attempt to net youth and sell them debt.

Consumer finance companies are legally permitted to charge interest at a maximum annual rate of 29.2 percent. Though this rate represents a reduction from 110 percent in 1983 and 55 percent in 1991, moneylenders can exploit a grey zone that exists between the two laws that govern interest rate limits and it's common knowledge that rate restrictions are flouted.

Loan sharks' billboards and TV commercials seem always to target the impressionable young. The sharks stepped up this feeding frenzy in the lost decade. The banking crisis that followed the inflation and collapse of asset prices in the 1980s forced commercial banks to tighten lending conditions. In doing so, they seemed to punish individual consumers more than corporations, and sharks circled the weak and wounded.

A woman in another ad said her role is to make new customers relax. She feeds at a consumer finance company. Yet another followed at what was now a suitably pornographic hour. Both adds employed doll-women. They infest life's waters. But society is turning on them with teeth. A court ruling in 2007 that invalidated coercive loan contracts has opened floodgates of litigation for refunds, and a new law will reduce the maximum interest rate to 20 percent in 2010.

Eric Clapton's "Layla" backgrounded a Mitsubishi Motors ad but for no particular model. "What'll you do when you get lonely and nobody's waiting by your side?" You'll drive a Mitsubishi car.

I left the TV on, too tired to sleep in silence. Late news showed a distraught man handing out leaflets at Ikebukuro Station on Tokyo's Yamanote loop line. He was appealing for information that might help police identify the person who had punched and kicked his student son to death on the Japan Railways platform at

this station. It was the anniversary of the death. The newscaster read the Ikebukuro Police Station telephone number twice and it was also shown at the bottom
of the screen.

Tokyo was changing, or perhaps this was another example of the existence of
a separate state —Tokyo — within Japan. Japan was safe. Tokyo wasn't. Japanese police solved most crimes quickly, but in Tokyo catching a killer could take
more than a year. Japan wasn't a place where parents appealed directly to the
public for help in solving crime. Tokyo had become so.

Dogwood flowers were in bloom in Utsunomiya Park, TV news said.

Oscar Wilde

Oscar Wilde was being quoted on Japan again (and again), in magazines,
newspapers, and online, more than a century after his time. Without ever having
visited the country, what had he realized? We visit his vision next.

CHAPTER 22. WHAT OSCAR REALIZED

> The whole of Japan is a pure invention. There is no such country, there are no such people. — Oscar Wilde, from "The Decay of Lying"

Add those with an interest in Japan to the roster of literary grave robbers who won't let Oscar Wilde rest.

It seems that almost every week a writer quotes Wilde's few words on Japan, turning the tragic figure of the Irish playwright into an early and improbable Japanologist, as though his ghost weren't busy enough variously as Irish rebel, subversive socialist, and gay martyr.

None of which he claimed to be.

Wilde wrote "The Decay of Lying," published in *Intentions* in 1891, as an imaginary dialogue between "Cyril and Vivian" — the names of his two sons — which takes place in the library of a country house.

In Wilde's dialog, Vivian declares:

> No great artist ever sees things as they really are. If he did he would cease to be an artist. Take an example from our own day. I know that you are fond of Japanese things. Now, do you really imagine that the Japanese people, as they are presented to us in art, have any existence? If you do, you have never understood Japanese art at all. The Japanese people are the deliberate self-conscious creation of certain individual artists. If you set a picture by Hokusai or Hokkei, or any of the great native painters, beside a real Japanese gentleman or lady, you will see that there is not the slightest resemblance between them. The actual people who live in Japan are not unlike the general run of English people; that is to say, they are extremely commonplace, and have nothing curious or extraordinary about them. In fact, the whole of Japan is a pure invention. There is no such country, there are no such people.

Wilde was writing at a time when impressionist painters were absorbing influences from Japanese print artists whose work had been exhibited in Paris and London. Monet in 1876 had produced "la Japonaise" of his wife in kimono against a sea of fans, and later Van Gogh would produce oil copies of Japanese prints. Japan's isolationist policies at an end, its art and artifacts made haste to Europe and ignited fad and fashion.

He declares the act of "thinking" to be the "most unhealthy thing in the world." People die of it. But what does he actually mean?

His essay attacks realism, memorably as he first simplifies, then exaggerates. He doesn't want artists or writers to think, because that would bind them to fact. He instead wants them to feel and imagine what can be, not boringly reflect what is. He declares that "Lying, the telling of beautiful untrue things, is the proper aim of Art."

He is also playing with Plato — compare his essay to the seventh book of *The Republic* — by borrowing the Socratic dialog form between a wise elder and a keen student and reversing the roles by making his younger son, Vivian, the teacher, and Cyril, the pupil.

Wilde praises Japanese art for its not being real. He gives other examples, asking, "Do you think that Greek art ever tells us what the Greek people were like?" In art, Athenian women were "stately dignified figures," Vivian explains to Cyril, whereas in reality they "wore high-heeled shoes, dyed their hair yellow, painted and rouged their faces and were exactly like any silly fashionable or fallen creature of our own day."

As for writers, the "modern novelist presents us with dull facts under the guise of fiction" whereas the "ancient historians gave us delightful fiction in the form of fact." And: "The only real people are the people who never existed, and if a novelist is base enough to go to real life for his personages he should at least pretend that they are creations, and not boast of them as copies."

Wilde writes of Japanese people only "as they are presented to us in art." He has never visited Japan nor, it is likely, ever met a Japanese. His Japanese people are "simply a mode of style" and "an exquisite fancy." The chord he strikes more than a century later among observers of Japan, though, is less about art than his intriguing notion that not much may separate Japanese from English people.

Patrick Smith noted that Wilde, in declaring that Japanese were "not unlike the general run of English people" was ahead of his time, separating orientalist fantasies from the reality of the country Wilde had not visited yet was, at the time of his writing, building factories and steamships, running department stores, operating universities and banks.

Pico Iyer, in his essay, "For Japan, See Oscar Wilde," in the collection *Tropical Classical* connects Wilde's comment that there isn't much difference between English and Japanese people to observations made by Kazuo Ishiguro, who was raised in England from the age of five and whose novel *Remains of the Day* is so quintessentially English that perhaps only a writer imbued with a foreign sensibility could have created it.

Iyer notes that Ishiguro grew up simultaneously as an English and Japanese schoolboy, and could see that the two were scarcely different. Ishiguro felt comfortable with actual Japanese methods of communication "because I have been brought up in middle-class England."

Iyer elaborated: "The very qualities that seem so foreign, even menacing, to many Americans in Japan — the fact that people do not invariably mean what they say, that certain distances separate politeness from true feelings, and that everything is couched in a kind of code in which nuances are everything — will hardly seem strange to a certain kind of Englishman."

Friends I quizzed don't believe that they share much in culture or outlook with English people. But they admit to an affinity with them, and are more familiar with the history of England's contribution to their industrialization during the Meiji era than with the Pacific War. They contrast the utility of the engineers England sent with the role of US missionaries and soldiers.

Wilde was writing also only a few years after the first production in London, in 1885, of the Gilbert and Sullivan musical, *The Mikado*. W. S. Gilbert's lyrics are an early marker of orientalism. The musical begins:

> If you want to know who we are,
> We are gentlemen of Japan:
> On many a vase and jar —
> On many a screen and fan,
> We figure in lively paint:
> Our attitude's queer and quaint —
> You're wrong if you think it ain't, oh!
> If you think we are worked by strings,
> Like a Japanese marionette,
> You do not understand these things:
> It is simply court etiquette.
> Perhaps you suppose this throng
> Can't keep it up all day long?
> If that's your idea, you're wrong, oh!

W.S. Gilbert, *The Mikado*, 1885

Ninety years later, Wilde may have been impressed that art still held sway over reality, as perceptions encased in *The Mikado* found a newer home in Stephen Sondheim's musical *Pacific Overtures*, first performed in 1976. The comparison isn't quite that neat, as Sondheim's work addresses a time 120 years earlier, when the US used naval power to intimidate Japan into opening trade relations. Commodore Perry, who led the four "black ships" into Tokyo Bay, was making, in his own words, a "Pacific overture."

But both musicals are the product of English-thinking minds attempting to appeal to popular notions entertained by English-thinking audiences, and their imagery can easily be swapped. Consider, from *Pacific Overtures*, the lyrics to "The Advantages of Floating in the Middle of the Sea."

> In the middle of the world we float,
> In the middle of the sea.

The realities remain remote
In the middle of the sea
Kings are burning somewhere
Wheels are turning somewhere
Trains are being run
Wars are being won
Things are being done
Somewhere out there, not here
Here we paint screens
Yes...the arrangement of the screens
We sit inside the screens
And contemplate the view
That's painted on the screens
More beautiful than true

Stephen Sondheim, *Pacific Overtures*, 1975

Perhaps we can sift Wilde's dust a bit more and apply what he said about Japanese people to place. Was a beautiful countryside also the "deliberate self-conscious creation" of certain artists? Or did it exist only in the mind of the orientalist? Why can't we see the beauty that only artists are entitled to imagine and produce?

The tag "orientalist" isn't a compliment. Imperialists bore orientalists. The type of screens and fans and trinkets they buy are manufactured for them and in a style not produced for local people in a century. But they are surely not wrong to want to see beauty in rural Japan.

When I conveyed to Japanese my disappointment with the bruised landscape that I encountered at most turns, they asked which places I'd visited. I gave the names of some villages and towns through which I'd walked. Invariably, they responded, "You went to those towns. But if you go to these other towns, you will find beautiful scenery." Beauty was always somewhere else, in another town, in another prefecture.

Looking out across finely manicured inn or temple gardens, in which plants had been pruned to perfect spherical or spiral death, or at the trunks of roadside trees — trunks because the branches had all been amputated (no one wanted to take responsibility for the fallen leaves, I was told) — it became clear that many Japanese don't respect natural forms. They instead feel a great urge to dominate and reshape nature, leaving a heavy human handprint. What isn't concreted is contorted.

Yet, friends said, the gardens do reflect nature, or rather superimpose a refined view of a natural state upon it, which, in Wilde's eyes, would disqualify them as art. They pointed out that they show none of the symmetry of circles, rectangles or squares that characterizes the planned gardens of England and France.

J. W. Robertson Scott, writing some 35 years after the first production of *The Mikado*, lamented that in place after place the "once beautiful countryside is now ugly and depressing." Farmers had completely cleared their arable land of trees, with not a clump left to shelter the farmhouse. They had created treeless plains.

Yet he also noted "unforgettable scenes of romantic beauty" in the gorges as he rode over suspension bridges and crossed the backbone of Japan.

———

There often isn't a middle ground in perception. Japan is either ugly or beautiful. It's hardly ever normal in the sense that it's some parts both. Isabella Bird remarked that the "whole country looked like a well-kept garden." Similarly, there's seldom a "normal" period of interest — popular or academic — in the country. Scott noted that for every worthwhile book on Japan, there were as many volumes of "fervid 'pro-Japanese' or determined 'anti-Japanese' romanticism." In nearly 100 years, that much hasn't changed.

Writers on Japan today still seem compelled to describe either miracles or massacres. The economic growth of the 1950s and 1960s is the most dissected "miracle," either proclaimed in extreme fashion or denied with equal extremity — there isn't a middle ground in extended essays on the subject; the killing of Nanjing civilians is the most revisited massacre. But these are subjects that require much research before anything new or meaningful can be said.

The shortcut to popular appeal is to employ the words "geisha" or "samurai" in a title and lace the narrative with the imagery of both. Using either word in online book searches bears this out.

On the subject of labeling, surely "miracle" is a backhanded word to use in describing Japan's advancement by Western measure. It's to say that unexplained phenomena produced the transformation in the economy.

English-speaking people wouldn't use the word "miracle" to describe their own success. They'd attribute their results to intelligence, effort, and perseverance, and other adjectives that would readily occur to them. They wouldn't be at a loss for words.

BALLOON BOMBS AND NAVELS

We now leave Wilde's imagined worlds and return to Numata where, in Tokugawa times, Macbeth would have felt at home. We see icons of America and encounter a fixation on navels in a town which time forgot.

CHAPTER 23. THE PATH OF GHOSTS

I skipped Hotel Aoike's cooked Japanese breakfast — ¥1,200 ($10) seemed too much and I'd found that it's exhilarating to walk for the first two hours or so after a breakfast as light as barely tea and yogurt — and paid the ¥8,160 ($68) bill. Later in the morning I'd set out for Shibukawa, a gentle walk of 18.7 kilometers (11.6 miles) out of the mountains and onto the edge of the Kantō Plain.

I hadn't understood the plaques in Numata Park — the names of historical figures in particular were beyond my reading ability — so I decided to ask for English translations at the city office, just a few minutes' walk from the hotel. Much civic material is translated into English but often the translations line the desk drawers of officials, as they do here. City office workers were busy at their laptops when I interrupted to explain my request. Soon translations were unearthed and I was kindly given photocopies.

The history, which Shakespeare could have rifled for ideas for Macbeth, spoke of betrayal, murder, and revenge, then more betrayal, more murder, and more revenge. In other words, Numata was an average castle town in recent feudal times.

One translation reads, "The history of Numata Castle: The castle was constructed in 1532 by Akiyasu Numata, the twelfth lord of the Numata family which moved here from the Makuiwa Castle in Yanagimachi. In 1566, Akiyasu transferred his castle to his son, Tomonori, and retired to the Tenjin Castle in Kawaba with his concubine and their son, Heihachirō. However, Akiyasu wanted to make Heihachirō the lord so, on the New Year 1569, he summoned Tomonori and killed him. Akiyasu and Heihachirō were forced to flee to Aizu pursued by Tomonori's family."

Heihachirō returned to Numata in 1581, intent on murdering daimyo Masayuki Sanada. Tables were turned and Sanada murdered him and, to convince all that he had died, had his head placed on a stone in the park. The body was buried at a different castle. Some say they can see a flying head in the park at night. They say it belongs to Heihachirō and is trying to locate and reunite with its body.

Before leaving this castle town I saw the park again, in better light, when ghosts slept. It's surrounded by mountains but there's a sameness to them that I didn't understand until I looked up their names and found that they're all of roughly equal height at around 2,000 meters (6,500 feet) — Mt. Hotaka, Mt. Shibutsu, Mt. Tanigawa, and Mt. Suzai. Only skullcaps of snow remained on their peaks in the warming spring.

Sounds assaulted the senses as I walked out of Numata around 10 a.m. Muzak infiltrated the air from a game arcade and met the chimed melody of "Greensleeves" from a kindergarten. Mothers had just dropped their infants off at a temple gate, and classes were in session within the precinct. Cheerful and so well dressed — and receiving an education from an early age — children such as these hold future's hope.

A friend said she was surprised to hear British prime minister Tony Blair mention children in a speech — "The key to our future," "The Britain they will inherit," or like phrase. She said she'd never heard a Japanese prime minister or cabinet minister speak of children. "They think only of themselves," she said.

Neither could I recall ever having heard a senior political figure allude to children in a speech, not in the three years I'd studied Japanese politics, not in the years since. The average age of politicians here is probably ten to twenty years higher than in the UK or the United States. The elderly don't inherit, and their children are adults in middle age.

We think of the people who are at home when we think of bequests. That may explain why the politicians' speeches, unlike Blair's, make no mention of the children who will inherit Japan, which may, in turn, explain the catastrophe of environmental wreckage.

————

Icons of America are never far from sight — if not a McDonald's or Kentucky Fried Chicken, then a Mister Donut or Starbucks. Or something else. In the district of Shimizu on the outskirts of Numata on Road 120, stood an imposing Delmonte research facility and factory. Nippon Delmonte Corp., which is majority owned by soy-sauce maker Kikkoman Corp., makes Delmonte ketchup and other sauces under license.

Two bridges, built in close parallel, lead to Road 17 across the Tone River. One of the river's banks was concreted. The older of the bridges — the Sagishi — doubled as an illicit garbage drop. I looked down from the Shinsagishi Bridge into a muddy torrent of snow melted by spring winds. Two barking dogs were tethered at the base of a pillar, no owner in sight.

A truck-stop restaurant and shops near Iwamoto Station on the Jōetsu Line were shuttered. The only retailers able to tempt motorists seemed to be convenience stores such as Seven-Eleven, owned by Itō-Yōkadō's global chain that includes US 7-Eleven stores.

A hairdresser in Iwamoto had posted one sign declaring "Men's Hair" and another, "Hair Men's." Colorful washing hung from his balcony. No matter how small the village, no matter what it may lack in amenities, it will have a hairdresser. Residents seem to say, "We may live in a small district of nowhere, but that's no reason why we shouldn't keep ourselves well groomed or utter English." They take pains personally to compensate for their surroundings.

At least they are free to visit a hairdresser. They haven't always been so. In the early 1900s, over-zealous, right-wing leaning "Young Men's Associations" in rural areas urged members to cut each other's hair to "save money" and "curb vanity," J. W. Robertson Scott reported. Centuries earlier, emperors had declared what their subjects could and couldn't do with their hair.

Road 17 follows the Tone River for about a third of the distance to Shibukawa. It meanders gently enough but is too narrow to walk safely. Ever mindful of trucks, I failed to appreciate the groves of cherry trees that grace the river banks and lower hillside.

The Ayado Dam, built in 1928 and operated by Tokyo Electric Power Co., assaults the Tone River in the district of Kawahake, Shōwa Village. It wasn't marked on my map. It appeared to serve as a debris trap. Ducks slow-paddled through layered flotsam. It was fed by an oil-green stretch of river and needed flushing.

The Ayado and the Makabe dams and a reservoir feed the Saku Power Station on the outskirts of Shibukawa. Neither was the Makabe Dam on my map. Later I learned that the Tone is dammed in at least six places — "at least" because regional geographies don't included some small dams.

Tokyo secures about half its water needs from rainfall and half from dams across the Tone. Dams aren't used much for generating electricity. Hydroelectric power accounted for just four percent of Japan's energy consumption in the year to March 2004, while the share of oil was 50%; coal, 20%; natural gas, 14%; nuclear power, 9%, and new energy sources, 2%.

As I write, earth-moving machinery is working the Yamba Dam site about 40 kilometers (25 miles) to the west of Numata along the banks of the Agatsuma River in the town of Naganohara. This massive concrete dam — height, 131 meters (430 feet); width, 336 meters (1,100 feet); reservoir capacity, 107 million cubic meters (140 million cubic yards); cost, ¥460 billion ($3.8 billion) — will submerge the inns and shops of the Kawarayu hot spring area, Kawarayu Onsen Station on the Agatsuma Line, sections of Road 145, and 340 houses over an area of 316 hectares (780 acres).

"Throughout history," a prefectural publication says, "man has continued to battle with rivers in his search for ways to control the flow of life-giving water in ways that best suit his needs." In the face of such entrenched thinking — of subordination, not coexistence — opponents of the Yamba Dam don't stand much chance of success.

Neither did the issue appear to interest news media. I found a seven-page article explaining and opposing the dam in the housekeeping magazine *Kurashi no Techō* (summer 2005 edition), though the magazine didn't advertise the article on its cover.

Perhaps advertising revenues in some cases influenced editorial policy. In the 5 October 2005 edition of the *Yamagata Shimbun*, the Ministry of Land, Infrastructure, and Transport had taken out a full-page advertisement feting construction progress on the Nagai Dam. The Nagai mayor said in a column in the advertisement that he "sincerely and happily celebrated from his heart" the achievement of concrete pouring for the dam having reached one million cubic meters.

Tokyo foists dam projects onto the regions. Some regional governors, such as those for Kumamoto and Nagano, resist this pressure. Gunma, though, isn't likely to engender political plurality. It appears as aligned to the Liberal-Democratic Party as that party's factions are to big business.

A young man driving in the opposite direction turned around, stopped and asked me if I was all right or needed a lift. When I said I was walking he seemed relieved that I was all right. Earlier worries that overly polite motorists would embarrass me by stopping and insisting on giving me a lift were unfounded. Only two had — the Sanjō-bound, fries-munching women and this caring man.

"They are too busy in their own lives," a friend told me, referring to people in their 30s and 40s who had ignored me at tunnel entrances or declined me accommodation. "Elderly Japanese assisted you because they have time." That may be so in some cases but I think historical perspective provides the larger reason. If the US-led Occupation wasn't all good, it was the lesser of available evils, which the elderly understand, and I'm an American to them.

Entering Komochimura, the inspiringly named "village with children" — this must be the boast all depopulating rural areas want to make — I said *konnichi wa* to three kindergarten children, they said konnichi wa back.

You see the future when you see children. Usually rural areas are bereft of them. Regional growth doesn't seem to be promoted much and young rural dwellers keep uprooting and heading in droves toward Tokyo in search of social stimuli and higher pay. Those who make a *yuu taan* — U-turn back to their home village or town, are few.

Oji san, the children said among themselves. I was mister to them. They hadn't learned the word *gaijin* — outsider — from their elders yet.

The "All-Japan Friends of the Moon" was signposted. What cult is this, I wondered. It isn't. *Zenkoku tsuki no tomo no kai* has been retailing clothes, bedding, health foods, and like goods since 1964.

A sense of foreboding enveloped me as I approached Shibukawa, the feeling you get when you know something is wrong but can't put your finger on what it is. The surroundings are tranquil enough — Mt. Haruna to the west, Mt. Akagi to the east — but the city, Gunma's smallest, sits uncomfortably at the confluence of two rivers — the Agatsuma and the Tone — which stopped being rivers a long time ago.

In the 50 years to 2004, the population of this smallest of Gunma cities grew 24 percent to just under 48,000, or an annual average 0.4 percent. The city grew out of the merger of villages — 12 in 1889 to which three were added in 1954. That may explain the lack of a sense of center, which disoriented me.

Road 17 diverges into two roads of the same number. One bypasses the city and the other forks into two. The larger of the forks also bypasses the city. The smaller, as Road 25, dissects the city in a line parallel to Shibukawa Station. By the time I realized my mistake in following the smaller of the two Road 17 bypasses, I was on the east and wrong side of the station on a lane between freight yards. A railway worker I asked for advice wouldn't speak and wouldn't listen. He crossed his outstretched arms back and forth at me as though trying to control a horse. Or perhaps signal a train. It took nearly an hour to correct my mistake.

A black limousine screeched to a halt just steps from me as I approached the station. I half-expected to hear a movie director call "Cut!" The driver, a flashily attired young man and his passenger, a fox of a young woman, stepped out of the car. He went to her side and tried to thrust money into her hand. She protested that she didn't need that much, but he forced the notes into her hand and clasped her fingers down on them, then sped away. She high-heeled to the station and was gone.

———

I'd erred in walking to the station. It wasn't in the middle of Shibukawa, but on the edge, as though the snub were deliberate. I needed to walk toward the center to find lodging but it was just after 5 p.m. and light would soon be lost.

Yamadaya Inn resembled a low-budget business hotel but it registered as a possible and I mentally noted the location. When you don't want to bother with the world, such a place suits, but I wanted to find something more Japanese and thus communal.

Ōtani Ryokan, walls darkly stained in the style of a daimyo's mansion, appealed as traditional but the 20 or so pairs of shoes in the entrance suggested it might be full. Still, *gomen kudasai*, I called. An elderly woman appeared from a tatami-mat room off the corridor, gasped for air, then raised her hand to her mouth as though she'd seen an apparition.

After regaining her composure she apologized profusely for not having any rooms available. Another time, I know she would have welcomed me, prepared the homeliest of dinners, heated the bath, and made up the warmest of futon bedding. Some people radiate goodwill and she is one of them.

I asked for recommendations. She gave directions to Yamadaya. It would have been unappreciative to break her off in mid-sentence and say, "I know." I listened to each word and left. Tonight I preferred company but the choice wasn't mine to make. Yamadaya it would be, if I wasn't turned away.

Reception at Yamadaya wasn't staffed, so I made my way to the inn's restaurant. Two waitresses were attending. One said the manager would return soon. I asked them both if they'd traveled. They said they wanted to leave Shibukawa but weren't confident that they ever would. One waitress said there was nothing for her in this town. Then the other said the same thing.

Over a passable pasta dish with salad I read material I'd collected about the city. No matter how bleak or small the place, it will stretch and strain to promote itself — "The strategic location of our city as a major traffic hub has led to developments in tourism and a broad range of thriving industries." In its desire to lure visitors it will say that it holds special attractions, celebrate its cuisine, list all its wares. Shibukawa is proud of its sausages, miso shiru soup, leaks, spinach, apples, strawberries and grapes.

Shinto gods here are removed from their shrines and carried through the streets in portable versions of the same in festivals half the year round — in April, May, July, August, October, and November. Heaven knows what they think of their earthly host's fixation on navels, which extends even to a festival. The chant *Heso dase, yoi-yoi, hara dase, yoi-yoi* — "show your belly button! Show your tummy!" sounds through the city during the July *Heso Matsuri* — Belly Button Festival — parade of funny faces jiggling on hefty bellies.

My map shows the Plum Month Belly-Button sushi restaurant, the Belly-Button Stone, and the Belly-Button Buddhist statue. The word *heso* is monotonously aired in civic promotions. Something other than Shibukawa's pride in occupying the geographical center of Japan may lurk behind this attention to navels. Perhaps it's the dread of the rural locale at severance from the mother mainstream. Perhaps it's something else.

When the manager returned she saw that I was already a customer who'd settled down to dinner. She would be disinclined to refuse me accommodation, which occurred as an afterthought as I'd not ordered a meal as a ploy to get a room.

Alan Booth in *The Roads to Sata* and *Looking for the Lost*, which recount his walks through Japan, I think secured accommodation in this way, though he doesn't admit to using the technique to do so. But frequently upon entering a town or village, he would stop at a noodle restaurant, order a dish, then inquire about what inns may be in the area. Soon enough, the restaurant owner would suggest one and even offer to telephone on his behalf. He had found in the restaurateur a travel agent, someone to vouch for him. He had put the matter of his accommodation into the hands of two Japanese who knew each other, and he was already a customer of one.

The manager told me that her husband's family had owned the hotel since the 1840s. Her husband, who didn't show himself, was the seventh-generation owner. She said the hotel had been rebuilt several times but couldn't say when the fires had occurred. It had thrived when Shibukawa was a post town on the Mikuni Kaidō, business made brisk by the daimyo trade for the last 20 or so years of Tokugawa rule. Its future was now uncertain. The city wanted the site for road widening as part of a project to revitalize the city center. She wasn't convinced that the sum the city had offered would be enough to rebuild on a new site.

Some people distance themselves from others as though under psychological siege. Their personal security thus secured, they remain in retreat. But the manager wanted to talk and we found common ground in journalism. She unearthed an article she had written about the history of Yamadaya for a local newspaper, and made a copy for me. She was still hurt that an editor's scythe had cut away three quarters of what she had written.

"I don't think my writing's that bad," she said. "And what they left in they rewrote. There's not much of me in this." She had wanted to see all she had written about this heirloom in print.

"It happens all the time," I said, trying to comfort her. "Even to journalists. They often lose control of their work once it is in a sub-editor's hands."

She was warmly engaging, her smile a friend's not a mother's. Not stick-thin or cuddly plump and not beautiful, she was attractive. There's something alluring in a woman of normal physique. But the shower in the room the manager assigned me may as well have run cold. The room was narrow, the bed a sliver, walls nicotine-caked. Feeling like a berated bedbug, I took to the night.

Shop fronts were rusted on the dimly lit main shopping street. Nothing was open. In Tokyo nothing would be closed. I passed the Ishizaka tatami-mat maker and a dentist and farm-machinery maker both of the Miyashita family name — a dynasty, I hoped, not wanting to believe that the same man attended to both businesses. I spotted a boilermaker and, conspicuously, two watch repairers. In throwaway, new-model Japan, it was good to see businesses built on demand for repairs.

Several private "hospitals" bearing family names were on the main and side streets. Takabashi Hospital typified the others in resembling little more than a private clinic with a few bedrooms attached. They made me shudder — someone dear to me nearly lost her life in such a place — and wonder why use of the word *byōin* is allowed in their case. Shibukawa has a public hospital which will meet its citizens' needs in ways that flimsy dens misappropriating the word byōin cannot.

———

Yamadaya's two washing machines were in use when I returned so I bagged my clothes and went out to search for a coin laundry. There's hardly ever any place to do your washing at a minshuku or ryokan — if you aren't bashful you can ask the owner to wash your clothes but the hard part is in the asking. Walkers need to launder daily and business hotels at least have coin-operated washing and drying machines.

Memories of student days flooded back at the laundry I found. While waiting for the machines to finish, I'd killed time by writing out ideographs in practice books. I should have washed my clothes more often. The hand as much as the mind must memorize ideographs, but they are as easy to forget as they are difficult to remember.

One other customer was here. He looked the type who uses laundries — unattractive, unmarried, no girlfriend. No woman to do his washing. That's fair and it doesn't mean that women are washerwomen. The man who offers to do laundry is regarded as unbalanced, so rigid is the assignation of domestic roles, so ingrained the habits. His wife would rather he attend to some manly task — or just go somewhere — than interfere in the kitchen or tamper with laundry.

———

Or this lonely man has been transferred and must fend for himself for some weeks or months. Companies often coldly transfer married men on a single basis. They like to maintain each individual as a mobile unit and the transfers are a loyalty test of sorts — employer above family. There's also the notion that the employer is family. Turning down transfers isn't sensible.

The transfers have loose historical parallel. Instead of taking husbands hostage, Tokugawa shoguns held their families. Mistrust in feudal Japan ran so deep that the shoguns required daimyo to leave their provinces and reside in Edo in alternate years. But there was a catch — in the years they went home, their families had to remain in Edo.

Daimyo were transported in palanquin and accompanied on their journeys to Edo by large retinues of attendants, on horseback and on foot. There were as many as 260 domains — more existed, but only briefly — and the processions of the daimyo to Edo supported inns and a host of roadside travel businesses.

The collapse of Tokugawa rule in the 1860s sounded a death knell for much of this highly developed regional travel industry. The routes fell into disuse and the post towns lost their patronage and became hollowed out and the habitat of ghosts.

I'd walked such a ghost route from Niigata. No one would regularly travel this road. When skiing took a toehold in the 1930s, rail was the preferred transport mode. Expressways later absorbed demand for transalpine road travel. Coastal freighters, not trucks, move rice and most other west-coast cargoes. The trucks I'd seen appeared employed mostly in regional earth-moving projects. The Mercedes-suited entrepreneur I'd met would have left and rejoined the Kanetsu Expressway at some points.

The laundry caretaker arrived. He looked unwell — it wasn't physical; he seemed small-town ill — and asked if I was with the church. An American priest, who had three children, came here to do his laundry, the caretaker said. But a missionary family would launder at home, and the caretaker is alone in confusing me with a priest. He fixed his whisky-glaze eyes to the side of my head and never looked at me when he spoke.

I resolved to locate this priest and talk to him about his washing. I'd try to visit him the following morning before leaving for Takasaki. Perhaps he was a long-term resident who could provide some insight into Shibukawa, which was bypassed ignominiously by its main thoroughfare, Road 25, by the Jōetsu bullet train to the west, and by even its own railway station to the east.

Guests were having too good a time for me to spoil in the breakfast room at Yamadaya on Friday morning, so I discreetly paid my ¥6,040 ($50) bill and stepped outside. Breakfast could wait.

———

I saw a church and went inside. The body attached to a crucifix told me it was Catholic. Bouquets of yellow, white and purple flowers lined the walls. Then I saw the portrait of the deceased, a late middle-aged man whom energy still seemed to occupy. It was positioned between candles and flowers on a bench in front of the altar. I unthinkingly put my hat down but quickly retrieved it when I realized I'd rested it on the coffin.

Children played outside a kindergarten in the church grounds.

A Japanese Catholic priest appeared after I knocked at the residence. He looked as weary as a parent. He said he had to drive a lot as his duty was rotational among Shibukawa, Numata, and Kusatsu.

"We held a wake for the deceased last night. We're saying our farewell today, from 11 a.m."

The American priest who the laundry caretaker thought still used his machines had left the city in 1999, the priest said, adding that he had moved to Kiryū, near the prefectural border, to join two others from his order at a convent called Francisco. I later read that Kiryū is home also to a Japanese extension of the Poor Clares sisters from Boston, though why Gunma attracts Christians is a question for another time, and it may not attract them more than other prefectures.

The past had imprisoned the laundry caretaker. His could have been the Laundry California, like the "Hotel California" in the Eagles' song, but unlike the unwitting guests of that perhaps mythical hotel, I could leave anytime I wanted.

The priest and I talked about the city. He said people these days bypassed the decaying downtown area and drove to big suburban malls on the outskirts of the city to shop. Gunma had the highest rate of car ownership — 1.6 million cars or 1 per 1.23 residents — in the country, he said, but hardly any parking was available downtown.

"This town is in decline. When people traveled by train more, it would have been more attractive."

It was now 10 a.m. Funeral attendants were beginning to arrive. One middle-aged woman suited in black frightened me by knowingly smiling at me. It was time to leave.

Shibukawa says, "The bountiful greenery of our parks serves as an oasis of charm and relaxation. Tranquility abounds as infants frolic, kids play ball with their parents and old folks talk together in our parks." The parks I'd seen were dormitories to the homeless but I didn't spend enough time here to appreciate those that weren't.

It adds, "Lights of cars form belts of light flowing north and south." We'll visit them someday. Treasures are hidden here but they are for others to find.

TURNING JAPANESE

We next visit the influence of Japan in popular song and consider the meaning of mirrors.

Chapter 24. Lyrics and Mirrors

The Vapors' song "Turning Japanese" has puzzled many in the years since it became a hit. David Fenton, the song's author and Vapors' leader, has said that the song means what you want it to mean and that he wrote it as a love song.

> I'm turning Japanese
> I think I'm turning Japanese
> I really think so

While walking, I could remember only two English-language pop songs that took something Japanese as a theme. One was the Vapors' 1980 hit, the other, Styx's "Mr. Roboto," released in 1983.

Surely there were more. Wouldn't traveling people and products spread Japan's popular culture? It seemed that only Japanese *anime* or cartoons had impacted Western media markets, though many children may not identify the source of *Dragonball* or other of the English-dubbed cartoons on TV as Japanese.

Japanese felt uncomfortable about their presence in the medium of an English pop song. One TV channel asked its New York correspondent to explain why "Turning Japanese" had become such a hit. The correspondent guessed it was about the fear of becoming a workaholic with no time to relax. A year earlier, an EC official had described Japanese as workaholics who lived in rabbit hutches, and the label had stuck. The correspondent emphasized "no fun" as he recited this lyric on-camera:

> No sex, no drugs, no wine, no women
> No fun, no sin, no you, no wonder it's dark
> Everyone around me is a total stranger...
>
> That's why I'm turning Japanese
> I think I'm turning Japanese
> I really think so

Some Vapors' fans contend that "Turning Japanese" refers to a shutterbug's obsession with taking photographs, as Japanese tourists are stereotypically portrayed. They cite these lines from the second and third verse:

> I've got your picture of me and you
> You wrote "I love you" I love you too
> I've got your picture, I've got your picture
> I'd like a million of you over myself

During 2002 World Cup soccer matches, tabloid and serious English newspapers latched onto the phrase "turning Japanese." Their use suggested that to "turn Japanese" was to provide good service or be a good host.

The *News of the World* offered "some tips to help you turn Japanese and impress your hosts." *The Sun* wrote: "Find out whether you're really turning Japanese with this fun *Sun* test." *The Times* captioned a photograph of soccer star David Beckham: "Turning Japanese: Beckham reveals the extent of his recovery by playing to the crowd in Kobe."

These examples have been pointed out by David Hills, a sports journalist writing for *The Observer*, who noted that newspapers stopped using the phrase after word spread that it was associated with a warning not to masturbate. "You'll 'turn Japanese' if you do that," the admonition was supposed to say, meaning that the eyes would narrow or the face contort.

Some British people say the slang is American; some Americans say it's British. Which suggests that it may be neither. And it's odd that newspaper sub-editors wouldn't be aware of such a slang term, if indeed it existed. I think it's more likely that some people — the type who resent a popular Japanese influence — tarred the lyrics of "Turning Japanese" to subvert the song after it became a hit.

One Vapors' fan has observed that a November 1999 edition of the animated US TV show *South Park* spoofed a *Pokemon* episode and turned all the *South Park* kids Japanese, except Kyle, who was slightly behind the times. This act of magic was the work of Japanese toy makers, who were bent on world domination.

"Fan" abbreviates "fanatic" and composers structure ambiguity so that the obsessed can choose and change meanings to suit. It's important to allow listeners this freedom of interpretation so that they can involve themselves personally in the music. As Fenton has said, his song means what you want it to mean.

Japan is modern and helps us escape drudgery in the Styx song, "Mr. Roboto:"

> You're wondering who I am — machine or mannequin
> With parts made in Japan, I am the modern man
> Domo arigato, Mr. Roboto, domo...domo
> Thank you very much, Mr. Roboto
> For doing the jobs that nobody wants to do

Lesser but sympathetic lyrics bind the English pop duo Alisha's Attic song "Japanese Dream" (1997) and the Bee Gees' song "Tokyo Nights" (1987). A verse in the Badfinger song "No One Knows" is sung in Japanese. Swedish pop group Ace of Base echoes centuries of careful Western observation in "Tokyo Girl" (1998):

> Though there's a fire burns inside her
> outside is ivory, silk and ice.

Ivory, silk, and ice — hard, smooth, and cold. What more needs to be said? Then:

> Deep in the heart of Tokyo
> found nothing there but a mirror.

The Ace of Base lyricist who wrote this is nicknamed "joker" but his use of the word "mirror" is serious. Some people uncannily are able to feel themselves in Japan's fabric and see themselves in its psyche. It holds a mirror to them — an old but tireless observation.

Helen Mears, in her 1948 book *Mirror for Americans — Japan* suggested that the self-scrutiny might extend to all of America, so self-serving, in her view, were some its occupation policies and methods.

Mears' thoughts likely were sound-tracked by lyrics such as "What a show, what a fight / Boys, we really hit our target for tonight," from The Song Spinners' "Comin' In On a Wing and a Prayer."

Or, closer to home, by Hoagy Carmichael's "I'll be ridin' my tank through a Tokyo bank, sure as I'm an Army buckaroo / And when I set my khaki down in old Nagasaki, I'll be singin' like a wacky jackaroo," from "I'm a Cranky Old Yank in a Clanky Old Tank."

But mirrors in Japan hold deeper meaning. The mirror that is handed down from ruler to ruler legitimizes authority, Kurt Singer explained in *Mirror, Sword and Jewel*. The mirror, Singer wrote, is seen as a source of fairness and justice as it enables things to be seen as they are, good or bad.

The mirror at a shrine entrance keeps evil at bay, and the discrete mirror inside the shrine is a body or *shintai* which gods can inhabit, though a stone, branch, sword or other item also can serve as such a receptacle. Robert Rosenstone in *Mirror in the Shrine* deftly shows how the contact with Japan of three Americans during the Meiji era gently changed their lives.

TOWARD THE EASTERN CAPITAL

Takasaki, where balloon bombs were made during the Pacific War, is our next destination and from there, in the line of the gaze of a goddess of mercy, we make our way toward Tokyo.

Chapter 25. The Gaze of the Goddess

A short walk of 18.7 kilometers (11.6 miles; the same distance as to Shibu-kawa), would take me to the city of Takasaki. I'd leave Road 17, which leads to Maebashi, and take Roads 35 and 25. The day had lost the sky by the time I left Shibukawa and I knew that I wouldn't visit the city again.

Some observers describe colored cloudy Japanese skies but apart from the bright white and blue of clear winter mornings, I can't see more than a low grey mass on most days. The day had lost its sky.

Pride of appearance soon collapsed. The base of a stream was concreted and strewn with rubbish — plastic drink bottles, vinyl bags — and a white cat lay dead on the footpath. Old futons, tins, and household waste smothered a house at roadside. Other garbage half-buried a car.

I could have been looking out the window of an Amtrak train coming into Jacksonville, Mississippi. After a friend died I had made that trip from Memphis to New Orleans to hear the sounds of the city while I lived. Later Katrina struck.

"Clever Noguchi's Any Work's," an auto-repair shop called itself. A smaller side sign misspelled "work" as "wark." A Japanese sign-writer must have said the word to himself and, as there is no "er" sound in Japanese, chosen "a" rather than "o." But the intended meaning was clear.

Some people make fun of Japanese for their misuse of English, but let's look again at Noguchi's sign, sympathetically. Clever Noguchi's Any Work's. It tells us that Noguchi is smart and can fix things. It isn't perfect but it doesn't need to be. It conveys its message. The atmosphere of his repair shop said the same. It was abuzz. Mechanics were busily, cheerfully fixing things, exuding confidence in their abilities. I'd bring my car here.

White wedding photos stood up showily in Maruyama photo studio's win-dow, alongside perfect-family portraits of conservatively clothed parents and school-uniformed boy and girl.

Lunch guests at the Ryūya noodle restaurant read newspapers and magazines and watched TV — always TV during meals. None talked or noticed me. Posters of young men sporting Elvis-style hairdos stared me down in front of Cut Shop Jail House, their models locked in the late 1950s.

An underfed dog was tethered to an undersized kennel in an open backyard cluttered with household and garden rubbish. Weeds carpeted the ground and crept through the rust holes of two car wrecks in the yard. A broken radio cassette player sat atop a wheelbarrow overturned on a heap of household rubbish.

If only the year were 1640 and my favorite shogun in power. J. W. Robertson Scott observed that strangers feel for the "unhappy demeanor" of dogs and cats. He thought that Japanese dogs suffered from having too much rice and few bones.

———

No-color new houses had been built of materials that looked like the products of a chemical company. Nothing even resembled wood.

Cycling, helmeted schoolgirls showed me the way into Takasaki, a former castle town on the edge of the Kantō Plain. In 1944, girls such as these were gluing mulberry paper for use in the manufacture of the large balloons that carried bombs across the Pacific to the US west coast. Schoolgirls whose nimble fingers were suited to the paper preparation were pressed into this labor also in Kokura, northern Kyūshū, in Yamaguchi Prefecture, and in Tokyo. It's a little-known history.

Kōichi Yoshino notes in *Fūsen Bakudan — Junkokusan Heiki [Fugō] no Kiroku* — "Balloon Bombs — A Record of the Indigenous Weapon 'Fugō,'" that launch plans for the balloons were finalized in the summer of 1944. Around 9,300 of the balloons, from a stock of some 17,000, were launched from November 1994 through April 1945, from the prefectures of Fukushima, Ibaraki, and Chiba, into the high altitude winds of the jet stream. The hydrogen-inflated balloons were around nine meters (32 feet) in diameter and laden with incendiary and conventional bombs at the base. The paper construction made the balloons invisible to radar.

There were 36 reported landings of the balloons in the US, with some reaching as far as the Great Lakes, according to Yoshino. The only recorded deaths were of five unsuspecting children and an adult who were killed in Oregon when they found a balloon and its lethal cargo intact in the woods and tried to drag it away. Washington had kept the public in the dark about the balloons to prevent panic. After these deaths the fact and danger of the balloons was publicized.

The balloons may have been intended to burn the northwestern forests in answer to the firebombing of Tokyo. There were earlier plans to sail such balloons from Manchuria to Vladivostok, to launch them from submarines, and to use them to carry biological weapons, Yoshino notes.

Takasaki was firebombed after the atomic-bombing of Hiroshima and Nagasaki, according to a city history. The air raid was made on 14 August 1945, one day before the surrender and when both sides knew that the war was over. It claimed eight lives and destroyed 701 houses. Perhaps Takasaki's role in the making of the balloons was revealed only one or two days earlier, and the bombing was last-minute payback.

———

Shaded by mountains to the north and west, Takasaki is situated on the west of Karasu River, a Tone tributary. Archeologists say people may have lived here as long as 1,400 years ago. It's a planned city — 15 districts are separately marked as industrial — that invests much in cultural pursuits. Maebashi to the east is the seat of the prefectural capital. Jōetsu and Nagano bullet train lines converge here, as did the Nakasendō and Mikuni highways to Edo when Takasaki was a castle town in Tokugawa times.

Hasegawa Hotel was a lazy choice this Friday evening. It's to the left of Takasaki Station on the west-exit side which gathers department stores and hotels while office buildings line the east-exit side. The late middle-aged manager recited to me the names of several hotels in this vicinity that charged less than his. It wasn't clear whether cruelty or kindness governed this effort but as I put my pack down and presented my wallet, he stopped his recital and reluctantly drew out a key from pigeonholes behind his desk.

At a department store where I bought bananas, oranges, and milk, staff competed for customers by loudly pitching their products and shouting out prices, as though nothing had changed from the old market-town days of open-cry, open-air stalls. The shopping baskets were no more than one-fifth the size of the obese carts in supermarkets in my country. Japanese shop almost daily, which makes them acutely sensitive to price fluctuations, food freshness, the arrival of new products and the withdrawal of old.

That evening, NHK showed staffers of the international department of the Gunma prefectural government speaking English. They do that one day a week, from 8.30 a.m. to 9.30 a.m.

Azaleas were blooming ten days earlier than usual, NHK said.

———

To survive in an Internet world where consumers search out and satisfy their specific interests and amusements, TV must secure a market of leftovers and left-outs. To do this, it calculates the lowest common denominator in content and taste. Thus news becomes the show of news, and personal failure, in shows such as *The Apprentice* or *The Weakest Link*, an entertainment.

Curiously, there's an inverse relationship between advances in broadcast signal and set technology and deteriorating program standards, as high-definition TV and plasma and LCD screens give greater clarity to sillier scenes and situations. Live sport and musical concert coverage may be the medium's strongest suits, because the winning goal or encore can't be contrived.

But for all TV's limitation, deception, and advertiser-only purpose, I sometimes channel-hop after a long day. Tonight I watched a *Dragon's Den*-type program in which four venture capitalists listened to presentations of business plans and decided whether to finance the applicant.

A Sri Lankan presented his case for cash most convincingly. A Japan resident of 12 years, this hopeful entrepreneur wanted to start a used-car dealership. He had bought and sold cars as a business in Sri Lanka. He spoke fluently and politely. He wanted start-up capital to target residents in well-to-do suburbs as a source of supply, and he would take his cash offer in hand directly to their homes. He would use a Japanese car valuer who would, he said, be more trusted than a foreign one. One panelist interrupted the pitch to say that he would trust the Sri Lankan more as a valuer, which drew expressions of wry concurrence from fellow panelists.

This plan impressed the panelists, though I hadn't thought for a second that they would finance this man. They would compliment him on his Japanese but advise that here business was conducted in different ways than in Sri Lanka. Perhaps they recognized that the affluent are sometimes asset rich yet cash poor, and here was cash on their doorstep. Suburbanites wouldn't have to drive to a car dealership and suffer the indignity of the low ritual of selling a car. No demand was made on their time. And a Japanese valuer was at their doorstep.

They would be unlikely to haggle, not within neighbors' earshot. They would sell, on the spot, and probably for less than their car was worth. They were the type of people who probably had maintained their cars well. The logic of the idea was now clear. Profits would be made more in the buying than selling of the product.

A panelist said: "This idea is the same as exchanging rolls of toilet paper for old cardboard and waste paper. I used to do that. We made money doing that." He allocated ¥5 million ($42,000) to the Sri Lankan, who was, after all, a salesman. He had sold his idea well. He could buy and sell cars equally as well.

The panelists savagely tore strips off the unsuccessful applicants and shouted "No money!" in their faces.

———

The walk this Saturday of 41.6 kilometers (25.9 miles) to Kumagaya in neighboring Saitama Prefecture would be my longest, and I'd add a couple of kilometers by visiting *Byakui-Kannon* — "White-Robed Goddess of Mercy." Since 1936, this goddess has stood atop the hill of Mt. Kannon, casting her gaze eastward to Tokyo.

I settled the hotel bill of ¥7,000 ($58) and no sooner was I into my stride than a string quartet's soothing sound, which lilted from a coffee shop, persuaded me that the walking could wait. At the table behind me, a man was interviewing a young woman. He spoke quietly but I understood from his tone that she had failed when he spotted a typographical error in her resume. The candidate left and was soon replaced by another.

I walked the few blocks to Takasaki City Office, which occupies a tastefully designed municipal building of 21 floors alongside the site of Takasaki Castle, which is now a park.

Unlike their forebears, city officials here work a five-day week. The office was closed — but I could still learn. I viewed the displays in the lobby and pocketed civic brochures and leaflets. Paper weighs a walker down, so every few days I posted the material I'd collected to a Tokyo address.

Products displayed include ham, cosmetics, soap, brews of sake, bean-paste sweets, canned green tea, wooden toys, silk, detergents, "pure, unscented bird oil," cakes, and rice crackers. A wall-mounted world map shows the time in major cities — maybe the mayor of Takasaki can tell the foreign minister in Tokyo where to buy something like this.

Also prominently displayed are gifts from four sisters — Battle Creek (Michigan, US), a linked formed in 1981; Santo Andre (Brazil, 1981); Chengde, (Heibei Province, China, 1987); and Plzen (Czech Republic, 1990). Battle Creek had gifted an Indian headdress; Plzen, a model of a crankshaft, which it described as a "powerful tool in the hands of thoughtful people," a machine tool for stamping metal, and beer bottles and mugs; Chengde, a painting of a panda bear, vases, calligraphic brushes, and metal-engraved jewelry boxes; Santo Andre, a cowboy hat, a stuffed armadillo, and a percussive instrument resembling maracas.

A Battle Creek plaque reads, "The citizens are hospitable and friendly by nature and the city's cultural and educational backdrop is instrumental in bringing out the best of its inhabitants." Battle Creek, it notes, is "home to an orchestra." This sister has paired well.

One out of ten Gunma residents travels abroad each year. Most go to the US, probably to Hawaii more than other states, then China. About 47,000 foreigners live in the prefecture (2005 year), the largest proportion of them Brazilians (37%), followed by Filipinos (14%), Chinese (13%), Peruvians (11%), and Koreans (6%). Gunma villages, towns, and cities have 37 sister affiliations abroad, the most in the US (14), Italy and China (5 each), Australia (4), and Czech Republic (3).

———

Gunma takes special pride in its orchestra, which rose from ruins in November 1945 as the Takasaki Citizens' Orchestra and was renamed Gunma Symphony Orchestra in 1947. The orchestra's 1994 performance in Prague is recorded as a milestone in prefectural history. It celebrated its 50th anniversary by performing Beethoven's symphonies — all of them — at home and in Tokyo.

I walked Symphony Road near the municipal building to see the Gunma Music Center and Symphony Hall, which fabulously provide the orchestra with rehearsal facilities and a main performance stage. Less fortunate orchestras must rent rehearsal space and in Tokyo's parks at night — winter cold or summer muggy — you can hear musicians practice, their sound too loud for neighbors. The orchestra also enjoys a local government subsidy of a reported 60 percent.

The Gunma orchestra is one of around 30 professional Japanese orchestras — probably the largest number for any country. Some think Japan's facility with Western music is related to mathematical ability. Apparently people who excel at math often do well in music.

There's another explanation. Music, in a sense, is a substitute for the English that isn't taught well. It's universal and global. The ability to perform and appreciate music serves to confirm world citizenry. Take the "Western" out of Western music and call it music because it belongs to us, too, Japanese seem to want to say.

Some people say that Japan's embrace of Western music should be restated as an embrace of German music. They point out that the NHK Symphony Orchestra, Japan's most prestigious, always appoints German honorary conductors. Less than 1 percent of orchestral music performed in Japan is by non-German composers, according to composer Shigeaki Saegusa. I wanted to test this claim, empirically.

I studied the music event brochures I'd picked up from the city office. The Gunma orchestra at its next subscription concert would perform Takemitsu's "Family Tree" and Mahler's "Symphony No. 1 in D." In the following three subscription concerts the programs were for Brahms' "Tragic Overture," Schumann's "Piano Concerto," Sibelius' "Symphony No.1," Cage's "Seventy-Four for Orchestra," Rossini's "Barber of Seville Overture," Stravinsky's "The Card Game," and Beethoven's "Symphony No. 5" and "Missa Solemnis." So, five out of the ten compositions were by German composers, and a Japanese, Finnish, Italian, American, and Russian composer were represented by one work each.

I extended this research method to the orchestra's forest program — once a year it performs in woods on the outskirts of Takasaki — and found advertised works by Beethoven, Brahms, Bizet, and Rodgers. Brahms was represented by two compositions; the others, one each. Let's not adjust for that and say the arithmetic is compelling: two out of four.

Choirs from Vienna and Hungary were scheduled to perform in Takasaki soon. A Japanese pianist was to hold a recital at the city gallery, and his program wasn't German-centric, containing one composition each from Schumann, Kabalevsky, and Debussy.

An exhibit of Belgian lithographer Felicien Rops was coming to the Takasaki Museum of Art. What would visitors interpret from the symbolism of his blindfolded woman walking a pig, naked except for her black gloves, blue silk sash, knee-high black stockings and high heels? There are crannies in Tokyo were no variety of eroticism is unknown and Rops may have found them. Clowns, toy clowns, jokers, angels, devils, fishermen and women were the subjects of some works selected for his Japan showing.

———

Prefectural police had embarked on a recruitment drive. Their brochure contained the English-language subheadings of "passion and mission," "message and advice," and "conscience."

These guardians of society in the 1930s were charged with protecting the Japanese language from the infiltration of foreign words. Now they were using English to attract young people to their ranks. Their brochure text in katakana also used the words "balance," "curriculum," "desk work," "event," "level up" (as a verb: to raise one's performance), "patrol," "private," "professional," "ranger," "rescue," "rule," "schedule," "stalker," and "start."

Stalkers were at large — I wondered if they were US-copycats or some indigenous malady. Indigenous, friends said.

Remains of feudal Japan appear in the most modern of associations, and I found a trace in a flier of the Takasaki Rotary Club, which was commemorating its 40th anniversary. *Sekai no naka no Nihon* — "Japan as a part of the world," the flier stated boldly in a red banner headline. This language is a conscious counter to the common expression *sekai to Nihon* — "Japan and the world."

The US, UK, Germany and others which are sure of their earthly place don't write "the US as a part of the word," "the UK as a part of the world," or "Germany as a part of the world." The descendants of Tokugawa isolationists who separated Japan from Europe for so long, however, still view themselves as apart from the world, not a part of it. The correction they now feel compelled to make, however, seems too self-conscious and a play to an audience.

"Mankind is our business," the Rotary Club's flier stated as a theme.

I made may way to the white-robed goddess. Souvenir, food and drink vendor stalls line the path up Mt. Kannon. Along the way, Shinto and Buddhist places of worship coexist peacefully — Japanese have never waged war in the name of religion though elements of the Pacific War may have been fought out of the religion of being Japanese.

Cloaked from the head, scroll in hand, the 42-meter-high (150 foot) goddess appears so man-made as to be ungodly, and there's military purpose in her bearing, for she memorializes fallen Takasaki soldiers of the Fifteenth Regiment who perished in China.

A cat skirted the statue base as priests chanted inside the adjacent Jiganin Temple. I didn't go inside the statue — it's a tourist marker that charges ¥300 ($2.50) for entry — but I read that it enshrines 20 Buddha images on nine floors. At the entrance a shop sells amulets for ¥200 each.

Outside, a trousered woman raised a leg and rested it horizontally against a wall as though stretching before a gym workout. She was talking loudly into a cell phone. I think she was talking to her daughter — it was a younger person who was asking for money. Someone had died and I think it was her sister.

"January? January!"

"But I won't have that much money in January! Not over the New Year! I'm by the statue of the Buddha. I arrived at 9.30 a.m. I'm leaving now.

"I left ¥1,000 yesterday, from the ¥10,000. I had to pay out all that money when your aunt died, to the priests and what have you.

"No. I don't have ¥100,000."

How unembarrassed some people are when discussing family matters — or anything else — in public. Or have cell phones made them that way since the death of phone-booth privacy? Perhaps this woman thought I couldn't understand a word she was saying but more likely she is the type who thinks nothing of sharing sundry and sordid detail of her life with a crowd.

A father was giving his daughter tips on how to sketch the statue. A touring motorcyclist, girlfriend at his side, started smoking. A man smoked as he pushed an invalid in a wheelchair uphill, giving the appearance of a sideshow skit.

I started down the hill. The whole place had appeared too modern but that's preferable to the structures being artificially aged. The woman who earlier was cutting away grass at the bottom of the hill was now cleaning gravesites. Five workers seemed over-employed making minor repairs to the road, but two of them were guiding pedestrians and controlling the light traffic — such is the fear of having to take responsibility in the event of an accident.

I crossed the Karasu River out of Takasaki, my direction toward Tokyo in line with the gaze of the goddess, and walked passed a yard for oil-tanker rolling stock and an oil-storage terminal. A diesel engine shunted in a freight yard. The warmly delicious aroma of freshly baked bread harnessed the air. Nothing here is congruent.

———

I'd closed out the night before by browsing the jazz selection at Tower Records and to enhance this Gunma experience I'd begun Saturday morning at Starbucks, drinking too-sweet coffee to the accompaniment of Simon and Garfunkel singing "Old Friends."

> Old friends, memory brushes the same years,
> Silently sharing the same fears

How universal a name this duo became on the strength of so few recordings. They issued only six LP records in their brief recording career, and five songs — "The Sounds of Silence," "The Boxer," "Homeward Bound," "Mrs. Robinson," and "Bridge Over Troubled Water"— sear their harmony, intelligence, melody, and universality into a Western as much as Japanese cultural fabric. Even people who don't care much for popular music probably can associate the duo's name with one or more of those songs.

It was possible that Art Garfunkel had heard his own voice here, inside this Starbucks in Takasaki. I read that he took up walking in the early 1980s. He "started walking vast distances, arriving in Japan on a freighter and deciding on the spur of the moment to walk across the country," he told London's *Sunday Telegraph* in an interview reprinted in a New Zealand newspaper in August 2000.

Garfunkel is quoted as having said: "It looked pretty narrow on the map. I carried my hat and in the hat I had a change of socks, a toothbrush, and a rubber ball." This sounded like the lyrics to a song not yet written. "Everyday I would buy some clothes and throw away the old ones."

I shouldn't doubt that Garfunkel walked across Japan but it's reasonable to ask how he managed to do so. Where did he eat and sleep? After reaching the coast, how did he make his way back? What type of map did he use, and how did he cope with perilously narrow road tunnels?

LANGUAGE AS DECORATION

Gunma police aren't alone in lacing their language with English. Japanese journalists in particular liberally import from English and other tongues. We next present examples of "borrowed" words from an edition of a daily newspaper, and discuss the danger of the decoration.

———

CHAPTER 26. STOLEN WORDS

When I couldn't get my prepaid cell phone to work in Tokyo, I telephoned a helpline. Menu prompts finally led to a voice, saying that in a moment I'd be connected to a *komyunikeetaa* — "communicator." Wasn't there a Japanese word for "communicator"? What happened to *tantō no mono* or *kakari no mono*? They used to communicate.

Languages are alive and trade with other tongues. It's more natural to import a word to describe a new foreign product or concept than conceive some awkward indigenous equivalent. So Japanese say *suupaa* for supermarket or *pasokon* for personal computer. *Yuumoa* for humor, friends tell me, must be allowed, as they can't find a Japanese equivalent.

But why say *baitaru riizun* for "vital reason" or *komyunikeeshon sukiru* for "communication skill"? Or *miitingu* for "meeting"?

How pervasive had usage of foreign loanwords become? To find out, I picked up a morning edition of the national daily *Yomiuri Shimbun*, and scanned it for loanwords, which I list at the end of this chapter.

I found 337 such words or expressions, or 284 when counting only the first instance of use, and reduced this number to 249 to allow for reasonable use of sports terms (*sukuramu* for scrum, for example) and names of office equipment (*sukyanaa* for scanner). But this is the usage in only a single edition of a daily newspaper. What would we find in the other 364 editions of the newspaper in a year? And in the weekly magazines? I counted words only in the editorial section of the newspaper. Had I counted the mostly outlandish or nonsensical examples in the advertisements, the list would have been much longer.

Steal-word is a more accurate term than loanword. People borrow things they intend to return. Borrow-words aren't returned and no one loaned them. They were taken without permission. "Near miss," too, means the opposite of what newsreaders intend it to mean. The planes that are said to have been involved in a near miss completely missed each other but nearly collided. Why don't people say "near collision"? We promote words that lessen our anxiety or camouflage the unthinkable.

When people don't say what they mean, ambiguity and euphemism infest speech, unattractive actions are window-dressed, and propaganda passes for information. George Orwell's essay "Politics and the English Language" in *Inside the Whale and Other Essays* could beneficially be made required reading in translation for students here and in the original in my country. And everywhere else. But I leave the campaign for the translation to others, mindful of the 23 years it took for Orwell's *1984* to appear in Japanese.

Stolen words are sometimes used to window-dress. Rather than say something unpalatable in Japanese, a foreign word is found to soften the blow of the meaning. The adult youth who, unmarried, lives with his parents, for example, is called a *parasaito shinguru* — "parasite single," because *kiseichū teki* — "parasitic," sounds harsh.

They are used more positively to dispense with centuries of role assignation. To describe his wife, for example, a Japanese can choose from, among other expressions, *uchi no mono* — "my thing at home," or *kanai* — my "inside the house." But by using steal-words, he can neutralize such terms by saying *mai waifu* or stake a middle ground and say, *uchi no waifu* — "my wife at home."

The new language of Japan is a hybrid. It may spawn a hybrid of communication. The un-English "vital reason," which may mean "most important reason" or something else, is an example. "But wasn't Japanese an earlier hybrid with Chinese?" asks an English friend, who says he's grateful to be able to use steal-words.

When English speakers are at loss for the right Japanese word, they can insert an English one into their Japanese sentence and pronounce it in Japanese. Depending on their company, they'll probably be understood. Some Japanese only half-jokingly discard their vocabulary and use English words in a Japanese grammar, as in *Mai raifu wa tafu da* — "My life's tough." A Shōgakkan electronic dictionary uses the word *koosu* — "course," to explain the word *reen* — "lane."

Puraibashii issues are topical as people rethink the practice of divulging addresses and birthdates to callers who sound official. But isn't there a Japanese word for "privacy"? Over sushi in Tsuruoka, I put this question to Prof. Shumpei Kumon of Tama University. After some thought, he offered *watakushigoto* — literally, "my affairs." He said Japan needed a new Yukichi Fukuzawa to consider carefully the meaning of foreign terms before rendering them into Japanese.

Does the prevalence of steal-words in Japanese matter? I think it does, because, unlike Chinese ideographs that were introduced for the precise meaning they contained, the larger appeal of steal-words seems to be onomatopoeic or ornamental. They hinder Japanese more than they help, especially students and the elderly.

The words are transcribed in katakana the way they would be pronounced in Japanese, so no lesson in English pronunciation is learned. Original meanings are often subverted. *Feminisuto* — "feminist," for example, means "gentleman."

Also, students who try to use these words in English conversation will likely pronounce them all in the singular, as the katakana renditions don't distinguish between singular and plural. And their usage confuses those students of Japanese whose native language isn't English, German, or French.

As we grow older, we can expect to understand more of our society. We have the benefit of hindsight, a little wisdom perhaps has accumulated, and we've had time to read and think. Here, the elderly will understand less as they age, because their young treat language as an imitative art.

Journalists of the mass-circulation dailies view themselves as an elite. Their journalistic license is a more powerful credential than in many other countries. They report on the establishment from clubs positioned within government ministries and agencies. They inhabit a private world and are privy to more information than they can ever report.

Their language has become the code of an inner circle whose members travel, browse foreign newspapers and magazines, watch satellite TV. They show off this familiarity with the foreign to less traveled colleagues and their readership. Like a sound-effects engineer, they strive to create atmosphere. Uncertainty of meaning doesn't deter them, as their purpose is to decorate more than communicate. Editors allow this, despite the availability of adequate Japanese equivalents for many of the stolen words.

John Black, an Englishman who founded the Japanese-language newspaper *Nisshin Shinjishi* in Ginza in 1872, became a thorn in the side of the government, which wanted to purge Japanese-language journalism of foreigners. The government itself offered him a job, which he accepted. This job was later taken away from him, and in the interim he had lost control of his newspaper. Editors today don't need to purge their ranks of any John Blacks. They need to purge their mindset of something else. And they should recognize the danger in their dalliance with foreign words as fashion, and understand that they are guardians of language.

Apart from showing contempt toward the elderly and those unschooled in foreign languages, these editors invite, sooner or later, a vehement reaction from segments in society who still cling to notions of racial purity. These are the political children of the right wing who reacted violently against what they viewed as foreign contaminants, including steal-words, in the 1930s.

I sympathize with those on the frustrated right. When they can't understand what they read in their own language, in their own land, their upset is understandable.

Here is the list of steal-words from an edition of the *Yomiuri Shimbun*, presented in alphabetical order from their katakana transcription.

adobaisu, advice; *adobaizaa*, adviser; *aidea*, idea; *akademikku*, academic; *akusesarii*, accessory; *ankeeto*, questionnaire; *ansanburu*, ensemble; *apaato*, flat; *apiiru*, appeal; *appu*, up; *arerugii*, allergy; *asufaruto*, asphalt.

baburu, bubble; *baitaru riizun*, vital reason; *bakkuguraundo*, background; *baio benchaa*, bio venture; *batafurai*, butterfly; *besutomenbaa*, best members;

betaahoomu kyōkai, better-home association; *borantia*, volunteer; *bukkufea*, book fair; *burendo*, blend; *buusu*, booth.

champion, champion; *chansu*, chance; *charitii*, charity; *chekku*, check; *chiifu*, chief; *chiimu*, team; *chiketto*, ticket; *chuutaa*, tutor; *consarutanto*, consultant.

daiaroogu, dialog; *dansu*, dance; *dassara*, to quit work as a salaryman; *deeta*, data; *depaato*, department store; *dezainaa*, designer; *disupurei*, display; *dorai*, dry in the sense of businesslike, unfeeling or without emotion.

ekonomisuto, economist; *eirian*, alien; *enerugii*, energy; *entorii*, enter (a competition or race); *eriito*, elite; *essei*, essay.

fea, fair; *fikkusu*, fix; *furumarason*, full marathon.

gaido, tour guide; *gaidobukku*, guidebook; *gattsupoozu*, gutsy pose; *gooru*, goal; *gubbai*, goodbye; *guddo purakutisu*, good practice; *gurafu*, graph; *guraundo*, ground; *guruupu*, group; *gyararii*, gallery.

hiiringu muubii, healing movie; *hiiringu myuujikku*, healing music; *hinto*, hint; *hitto*, big hit; *hittomedoree*, medley of hits; *horumon*, hormone.

ibento, event; *iningu*, inning; *imeeji*, image; *infure*, inflation; *intabyuu*, interview.

jaanarisutikku, journalistic; *jaanarisuto*, journalist; *janguru*, jungle; *janpu*, jump; *jendaa*, gender; *jenerarisuto*, generalist; *junia*, junior.

kabaa, cover; *karikyuramu*, curriculum; *karisuma*, charismatic; *keesu*, case; *kiiwaado*, key word; *kikku*, kick; *koa karikyuramu*, core curriculum; *komedian*, comedian; *komedii*, comedy; *komento*, comment; *komyunikeeshon*, communication; *komyunikeeshon sukiru*, communication skill; *konbi*, combination; *kongurachureeshon*, congratulations; *konpe*, competition; *kontesuto*, contest; *konto*, comedy skit; *kontorooru*, control; *koodineetaa*, coordinator; *koonaa*, corner; *koosu*, course; *kooto*, coat; *korusetto*, corset; *kosuto*, cost; *kurinikku*, clinic; *kyanpeen*, campaign; *kyanpu*, camp; *kyarakutaa*, character; *kyasuto*, cast.

maaketingu, marketing; *maaku*, mark; *manaa*, manner; *maneegeemu*, money game; *masutaa*, master; *medaru*, medal; *media*, media; *medoree riree*, medley relay; *meekaa*, maker; *meeringu risuto*, mailing list; *meritto*, merit; *messeeji*, message; *miitingu*, meeting; *misairu*, missile; *misu*, miss; *misuterii*, mystery; *monsutaa*, monster; *mooru*, maul or attack; *muudo*, mood.

nanbaa tsuu, number two; *nanbaa wan*, number one; *nareeshon*, narration; *noomisu*, no mistake; *nootorai*, no try; *noohau*, know-how.

obuje, ornaments; *onrii wan*, only one; *oodishon*, audition; *ookushon*, auction; *oonaa*, owner; *oopun*, open.

paafekuto, perfect; *paatonaa*, partner; *pabirion*, pavilion; *paipurain*, pipeline; *pan*, pan; *paneru disukasshon*, panel discussion; *paneru shiataa*, panel theater; *pasu*, pass; *pasuwaado*, password; *pea*, pair; *peesu*, pace; *piiku*, peak; *pointo*, point; *pojishon*, position; *poriipu*, polyp; *puraibashii*, privacy; *purasu*, plus factor; *puree*, play; *pureeto*, plate; *puro*, professional; *puroguramu*, program; *purojekuto*, project; *purosesu*, process.

raibaru, rival; *raifurain*, lifeline; *rankingu*, ranking; *rasuto*, last; *reberu*, level; *reesu*, race; *regyuraa*, regular; *rejume*, resume; *ressun*, training; *riberaru*, liberal; *rihabiri*, rehabilitation; *riido*, lead; *riigu*, league; *rimokon*, remote control; *rinku*, rink; *rirakkusu*, relax; *risutora*, job-cutting or restructuring; *riumachi*, rheumatism; *rizumu*, rhythm; *roon*, loan; *ruuru*, rule.

saakuru, circle; *saido*, side; *saito*, site; *samaa taimu*, summer time or daylight saving; *sapooto*, support; *sateraito seminaa*, satellite seminar; *sekuhara*, sexual harassment; *sentaa*, center; *seorii*, theory; *serufu imeeji*, stereotype; *shaapu*, clear or definite; *shiizun*, season; *shikku*, chic; *shinajii*, synergy; *shinario*, scenario; *shinemapaaku*, cinema park; *shinpojiumu*, symposium; *shisutemu*, system; *shokku*, shock; *shoowindoo*, show window; *shuuto*, shoot; *soro*, solo; *sutoreeto gachi*, win straight sets; *sukeeto sentaa*, skating center; *sukiru*, skill; *sumaato*, smart; *sumuuzu*, smoothly; *supairaru*, spiral; *supaisu*, spice; *supesharisuto*, specialist; *supin*, spin; *supookusuman*, spokesman; *supootsu jaanarisuto*, sports journalist; *supootsu kurabu*, sports club; *supootsu kyasutaa*, sports commentator; *supootsu senshu*, athlete; *surippa*, slippers; *sutaataa*, starter; *sutaato*, start; *sutamina*, stamina; *suteeji*, stage; *suteeki*, steak; *sutoraido*, stride; *sutoreeto make*, lose straight sets; *sutoresu*, stress.

taimingu, timing; *taipu*, type; *taitoru*, title; *tankaa*, tanker; *teema*, theme; *teema paaku*, theme park; *tekunikku*, technique; *tenisubooru*, tennis ball; *tero*, terror; *terorisuto*, terrorist; *tesuto*, test; *toppu*, business head; *toppu rannaa*, top runner; *toppu riigu*, top league; *toraberu karute*, medical record; *torai*, try; *toreenaa*, trainer; *toreeningu*, training; *tsuaa*, tour.

ueitoresu, waitress; *waakingu chiimu*, working team.

yuumoa, humor.

zero, zero.

Diesel and dust

The next prefecture through which we walk, Saitama, takes us to the edge of Tokyo, and reminds that, over centuries, some characteristics of a country don't change much. We stumble across pimps, prostitutes, and massage parlors and find accommodation in a love hotel.

CHAPTER 27. SLEEPLESS IN SAITAMA

A scattering of roadside love hotels — Hotel Bob, Elegance, Hotel Ring Bell, Carlton, Princess, QE II — ushered me into Saitama Prefecture after I crossed the Jieitai Mae Intersection in the town of Shinmachi just before the Kanna River.

Gaudy and garish, the hotels may appear "modern" but they have held their place in various forms along highways for at least 300 years. They are an offshoot of inns that supplied prostitutes to the retinue of regional daimyo and others who regularly traveled to Edo.

Engelbert Kaempfer, who twice made this trip from Nagasaki to Edo in the 1690s, wrote that it was "impossible to deny that every public inn on the island of Nippon is at the same time a public brothel."

When talking about the crowds on the road, Kaempfer said he couldn't "omit the prostitutes of large and small inns and roadside tea and food stalls in villages and towns...As soon as they are dressed and made up, from around noon, they sit on verandas constantly eyeing approaching travelers; with amorous cries from here and there, they try to outdo each other calling him to their inn, the prattle ringing in the traveler's ears." He reported that some Chinese had dubbed Japan the "brothel of China."

Kaempfer also wrote that "the prostitutes' quarter is frequented no less than the temples." Girls were "traded for a sum of money when still children for a certain number of years." The prostitutes could marry and "pass as honest women" as they had been educated, but the brothel keepers, no matter how wealthy they became, couldn't pass as or associate with honest people. They were so distained that they were required to lend their male staff to the class of outcasts who were charged with slaughtering animals and executing criminals.

A monotonous vista of car sales yards and small, look-alike businesses tied to the farming and construction industries numbed my senses along Road 17, which from Shinmachi follows a more or less straight path for 29.4 kilometers (18.3

miles) through the smaller cities of Honjō and Fukaya into the city of Kumagaya. But Japan's traditions are rooted in agriculture, and nothing represents more the country than the automotive and construction industries, so it was Japan that I faced.

Clean Car Fukaya brought to mind a friend who once sold cars. Most customers, he said, didn't understand cars and, he admitted, neither did he. But he knew that if he cleaned and polished a car — top to bottom, inside out — it would sell. He also noted competitors' prices and set his own at the lower end of their range, reasoning that he prospered more through a high sales volume than by pricing each car to the market maximum.

But I'd stopped noticing a hotel called Hotel that wasn't, or much else. The road runs roughly equidistant from the Tone River to the left and Jōetsu bullet train to the right, and it might be more rewarding to rush with the river out to sea.

It was cold, and the White-Robed Goddess turned out to be near-sighted. She watches over and welcomes only train travelers. This I learned later when I telephoned Takasaki City Office to ask why the goddess faces east and was told her gaze is fixed on Takasaki Railway Station.

An office building was sign-painted Urban Communication Space — the language of architects. Like lawyers, architects live in a language of their own. They turn functions as basic as eating or sleeping into a science for city dwellers. They talk about communicating in urban spaces, while others talk to people in the city.

––––––––

Urban Japanese look down on Saitama Prefecture residents as bumpkins. They call them *imo* — "potatoes." And they tag the Tōbu-Tōjō Line, one of the main rail routes into Tokyo, the *imo densha* — "potato train." Small-lot farmers — elderly women conspicuous among them, tall vegetable loads strapped to their back — used to take this train into Tokyo to sell their produce at station steps or curbside.

Some youth refer to the prefecture as *dassaitama*, collocating the word *dassai* — "uncool," with the prefectural name.

In turn, Saitama folk don't think much of their ruling neighbors. There's a history to this animosity. More than 6,000 farmers from the western region of Chichibu marched on Tokyo in 1884 to protest the government's deflationary economic policy. They harassed government offices and moneylenders. They fought police and troops. Tokyo responded by arresting some 3,000 of them, fined most, jailed some for five to eight years, and hanged five ringleaders.

About seven million people live in Saitama (2005 year), making it the fifth largest prefecture. Its economy, which recorded economic production of ¥21.8 trillion ($182 billion) in the March 2005 year, is comparable to that of Norway. It has its share of omnipresent clusters of machinery and electrical equipment factories but to Tokyo it's a farm, supplying spinach, broccoli, tea, wheat, rice and beef. It's also host to some 110,000 foreigners (as of December, 2006), led by Chinese (33% of the total), Koreans (17%), Filipinos (14%), and Brazilians (12%).

___

Concrete slabs buttressed the banks of the Kanna River, which feeds into the Karasu River, and the riverbed was spiked with tetrapods. Some observers deplore such ugly canalization of rivers and see large sums of money changing hands between construction companies and government regulators for concrete pouring permits.

The prefecture has set up a "river museum" in the town of Yorimachi on the banks of the Ara River, to the west of my route. Some people fear that the inside of a museum may be the only place where they'll be able to see traces of Japan's rivers in the future. It's troubling that the tragic irony of consigning rivers to institutions that preserve the past may not be understood.

The museum contains a one-thousandth scale model of a segment of the Ara River. You can push a button to control the water flow. I haven't visited this museum but I obtained a brochure about it from the Saitama prefectural office in Tokyo. The museum houses a "river hall," "adventure theater," "display rooms," "meeting and lecture rooms," "information office," and a restaurant and a shop which sells "original goods."

___

Between Shinmachi and Kumagaya, Road 17 overlays the feudal highway called Nakasendō, which was one of five main roads the Tokugawa shogunate used to control access to Edo. The Tōkaidō, linking Tokyo with Kyoto and Osaka via the eastern seaboard, was the most used of the roads. There's still a local railway called Tōkaidō, and the name recalls the time when daimyo processions, samurai and couriers walked or ran the route, staying at post-station towns along the way.

The Nakasendō, like the Tōkaidō, also connected Tokyo to Kyoto, which, rather than Osaka, served as its terminal, but via a mountainous inland route. I'd joined this 500-kilometer (310-mile) road at a northwestern point just as it arcs toward Tokyo. I couldn't see any plaque commemorating this history, only smashed vending machines, which crumbled outside an abandoned drug and liquor shop whose car park was strewn with rubbish and deadened by car corpses. Stacked car wrecks bordered a nearby golf driving range.

In feudal times, travel on roads to Edo was monitored as strictly as commercial flight paths to New York. Assassins and saboteurs were as likely to travel the roads as were poets and priests. Domestic travel was by permission, and travelers had to present their travel documents at checkpoints such as that at icily xenophobic Sarugakyō along the way.

They also had to stay at designated inns, which police visited periodically to examine the guest register. Police scrutiny of travelers extended into the Meiji era, as Isabella Bird noted police were in the habit of making monthly visits to some of the inns at which she stayed in western and northern Honshū in the late 1870s.

Reports from the checkpoints and the innkeepers kept the shogunate informed about who was traveling on which route and their whereabouts on that route at any time. Letters were carried by runners who worked in relay to provide a swift courier service. Couriers on the Tōkaidō, for instance, offered three speeds between Edo and Kyoto — extra fast, of three days; fast, of six days; and regular, of nine days, according to Dōshisha University research. The runners, too, would have reported suspicious activity along the route to authorities in Edo.

A Tanaka of the time couldn't make political capital out of bridge construction as shoguns disallowed bridges on the route to slow the movement of potentially hostile travelers. Instead, strong men were available for hire to carry individual travelers across rivers at shallow points they knew to be safe.

––––––

Dogs of the World advertised its stock at roadside, and various breeds were caged only a meter or so from a procession of thundering heavy trucks. Diesel fumes blew across their faces. Three, four, or five to a cage, the dogs' nerves appeared shattered. The noise, vibration, and pollution would have shattered mine.

The dog seller was conducting a *haru no wan wan seeru* — "spring bow-wow sale," to the drone of country music. Prices ranged from ¥50,000 to ¥130,000 ($420–$1,100) for a Black Labrador, Irish Setter, Brittany Spaniel, Welsh Corgi, miniature Dachshund, Saint Bernard, and Chihuahua. Zoom Pet Land Shampoo and Cut Hotel offer grooming and short-term accommodation on the same premises.

A couple stopped to view the cages. I cautioned them about the likely poor health of such dogs keep at roadside. I put them off the idea of buying from this shop. Minutes later, when it was too late, I realized that this couple might have offered one of the dogs a life out of the diesel fumes, with a family, and I regretted my interference. The point I wanted to make I should have made to the owners of the facility, not to prospective buyers.

Animal-protection societies advise not to buy dogs from such places, because puppies don't receive the individual attention they need when mass bred by puppy mills for the pet-shop market. Pet shops try to tempt impulse buyers by showing exotic and cute-looking breeds. Such buyers may not have thought through the suitability of the dog as a pet or themselves as an owner. Dogs bought at pet shops are more likely to exhibit behavioral problems than dogs bought from breeders. But I still felt guilty that I may have deprived a dog of the chance to escape the edge of a highway and enter a home.

My mind wandered to the thousands of stray dogs that inhabit the suburbs of Athens. City authorities would have killed as many of them as possible in their cleanup campaign for the 2004 summer Olympic Games.

I lunched at an "Italian" restaurant. Such eateries boasting various pasta dishes are sometimes the creation of entrepreneurial *ramen* or noodle joint owners. They can charge from ¥400 to ¥600 ($3.30–$4.60) for basic noodle dishes, but three times that amount for dishes tagged as Italian. It takes longer to boil pasta and finely chop mushrooms and herbs for the sauce, but adaptable ramen cooks seem to find the effort worthwhile. I think such a cook prepared my lunch. But this restaurant was clean, quiet, the food passable and the service good.

Toward Honjō, Onuma Book's towering billboard boast of a stock of 100,000 books confirmed the voracious reading habits of most Japanese and how sensibly they use their leisure time while the pachinko parlor Try confirmed how well they waste it. But no one had tried Try in a long time, the building abandoned and reduced to a shell. Try may have failed to stay abreast of pinball machine technology and not installed the latest, most alluring models, which is how the parlors compete.

Onuma also advertised a stock of 500,000 videos, but Japanese appear to read as much or more than other peoples. Business people, homemakers, the young, and the elderly all pack Tokyo booksellers during lunch and after hours. It's misleading, too, to think that people read mostly "comics" for "comic" isn't an adequate translation of *manga*. The almost unfathomable range of manga defies casual description — the pornography from soft to violent is there, but so in equal or larger volume are the finely crafted and illustrated novellas and histories.

―――――

Some places look better in the dark, but Kumagaya isn't one of them. I'd entered this former post-station town in northern Saitama via its underbelly. It didn't exhibit quite the moral mayhem of Barter Town in the film *Mad Max Beyond Thunderdome*, but it was on its way.

Touts, prostitutes and their pimps, clip joints and massage parlors occupy the main and the maze of side streets. Second- and third-floor curtains on the pencil buildings were drawn. "Hello Miistaa," a woman called out, in thick Filipina accent.

The history of prostitution shows the history of the transfer of wealth and power among nations. J. W. Robertson Scott reported that there were "thousands" of *jorō* or Japanese prostitutes at Singapore and other Asian locales in the years of World War I. He believed that many had been deceived into going to these places and saw some returning from Singapore and being "shepherded by an evil-looking fellow" on the ship that took him to Japan.

Police required brothels to keep exact records of their workers and customer numbers. In Aichi Prefecture in a particular year, for example, Scott was able to report that 725,598 customers, of whom 2,147 were foreigners, had visited 2,011 girls in 222 houses. He learned that parents sold their daughters for ¥200 to ¥500 for a three-year term, but the girls were "almost invariably drawn into debt to the keepers, and not more than 15 percent were able to return to their villages."

Police today aren't able or inclined to exercise such control. But in a purification rite of sorts, they seem to be making life harder for foreign prostitutes who overstay their tourist visas. Along with other foreign workers in menial jobs who overstay, they are fined, imprisoned, and ordered to pay for their imprisonment cost before deportation.

―――――

It was already around 7.30 p.m. and I'd walked 41.6 kilometers (25.9 miles) — that was a mistake; this wasn't supposed to be an endurance test — and no reputable inns or hotels were in sight. Perhaps I was on the wrong side of the tracks. Weaving my way among stumbling drunks, and taking care not to shoulder brush any of them lest I provoke a reaction, I found the station. A couple of revelers had passed out on the steps. Buskers punished acoustic guitars and saxophones.

Back-street neon on the other side of the station led only to love and business hotels. I chose Kogetsu, which had aspects of both. One entrance led to another — it was a love hotel — and a matronly woman responded to the buzzer. You could see her, in uniform starched stiff and white, running a hospital ward. She admitted me to an eight-mat room that reeked of disinfectant. Later she brought tea. After stepping out to buy yogurt and orange juice, I returned to watch a TV documentary suitably about the homeless.

The homeless can't return to society unless they can prove that they have a home, which they can't because they don't. They need an address, for employment applications, welfare registrations, opening a bank account. The program thus introduced the dilemma of the homeless and the anchor of an address.

Some homeless are so by choice and don't wish to attach to an address. For those who do, the program showed a lodging house in Osaka that supplies the destitute with a suit of clothes, and allows them to use its address as their own and stay for at most six months. Within that time, they must get a job and save enough money to rent their own apartment. Only a few manage to do so. Most can't put together the gift and deposit money, which amounts to several months' rent, that landlords demand in advance.

The documentary included footage of Rudolf Giuliani, a former major of New York who was credited with having reduced homelessness in his city in the 1990s, saying in a speech that New York needed to "replace the culture of welfare and dependency with the culture of work." Though elements in Japanese society encourage a culture of dependency — the child on the mother; the employee on the company — the state can't be accused of doing so. This shows in the naming of unemployment bureaus, which dispense benefits for a short time until a job is found, as *Haroo Waaku* — "Hello Work."

Still, the public health system is more generous than popular notion holds. Health insurance and disability benefits, for example, are available equally to non-Japanese. A friend who had undergone surgery said he benefited hugely from public health insurance, and another had arranged to have an insurance card issued to an older associate.

The problem of domicile is one foreigners share with the homeless. A friend's bank, even when he was in debt to it, wouldn't send an account statement to him at a foreign address. And his life insurance company, despite a long record of premium payments, wouldn't send notifications to him abroad. The thousands of Japanese who work overseas don't receive letters from their local government offices or banks or insurance companies. Instead, before they leave Japan they must ask a parent or relative for the use of their address. Japanese can't contest the assumption that because they are Japanese they live in Japan.

Some people become defensive when you point out that this reluctance to recognize a foreign address must be a psychological remnant of the Tokugawa era. They say it's probably the case that English-language addresses can't easily be entered into computerized Japanese-language mailing lists. But it's a Tokugawa mindset in the first place that would write software that can't accommodate foreign addresses.

Some states of tiredness will allow sleep through any disturbance or malodor. But at Hotel Kogetsu the stench of disinfectant was overpowering and I slept fitfully. I didn't need to check out as payment of ¥5,800 ($48) had been required the night before.

I learned later that if I'd kept walking just a short distance further along Road 17 and not detoured to the station, I would have happened upon MarRoad Inn, replete with bar, tea lounge, and Chinese and French restaurants, and with a single-room rate of only ¥100 more. Occasionally the traveler wishes he were a tourist.

A SYMPHONY ON A CD

We next visit an obsession with a symphony whose recorded length set a standard for CDs.

CHAPTER 28. 74 MINUTES

Anniversaries had occurred as I walked. "It was 20 years ago today…" begins the Beatles' song "Sgt Pepper's Lonely Hearts Club Band." It was the 20th anniversary of Sony Corp.'s introduction of the compact disc player in 1982.

For anniversary junkies, almost 40 years had passed since Philips of the Netherlands introduced the compact cassette in 1963 and since Japan overtook Germany as a camera maker. And 50 years had passed since Japan regained its independence after the end of the US-led Allied Occupation.

The CD was most on my mind. Its invention had changed lives. People lent, borrowed and copied recordings more than they ever could when bulky, fragile LP records were the main medium of recorded music. CDs spread music wider and faster. It seemed that CDs a short while ago were novel and new. More than 20 years had passed.

But why was the playing time of the first CDs 74 minutes? Why add four minutes to 70? Wouldn't a manufacturer duplicate the playing times of tape cassettes, which were available in lengths of 30, 60, 90, and 120 minutes? To Sony, the number 74 meant something special. It had nothing to do with technology.

The question hadn't occurred until I read Bob Johnstone's *We Were Burning*. The title isn't about the victims of atomic or firebombing but relates how electronics engineers described their feelings when they knew they were on the verge of a technological or product development breakthrough.

Philips had argued for a 60-minute CD length. Sony and Philips had wanted to agree on standards in order to ensure that the new technology spread and became standard. Sony had learned its lesson from not sharing its Betamax video format which, though believed by many to be superior technically to the competing VHS format, died an early death while the shared VHS went on to rule the world. But Sony argued vigorously against a 60-minute CD length, as a result of the classical music knowledge of one executive.

Sony's deputy president, Norio Ōga, had trained in Germany as an opera singer, and kept company with music luminaries such as conductor Herbert von Karajan. Ōga argued that listeners should be able to enjoy Beethoven's "Ninth Symphony" without having to change discs. His wishes were met, and the CD playing time was accordingly set at 74 minutes 42 seconds. Perhaps that was the length of the particular recording Ōga owned, or the longest version he could reference. Mine is 72 minutes 34 seconds.

For some reason, Beethoven's Ninth — *dai-ku* (number nine) means only this symphony in Japan — has wedged itself deep in the country's psyche. Perhaps Japanese yearn for a freedom they don't have in their daily lives. Perhaps they can feel, when they listen to this symphony, the meaning of the lyric "rescue from the chains of tyrants" in the poem "An die Freude" (Ode to Joy) by Friedrich Schiller, which inspired Beethoven. Or perhaps they want to feel loved and included in a world that might include Japan — "Be embraced you millions! This kiss is for the entire world!"

The symphony is performed throughout the nation in December and the "Ode to Joy" choral finale is sung on New Year's Eve in a tradition as set in stone as the ringing of a Buddhist bell. It was the music of choice, displacing all traditional music, to mark the opening of Ryōgoku Kokugikan, Tokyo's arena for sumo wrestling, the most traditional of sports, in 1985.

German prisoners of war may have staged the first performance of the symphony in Japan during World War I. Around 1,000 German POWs were interned at Bandō Prison near what is now the city of Naruto, in Tokushima Prefecture on Shikoku. They had been captured in the Chinese port city of Qindao when Japan fought as a British ally. Naruto City records that an orchestra formed by some of the POWs performed the work on 1 June 1918. A museum called German House in Naruto contains a model of the orchestra.

Japan isn't alone in its enchantment with this music. "Everywhere, we hear the echoes of its mysterious opening...its publicly waged struggle for coherence and resolution," Michael Steinberg noted in *The Symphony — A Listener's Guide*. As he put it, a performance of this work can never be an ordinary event.

Leonard Bernstein conducted performances of the symphony in both sections of Berlin in December 1989 to celebrate the fall of the Berlin Wall the month before. Earlier that year, Chinese students played it in Tiananmen Square in Beijing as an anthem for their hopes for democracy. Anthony Burgess used it to background the rape of two girls in his novel *A Clockwork Orange*.

And so CDs were first designed to hold 74 minutes and 40 seconds of music.

A SHOGUN'S TOWN

We next visit Kawagoe, a former castle town established by the first Tokugawa shogun as a military base for the defense of Edo. We pass an army base, consider the reasons for the immobility of soldiers, and note the arrival of Brazilians of Japanese descent.

Chapter 29. Kawagoe Comfort

This Thursday I would farewell Road 17 and the course of the Nakasendō and take Roads 407 and 254 to the city of Kawagoe, a distance of 29 kilometers (18 miles). I found Road 407 a few blocks north of Kogetsu, crossed Arakawa-ōhashi Bridge — it's best not to look underneath — and was in the rhythm of my stride.

Warner Mycal Cinema's billboard loomed large. So did one for a B.B. King — King of the Slot pinball and slot-machine gambling den. What would the blues guitarist think if he saw his name branding this establishment? I would write and alert him to the insult and illegality. My letter would spur his management into taking stern action. Headlines such as "Famous US Guitarist Sues Saitama Pinball Parlor" would follow.

I would confront the manager, ask if he knew who B.B. King is, then, in an accusatory tone, ask if he had no *haji* — "shame." Disciplined from infancy by threats of shaming, people here can be held in check by the mere utterance of the word.

The entrance resembled the ticket-office of a railway station, with semicircular cutout at the base of the receptionist's window. Through a small side-door gambling prizes such as toiletries or groceries would be exchanged for the balls, and that contraband, at a hole in the wall one or two blocks away, exchanged for cash. Gambling is illegal but entrenched in circuitous forms such as this.

I pushed the buzzer, pushed it again, and kept pushing. A late middle-aged woman, auburn hair thinning from over-dyeing, appeared at the window. In no mood to converse, she stated the opening time and, as I began a question, repeated that time, then disappeared behind a door. Again a rehearsal of indignity had come to naught, but this wasn't my battle, and I wouldn't write that letter. I've heard B.B. King play, and I've seen the B.B. King — King of the Slot den, and for what it teaches of shamelessness, the sign can stay.

The crime and irony of the den would be lost on the suitably balding woman, for Japan has inspired blues and jazz musicians to produce some of their finest work, but not all of the recordings have been widely distributed. Some recordings were pressed only in Japan for the domestic market. B.B. King's *Live in Japan* CD was issued in 1999, 28 years after the concert, as his US record company had not wanted it to compete with a recording of a concert he had performed the same year in London. The Japan concert is now recognized as one of King's finest.

Otis Rush, a Mississippi-born blues guitarist who made his name in Chicago, played his soul out at Hibiya Park, Tokyo in 1975. Flowers and an appreciative audience served as an unlocking key. He said he'd never seen so many flowers in his life — at Haneda airport, over his baggage, in his car, with people who stood around him. Steve Tomashefsky, who produced the Tokyo recording for release in the US, wrote in liner notes that the "audience was so far removed from the sociological realities of the blues that it was able to experience the blues profoundly as art, timeless and soul stirring."

Higashiyama Pet Memorial Park, spread out over 1.3 hectares (3.2 acres), said in a sign that pets are "your friends, even after they go to heaven." Friends of mine, I recalled, had held a Buddhist funeral for their departed dog. A priest had visited them and offered prayers and still visits on the anniversary of the death.

A burial mound with a circumference of about 20 meters was visible in fields near the town of Ōsato. No plaque advised whom it contained. I'd associated such mounds with emperors or national figures of great importance but throughout Japan leaders down to the level of local village chief had mounds built for themselves, mostly in the sixth and seventh centuries, and hundreds of them dot the landscape. They're commonly found along the Japan Sea coast from Shimane to Kyoto prefectures, and suggest a transfer of Korean burial style to Japan.

An old American gas-guzzler — a Buick 8, the Dynaflow model, status symbol of the days when some Japanese thought that things American were best because they were big — sat stately in a roadside garage. At Kawajima Hibarigaoka I passed a school named in English "A school for children with special needs." It wasn't clear what those needs were but I felt happy to see non-discriminatory terms in use, even if they weren't in Japanese.

———

I left Road 254 at the Miyamotomachi Intersection and took Road 39 toward Hon-Kawagoe Station. A beauty salon named Marry (a pitch to single women) and Candy Home ushered me into the city of Kawagoe, a former castle town and military base for the defense of Edo. The first Tokugawa shogun, Ieyasu, established Kawagoe as a *han* or feudal prefecture in 1590, and its development roughly parallels that of Edo.

An elderly woman sat scraping bamboo shoots inside Candy Home, where I bought some sweets. Refreshments — beer and Japanese-style coffee (strong, in small cups; regular coffee is called *amerikan*) — were served inside, the spring air overcooked by a gas heater.

Toys and trinkets of a 1950s' childhood cluttered the interior — candy jars with screw-on lids, plastic baby dolls, painted tin and wooden toys, small bamboo flutes, a drum, porcelain cat, and motorboat model. The valve radio and handle telephone removed me to a childhood in rural New Zealand. We'd listen to make sure that a neighbor wasn't using the line, then crank the handle to raise an operator, and ask for a number to be called.

Candy sticks made to resemble burning cigarettes stood out amid plastic whistles and miniature bamboo umbrellas. The candy-cigarette package advertised "fine chocolate." Marketers seize upon the image of product forbidden to children in order to sell them something else. They, and collusive cigarette makers, know that from age ten to 20 it is a short jump from chocolate to cigarettes. Nippon Kashi, the candy maker, should know that, too.

A customer who said he was a high school employee lectured me that all Japanese are kind. Most Japanese are kind, I rebuffed. The worker twice stressed that he wasn't a teacher. He seemed too aware of his status as an employee in school administration. His school sent students on exchanges to Canada and New Zealand.

Something is different in Kawagoe. It's the uncluttered view of the sky from the inner streets. The city has buried its power and telephone cables, but only in the historic center of preserved Edo-era architecture. The clarity and brightness bring an unsettling dimension to the surroundings.

I walked past clusters of candy sellers, a wooden bell tower, and Hōzenji Temple, as afternoon turned to dusk. Black-tiled roofs and dark-stained wooden buildings transport you to the last century of the feudal era. The buildings, once military-supply storehouses of the Tokugawa shogunate, now retail souvenirs but their Edo-style architecture is no less real.

Four elderly smoking Japanese occupied a small playground which bordered a shrine; there were no children. I'd seen them more often playing around shrines than temples, and a stronger community spirit seems to attach to the shrines.

Festivals begin and end at the shrines, as gods are transported from and returned to them. Japanese generate a palpable sense of togetherness when they participate in a festival. Shinto priests officiate for the newly born and newly wed. Temples, on the other hand, administer education and funerals.

Apart from some small establishments masquerading as museums — their entrance fee covers green tea but exhibits are sparse — this destination is worth while. The only unpleasant aspect was the speed at which local tourists walked, as though under pressure to meet some deadline. I wanted everyone to move slowly.

Kawagoe teems with tourist markers, but that isn't off-putting. It's like New Orleans, with much to explore within the French Quarter and outside it, and the quarter isn't a reason not to visit the crescent city.

I'd like to spend time at Tōshogu Shrine where Tokugawa Ieyasu's remains were rested on the way to their final resting place at Nikkō. I also want to see the 500 or so stone statuettes of disciples of Buddha within the precinct of Kitain Temple, for the poses they assume and the moods they show. Soon, I will.

After the experience of Kogetsu, comfort could claim me and I chose Kawagoe Prince Hotel, on the southwest edge of the tourist quarter. It's a short walk from Hon-Kawagoe Station on the Seibu Shinjuku Line, not to be confused with the nearby, similar sounding Kawagoe or Kawagoeshi stations on the Tōbu-Tōjō Line.

Kawagoe Prince is a Western-style hotel in the American sense that you pass through large glass doors into a supermarket-style reception area, not the discreet, family-home atmosphere of a European hotel. Prince hotels are a chain and the business logic of the chain is that customers can expect the same standards of product or service at any link. Risk of choice isn't theirs to take.

There's a glassy coldness inside, the grand piano too large and white at center stage, the pianist remote and controlled. Everything is neat, ordered and operating. Here there can be no rejection of a traveler such as myself. It doesn't matter that I don't have a reservation. It only matters that a room is available and one is. Nobody can turn me down here. But it isn't me that reception is accepting. It's my credit card.

At last in a clean room with an easy chair I can sit and relax. The custom of doing nothing in particular isn't supported in a Japanese-style room. I left this luxury only to retrace my steps through the tourist quarter and find the city office, where I collected some brochures. And unwilling to indulge in can-you-use-chopstick conversation or dine at elbow's distance to others — not tonight — I bought bread, yogurt, and orange juice at a department store.

The throng of people had caused a mental exhaustion that had tired me more than the walking, and I slept, secure in a privacy that much advantages Western-style hotels over local counterparts. When I checked out I didn't scold myself for paying ¥13,410 ($112) — more than double the accommodation charge I'd paid elsewhere. It's important to treat ourselves sometimes.

The dream of Kawagoe ended at the Shinjukuchō-kita Intersection — an ugly crossing of Roads 18 and 254, among others I couldn't name, and the Kawagoe and Tōbu-Tōjō lines. There I entered the Kawagoe Kaidō and headed south toward Tokyo. Pachinko and Thai massage parlors, one called Haroo — "Hello," showed the way, in tandem with Tijuana Inn.

Segments of the Kawagoe Kaidō are richly tree-lined and bordered by large traditional wooden homes, at least up to Road 334. This aura of permanence soon gives way to a gray-brown patchwork of apartments and small factories that haven't been built to last.

Central Club, an all-night Internet café, provided a stock of comics, snooker and karaoke rooms, and computer game machines, in addition to a bank of computer terminals. The charge of ¥100 (91c) for 15 minutes included free soft drinks and coffee. The words "all night" and "karaoke" and "room" suggested low-budget nests for lovers, like the cabins near Shirone in Niigata Prefecture.

Gulliver isn't recognized for his cultural insight and acceptance of people but as the brand of a used-car sales chain, opposite a link in which before me were the hotels America, Canada, and Muse Rex. Who names a love hotel "Muse Rex," I wondered, then the restaurant *Bikkuri Donkii* — "Surprise Donkey" (The diner was surprised to see donkey on the menu? The donkey was surprised to be on the menu?) — caught my eye and I decided it wasn't worthwhile to dwell on these names. Service businesses here were choosing words for their visual image and perhaps for the sound they make in Japanese transliteration.

A "Korea Esute" parlor looked like what it was. "Esute" as a contraction of "aesthetic" was new to me, but this wasn't a beauty salon. Korea Esute's charges began at ¥12,000 ($100). A one-hour "VIP Course" was advertised at ¥17,000 ($142).

Rich market-garden land contrasted with multi-storied apartment blocks as I entered the city of Niiza. Near the turnoff to the Niiza municipal cemetery and city office, two army trucks and two jeeps sauntered passed.

Japan's constitution, which the US wrote, bans the maintenance of armed forces. The ink barely dry on this inadequate document, the US directed Japan to rearm in a world changed by the Korean War and the Cold War. US defense contractors cruised in the political slipstream, and Japan provided them with a large market, particularly for missile systems. Japan's armed forces are now among the world's largest. Language was bent to circumvent the ban: army, navy, and air force were called Ground, Maritime, and Air Self-Defense forces. But aren't those the best names for all nations' armed forces?

———

The perimeter of an army base joined the road at Asaka Jietai Intersection. Scores of trucks, bulldozers, long trailers with drop-down ramps for heavy-vehicle transport, and a range of construction machinery, were parked in football field-length rows. This civil-engineering branch of the army in wartime would build bridges, roads, and runways. In peacetime — all the time, for Japan since 1945 — the equipment would be used in disaster relief and post-earthquake reconstruction. Or should be.

I was working in Tokyo on the January 1995 morning of the Kobe or Great Kansai Earthquake, in which around 5,300 people perished. The numbers of dead and missing were updated by news media at regular intervals, but it soon became clear that each decrease in the number of those missing was all but matched by an increase in the number of those who had died.

Later, a diplomat told me that he understood that the Japanese government had held two cabinet meetings on the same day. The earthquake wasn't on the agenda of the first, scheduled cabinet meeting and a second meeting had had to be called in the afternoon to discuss earthquake measures. Yet that morning from around 7 a.m., business leaders in the Osaka region had begun their own rescue efforts.

Presidents of a large department store and a heavy machinery maker were chartering helicopters and organizing fleets of motorcycles to bring immediate aid to the injured. It was as though they knew that their government would be slow to act and that they couldn't rely on Tokyo for help. As hours of official inaction passed, their skepticism seemed warranted.

———

One thoughtful TV documentary at the time showed a diagram of the workings of some central government ministries and agencies. Myriad lines connected as many boxes. These showed the channels through which regional governments had to request emergency assistance. It was more a maze than a diagram. The documentary presenter said he couldn't follow it. I couldn't follow it, either, and wondered who could. Which was the point of the documentary. As E. H. Norman wrote, "It would be a bold Theseus who could thoroughly explore this maze with its weird crepuscule and hollow echoes." Norman was noting, though, the lack of transparency in government in the Tokugawa era.

Lessons from the Pacific War had made it hard for the national government to throw military weight around. Postwar laws don't permit Tokyo to send soldiers into the regions before receiving detailed and specific requests to do. So, as Kobe residents — mostly the elderly whose flimsy wooden houses had collapsed under the weight of tiles designed to withstand typhoons but not earthquakes — lay buried alive and dying in rubble, the Ground Self-Defense Force, a force not permitted to fight overseas, was also unable to fight at home.

————

Around 5,000 Brazilians of Japanese descent have settled in the town of Oizumi, about 12 kilometers north of Kumagaya near the prefectural border with Gunma. They make up about 11 percent of the town's population. Many work at a Sanyo Electric factory. Around five to ten Brazilian teenagers are arrested each year for some offense or other. I read that Oizumi folk describe such numbers as a "crime wave" but in my country police would use the word "whimper" and not bother to make arrests, so stretched are they dealing with adult criminals.

History visits ironies upon Japan in its interaction with other countries. An immediate economic consequence of opening ports to US and European traders in the 1850s was that demand for Japanese goods surged beyond the capacity to produce them. Prices rose sharply and Japanese, in the way that locals are out-priced when their town becomes a tourist destination, were pressed to make ends meet. To counter that inflation, the government deflated the currency, which reduced farm incomes.

Hence Saitama farmers' angry march on Tokyo in 1884, and later, to relieve social pressure, the arranged exodus of farmers to Brazil. Rural Japanese were dispatched to Brazil in three waves — about 40,000 from 1908 to 1924; 150,000 from 1925 to 1941; and 54,000 from 1953 to 1989. Now their descendants return.

A CRUEL PEOPLE

In the way that a dog understands that big things are dangerous and make low noises, it seems a fact of nature as English people understand it that Japanese are a cruel people. Our travel next perambulates this perception.

CHAPTER 30. AS WE SEE THEM

The movie *Bridget Jones' Diary*, based on the book of the same name by Helen Fielding, repeats the stereotype of Japanese as a "cruel" people. Dinner party guests knowingly whisper the word as though it were part of an in-joke.

In the book, Bridget's mother, in her pitch of divorced lawyer Mark Darcy as a partner to Bridget, explains that Mark has had a "terrible time" with his Japanese wife, who has left him. She concludes: "Very cruel race."

The remark doesn't seem out of character for a late middle-aged English-woman, and the labeling isn't used as a device elsewhere in the diary. But the script demands that young people repeat the remark, out of character and context. The underlay is spread that Japanese are un-Christian as the "cruel" wife of the "cruel" race left Darcy on Christmas Day.

Friends said, who cares what movie scriptwriters think or write? I said, I do. I didn't enjoy the movie as much as I would have without the anti-Japanese undercurrent.

The *Bridget* scriptwriters may not have understood the depth of the racial vein that they were mining. They may have thought that its genesis lay in the World War II generation, but the Western notion that Japanese are a cruel — and violent — people is centuries old. It took hold strongly in the US during the mid-1800s when Japan badly treated shipwrecked American whalers.

When Atlantic whale stocks became depleted in the 1800s, whalers pushed out into the Pacific — to Japan, Australia, and New Zealand. Herman Melville noted that the American whaling industry then was larger than the rest of the world's combined, employing 18,000 men aboard 700 ships. Revenue from a whaler would exceed its expenses by nearly 100 percent, making the business as profitable as perfume. Japan became one of five established Pacific whaling grounds, and whales were so plentiful in Japanese waters that whalers didn't even need to chase them. In Melville's *Moby Dick*, Ahab is "dismasted off Japan."

Whalers from the shipwrecked *Lawrence* in 1847 found themselves ashore on Hokkaidō at a time when Japan forbade its people to leave the country or foreigners to enter, Peter Booth Wiley documents in *Yankees in the Land of the Gods — Commodore Perry and the Opening of Japan*. They were captured and caged in a Nagasaki jail, as were sailors who a year later deserted the American whaler *Lagoda* and landed on Hokkaidō.

Thus caged, the sailors were exposed to the elements, at times confined in stocks, bound, beaten, and denied adequate food and clothing. The corpse of one of the *Lagoda* sailors who had hanged himself wasn't removed from the cage for two days. Another had died from poisoning after receiving medical treatment.

Survivors were repatriated aboard the Dutch trading ship which visited once a year. Between those Dutch visits, two American warships had visited but Japan had not volunteered to them the information that it was holding the Americans. The whalers finally were rescued at Nagasaki by the American naval corvette *Preble* in 1849.

Ships then published accounts of their years-long voyages which brimmed with detail of adventure at sea and in foreign climes, and the report of the Japan visit of the *Preble* would have been widely excerpted. The *New York Herald* later would describe Japan's treatment of the sailors as "inhumane barbarity" and their imprisonment as "ignominious and cruel." A US government report stated that the "narrative of the imprisonment of these unhappy mariners shows the cruelty of the Japanese government."

Mutineers were among the stranded whalers and had fought among themselves and more than once attempted to escape from confinement on Hokkaidō. They couldn't have been easy men to deal with and, as illegal entrants, they had broken known laws forbidding landing in Japan. But Americans wouldn't tolerate such treatment, which was, in the words of James Glynn, commander of the *Preble*, "a good cause for a quarrel."

Japanese are perceived as violent, too, in formal and popular writing. Roy Andrew Miller, in *The Japanese Language*, wrote: "The violence of Japanese nature is reflected in elements of violence which are never far below the surface in Japanese society, though centuries of Buddhist culture have helped conceal these deep-seated veins of fire with a brittle lava of elaborately structured manners and formalized behavior."

Jim Melly, in *Last Orders, Please — Rod Stewart, The Faces, and the Britain We Forgot*, described an altercation in a Tokyo hotel between a Faces musician and another guest. The guest had complained about the noise the musician made playing soccer in a corridor. Unhappy with the response to his complaint, he decided to settle matters with a wooden shoetree. Tetsu Yamauchi, then the band's bassist, intervened. Melly quotes a band member as saying that Tetsu "went all Japanese and beat the living crap out of him." To "go all Japanese," then, means to fight as though it's a national trait.

But the source of the belief that Japanese are a cruel people rests in religion, and predates the experience of the whalers by some 300 years. Learning from the example of Christ's fate, Japan crucified Christians.

Portuguese missionaries in the 1500s came to be viewed as a political threat for their allegiance to Rome and as plunderers of natural resources. They defied orders to leave upon pain of death, which they met. Twenty-six Christians — foreigners and Japanese — were crucified at Nagasaki in 1597. Fifty-one more were executed by various method in Nagasaki in 1622, and two years later 50 were biblically burned in Edo.

The Christians' faults, Engelbert Kaempfer explained, were the "arrogance they showed toward the mighty and the greed they showed toward the common-ers." They had considered themselves higher in status than daimyo, which was asking for trouble.

Torture wasn't declared illegal until as late as 1876. Police had inflicted pain as a prod for information and as punishment. The legacy of torture is seen today in the high conviction rate that police achieve mostly through obtaining confessions. In usual years 99.9 percent of the accused are convicted and 92 percent of suspects confess. Fear prevents crime — people know that they must never become a suspect — for newspapers and neighbors often judge suspects guilty until proven innocent. The damage has been done by the late time a verdict is reached.

A preference for blade over bullet, too, has surely bolstered Western notions of Japanese cruelty. If soldiers had shot everyone that they cut, English eyes may have viewed them as a more civilized people.

And the soldier of rural background with bayoneted rifle in hand may have suffered from delusions of samurai grandeur and wielded that bayonet against enemy soldier and civilian alike in the way that samurai were licensed to do. Samurai were permitted to cut down anyone who they believed had insulted them. No judicial process later asked whether the insults were imagined or real.

Xenophobic samurai also cut down Europeans as a slap in the face of the shogunate for concluding trade treaties with foreign powers in 1858. Ernest Satow wrote, "The Japanese sword is as sharp as a razor, and inflicts fearful gashes. The Japanese had a way of cutting a man to pieces rather than leave any life in him. This had a most powerful effect on the mind of Europeans, who came to look on every two-sworded man as a probable assassin, and if they met one on the street thanked God as soon as they had passed him and found themselves in safety."

But centuries before the arrival of Christians, Japanese recorded heinous acts of torture perpetrated among themselves. In the *Nihongi* arms are boiled in mud, babies are abandoned on beaches, faces are branded, feet are flayed, nails are plucked, nuns are flogged, a pregnant woman's belly is ripped open (by an emperor, no less), and capital punishment by burning or scalding is common.

Still, I don't believe that any one people are inherently crueler or more violent than another. Humans appear to be the only species in the animal kingdom who kill for reasons other than food, and it's hard to see that any one tribe more skillfully inflicts pain than another. The proud, boastful exhibit of sundry instruments of unspeakable torture throughout European museums supports this view.

———

Something else may be at work in perceptions of cruelty and violence. It may be as simple as a like or dislike. Europeans — English or latterly Americans — in the main don't appear to like Japanese people, and those who do are often viewed as oddball or even traitorous.

Miller also wrote that Japanese are "unwelcome immigrants almost everywhere in the world, except for certain desolate reaches of South America...With no place else to go, the people of modern Japan must continue to fight their daily battle for survival with an ingenious combination of intensive agriculture, large-scale imports of foodstuffs, and a life-and-death struggle for export markets for the products of their own heavy and light industry."

Unwelcome almost everywhere in the world. Not in South Wales, a friend countered, where there are around 60 Japanese companies and 1,300 nationals. Some trace this warmth to the Welsh coal that Japanese warships burned while humiliating the Russian navy in the Japan Sea in 1905. And is Sao Paulo, where many Japanese settled in Brazil, a "desolate reach"? It isn't, but the tracts of land which early Japanese immigrants had to break to farm weren't suburban. The open arms for investment that produces jobs aside, Miller may be right.

Miller, a brilliant though disaffected linguist who late in his career grew contemptuous of Japanese for perpetuating the mythology of their uniqueness, identifies, I think, a large element of the issue of dislike or prejudice. Emigration requires willing leavers and immigration willing receivers. Japan has seen neither. Japanese governments at different times have forbidden or discouraged emigration. Expressed as a percentage of population increase between 1850 and 1950, the emigration rates of England and Italy at 74 percent and 47 percent compare with 1 percent for Japan. Japanese emigration in the examples of Hawaii and Brazil occurred only because of governmental agreement and arrangement.

Yet the 1700–1900s were centuries of emigration from the old world of Europe to the new world of the Americas and the South Pacific. Europeans, though, hadn't expected the mobility afforded by sail and steam to spur any relocation of Chinese or Japanese to these new countries. But individuals from China and Japan of course wanted the same new life of new opportunity. As racial equals, it would have been hard to find a basis to deny them the right to immigrate. So don't declare them so. The US and Australia, among other countries, didn't.

Fearing that one result would be pressure to accept immigrants, neither Washington nor London supported Tokyo when in 1920 it argued for the inclusion of a "racial equality" clause in the League of Nations Charter. Australia in particular objected to such a clause, Morinosuke Kajima wrote in *The Diplomacy of Japan 1894-1922*. Australia's prime minister, Charles Hughes, had said that 95 percent of Australians would oppose the "underlying idea" of racial equality, according to Kajima. Australia's ban on non-white immigration in 1886 at heart targeted Japan and was prompted by uneasiness over Japan's defeat of China the year before, Henry Frei asserted in *Japan's Southward Advance and Australia*.

Earlier, San Francisco had expelled Japanese-American children from its public schools and ordered them, along with Koreans, to attend a segregated Chinese school. The US banned Chinese immigration in 1882, the entry of Japanese laborers via Hawaii, Canada, and Mexico in 1907, and the immigration of all Asians except Filipinos, who, colonized, were US nationals, in 1924. The United States further interned Americans of Japanese descent during World War II, though admitted — decades later — that this had been a mistake and apologized to surviving internees.

The Hawaiian case says much. Between 1885 and 1893, some 30,000 Japanese had immigrated to Hawaii as sugarcane laborers by agreement between the Japanese and Hawaiian governments. Arrivals grew to around 180,000 by the mid-1920s. But Hawaii became a US state at the turn of the century, and its Japanese immigrant population seemingly free as Americans to settle in any US state. Naturally, they would want to go to California, and some 30,000–40,000 did. White reaction was hostile. Laws stopping them were quickly enacted.

Today people talk about Asian Americans or Japanese Americans but these are new terms. As recently as the 1960s such people were more likely to have been called Orientals in a blanket reference with no thought or allowance of indigenous culture.

The denial of equal treatment among nations must be the stuff of war.

DOTTED LINES

Tokyo and Yokohama have grown into each other and only the dotted lines of maps separate them now. So we, too, visit one after the other, and put nothing in between.

CHAPTER 31. THE CITY THAT WORKS

Into the stride of my walk, I left the Asaka army base behind and entered the city of Wakō on the southern border of the prefecture.

The national flag bellowed in the breeze above a research facility of the Honda Motor Co. on Road 254. I've thought of raising the flags of Japan and New Zealand in my small yard but I don't have the courage to do this. Hotels can fly the flags of their guests' countries but individual expression of national pluralism is seen as a conflict and contradiction.

Though 60 years have passed since the Pacific War, it may be too soon for a resident to raise a Japanese flag in my neighborhood. I'd need to survey my neighbors first, but even if they saw no harm in the gesture, passing traffic might, and I could become the target of vandals or worse.

But we should lower not raise flags. We should declare the age of nation states dead. It's dying and we should hasten its end. We must bring the borderless Internet to earth, and live here as we do there. Olympic athletes not countries win medals and we must celebrate the individual.

There isn't a case for a border between Korea and Japan, Canada and the US, the US and Mexico, Ireland and England, or Australia and New Zealand, or on any continent or ocean. In this thinking, we can solve the problem of warring states whose conflict has always been rooted in misconceived notions of nationalism and the lust for unfair shares of resources that belong to all.

We can also solve the question of the security of Israelis and the aspirations of Palestinians. Both live on land they recognize belongs to the same god. Christians, Jews, and Muslims don't argue the identity of this god. They dispute only the path or the prophet. The land of their shared god is thus a free region — their god would say this — and within it should exist the right of all to study and work and worship as they wish. There are no borders to cross as none exists except in the mind.

This is a great benefit of walking long distances. One can single-handedly solve some of the word's intractable problems. I don't believe that anyone is a Japanese or a German or an American. We should strip these accreted coatings as we strip peeling paint from wood, leaving only the grain and texture of the native timber to show through. The coatings seem always seized upon to impress that one people are inferior or superior to another, with no good and frequent fatal result.

I turned left onto Road 68, only a kilometer or so from Shirako and, after a misstep or two, found the house of acquaintances. Up a stepped, narrow path, a snake had nestled itself into the gaps of a brick wall. It was about a meter long and looked like a grass snake. I alerted people nearby and they came to look.

"Aren't you going to kill it?" a young man asked.

"No. It's bad luck to harm a snake," an older man replied.

———

I slept upstairs in a six-mat room that had been vacated by the family's un-married middle-aged son for the two days I would stay. He slept on the floor of the single downstairs room, which served as a living room by day and bedroom at night.

When I descended the stairs to use the bathroom after midnight, the oversized TV was on but muted. The mother, nearly 80, was holding her face to the screen at a thumb's length, and nodding in time with the moving pictures while her hus-band and son slept seemingly undisturbed.

When I looked again the three were asleep in a row, the son in the middle, hence the expression, *kawa no ji ni natte neru* — "to sleep in the pattern of the three strokes of the ideograph for river." They would have slept like this some 40 years ago. Most mothers insist on this arrangement after a child is born, and the custom probably marks the beginning of the end of some marriages, as the mother is gained and the wife is lost, in the way that the wife is gained and the girlfriend is lost, and the losses are irreversible.

After a breakfast of miso shiru soup, deep-fried shrimp, rice, and pickles — and toast and yogurt as a concession to me — the family transferred their attention to the TV and it consumed them. I rested upstairs, dozing and reading Fumiko Enchi's *The Waiting Years*. A stereo set soon accommodated my other traveling companions of Bud Powell and Rita Coolidge.

I was tired, but lighter — if you walk several hours a day for a few weeks, and eat sensibly, you will probably lose at least one-tenth of your weight.

That night I succumbed to the family TV ritual. The cheapest of filler fodder are quiz shows, which induce a state of stupefaction, put brains in brine. Tired, exchanging one state of numbness for another, I watched one of them. Was it pos-sible to learn anything? It might be.

A conveyor belt in a sushi restaurant moved a selection of dishes on color-coded plates in front of diners seated at the counter. The snaking belt was 186 meters (170 yards) long. Would it take more or less than 30 minutes for the belt to go around once?

———

One contestant said less, as sushi must be kept fresh; another said more, because the restaurant would attract families whose children would need time to choose from among the dishes. The belt made one revolution in 22 minutes. I reflected on the logic of the response, "Children would need time to choose."

A taxi driver had memorized "Thank you" in a number of foreign languages in his 48 years of driving. We see a black and white photograph of a young man in a large sedan taxi, the absence of color adding a sense of history. Would he have memorized "Thank you" in more or fewer than 30 languages? One contestant said more, arguing that the driver would have surpassed the 30 mark even if he had remembered less than one a year. Another said fewer, doubting that foreigners from so many countries would have visited Japan.

The driver was put to the test. He recited the names of 50 countries and said "Thank you" in each country's language — the Chinese, Korean, and Arabic were correct (I don't know much more than "thank you" in those languages), so I didn't doubt that he knew the others. The studio audience vigorously applauded, and I felt proud, too. The reasoning behind one response was telling — "Foreigners from so many countries wouldn't have visited."

At night in the upstairs room I looked through photo albums. I saw photos of reunions of war veterans who had fought in China and Southeast Asia in the Pacific War. The veterans each year had gathered at a hot spring resort to have an outing and reminisce. It seemed that at most 30 or so veterans participated, but each year their numbers dwindled with death.

The father and grandfather of this house was a war veteran. He had been drafted into the army at age 17, sent to China, then redeployed to the Solomon Islands. He told me that in the sea after his ship had been hit, a soldier tried to pull others toward him, saying, "We will be all right if we can only swim home. This way!" The soldier had lost his mind, the others pulled free of him, and he drowned.

Too few veterans now survive to hold the reunions. The government seems to look after old soldiers well, though some after the war were destitute and reduced to begging. Perhaps some status separated regiments. This householder in peace had found work in the fire service and then as a receptionist in a police hospital. It seems that such public-service positions fall into the lap of able veterans.

On a muggy spring morning I left this house and entered the metropolis of Tokyo after crossing the short bridge over the Shirako River — both banks concreted; a canal — at the segment which serves as a boundary with Saitama Prefecture.

Tokyo as a metropolis encompasses 26 cities, three towns, one village, and the Ogasawara and Izu and seven other islands southeast of Honshū, as well as the 23 wards which make up the "city" of Tokyo. Commuters from the neighboring prefectures of Saitama, Chiba, and Kanagawa increase the population of the metropolis from 12 million (2005 year) to nearly 15 million during the day. The wards accommodate some 8.3 million. The scale of the economy, with production of ¥90 trillion ($750 billion; year to March 2005) exceeds that of Korea or Mexico.

Apart from enclaves of original Tokyo inhabitants — called Edokko — in the eastern part of the city, Tokyo is home mainly to new and older generations of *dekasegi* — "leave and (work and) save," migrants from outer prefectures.

This Wednesday I'd walk 16.6 kilometers (9.7 miles) through the wards of Itabashi, Nerima, Toshima, Bunkyō, and Chiyoda, to Tokyo Station. I would follow Road 254 to Ikebukuro, an unfashionable crossroads of two subway and three overland lines.

I made my way through Kitaguchi Ave. mall to Narimasu Station on the Tōbu-Tōjō Line. Commuters waited impatiently at a level crossing for the bells to stop clanging and the arms lift. At this time — the morning rush hour — a local or express train comes every two or so minutes, so the crossing arms come down almost as soon as they are raised.

Some commuters pushed one of the arms aside, glanced down the tracks left and right, then dashed across. First one commuter, then another, then more. Three trains passed without the arms being raised once, and between their coming and going, nine commuters had risked their lives. Then another three darted across after pushing aside the arm.

They had nothing to fear. They were making their dash together. *Minna de aka shingō wo watareba kowakunai* — "We have nothing to fear if we all cross against the red light at the same time." It's a saying often heard in reference to the euphemistically termed "night tours" of male tourists to mainly Southeast Asian destinations in the 1970s and 1980s.

Commuters couldn't wait to get to work, or bother to walk a further 100 meters or so to use an overhead bridge. Perhaps it was both. I recall that during the train strikes of the 1980s commuters walked and ran down the tracks to work. Their behavior this morning suggested they would do so again.

Tokyo is mobile and civil and it works. It works so well that some suspicion is cast upon it. That may be why the smallest misstep in the city's administration is seized upon by local and foreign media alike as a portent of imminent disaster.

It works because that is the purpose of the millions who live in and commute into it each day. Its mindset is work — and to make things work. Commuters can't wait to get to work, and work is respected as a privilege.

Even the city's nighttime inhabitants are likely to work the same hours as those of the day. Bus and train schedules are set to ensure that almost everyone is under his futon by 1 a.m., thus the Edo curfew extends itself by one hour a century. As for the stragglers and drunkards, capsule hotels accommodate them, and they are as likely as the others to be on time for work the next day.

Road 17 — buddy of sorts — joined me again, but it was doing a double act. I'd bid it farewell at Kumagaya. Now it had metamorphosed as the New Omiya Bypass, which fed into Road 254 a short distance from Shimoakatsuka Station. The original Road 17, still following the path of the feudal Nakasendō in an easterly direction, continues to its terminus at Sugamo, which was the Itabashi post station.

Itabashi was one of four entrances to Edo, along with the post stations of Shinagawa, Shinjuku, and Senjū. Brothels catered to travelers at these locations. Edward Seidensticker in *Low City, High City* said that city residents flocked there, too. Bonded prostitutes — slaves, really — were liberated as free persons in 1872, and thereafter the brothels were renamed as *karizashiki* or rental rooms. These are the precursor of the love hotels.

Low City, High City, and its companion volume, *Tokyo Rising*, are out of print. I was able to acquire used editions but books such as these should always be available. *Edo, the City That Became Tokyo*, written by Akira Naitō and illustrated by Kazuo Hozumi, is also a treasured reference.

On the subject of out-of-print books, Ian Buruma in his recent short history *Inventing Japan*, recommends 49 English-language books for further reading. Of those, 17 appear no longer available new.

A Ground Self-Defense Force camp is sited on Road 254 near Tōbu-Nerima Station. I counted at least 20 substantial buildings in the compound. This road appears to have preserved its feudal role as a military supply route between Kawagoe and Edo.

I continued toward Ikebukuro, pausing outside the Church of Christ at Kami-Itabashi Station. It looked insecure in its three-story pencil building. The church occupied the middle floor, below a family residence and above a car park. An elderly woman swept leaves from the path until none remained, and I thought of the savage maiming of trees because of the leaves they shed.

Chōmeiji Temple shared the intersection of Road 318 with Handsome Noodles. Shrubs in the temple precinct were groomed to near perfect spheres, not one twig too long or short, and the priest's residence was a definition of understated opulence in dark and polished wood.

Pedestrians wore the *kyodatsu* expression of weariness redolent of the exhausted faces of a defeated nation in the late 1940s. They look this way especially when shopping when they receive so little for what they pay. There is a deceit in the ritual of wrapping. After unraveling the ornate, wasteful packaging, so little is left. I wonder what the impact on oil prices would be if Japanese demand for petrochemical products such as plastic and polystyrene were to plummet.

Fast-food joints blight Tokyo. The oily protuberant face of foreign-franchised chain or domestic look-alike sneers in station areas and malls. They are part of choice but inside their acceptance is the cynical association that what is American is quick and cheap. Diners damage their once-clear complexion and become ungainly by succumbing to this fare.

McDonald's is among the most prolific of the chains, with 3,500 or so outlets, but its fate seems aligned with that of tenpin bowling — once the rage, then the alleys deserted, the pins scuttled and unable to right themselves. The chain neglected a key ingredient, essential to health.

McDonald's retails a fickle product called peace of mind. It eliminates a diner's risk of choice through strict food ingredient and meal portion control.

Diners more or less know, before they buy, the taste and volume of what they'll be served.

But McDonald's diners here are smokers' dens. They replace the cheaper of the coffee shops at which idle students and workers used to wile away the hours. While McDonald's ran its outlets along local lines, which include generous concessions to smokers, customers were somewhere else. They were favoring a more American, smoke-free environment. McDonald's appeared not to grasp the trend, or irony.

Investors punish corporate failure to lead or pace a trend. But mainly individuals had trusted the McDonald's brand and bought shares when they were floated at ¥4,300 ($36) each. When I last looked, they had declined 53 percent to ¥2,015 ($17). Institutional investors, which had been more circumspect, began to view the price-cuts McDonald's made to win back customers — to ¥59 or 49 cents for a plain burger — as a deflationary indicator for the economy.

Fresh air was the missing McDonald's ingredient. Against local advice, I heard, the Starbucks coffee chain stuck to its non-smoking guns, and now its green goddess logo is omnipresent. There may be more to it. Friends talk of people they know who are *Sutaba bimbō* — "Starbucks poor," because they spend too much at Starbucks. They get hooked on the high sugar content of the coffee.

Sometimes in Tokyo you lose the natural light from your path as the sky recedes like a sliding tray being pushed back into some compartment. You've come under a segment of the colossal structure of the metropolitan expressway. There are 24 or so routes of this expressway of a total 283 kilometers (176 miles), and more are planned. I lost the sky as Road 254 fell under the path of the Ikebukuro route at the intersection with Yamate Ave., then found it about two kilometers further along at the intersection with Meiji Ave.

The Sunshine 60 and City buildings clutched clouds to the left. They contain the usual — offices, restaurants, hotel — and perhaps paranormal. They were built on the site of Sugamo Prison where the US hanged Japanese it convicted as war criminals and where Japanese hanged their own criminals before and during the war years. Ghosts in full military regalia are said to walk floors of the 60-story skyscraper.

Sometimes you feel that your feet have lifted from the ground, because there is none. Segments of the expressway combine with multiple levels of overhead and underground trains to produce this effect, which you can dissipate by walking more quickly. But if you slow down, one or other layer seems to shift underfoot like a portable plain.

And when a length of the expressway snakes overhead, stealing light, you may suspect that you are being showered by particles of diesel soot and dust. Considering that a daily average of 1.1 million vehicles, or 12 per second, enter the expressway's on-ramps, your suspicion is probably well founded.

I followed Road 254, which here is also Kasuga Ave., to its intersection with Hakusan Ave., and looked across to Tokyo Dome, a baseball park which converts into a concert arena. It's also a publicly listed company. A certain stock analyst in the late 1980s wished to recommend that investors sell the stock because of a bleak profit outlook. Michael Jackson made him change his mind. The singer had announced that he would perform at Tokyo Dome, and such were the times that that was enough to inspire confidence.

I turned into Hakusan Ave., then Uchibori Ave., which leads to Marunouchi and Tokyo Station. In taking this route, I was more or less following the divide between east and west, low city and high city, downtown and uptown, the wrong and right side of the tracks, those who watch TV and baseball and those who listen to orchestral music and see opera.

People who delight in what remains of the lifestyle of the Edokko will favor the east side, but few who are wealthy will want to live there. Western-style hotels and residences and the most prestigious concert halls are all on the west side. You can roughly demarcate the two sides by bisecting the Yamanote loop line between Ikebukuro and Tokyo stations.

Tokyo works for another reason. Contrary to foreign folklore, it has been meticulously planned. Villages have grown into each other but not without overlays of rail and road. Though roads were neglected at the expense of investment in rail and coastal shipping from the late 1800s through the mid 1900s, they received much funding as part of preparation for the 1964 Olympics.

Apart from the expressway, the network of main roads forms the pattern of a web of three rings and nine radials. The radials have been completed but links are still missing in the rings.

This web-like design enlarges the spiral design of Edo. For security reasons, the road that led to the shogun's castle followed a diminishing circuitous route and travelers were inspected at numerous gates or *mon* along the way. The suffix of mon in place names such as Hanzomon, Kaminarimon, Onarimon, Sakuradamon, and Toranomon indicates the location of the gates.

The design may explain the brisk growth of Edo, as roads wound outward to accommodate but also contain the expansion within one mass. Edo was probably the largest city in the world in the late 1700s and 1800s, according to Seidensticker, with a population believed to be between one and 1.3 million at a time when the population of London, then Europe's largest city, was less than a million.

Tokyo isn't the museum which is London nor is it as electric as Manhattan. But it's in their company as a truly great city. Too vast and deep ever to explore fully in a lifetime, whatever exists in the world, you will find one or more of those in Tokyo — if you know where to look.

If you live here for a long time, you'll live in a corner or along a short side, but there'll be no beginning or end to either dimension.

It's a sensual city. Women dress provocatively in light clinging cotton in summer and calculate precisely the charge they exude. Students and school leavers who arrive from the outer prefectures for university or a higher paying job are, for the first time, without teachers and parents and soon embark upon orgies of discovery. Sexually the city accommodates the imaginable and more. It's also a center of low and high fashion — both ruinously short-lived for those who bow to trends.

Among its millions, you can be alone in Tokyo in a way that villages or towns, where people make your business their own, never allow. No one here is bored enough to make inquiries of you. There's luxury in this privacy. Yet people will recognize and welcome you where you live and shop, because the magic of the metropolis is that it's also a village or, rather, clusters of them.

Seidensticker concluded *Tokyo Rising* on notes of pessimism. He wasn't confident that Tokyo, even with its new money, could match the grandeur of New York or be as tasteful in its architecture as London. More disturbingly, he maintained that it was a "very insular city" and that foreigners are in "no significant way a part of its life." Inhabitants were "far from ready to accept the pluralism of a New York." He was writing this in the late 1980s. These judgments fit some of the places I'd visited — Koide and Sarugakyō, for example — but not the Tokyo I knew or now saw.

With such large numbers of foreigners living and settling in Tokyo, the city may have no choice but to adapt and accommodate. It's now home to some 360,000 non-Japanese (as of October 2006; an increase of 20 percent from the October 2000 total).

The largest contingents are Chinese (34% of the total), followed by Korean (30%), Filipino (9%), and US (5%). There are several thousand each from Australia, Brazil, France, India, Thailand, and the UK. Most live in the western wards of Minato and Shinjuku, followed by the eastern wards of Adachi and Edogawa.

Many of the Chinese and Korean residents are students who have put the wartime experience of their grandparents behind them and look to an education in Japan as a passport to a brighter future. Such people had been my fellow students. Language similarities enable them to study in Japanese at university level after only one or two years of language study, and it isn't unusual in Chinese and Korean business and political circles to encounter fluent speakers of Japanese.

———

I was beginning to regret my decision to walk through this organized chaos. Inhabitants are hurried, and the crowding makes it hard to walk at a brisk pace. It's air-conditioned on the inside but sticky on the outside. Alan Booth didn't walk through it. In Honshū, he more wisely stuck to the rustic west coast, altogether skirting the urbanized, industrialized east coast.

A few years before Booth made his walk, another person was talked about who was said to be walking the length of the country, or rather traversing its mountain ranges. Students I knew said this walker was avoiding not only cities and towns but also villages and hamlets. His aim was said to be to walk through a natural state of Japan, as a challenge first to see if he could find continuously such a state and second for the exercise. So much then was new that I'd no thought of identifying this mysterious person and heard no more about him.

Tokyo isn't suited to cyclists, either. They are safest using footpaths, which nearly all do, as roads are too narrow for them to coexist with cars. When they reach some intersections with overhead pedestrian bridges, they must carry their bicycle up and down the steps in order to cross the road.

————

Amid markets sprung by wealth, "classical" music has blossomed and Tokyo surely offers more concerts than any other city in the world. In a usual year there are likely to be 3,000 to 4,000 concerts, and visiting orchestras and musicians will perform from 600–800 of those. Within that total there are likely to be 600–700 orchestral offerings, 300–400 chamber concerts, 700–800 piano recitals, 200–300 operatic performances, and 300–400 solo vocal recitals.

These figures don't include the many performances by student and amateur Japanese orchestras and ensembles. It all builds to a crescendo in December, when orchestras and choruses offer multiple performances of workhorses such as Handel's "Messiah," Tchaikovsky's "The Nutcracker," and Beethoven's "Ninth Symphony."

Once at a Mischa Maisky recital at Tokyo's Suntory Hall I saw the audience goad the cellist back at least five times for encores — this after he had breathtakingly played a generous program, two encores, and let enthusiasm snap an instrument string. But can we bring him back on stage one more time? A respect for the musician and the music wouldn't have produced such a spectacle or sport. This scene made clear to me the difference between hearing and listening to music, and Japan's appreciation of classical music sometimes appears imitative of the appreciation which is understood to be shown in Vienna or New York.

"I think they are learning," an English friend said. "When the Royal Opera Company came to Tokyo, Britten's *Peter Grimes* was the least attended of its three offerings but received the warmest reviews and enthusiastic audience response."

Naomoto Okayama, chief executive of the Association of Japanese Symphony Orchestras, believes that audiences have developed a deeper appreciation of classical music through exposure to performances by first-class orchestras. And thanks to municipal building sprees in the heady 1980s, as many as 2,000 concert halls are available. But it's best not to ask about the quality of all performances, Okayama has advised.

Okayama traces appreciation of Western music to lessons given to the army by a British military band in 1888. It may be earlier. Commodore Perry brought brass bands to Japan on his trade-opening missions in 1853 and 1854. On the first visit, his band at Kurihama played "Hail Columbia" and "Yankee Doodle." On the second, he had three bands play "The Star-Spangled Banner" before the signing of the Treaty of Kanagawa at Yokohama and "Home Sweet Home" afterward. To a people accustomed to hearing the delicate-sounding koto or shamisen, this spirited audio assault must have made a lasting impression.

While walking I didn't once hear traditional music, such as played on the koto, but foreign TV producers use it often enough to background their snippets on the country, so I hear it at home. The music isn't played because it isn't sold. At large music retailers in Tokyo — say, Shibuya HMV or Tower Records — I don't know where to find traditional music, and these are shops I visit often enough.

Japan is the second largest market for recorded music. Sales of CDs, tapes, LP records, and digital downloads were worth $5.4 billion in 2005, according to the Recording Industry Association of Japan. This compared with $12.3 billion in the US, $3.4 billion in the UK, and about $2 billion each in France and Germany. These five countries belong to what can be called the billion-dollar music sales club, and no other markets approach their size.

What music sells so much in Japan? I'd expected to find that CDs of foreign popular music sold most, followed by mainly European "classical" music. I was wrong. Data for new releases of music by genre in 2005 showed that, if most of what is released sells, sales would be greatest for Japanese popular music (42% of the total), followed by foreign popular (33%), and foreign classical (10%). The fourth largest category is anime or cartoon soundtrack music (4%). The share of traditional Japanese music — only 158 CD album releases out of a total 14,100 — barely exceeds 1 percent.

Later, with grandfatherly kindness, Okayama explained to me in his Tokyo office that the appeal to Japanese of European orchestral music lies much in the fullness and loudness of the sound in large concert halls. This "power of sound" contrasted with traditional Japanese music, which is composed to be played in small rooms by only a few musicians. He welcomed the greater frequency of concerts of Chinese and Korean music in Japan but observed that the sound of traditional Asian music seems small and fragile for audiences who enjoy orchestral sound.

Edward Morse, an American zoologist who taught in Japan in the late 1870s and set up the country's first museum of natural history, declared that he had "heard as yet nothing in Japan that we could regard as music," Robert A. Rosenstone recorded. Ensembles of flutes and drums at temples and shrines produced "one constant wail of the saddest sounds," Morse said. But he kept an open ear — "it may be that their music will ultimately prove to have merits of which we get no hint at present"— and later found himself moved through a range of emotions from sadness to excitement and fear by a vocal accompaniment at a kabuki performance.

Between the times of Okayama and Morse, the writer Nagai Kafū, who nostalgically chronicled the transformation of quaint Edo into mechanized Meiji, also weighed the two music types. A residency in Paris had acquainted him with the music of composers such as Berlioz but he may not have been moved by the fullness or the loudness, as he was later to write: "In the music of our ancestors…frail notes from three thin strings are enough to call up emotions as deep as the moment of death. Such music has no need for the complicated structures of Western music, harmony, polyphony and counterpoint."

I browsed the book *New Tokyo Life Style Think Zone*, a gift from a friend. The words "think" and "zone" hinted that it was the offspring of architects, and so it was.

Their creations born, the architects had become curious about the beneficiaries of their structural largesse. They had been reading surveys. I wasn't privy to the wording of the questions, and questions can be constructed in such a way as to elicit a response that satisfies some demand of the sponsor of the survey. But responses cited here seemed instructive:

— More than 70 percent of Tokyo workers sleep six or fewer hours a night; three out of four commute for more than one hour a day; only 5 percent of Tokyo is devoted to parks, compared with 30 percent of London; of married workers, 41 percent spend 15 minutes or less a day talking to their spouse, including 10 percent who don't talk with their spouse.

Tokyo was less humane than New York or London, these responses implied. But mobility and security are greater here, and personal possibilities seem so, too. Architects talk their own book — if you commission our designs the city will become more humane — but they are surely correct in pointing to inefficient uses of land which reduce the quality of life.

In the rush to rebuild after the Great Kantō Earthquake of 1923 and the firebombing of 1945, the entitlement of private and public space of an individual can't have been a measured unit in design.

The Empire State Building was built to a height of 1,250 feet (381 meters) in Manhattan in 1930. Japan, 20 years later, was still limiting the height of buildings to 33 meters (108 feet), in Tokyo as elsewhere, and the resulting sprawl of low buildings reduced the availability of land for parks and other public amenities. A revision to building standards in the 1960s permitted the construction of skyscrapers but on a zoned basis, so they have sprouted unevenly in isolated clusters, mostly in Shinjuku.

The city mutates. Renewal and change are its only constants. It is building up. It is showing its intent of matching, in time, younger sister Manhattan, leaving ever further behind the other siblings of Berlin, Jakarta, Moscow, Paris, Rome, Sao Paulo, and Seoul.

CHAPTER 32. LOOKING OUT TO SEA

Today, after a 16.5-mile (26.5-kilometer) walk along mostly flat and straight city roads, I would look out to sea. I'd crossed the country but, unlike Alan Booth, I hadn't walked its length.

Unlike, too, the lone Japanese youth who was seen walking toward Cape Reinga at New Zealand's northernmost tip. His appearance gave the impression of a long-distance walker. Some people who saw him wondered, has he walked from Bluff in the far south? He had. They joined him on this last stretch, as a celebration of his feat and of him.

But my purpose wasn't athletic. It was to connect windows on the world, and view a profile of the land in between. This I'd almost done, and it had given me much to consider. And I'd already decided to break a foolish rule of travel. I'd go back.

Now, in Tokyo, it seemed strange to walk in a city in which all rushed. Though commuter trains arrive every few minutes people nonetheless run up and down station stairs to catch them and fast-walk or run to their offices. If none did that none would be late.

Yaesu Fujiya Hotel's bill of ¥19,675 ($164) was two to three times what I'd paid in Niigata and Gunma. Tokyo is reputed to be the world's most expensive city but grocery prices at supermarkets for expatriates, which I read was one UN comparative measure, don't tell us much. Tokyo's range of cost is from one to 100 or even 1,000 — from the flophouse to the luxury suite, from the station noodle bowl to the most expensive of French — or almost any country's — cuisine.

It felt strange to be using a credit card again. Most minshuku and ryokan had accepted only cash. I didn't have a savings account with the post office, whose banking facilities can be used at branches nationwide. Booth sensibly used a post office account to fund his four-month walk, withdrawing money as he needed it. I found later that the cards of Tokyo banks can be used at machines outside Tokyo, but at exorbitant fees. Cash still reigns regionally in the new century.

———

A Fujiya hotel — it's now a chain — wasn't my first choice. Isabella Bird wouldn't have stayed at this hotel in its first incarnation in 1878, the year she arrived. It then targeted moneyed foreigners as a niche, replicated their comforts, and felt duty-bound to "explain Japan" to them. You always want to escape from Japanese who try to do that, because they sanitize and mythologize. Bird did, heading west and north, while the tourist track took foreigners mainly south, to Hakone — Fujiya is well represented among hotels there — then Kyoto.

I'd wanted to stay at Tokyo Station Hotel but it was full, and I briefly regretted my decision not to reserve accommodation. The hotel was built in 1914 in red brick and looks English. It exudes the cosmopolitan charm of the short-lived Taishō era and is remarkable for having survived — touch its paneled wood — the several attempts by developers to erect steel-glass towers in its place.

Slow-moving and disoriented in the city I thought I knew well, I lost my way. I searched for Road 1 on the Yaesu side of Tokyo Station, not understanding that it doubled as Eitai, Hibiya, and Sakurada avenues. I realized my mistake only in Nihombashi, a district whose name translates as the bridge of Japan, though I didn't reached the actual bridge, to which all distances to Tokyo are measured.

In feudal times the bridge of Nihombashi served as the gateway to Edo for travelers who walked the Tōkaidō that connected the city with Kyoto. In a way I'd missed an opportunity to indulge in nostalgia and symbolism, but it wasn't my purpose to trace a feudal route, and ports symbolize more for me than bridges. Road 1 later in Kanagawa Prefecture is also named Tōkaidō, but I can't say how faithful is the course to the original highway.

I crossed to the Marunouchi side of Tokyo Station via a passageway underneath the myriad tracks, then took Hibiya and Sakurada avenues to the Iikura Intersection.

———

"Mum! Just imagine how I'm feeling! Stop it!" I overheard a young, disheveled Englishwoman say. She was walking in Toranomon. I shuddered. At least she was alive. She looked like she hadn't slept in days. I wasn't near enough to catch the content of the lecture, but her mother seemed to have rescued her in some way.

Toranomon is walking distance from the wasteland of Roppongi, a foreigners' ghetto and home to bars from the hole-in-the-wall hovel to clip joint and members' club. It's also a pairing stage for one-night standers where lost foreigners are found. Not as ugly as it used to be, it's still ugly. It's un-Japanese, too. Foreigners at some bars are asked to pay in advance for their drinks.

Foreign hostesses pour drinks, light cigarettes and feign interest in pawing men at Roppongi bars. Some hostesses disappear off the face of the Tokyo asphalt, believed stalked, raped, and killed by men who live out their fantasies toward white women.

That was the evident fate of blonde, blue-eyed Lucy Blackman, a former British flight attendant who disappeared in 2000 and whose dismembered remains — head encased in concrete — were found the next year on the coast at Miura south of Tokyo. She was 22. She had come to work Roppongi for quick cash to erase credit-card debt.

As I write a Japanese man is on trial for Blackman's murder, but he may not have been without the strenuous, persistent efforts of her father who lobbied at home and in Japan for his daughter's disappearance to be taken seriously. A call to the hotline he set up in Tokyo led to the suspect's arrest.

————

There are other roads to Yokohama. There's Road 15, also named Dai-Ichi Keihin (No.1 Tokyo-Yokohama Highway), and Road 446 or Dai-San Keihin (No. 3 Tokyo-Yokohama Highway, an expressway). Both are radials in the web, and between them is Road 1, also a radial, and the second of the three Keihin highways. This middle radial is the sensible one to walk. It isn't hard against the factories of Kawasaki or the heavily industrialized Keihin waterfront district, which exemplifies Japan's cluttered and concreted factory coast.

Tokyo spills into the cities of Kawasaki and Yokohama or they into it, turning the three into a megalopolis. At least some greenery separated Tokyo and Yokohama in the 1970s. It doesn't now. The Yokohama that Bird described as "beautiful, with abrupt wooded hills, and small picturesque valleys' is a memory of the dead.

Road 1 is straightforward from Iikura, and I sped along it, impatient to reach the port. I should have scrutinized my surroundings more, though some things stuck out. Japan Pet Fish Trading Co. was one. You still see exotic species of fish in tanks in furniture shops and some restaurants. Like places which confine animals, those which keep pet fish seem always unclean.

I left Tokyo at the Tama River, and crossed into the Saiwai district of Kawasaki City in Kanagawa Prefecture. The word prefecture, which suggests a subordinate province, misleads. Kanagawa, with a population of some 8.8 million (2005 year) and economic production value of ¥32.5 trillion ($271 billion; year to March 2005) is comparable to Switzerland.

I'd thought that *Kawasaki byō* or illness was caused by the pollution of the city of the same name. It isn't. That illness, which mysteriously attacks children under four years old, giving them fever and making their lips bleed, is named after Tomisaku Kawasaki, who identified its symptoms in 1967. The cause of this illness isn't understood, but 25 to 50 children die from it each year. Kawasaki asthma, though, is named after the city, and fed by the sulfur and nitrogen oxides released by petrochemical and other plant.

I didn't feel poisoned as I walked. Controls on harmful emissions from industrial plant are stricter now than they were in the 1970s when I recall walking through blankets of thick gray air in the Tsurumi ward of this prefecture. It's the diesel exhaust from trucks that now needs cleaning.

Kanagawa boasts the highest ownership of personal computers of any prefecture at 77% of household occupants, compared with 54 percent for the nation (2004 year), according to the Statistics Bureau of the Ministry of Internal Affairs and Communications.

The national figure is similar for Internet usage, which tells a story. Only 50 percent of Japanese use the Internet, a lower percentage than for Sweden, which leads the world at 76 percent, or Singapore or the US, according to data compiled by the International Telecommunication Union for 2004. Some observers claim that the cumbersome writing system slowed the diffusion of personal computers and Internet usage. That may have been a part of the reason, but it was a small part. The use of ideographs had never slowed much else down.

The greed of the telecommunications monopoly, then Nippon Telegraph and Telephone Corp., which charged usurious rates for Internet access, put the Internet out of reach for average-income families. I'd made quite limited use of the Internet and recall being invoiced amounts from $200 to $300 a month by NTT.

But more than greed was at work. There was a view that ordinary people wouldn't — or shouldn't — much use this tool. For one, it connected them with ease to information and to the world. Second, it was a wholly unregulated sphere, and it contained a microcosm of what was bad as well as good.

NTT behaved like a government agency and in its protective paternalism was showing how Tokugawa edicts persist in spirit and practice. One edict said, "It is enough to follow the books of old, there is no need to write new ones." And the word *gumin* — "stupid commoners," used by samurai and others of high social order, was in vogue then, and is still heard today.

As the choice of connection device has expanded to include mobile phones, other hand-held devices, and game machines, more — and younger — Japanese are accessing the Internet. According to a Ministry of Internal Affairs and Communications survey, Internet users in 2005 had reached 85 million, or 67 percent. This survey was of users aged from six years.

An unkempt man in a park was stomping on drink cans. His bag of flattened cans was almost full. A shopping cart contained what appeared to be the sum of his possessions. He wasn't alone. The homeless are here not for the benches but for the clean water. Most parks have hydrants for watering plants and the homeless draw their drinking and laundry water from these.

A friend said some of the homeless make money by selling their identity to criminals. They can give a criminal a name and perhaps an address which is still on a family register, which can be used for the issue of identity or cash or credit cards.

Dean MacCannell, in the introduction to his 1989 edition of *The Tourist*, wrote that "no doubt someone will be tempted to squeeze the homeless and the impoverished for symbolism even after their last dollars are gone." MacCannell cited the tours of Appalachian communities and northern inner-city cores as examples of "negative tours" which provide a "moral stability to the modern touristic consciousness."

The homeless — I saw them also on a riverbank in Gunma — are entitled to keep their stories to themselves. I felt no inclination to encourage them to share their heartbreak or life-break. And, unlike Orwell as tramp and scullion in *Down and Out in Paris and London*, I wasn't prepared to live as they do to qualify to write about them.

Cold drizzle fell as I entered the Tsurumi ward of Yokohama City at Shitte Station on the Nambu Line at around 1.45 p.m. Near the station, on the right side of Road 1, a ShinMaywa Industries' factory recalls the flying boats which ushered in the age of air travel and were used in anti-submarine warfare.

There's no longer a naval use for flying boats, but the Defense Agency still orders them from ShinMaywa. They can be used in fighting forest fires and for search and rescue at sea. I haven't read of them being put to either use here, but Japan still clings to the manufacturing capability.

There's history in ShinMaywa. The company is a reincarnation of Kawanishi Aircraft Co., whose flying boats and fighter planes were used in the Pacific War. After that war, the US imposed a ten-year moratorium on the production of aircraft by Japan. This allowed the US and Europe to lead in the manufacture of commercial aircraft and no commercial plane of Japanese make flies today.

Instead, companies such as ShinMaywa, Fuji Heavy Industries, and Mitsubishi Heavy Industries, all pre- and postwar defense contractors with a record in the manufacture of military aircraft, have become subcontractors to The Boeing Co. I once tried to calculate the percentage of a 747 jetliner which is made in Japan, but Boeing became upset with my efforts and declined to answer my detailed questions, and I decided it wasn't worthwhile to pursue the matter.

Japan's supply of fuselage and wing components and precision equipment such as actuators to Boeing is part of an offset deal for the Boeing planes which Japan Airlines commits to buy. But it also signifies that, in defeat, Japan lost a measure of industrial as well as political independence.

The Boeing subcontracts today are one of only two opportunities Japanese companies have to make aircraft parts or aircraft. The other is in fighter jet production for the Defense Agency, but these jets are mostly reverse engineered from US models.

The Tsurumi River flowed black and gray.

A man expertly maneuvered a Harley Davidson motorcycle with sidecar out of the rain and into Sunrise Auto Motor shop. Here, too, urban professionals who claim this *Easy Rider* icon as a lifestyle accessory have overridden the imagery of Hells Angels. They are the buyers of motorbikes such as these. Japanese bikers ride much smaller bikes — less than 100 c.c. — and swarm at night in large groups. The high-pitched din of their engine revving pierces the still night over entire suburbs.

The friendly owner seemed relieved when I said I wasn't a motorcyclist and wasn't going to buy a Harley. He didn't have to waste sales patter on me in the way that he must waste words most of his day. I parroted a comment about Harleys needing a lot of care.

"The newer models are more reliable," the owner said. "But their engine sound isn't as good as that of the older models. They do have style and history, and some Japanese like that. Still, you don't need much money to run a Japanese motorcycle. Harleys tend to overheat."

Two of the Harley models had sidecars. One model was fitted with a pedal clutch and gear stick in a concession to armchair motorcyclists who had rejected cars but who were more comfortable driving than riding. A 1990 Harley Sotel was priced at ¥1.5 million ($12,500).

———

I'd walked from Kawasaki almost the length of the Keihin waterfront district, which stretches for about 17 kilometers (11 miles) from Haneda airport on the ocean southeast of Tokyo, to Higashi-Kanagawa and Yokohama. It's an industrial zone on an artificial edge of ocean where, as Seidensticker has put it, one mile of dust and concrete leads to another. I couldn't see any of the petrochemical or power-generating or other plant from Road 1, but the air is thick with their presence.

I wouldn't linger at Yokohama Station, which doesn't exude the cosmopolitan or maritime atmosphere of the city. It's an impostor of sorts. It was sited here in 1915 so that it would connect directly to the Tōkaidō. The original Yokohama Station is today's Sakuragichō Station — the next stop south — which only borders the portside of the city.

The atmosphere of the port city is felt strongest between Kannai Station, the next from Sakuragichō, and the ocean. Here the wide avenues are tree-lined and buildings look distinctly European. The city and prefectural government, district court, offices of the national government, and stadium are closest to Kannai, and if you are meeting someone in "Yokohama," you will probably meet them here.

Road 1 turns seaward between Kanagawa and Yokohama stations and crosses several sets of railway lines, before falling under the cold shadow of the Kanagawa section of the Metropolitan Expressway that links Yokohama with Haneda airport. Rather than loose my sense of a level earth, I made my way down Minato Mirai Ōdori Ave., which flanks Landmark Tower, crossed the mouth of the Ōoka River, and entered Honchō Ave., which leads to Yamashita Park.

Much of Yokohama looks new but the city is steeped in history — imagined and real. It looks new because it has twice in one century been destroyed — by earthquake in 1923 and by an estimated 30 rounds of US firebombing in 1945. On the heaviest day of the firebombing, 29 May 1945, Burritt Sabin recorded in *A Historical Guide to Yokohama*, 517 B-29 bombers and 101 P-51 fighters dropped more than 350,000 bombs in 68 minutes, or 85 per second. Earlier some 60,000 residents had fled to the countryside, but this raid still claimed an estimated 7,000 to 8,000 lives.

Jules Verne deposited the fictional Phileas Fogg here in 1872 as he made his way east around the world in 80 days, via the ports of Calcutta and Hong Kong. Rudyard Kipling was in slow pursuit, sailing this same route in May 1889, also, like Fogg, on his way to San Francisco.

Kipling must have liked what he saw at Nagasaki and Yokohama on this visit of just three and a half weeks, as he returned to Yokohama in 1892 and honeymooned for three months. His wife, Caroline Smith, had a strong Japanese connection through her grandfather, the eccentric Peshine Smith, who was attached to Japan's Foreign Office as an international policy advisor in the 1870s, Charles Carrington noted in *Rudyard Kipling*.

Kipling was all but bankrupted here as a result of the failure of the Oriental Banking Co., despite the knowing efforts of a teller to urge him to withdraw much more than he requested, but world fame then lay in wait and his finances would more than recover.

––––––

Japan and the US signed their first treaty in Yokohama in 1854. Informally called the Treaty of Kanagawa, it notionally gave US ships access to the ports of Hakodate and Shimoda and, tellingly, required good treatment of shipwrecked sailors. In the follow-up Harris Treaty of 1858 and in treaties signed with France, Great Britain, the Netherlands, and Russia the same year, Japan agreed to open more ports. Thus was Japan drawn into the web of the West.

Though the 1958 treaties permitted foreigners to reside in the towns of the opened ports, their movement was restricted. In the case of Yokohama, foreigners weren't allowed to venture beyond a distance of around 40 kilometers (25 miles) in all directions from the port or the banks of the Tama River between Tokyo and Kawasaki.

Edo and Osaka opened in 1862 and 1863. Shimoda, the first to be opened, was closed after six months of the opening of Kanagawa. The agreement on Shimoda, whose unsuitable geography wasn't understood until after the concession had been made, had been a short-lived masterstroke of last-gasp isolationists.

The shogunate tried to turn Yokohama into another Dejima by isolating it within the watery bounds of river and canal, but this intention was seen and thwarted by US and other foreign residents. It wasn't until 1899 that the foreign settlement and extraterritoriality were abolished as part of revisions to the treaties.

Some 71,000 foreigners reside in Yokohama (2006 year), mostly Chinese (36% of the total), Korean (22%), Filipino (10%), Brazilian (5%), and American (4%).

The city's Chinatown, which lies between Yamashita Park and Ishikawachō Station, is reputedly the world's largest, and from within its confines Sun Yat-Sen plotted revolution against the Qing dynasty. Apart from their role as traders, the Chinese, like the Dutch, were language intermediaries between Japan and English-speaking peoples. Japanese trade documents would be translated first into Chinese or Dutch, then English.

––––––

But Yokohama showed Japanese — in particular educator Yukichi Fukuzawa when he visited in 1859 — that the world was larger than they had seen through the eyes of their Dutch agency and that their need was greater for English. Has the lesson been learned? After nearly 150 years, English isn't spoken well.

There are fine speakers of the language, as there are of French or Spanish or any European tongue. But these are people who have determined to use a particular language in their career, then, assisted by private or corporate tutors, made an extraordinary personal effort to master it.

The curricula of public or private schools don't seem to focus on oral communication. English is taught mostly as an exercise in translation, so that it can be used, as it was in the Meiji era, for the introduction of things foreign — developments in medicine, science, technology. It's learned for the reason that Dutch was learned.

In the vacuum has sprung an industry of private English "conversation" schools and companies take it upon themselves to provide English tuition to employees who need the language in their work. The government does contract foreign English teachers but mainly for dispatch to rural areas where they rotate among small schools that don't attract Japanese teachers.

Some foreign residents with a penchant for conspiracy theories maintain that the government doesn't seek to produce English speakers because it fears that increased interaction with foreigners would dilute indigenous culture. I believed this notion for some time, but after discussing it with friends who have children in schools in Tokyo, I'm not so sure. They say that, within the time constraints imposed by an ever more demanding regular curriculum, a genuine effort is made to teach spoken English.

The cultural conspiracy theory, though, is deep-rooted. Its proof, proponents say, is in the results that schools produce, which don't include English speakers. Those of more mild persuasion point to the hours which students must devote to memorizing ideographs, but others say that task is more assigned to homework. Still others say the large amount of time spent on socialization, on teaching students how to behave as Japanese, shortens the time that can be spent on everything else.

Samurai fought the dilution of indigenous culture and were contemptuous of foreign languages. Ernest Satow in the 1860s refused the title of interpreter because the position was "looked upon as only fit for the lowest class of domestic servants, and no one of samurai rank would ever condescend to speak a foreign language." The descendants of samurai, whose social class was the highest, today are less likely to populate the armed forces than they are government agencies and ministries. The prejudices of samurai may fade more slowly than the samurai.

Yamashita Park was built on reclaimed land using earthquake rubble. Occupation forces requisitioned the park in 1945 and built Jack and Betty cookie-cutter houses on it, Sabin has noted. Thankfully, they don't survive.

I walked down to the park and at the parapet stood facing the ocean. The horizon seemed to set not on sky but on the outline of a thermal power plant, a gas works, a chemical factory, a steel works, and a glass company — all on a stretch of reclaimed land beyond Daikoku Pier.

For an hour or so I'd walked through drizzle yet I'd so wanted warmth. And I'd wanted to look out toward the vast container handling terminals of Honmoku Pier to the right, and see ships.

The pier has 25 or so berths, but even on a clear day you can't see more than a silhouette of the gigantic cranes that load and unload the trucks of the ocean. But I wanted to know that they are there, as symbols of this country's place in, not outside, the world.

The ships are there. As many as 11,000 foreign-flagged ships enter this port every year, or more than one an hour, making Yokohama one of the world's busiest ports. Though the beneficial ownership of many of these ships is Japanese — the flags will be of convenience — that doesn't lessen the symbolism of their connectivity.

In bright sunshine I'd wanted to feel the music *Harbor Narrative*, composed by George McKay. The nine segments of that composition — "Sea Horizon," "Enroute," "Voice of the City," "Chanty," "Men and Machines," "Gulls," "Waterfront March," "Outward Bound," and "Into the Distance" — speak to Yokohama.

I could hear only "Men and Machines."

The day was bleak, and I was cold. But I wanted to celebrate. I decided to treat myself to dinner at a family restaurant called Jonathan's on the strip facing Yamashita Park. Jonathan's was hosting an Italian "fair." I obliged, ordering garlic bread, minestrone soup, deep-fried zucchini and chicken, and coffee.

"Is garlic bread all right?" the waitress quizzed, thinking I may have mistakenly ordered it.

"I'm not a vampire."

She laughed. I felt good. I'd chosen this restaurant for another, personal reason. It was part of a celebration.

Before turning back toward Kannai Station, where I would board a train to Tokyo, I walked across the park. Two cruise liners and tugs came into view. I watched them from the parapet, looking out through the cold spring rain.

———

Too late it occurred that perhaps I should have followed in the figurative footsteps of those who walk with more altruistic purpose than I'd contrived. For example Ian Botham, who understood that as a cricketer he should entertain, has raised about five million pounds ($9.2 million) through walking some 4,000 miles (6,400 kilometers) for good causes, according to a BBC report. His most recent effort was a 220-mile (350-kilometer) walk across Wales to raise money for a Welsh children's hospital.

And my walk can't compare with the distances routinely covered in earlier centuries by rural or city-dwelling Japanese with business in other parts of the country.

Political refugees and economic migrants today walk great distances through troubled regions. Some of these journeys — through desert and mountainous terrain, clothing and food inadequate — will not end in a lifetime. Parents will bequeath them to children who also must walk.

I met no dangers from rivers, from robbers, from my fellow countrymen, from foreigners, from false friends, or in the country or in towns or at sea. I didn't go without sleep and neither was I hungry or thirsty. Nor did I suffer from cold or exposure. There was little travail in my travel.

There's no hardship in spending several hours each day walking along Japan's country and city roads, nearly always safe and comfortable at the end of each day. It's a luxury to ponder questions of acceptance, and children, the elderly, and those of similar age or profession had welcomed me.

Part out of cowardice and part out of good sense I drove my route before walking it. There was no point in driving the route in both directions — from Yokohama to Niigata and back — so, starting from Shin-Yokohama Station, I took the Kanetsu Expressway to Niigata, then drove back. This may have saved my and other lives, as it convinced me of the folly of trying to walk through road tunnels.

I entered the telephone number of a Niigata hotel into my car navigation system, then followed the arrow on the digital map and obeyed the soft female voice prompts. She wasn't real but she was nice.

"You've been driving for two hours without a break," she said. "Won't you have a rest?"

LATER IN TOKYO

My cell phone rang.

Chapter 33. He Loved His Wife

I took the call in a Tokyo hotel room. The reporter from the Niigata bureau of *Nihon Nōgyō Shimbun* called to say said that the husband of the snow country geisha had passed away soon after his wife had died. There would be no point in my returning to Sanjō.

He called back an hour or so later. *Me ga deta* — "A bud has come out," he said. There's hope. He had asked around. A reporter on Niigata's daily newspaper, *Niigata Nippō*, had told him that he knew the whereabouts of neighbors of the geisha. Would I like to visit Sanjō and talk with them?

He gave me the reporter's name and telephone number. I said I'd call and visit. The opportunity was too good to pass up. I was trespassing through hearts but years had passed.

A nervous excitement welled inside me, and I marveled that this trail had begun at Jazz Mama. I called the reporter and arranged to meet him in Sanjō in about a week's time. He said he commuted by car from Niigata to his newspaper's bureau in Sanjō, where he sometimes slept over.

A bullet-train ride later and over lunch, the reporter told me that Kiku and her husband had rented an apartment in the neighborhood of the distributor of his newspaper. The apartment, which the couple had rented for ¥4,500 a month, was a few doors down from the general store that still serves as a distributor for the *Niigata Nippō* in the Sanjō town of Nishiyama.

The reporter drove me to the store, which fronts the storekeeper's house. It sells rice and groceries and carbonated drinks and sweets. It gets the newspapers out. It's the type of store I used to pay rent to as a student, and the type that late-night convenience stores put out of business.

In a few minutes the neighbor who had been Kiku's landlady joined us. This woman was 81, and the storekeeper, 88. Neither knew of Kiku's life as a snow country geisha when she came to live as Mrs Otaka in this neighborhood.

235

The storekeeper was seated on a tatami mat. The neighbor and I sat on chairs as small as those in a primary school classroom. The neighbor's memory was clearest.

"I was surprised that a tailor as skilful as Otaka could be found in Sanjō. You could make a living as a tailor then," the neighbor said. Otaka had hired more than ten seamstresses at the peak of his business.

The shopkeeper, age 88, was proud of being able to work. "I'm busy," she said several times during our conversation, but not rudely. Her face beamed. She was proud to be busy.

The neighbor, originally from Tokyo, was beautiful. Features fine, skin clear, smile warm but crisp, voice soft and manner gentle, she was aging gracefully. Her intellect was intact. She spoke in sentences, each word in its place, and never began a sentence until either the storekeeper or the newspaper reporter or I had stopped talking. I hope that I can age as well as her.

"You wouldn't know Kiku was a geisha," the neighbor told me. "She never talked about Kawabata or the Takahan Hotel. Not at all. Not to anyone.

"She was an intelligent and good person. She always wore kimono, never Western dress. She was happily married. There was no bath in her apartment. She and her husband went to the public bathhouse together. There was a Buddhist altar in her apartment.

"She didn't have any children, but she adopted her niece as a daughter. She was kind to children in the neighborhood."

"What did Kiku do in her spare time?"

"She was always reading novels."

But not Kawabata's. She'd read historical romances and detective fiction. She didn't read but lived love stories.

Around the time the first screen version of *Snow Country* was released in 1957, the neighbor and storekeeper became aware that Kiku had led a very different life before settling in their city. They couldn't recall the circumstances that led to the exposure of Kiku's past.

It's likely, I think, that they were alerted by the arrival of movie people from Tokyo who, touring as an intrusive mob, would have traced Kiku to this neighborhood. They would have accosted her and clawed for insights that would help actress Keiko Kishi play the role of Komako.

"I was upset when I read *Snow Country*," the neighbor said. "Kiku was a wife, an ordinary person." And the movie had disappointed her husband. "He told me the actress's hands were small and her fingers thin. He said that wasn't a snow country woman."

Kiku's mother had hidden newspapers which carried articles about the movie so that her daughter wouldn't see them. Soon after the movie's release, Kiku and her husband moved to another part of Sanjō.

Though Kawabata had stopped visiting Yuzawa around 1938, some 30 years later he is understood to have visited Sanjō, telephoned Kiku, and reminisced with her at a coffee shop. I wonder if, after all, he was the sponsor who had paid down her geisha house bond and freed her. Who else could it have been?

The neighbor and storekeeper responded silently when asked their opinion of Kawabata's winning of the Nobel Prize and his suicide. A resignation bordering on disappointment filled their faces but they voiced no thoughts.

The reporter took a small digital camera from his shoulder bag and took some photographs. I was being set up. Later an article would appear in his newspaper, about an outsider collecting memories of a snow country geisha. He didn't tell me that he would write the article, but was courteous enough some weeks later to send me a copy of it. It was more than a fair trade. I'd left Sanjō carrying history in my hands, and the answer to a question.

How could Mr. Otaka have made a life with someone who had been the obligated lover of snow country travelers and the companion of a celebrated literary figure? That he had so soon followed his wife into death answered the question. He had loved his wife.

IMMIGRATION MAN

I returned to Tokyo and took a train to Kannai in Yokohama. I had more questions to ask, but not of a deceased geisha's neighbors. I wanted to ask immigration authorities whether I could become a Japanese, and this was more than a new take on a vaporous song.

CHAPTER 34. UNTIL THE END

We all thought we would leave, and so did, we believed, the immigration authorities. That was why they treated us more kindly than they did Asians, who they believed wanted to settle in Japan for the richer life it offered and who would never go home.

But eventually we would go home, so let's be nice, we thought immigration authorities thought.

Then feelings changed.

This change was that it was all right to stay in Japan, until the end. People who had always believed they would leave had stopped seeing their departure as inevitable and instead were resigned to never leaving.

"It's all right to die here," Henry told me, when I visited him before leaving.

But how difficult was it to become a Japanese?

I took a train to Kannai Station and walked almost the length of Bankoku-bashi — the bridge to 10,000 countries — Ave. to the building which houses the Yokohama branch of the Justice Ministry. I would visit the ministry's Naturalization Department and discuss my credentials.

Becoming a Japanese was a more common occurrence than some may think. In 2005, 15,251 naturalization applications were accepted, or about 293 a week. Approvals for Koreans numbered 9,689 or 64 percent of the total; for Chinese, 4,427 (29%); and for "other," 1,135 (7%). Only 166 applications were rejected.

The "other" category likely would include Brazilians of Japanese descent and perhaps a Hawaiian sumo wrestler or soccer star or other sports prodigy whose applications seem to be fast-tracked. I checked data going back ten years, and found that each year from 14,000 to 17,000 people had become Japanese.

I sat down with an official of the naturalization department to discuss my case. I thought I could meet all the requirements. The official told me that he counsels mainly Chinese and Koreans who seek to become Japanese. He said he had never interviewed a New Zealander. Eligibility to become a Japanese was one thing, he said, but the need to become one was another.

We went through the list of requirements — copies of your driver's license, if you have one; graduation certificate from the last school attended; your bank savings balance; any land or building ownership registration; alien registration certificate; documents that evidence date and place of birth, arrival in Japan, residence qualification and period; residence record for the past five years; and two or three family photographs.

You have to have lived and behaved well in Japan for five consecutive years, or three if your spouse is Japanese; be 20 years or older; have the ability to make a living by yourself or by the skills or assets of family members; and be willing to forgo your present nationality.

But did I need to become a Japanese? the official asked. Could I not make a living or did I suffer from political or religious persecution in my country? Though the answers were "No," he nonetheless offered to proceed with the interview. He began by requesting that I draw diagrams of my family tree, beginning with paternal and maternal grandparents. He helped me connect the bodies with lines as though we were playing a dot game.

He examined each page of my passport and noted that, though I held a residence permit, I'd recently absented myself for more than six months at one time. That was enough to disqualify me.

The official concluded the interview by discussing the elements of need and judgment. People who qualify for naturalization may not necessarily be accepted, he said. The ministry would exercise its judgment in each case. It was, he repeated, a matter of judgment.

He didn't need to suggest that my application probably would be rejected. As a permanent resident I'd absented myself for longer than the permitted period of six months. That was little more than a technicality, but it could be seized upon. Japanese for whom Japan lacked nothing didn't leave for that long.

Before leaving I wanted to collect my thoughts. Like a patient I sat down in the small waiting room in the naturalization department, and looked at wall posters. One showed flags of the world. Another proclaimed that leprosy wasn't a hereditary disease and beseeched people to rid themselves of prejudice toward lepers. This poster used the term Hansen's disease, not *raibyō*. Another poster, showing the portrait of a youthful woman, fresh and full of life, extolled all to live *sawayaka na egao de* — "with a pure and smiling face."

A TV was on. The prime minister, Junichirō Koizumi, kicked a soccer ball to mark his first year in office. The introductory bass riff to the Pink Floyd song "One of These Days" thumped the commemoration. The producer can't have understood that the song's short lyric is, "One of these days I'm going to cut you into little pieces."

I've read cases of some westerners who in later years regretted their decision to become Japanese. Their love affair with the country in tatters, they realized that, after all, they weren't Japanese, and no Japanese recognized them as such, no matter what passport they carried. Lafcadio Hearn, who wrote voluminously on Japan from the time of his arrival at Yokohama in 1890 till his death at age 54 in Tokyo in 1904, may be one such example.

Hearn married a Japanese, adopted a Japanese name, and became a Japanese national. I learned in a lecture that his employer, Tokyo Imperial University, had become dissatisfied with his tenure and seized the opportunity of his becoming Japanese to reduce his compensation from that for an expatriate to the lower amount paid to Japanese professors. The university had calculated that he would leave rather than temper his lifestyle. This was a rejection, and the heartbreak of it by the society he had so embraced may have extended to his fatal heart attack.

I couldn't imagine that end for James Abegglen, an author and business consultant who became a Japanese national in the 1990s. He told an interviewer in 2001 that it was harder to renounce his US citizenship than acquire Japanese nationality. He had to engage accountants and lawyers to complete the US paperwork. He said he should have become a Japanese earlier than he did. Japan had been very good to him, personally and professionally, he said. Later Abegglen told me that obtaining Japanese nationality, while requiring a "longish, bureaucratic time span, was quite simple with no intrusive interviews or other unpleasantness."

As a US marine in the Pacific War, he was wounded on Guam and Iwo Jima. After the war, he transferred to Tokyo to work with the US Strategic Bombing Survey, which was tasked with quantifying Japan's destruction. He returned to the US to earn a Ph.D. in anthropology and clinical psychology from the University of Chicago. He has since taught, consulted and lived in Japan on and off for 30 or so years.

As a footnote, some Japanese believe that applicants for naturalization are required to submit records of their tax payments. They say that that prevents many resident Koreans from obtaining Japanese nationality, as they work mainly in cash businesses such as night trades or pachinko parlors and don't pay taxes. I was glad to have visited the Justice Ministry's Yokohama branch. I learned that such talk didn't contain even half-truths. There was no requirement to submit tax records, and Koreans do become Japanese — they become Japanese every day of the year.

COUNTING

We find within a Buddhist temple in Yokohama a memorial plaque for the man who authorized the attack on Pearl Harbor. Then we try to count the dead.

CHAPTER 35. THE UNCOUNTABLE DEAD

> Japan's emergence as a modern nation was stunning to behold: swifter, more audacious, more successful, and ultimately more crazed, murderous, and self-destructive, than anyone had imagined possible. — John W. Dower, in *Embracing Defeat*

> There is no more amazing or portentous phenomenon in modern history than the way in which sleeping Japan, roughly awakened by the cannon of the West, leaped to the lesson, bettered the instruction, accepted science, industry and war, defeated all her competitors either in battle or in trade, and became, within two generations, the most aggressive nation in the contemporary world. — Will Durant, in *Our Oriental Heritage*

> I have no desire for any man's death. This is the very word of the Lord God. — Ezekiel 18.32

In the early hours of 23 December 1948 the freshly hanged bodies of seven Japanese "Class A" war criminals were carried by US army vans from Sugamo Prison to a crematorium in Yokohama. I looked up at the gate of this crematorium, Kuboyama Kasōba, which stands now on the site it did then, on a morning in May.

One of the corpses belonged to Hideki Tōjō who, as general, war minister, and prime minister, prosecuted much of Japan's war in China, Southeast Asia and the Pacific. He authorized the attack on Pearl Harbor. By failing to anticipate the results of that attack, he showed he was as removed from the world as a Tokugawa shogun.

For some reason Tōjō changed his first name from Eiku to Hideki after becoming prime minister in 1941. Identities exchanged in death as in life, Tōjō was, some said, the "Hitler of Asia." The comparison doesn't stand in terms of numbers of dead at one person's hand but to some people the symbolic value is probably of equal measure.

People who today can't recognize Japan's emperor or prime minister probably can recognize Tōjō, who seems perennially to occupy TV screens as the symbol of choice to illustrate Japanese militarism in documentaries about the Pacific War. It's as though some innate need possesses us to acknowledge his presence.

Did Tōjō also personify Dr. Fu-Manchu? Sax Rohmer launched his "sinister chinaman" as a fictional character in 1918, the year before Tōjō was posted to Berlin as a military attaché. In the ensuing years, Europeans came to recognize both — the flat, bespectacled, mustachioed faces weren't the same but they weren't that different — as symbols of the Yellow Peril.

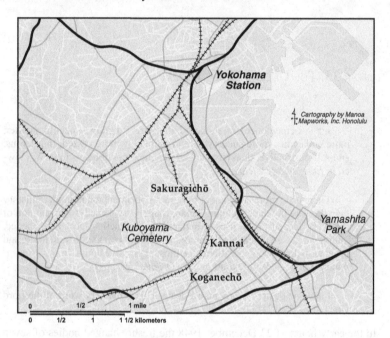

Key locations in the city of Yokohama.

The insidious doctor was bent on world conquest; Tōjō tried to conquer a large part of the world or oust Europeans from it. Both had to be stopped. That one was Chinese and the other Japanese couldn't be expected to dilute the European association of the images, which seemed to lodge deep in the subconscious.

So I was intrigued to read in John Carroll's *Trails of Two Cities* that Tōjō's ashes rested in Kuboyama Cemetery, on a hilltop near the crematorium where I stood. Could this be true? Didn't the Americans destroy the ashes out of fear that if Japanese got hold of them they would enshrine them and martyr this symbol of militarism?

I can't explain the compulsion I felt to clarify the matter of where Tōjō's journey had ended. He had tried to end it by shooting himself, and a certain obscenity attaches to the photograph of American military medical staff making him well enough to be hanged. Could crematorium workers have succeeded in cheating their American rulers where Tōjō had failed?

After my walk I took a train to Yokohama to try to answer this question. The effort didn't seem misplaced. Port cities terminate journeys. In a way, I'd already begun to trace Tōjō's, as my route into Tokyo had taken me within a slingshot of the site of the prison that had housed and hanged those judged guilty of war crimes at the International Military Tribunal for the Far East, also called Tokyo Trial.

I took a bus from the north exit of Kannai Station to the Kuboyama Reidōmae stop rather than walk the kilometer or so from Koganechō Station to the cemetery. It was a ride of about ten minutes across the inland ward of Nishi where people dress as laborers or carelessly, not in the smart casual which is uniform on the south or portside of cosmopolitan Yokohama.

A segment of the Keihin Kyūkō Line snakes in parallel with the Ōoka River, which the bus crosses before climbing the steep hill after which the cemetery is named. The river is more canal, sides concreted and the green black water still. Trades of the night couch in ramshackle pockets near the railway tracks.

Kuboyama Cemetery. April, 2007. Photo by the author.

Strip-carved into the hillside like terraces for the dead, and forming part of the skyline like a gate, the cemetery is eerie enough. Visitors were watering and weeding and sweeping around tombstones as though possessed to visit the neatness of their life upon the dead. A woman was pouring water into stainless-steel vases at the base of a tombstone. Then she poured water over the stone. My eyes caught the glistening blue of her bucket. Engravers chiseled new stones.

The memorial to Hideki Tōjō at Kōmyōji Temple. April, 2007. Photo by the author.

It could take days to find a particular tombstone among the 30,000 or so said to be here. The help I needed I found at a coffee shop near the entrance. Several such establishments beckoned passersby on the hilly road. They must do a brisk trade, serving refreshments on hot days to those who tire after trekking up and down the cemetery's goat hill-like trails.

The shop proprietor told me that Tōjō's tombstone wasn't in the cemetery, but Carroll was close and I'm grateful that his book guided me here. The proprietor summoned a younger man who explained that a memorial plaque for Tōjō had been erected inside Kōmyōji Temple, one of seven Buddhist temples on the Kuboyama-zaka or south side of the cemetery.

Crematorium staff did salvage some of Tōjō's ashes, the man said he had heard priests say. These ashes at first had been kept in an urn at nearby Kōzenji Temple, then moved to Kōmyōji. The Kōzenji head priest would be able to elaborate, the man said. But this priest was away when we visited, so we made our way to Kōmyōji, where the man left me at the gate, saying he would guide me through Kuboyama Cemetery later in the afternoon.

I entered the precinct of Kōmyōji disbelieving that a temple would have fostered some resurrection of the most symbolic of convicted war criminals by allowing a memorial plaque within its grounds. But that's what this temple has done. Inside, to the left of the gate, is a plaque standing about two meters tall. On its reverse side are engraved the names and rank of the 60 "loyal followers" of Tōjō who were hanged at Sugamo Prison.

Why wouldn't a temple memorialize Tōjō? After Japan regained its independence under the San Francisco Peace Treaty of 1952, it legislated so that the families of the war criminal dead would receive the same benefits as the war dead. Tōjō and other "war criminals" had been prisoners of the Allies at a time when Japan wasn't at peace: they had been prisoners of war.

A Kōmyōji office employee approached, exchanged pleasantries, then brought me some photocopied sheets of a history brief about the memorial. The brief was written by the "Japan Association," a catch-all name suggestive of a right-wing political lobby. Or a nondescript umbrella under which the memorial's sponsors can conceal their identities but the brief at least names an association director as author.

The brief states that an unveiling ceremony for Tōjō's memorial was held in October 1968. Family members visited for a time after the unveiling, but none was seen to visit now, the Kōmyōji employee said.

Like other histories that address the subject of the Tokyo Trial and execution of Japanese war criminals, the brief is a confused document. It includes Tōjō's name among his "loyal followers." It states that the 60 were judged war criminals and sentenced to death at the Tokyo Trial. They weren't, not at that particular trial, but the number is about right.

The Tokyo Trial passed judgment on only 25 of the original 28 Class A war criminals (two had died during the trial and another was declared mentally unfit). "Class A" refers to the political and military leaders who planned and prosecuted the war, and their cases were heard at the Tokyo Trial between May 1946 and November 1948.

A much larger number of Japanese "Class B" and "Class C" defendants were convicted of war crimes in tribunals held in and outside Japan, before and after the Tokyo Trial. These tribunals were poorly documented. ("Class B" was first applied to those who had broken the rules of war while fighting; "Class C" to those who failed to stop such transgressions but later the distinction became blurred and the two categories were combined as "B/C".)

Though individual Allied powers tried and executed "B/C" war criminals outside Japan, within Japan the several tribunals and the Tokyo Trial were managed by the United States.

From April 1946 to April 1950, the US hanged 63 prisoners at Sugamo Prison, according to Bill Barrette's detailed paper for the Japan Policy Research Institute, which backgrounds his collection of the art and other objects made by Sugamo inmates. This implies that 56 of the 63 were "B/C" criminals as the total includes the seven hanged "Class A" criminals.

Barrette cites as his source a privately printed compilation of documents from Sugamo retained by a Lt. Col. Lee Vincent when the prison was turned over to Japanese control in May 1952. The collection is called *Sugamo Prison Tokyo Japan, APO 500* (eds. Charles F. Smedley, Tommy M. Hight, and Charles W. Patterson).

I was fortunate that Barrette had gone to such lengths in his research, because I couldn't comprehend this subject without his and Dower's thoroughness.

Barrette notes that US military tribunals in Manila, Shanghai, and Guam resulted in 85 executions of Japanese military personnel. Adding the Sugamo 63 produces a total of 148, made up of the 141 "B/C" and the seven "Class A" war criminals. The figure of 141 compares with Dower's 140, which is remarkably close given the imprecise nature of counting these dead.

During the longer period from 1945 to 1951, Dower's research shows, the Allies executed around 920 Japanese "B/C" class criminals out of an indicted total of around 5,700.

These 920 B/C defendants were tried at "minor" tribunals throughout Asia. The Netherlands held 12 such tribunals (and upheld the most death sentences at 236); Britain held 11 (223 death sentences); China, 10 (149); Australia, 9 (153); the US, 5 (140); France, 1 (26); Philippines, 1 (17). The total of 944 upheld death sentences implies that some of the condemned died awaiting execution.

Japan — An Illustrated Encyclopedia describes the record of the many tribunals as "fragmentary and scattered." Dower notes that sentences of capital punishment were sometimes reviewed and altered and precise records were not always maintained or made available.

Kōmyōji Temple's brief quotes *Seiki no Isho* — "Testaments of the Century," as recording that the Allies executed 1,068 Japanese war criminals in and outside Japan. This total implies that 1,005 (1,068 less the Sugamo 63) were executed outside Japan, compared with Dower's (and Kōdansha's) 920. It's possible, I think, that this variance of 10 percent — not bad in a ballpark business — dead or alive may be explained by the summary score settling, by former prisoner against former guard, which was understood to have occurred at the instant power changed hands.

Seiki no Isho records the last letters, poems, and words of some 692 executed war criminals and was intended to restore their honor as individuals. It appears to have done that. Surviving war criminals were pampered, released, rehabilitated. Some, with the tacit support of the US, resumed powerful positions in business and government as the US reasoned that it needed them in a new Japan that would serve as a bulwark against communizing China and, in a changed world polarized by the Cold War, the Soviet Union.

Rohmer, too, had softened his theme. He had begun to present Asians in a more positive light, and Dr. Fu-Manchu himself — the once "yellow peril incarnate" — had joined Western forces to fight the Chinese communists. Life was imitating farce.

History guesses at much that occurred at the Tokyo Trial, unlike the case of the fully documented Nuremberg trial of Nazi war criminals, which served as a model for the Tokyo effort. No Allied government ever obtained a definitive set of the trial proceedings, according to Dower. "For all practical purposes," Dower wrote, "the record of the trial was buried."

A friend found a Japanese history book on the subject, which was published in 2002. I haven't named this book because I haven't read it, but a summary of its account of the trial showed that most of its facts are wrong. Other friends I quizzed knew little.

At least reporters and members of the public could attend the Tokyo Trial sessions, and though the records are fragmentary at least there are fragments. There was no public witness to the separate military tribunals that convicted and hanged the many more B/C war criminals. Too, the trial was designed to fix in our collective memories, not through documentation but through the selection of figurehead defendants and an elaborately staged performance — some compared the exceptionally bright courtroom lighting to that of a Hollywood movie set.

Barrette said he had "only the vaguest notion" of the postwar period in Japan, and his first response was, "How is it that I do not know anything about these trials?" His father, too old to serve in the war, had no stories to tell. But in rural Rhode Island, early memories were framed by references to the personalities of the war — MacArthur Boulevard, Doolittle Street, and Marshall Circle bordered a housing development called Truman Heights.

Barrette probably spoke for a postwar generation and their children when he wrote: "The significance of the war in the Pacific as a triumphant and defining moment in American history was inscribed in the landscape and seemed to silently validate the heroism of those who had participated. But, in what I can only attribute as a failure of our educational system, I learned little of substance about the complex and closely entwined relations of the US and Japan before, during, or after the war."

The fountain of bloodlust which possessed the US and its allies in their postwar dealing with those Japanese they judged as war criminals was filled by accounts of maltreatment of prisoners. That this would be a focus of the war crimes tribunals was made clear in the July 1945 Potsdam Declaration, which warned that "stern justice would be meted out to all war criminals, including those who have visited cruelties upon our prisoners." Roughly three-quarters of the B/C defendants were accused of crimes against prisoners, Dower's research shows.

Like the dead, prisoners weren't counted equitably. An enduring statistic to emerge from the Tokyo Trial was that 4 percent of American and British servicemen taken prisoner by Germany and Italy died in captivity compared with a 27 percent death rate for American and British Commonwealth prisoners of Japan. Excluded from this calculation are greater numbers of Asian prisoners who died in Japanese POW camps, of Soviet prisoners who died in German hands, and of Japanese prisoners who died while held in China and Russia after the war. Jewish victims of the Holocaust are counted separately.

Later I wondered how special the Tōjō memorial at Kōmyōji is. Albert Axelbank noted in *Black Star Over Japan — Rising Forces of Militarism* the unveiling of a like memorial near Mt. Fuji, also in the 1960s. A search may reveal more.

A Japanese friend said she believed that the emperor could have stopped the war. She said that it was no accident that, in old age, he bled to death.

———

Tombstones teach nothing of time's march and I hesitate to tread among them. But the offer of a private tour was too generous to pass up, especially in Kuboyama Cemetery, which isn't a tourist marker such as the foreigners' cemetery near Bluff on the fashionable port side.

Inside, my gaze fixed upon rows of unnamed, unadorned, knee-high tombstones which carried no inscription except for a number — 1, 2, 3 and up to 60. The numbers identified prisoners who had lost in their crimes the right to an identity beyond death. I wondered whether they had died nameless in prison or had been executed.

The corpses of the hanged in Japan are returned to family — if they care to claim them and foot the cost of transport — and families wouldn't assign a number to a tombstone. Perhaps their family was unknown, or the numbering was part of the punishment in their desolate end. More dignity attaches to unhewn stone than a numbered mortuary tablet.

We walked to the tombstone of Shigeru Yoshida, the long-serving postwar prime minister who is credited with overseeing Japan's reconstruction from ruins. It's set in a plot all of six meters wide and ten meters long, several times the area of neighboring plots. Six stone lanterns stand inside as if on guard duty, and the plot contains a number of smaller tombstones of family members. Flowers were set at the base of one of the tombstones, a cup of sake at the base of another.

The guide stamped out a cigarette inside the plot.

Yoshida was said to be adept at getting things done by bringing to the same table powerful factions from within business, the bureaucracy and political parties. The larger truth, I think, is that his efforts were guided by the US at each step, and in return he consented to align Japan economically and militarily with its former foe.

When Japanese today think of Yoshida's legacy, they think mostly of the security treaty he signed with the US, which allows the operation of US air, army, and naval bases throughout Japan. These bases today appear as traditional as a temple and, except those on the southerly island of Okinawa, are seldom the target of any sustained protest or even discussion.

Yoshida wrote a book called *Sekai to Nihon* — "Japan and the World."

Between tombstones the guide lowered his voice to confide that in the Edo era a red-light district occupied the current site of Yokohama Stadium, near Kannai Station. We paused alongside a memorial to victims of the 1923 earthquake, which borders a playground on the edge of the cemetery. A cloud of insects hovered before our eyes, blackening the view.

Later I returned to the house of a friend and that evening learned from a TV program about four Japanese women self-defense force personnel stationed in East Timor as part of a peacekeeping operation. One said that she wanted to work overseas, and look at Japan from the outside. She was a radio operator.

In some histories, fact selection, accent and emphasis are culturally calibrated to produce accounts that conform to one generation's view of what is correct in the world.

England, France, Germany, the Netherlands, Russia, and the US each occupied parts of Asia in the 19th and 20th centuries, and Europeans believed that a Eurocentric world was correct and in their missionary zeal declared it a part of their cause. It's better understood now that the objective was commercial interest and expansion, and that religion was the greatcoat over the uniform. A lot of things are about money.

As a student this history brushed me only lightly amid English and Dutch brooding over "What the Japanese did to us." Later I began to study it in detail by reading as broadly as I could. It's more a fascination with the present than the past, as silting the base of feeling toward Japan today so often is the war that was fought more than 60 years ago.

Some people think that our collective pasts belong to the dead and are documented well enough. Others feel we should rethink our forebears' work, not merely out of regard for it as the journalism which is history's first draft, but in a larger, sustained effort to "correct and recreate the historical memory," as Dower wrote in *War Without Mercy*. Without doing so, we can never, in Dower's words, "hope to understand the nature of World War II in Asia, or international and interracial conflict in general."

Some recent works, balanced by the benefit of hindsight and rigorous scholarship, curiously are more passionate in their expression than earlier histories that fail to transcend the atmosphere and bias of their time. It's hard to imagine a more thoughtful and balanced account of Japan's immediate postwar years than Dower's *Embracing Defeat*. This book's triumph is that victor and vanquished consider it fair.

Rob Havers' *Reassessing the Japanese Prisoner of War Experience — The Chiangi POW Camp, Singapore, 1942–5*, documents a more civilized than brutal existence for prisoners at Japan's POW camp in Singapore, though Havers doesn't deny the brutality of Japanese soldiers toward POWs at other camps or on the Burma-Thailand railway.

Henry Frei's *Guns of February* recounts Japanese soldiers' view of their Malayan campaign and the fall of Singapore. He shows how the success of the campaign was subverted by the murderous end meted out to Singaporean Chinese civilians by Japanese troops. He traced the killing orders mostly to a Japanese army officer, Col. Masanobu Tsuji, whose designation as a wanted war criminal the US lifted in 1950.

I visited Henry at his home in Tsukuba, Ibaraki Prefecture, when he was writing *Guns of February*, which was published posthumously. We'd studied at the same language school in Tokyo. He had forfeited his early career in business to become a scholar. He said he wanted to write history in the way that Stephen King wrote fiction. I don't know if he had read much King but I knew he so wanted his writing to be read.

Some works of the time and earlier show objectivity and a remarkable pre-science. They also suggest that whatever the Pacific War was, it was no surprise. Will Durant, writing in 1934:

> Must America fight Japan?...By the sardonic irony of history that same Japan which America awoke from peaceful agriculture in 1853, and prodded into industry and trade, now turns all her power and subtlety to winning by underselling, and to controlling by conquest of diplomacy, pre-cisely those Asiatic markets upon which America has fixed her hopes as potentially the richest outlet for her surplus goods. Usually in history, when two nations have contested for the same markets, the nation that has lost in the economic competition, if it is strongest in resources and armament, has made war upon its enemy.

There are killings and in the political vocabulary of the last century there are mass killings. The scale of these defies tallying or tabulation.

So complex is the subject that it's now tackled by academics as a social or political science, replete with rigorous categorizations and definitions. Benjamin Valentino, in *Final Solutions*, for example, puts the mass killings of the 20th century into categories such as communist, counter-guerrilla, ethnic, territorial, terrorist, and imperialist. He defines a "mass" killing as one that claims more than 50,000 lives.

Between 60 million and 150 million people perished because of such killings, Valentino calculates, compared with the approximately 34 million battle deaths in international and civil wars in the same, bloodiest of all centuries in human history.

Valentino states that mass killings in history's most murderous states of the Soviet Union, China, and Cambodia caused between 21 million and 70 million deaths. It seems surreal to note that 50 million people may or may not have died, but precision seems beyond any science that deals with the dead. (R.J. Rummel in *Death by Government* puts total communist killings as high as 110 million.)

Valentino's "terrorist" category includes attacks on civilians in wartime. He thus cites as an example British and US bombing of cities in Europe during World War II which he estimates killed from 300,000 to 600,000 people.

Japan's occupation of East Asia (especially China) in 1937-45, in which from 3 million to 10.6 million were killed, is cited as an imperialist example — seven million people may or may not have died. Nazi territorial expansion in Eastern Europe in 1939–45 is estimated to have killed from 10 million to 15 million.

The genocide of Tutsi in Rwanda in 1994, which killed from 500,000 to 800,000, is given as an example of ethnic mass-killing, and Indonesia's sup-pression of East Timorese secession in 1975–99, which caused from 100,000 to 200,000 deaths, is cited as an example of counter-guerrilla mass killing.

I thought, those most able to count the dead probably are most culpable in the killings. Counting won't be on their mind.

Across all categories, Valentino gives 38 examples, and adds another six as "possible cases." So, on average, a mass killing occurred at least once every two and a half years in the last century, and that isn't counting cases in which fewer than 50,000 people were killed. The frequency alone suggests that such killings aren't the result of errant armies occasionally running amok but are part of deliberate and reasoned policy.

Valentino leads us to this conclusion. He finds that the primary cause of mass killings often isn't, as we'd suspect, ethnic hatred or dysfunctional society. Rather, it originates as policy from small groups of powerful leaders as a political or military strategy designed to counter threats to their power and advance their ambitions.

———

Did Tokyo direct the rape of Nanjing as a deliberate, terrorist softening exercise in order to weaken Chinese resistance to Japan's occupation, or was it ordered by vengeful field officers and soldiers operating under a loose mandate?

A journalist I worked with in Tokyo researched the background of soldiers who fought in China. He found that many were farmers' sons and that a large number had come from Ibaraki Prefecture, an hour or so north of Tokyo by train. He can't say why this particular region should have supplied more brutality than any other. We who had lived in Japan didn't want to believe that the country could have committed atrocities such as Nanjing.

There's some logic to blaming farmers' sons. Japan conscripted farmers' second sons first. As second-born, these soldiers had already been dispossessed of their family's land. Perhaps this rule of inheritance made it easier for them to dispossess others. Some pin blame on those Koreans and Formosans who as Japanese colonial subjects were conscripted into the army and tasked with guarding defeated foreigners — the lowest position. Their own national and with it personal identity first denied then lost, perhaps it came easy to them to look upon their captives as non-persons. People can do terrible things to an object.

We were, I felt, stumbling upon parts of a larger truth, but couldn't escape our conditioned belief that Japan operates more collectively than individually. As we studied and worked in Japan we were dismayed by the lack of overt individuality. We witnessed all manner of group behavior and were dismissive of Japanese who seemed incapable of thinking or acting for themselves. Seeing them helped us understand how deeply ingrained was our individualism, so stark was the contrast.

Yet when confronted by accounts of atrocities suddenly we became consumed by a desperation to identify culpable individuals and claim that they had acted on their own initiative. I don't think we were wrong to do that. Individuals, not groups, issue orders. In Japan, the skill of the successful leader lies in the invisibility of the leadership. Decisions appear to result from group thinking and consensus, but of course they don't. They are the product of an individual mind and determination, as they are anywhere else. Leaders don't wish to be seen to lead because of the inborn dread of the consequences of responsibility.

———

Because torture or beheadings or forced suicides in the bloody Tokugawa period — Japan may have been at peace with the world but it wasn't at peace with itself — were so common a punishment for those who made even small mistakes, or for those who were obliged to assume responsibility for the mistakes of others, the word *sekinin* — "responsibility," stalls or freezes all who hear it. It transmits a tension and a terror. It also instantly dissolves the courtesy or convenience of ambiguity in social relations. It's the heaviest of words. The language reflects that weight in phrases such as *sekinin mondai* — "the problem of responsibility" and *sekinin tenka* — "the transfer of responsibility." The ideograph for the first part of the word [seki or se(meru)] is used in the words censure, condemn, persecute, and torture.

A CLASSICAL CONCEIT

We now imagine the destination to which Krzysztof Penderecki's composition "Threnody for victims of Hiroshima for 52 stringed instruments" transports us, and consider the virtue of popular music over the conceit of "classical" sound.

CHAPTER 36. WAR AND MUSIC

Krzysztof Penderecki's composition "Threnody for victims of Hiroshima for 52 stringed instruments" unsettled me. Mieczyslaw Tomaszewski wrote in the liner notes to the Naxos CD *Penderecki Orchestral Works Vol. 1* that the music "ushers in an orgy of hissing, 'noise' and rasps, played in all possible ways." The notes add that the composer once reminisced that he had named the work, which he wrote in 1960, numerically as "8'37."

Penderecki is quoted as having said: "But it existed only in my imagination, in a somewhat abstract way." After listening to a recording of the composition, he said he was struck by the "emotional charge" of the work. He thought it would be a "waste to condemn it to such anonymity, to those 'digits.' I searched for associations and, in the end, I decided to dedicate it to the Hiroshima victims."

I felt uncomfortable that Penderecki had rifled recent history for a peg upon which to hang his composition. Hiroshima's victims hadn't inspired the music. I imagine, too, that after the bomb detonated the city was silent. Perhaps composers who have music inside themselves don't need inspiration. They compose involuntarily, and it's to satisfy us that they label their work. Then again, perhaps we should be grateful for any artistic commitment to memorialize such a tragedy.

When I first listened to Penderecki's piece, I thought I heard his strings play a tritone interval to create the sound of an ambulance siren. They do, but on the composition immediately following, "Fluorescences for orchestra." It still makes one think, what use an ambulance? What treatment would medics in an ambulance administer? Where would the ambulance go?

In his essay "On Medicine and the Bomb," Lewis Thomas, a medical doctor, writes that "no medical technology can cope with the certain outcome of just one small, neat, so-called tactical bomb exploded over a battlefield." Thomas was responding to a US presidential directive of 1980 that attempted to justify the "tactical" use of a nuclear bomb in a "prolonged, limited" nuclear war.

He asked: "As for the problem raised by a single large bomb, say a twenty-megaton missile (equivalent to approximately two thousand Hiroshimas) dropped on New York City or Moscow, with the dead and dying in the millions, what would medical technology be good for? As the saying goes, forget it. Think of something else. Get a computer running somewhere in a cave, to estimate the likely numbers of the lucky dead."

Thomas's essay is one of two that address questions posed by nuclear bombs and are contained in his book *Late Night Thoughts on Listening to Mahler's Ninth Symphony*. In the other essay, "The Unforgettable Fire," Thomas notes that any one of today's nuclear bombs would produce at least one thousand times the lethal blast, heat, and radiation that resulted from the Hiroshima or Nagasaki bombs, which were "primitive precursors of what we have at hand today." This essay takes its title from the book *The Unforgettable Fire: Pictures Drawn by Atom Bomb Survivors*.

Wars invade music. The Vietnam War is said to have inspired George Crumb's composition *Black Angels*. This work "draws from an arsenal of sounds including shouting, chanting, whistling, whispering, gongs, maracas, and crystal glasses," explain the liner notes to the Elektra Nonesuch CD *Black Angels*, performed by Kronos Quartet. The composer is quoted as having said that the music was conceived as "a kind of parable on our troubled contemporary world."

It isn't music in the Japanese sense of *ongaku*, whose two ideographs mean "sound" and "enjoy." Much of last century's Western music can't have been composed with the enjoyment of listeners in mind. It's morbid and jarring. It's also esoteric — composed for the private consumption of knowing people in the way that one academic writes for the benefit or scrutiny of another. Nobody should be upset if the CDs don't sell.

This music sends listeners to caves of private agony. Its redeeming feature is that it spurred by negative example an appreciation of cheerful, energetic, intelligent popular music that entertained. The Beatles and other popular music groups that struck such a chord among people of different ages and interests in the latter half of the last century seemed able to do so because they filled a void drained of life by so-called "serious" composers.

Some say that "classical" music is "serious," which infers that pop music is frivolous. Others appear uncertain what "pop music" means. *Gramophone* magazine has argued editorially that "popular" and "pop" music aren't the same. I wrote to the magazine's editor to ask him to explain the difference. No reply. No surprise.

Duke Ellington — our honorary citizen of Niigata — distilled the essence. There are, he said, only two types of music — good and bad.

It may be that some composers, like some writers, first compose to satisfy themselves, not wishing to sell or become popular.

"The majority of my symphonies are tombstones," Russian composer Dmitri Shostakovich is recorded as having said, in his biography by Solomon Volkov, as quoted in the liner notes to *Black Angels*.

"I feel eternal pain for those who were killed by Hitler, but I feel no less pain for those killed on Stalin's orders...Too many of our people died and were buried in places unknown to anyone...Where do you put the tombstones? Only music can do that for them. I am willing to write a composition for each of the victims but that is impossible, and that is why I dedicate my music to them all."

KILLING FIELD

New Zealand guards shot and killed 48 Japanese prisoners of war in February 1943. We visit the park that memorializes some of them, then consider the prisoners of imagery.

CHAPTER 37. FEATHERSTON

Featherston is a world's-end town about an hour's drive northeast of Wellington. New Zealand guards shot and killed 48 Japanese prisoners of war at an army camp there in February 1943. They wounded a further 74. It's a history New Zealand doesn't teach and can't bring itself to confront.

One guard machine-gunned some of the prisoners in the back while other guards shot them with rifles from the front. This followed an agitated reaction among assembled prisoners to the wounding of their leader by a warning shot fired by the camp adjutant. This first shot was the culmination of tension that had built up over prisoners' refusal to work.

At dusk on a winter's evening I drove into Featherston. I wanted to read the memorial plaques at a park on the site of the former army camp where the killings occurred. It's a blink-and-you'll-miss-it park and I did. A fish-and-chip shop gave me wrong directions. Someone else said drive west. The park was north. It isn't a landmark for townspeople.

I called Mike Nicolaidi, who wrote *The Featherston Chronicles*, to ask for directions, and found the park by retracing my route for a couple of minutes. Mike had insisted that I visit the memorial before interviewing him, which I was to do the following day.

In the day's last light I found the park and copied plaque inscriptions. To the right of the park gate, a sign reads, "This site is a memorial to the Featherston W.W. I camp and the soldiers who passed through it. It also emphasizes Featherston's 'Twinning' with Messines in Belgium, and recalls the W.W. II Japanese prisoner of war camp."

Words and their order give people away. The site "recalls" the Japanese POW camp, more important than which is a Belgian sister-city relationship. Like the gate sign, plaques inside appear uncomfortably constructed and positioned. They are sited in unobvious spots and I became disoriented trying to locate them all.

One plaque carries a haiku by Bashō: "Behold the summer grass / All that remains / Of the dreams of warriors."

Another memorializes the only New Zealander to die in the shooting: "Private Walter Pelvin / No. 496685 HD / N.Z.T.S. / Died 28.2.1943 / As a result of injuries received on duty during the disturbance at the POW camp, Featherston on 25 February 1943.

Lines from a Robert Frost poem were inscribed on another: "For I have promises to keep / And miles to go before I sleep."

Another reads: "Repose of Souls, Japanese POW WW II."

Only one of the plaques appears official. It was donated by the Japanese Embassy in Wellington. It's part of a three-seat park bench. To the bench back is fixed a slab of concrete, into which is inlaid a brass plaque, which baldly reads, "In memory of 58 servicemen who died here in W.W. 2." It's hard to imagine sitting on the bench to relax, your back resting against the inscription.

After sifting through Wellington crematorium records, and delving deep into army and government archives, Nicolaidi learned that 67 Japanese POWs — 48 in the shooting; 19 from other causes — had died in New Zealand during the war years, nine more than Japan's official count. The New Zealand army had been casual in its counting, too, with one memo putting the number of sets of ashes of Japanese dead at 76.

Other plaques tell the history of the camp. It opened in January 1916 as a training ground for the 30,000 New Zealanders sent to fight in World War I. Soldiers camped here in "canvas town" before being "hardened up" in a march across the Rimutaka Range to Wellington where they boarded troop ships for Europe.

The memorial park is makeshift, the well-meaning but incomplete work of individuals. It hasn't been addressed as a national task. The New Zealand government, which views itself as a non-nuclear peacemaker, can't make this peace with Japan. Rather, it has devolved responsibility for the memorial to the local council, with predictable result in a small, rural town. The memorial contains, for example, no list of those who died here.

The park might have memorialized only New Zealand soldiers and no Japanese POWs, were it not for the efforts of a former Featherston mayor and returned serviceman, Bill McKerrow, who welcomed Japanese to the region and worked to ensure that the Japanese dead were not forgotten. "I was very dedicated to helping heal a wound," McKerrow has said. The say-nothing-in-particular obliqueness of the park's main sign seems to bear witness to the local sentiment that McKerrow must have faced.

It doesn't seem useful to apportion blame for the Featherston incident. Nicolaidi quotes a former New Zealand army intelligence officer and interpreter, Eric Thompson, as saying, "You could either blame both sides or no side." Thompson spent much of his later life trying to understand what had happened. He talked at length with survivors from both sides and helped organize a ceremony for the consolation of the spirits at the site in 1986.

Both sides broke Geneva Convention rules, which govern the treatment of war prisoners — some of the Japanese by refusing to work; the New Zealanders by failing to post the rules at the camp in the language of the prisoners. Japan had signed but not ratified the 1929 convention. It hadn't expected large numbers of its military to be taken prisoner — their training had psychologically conditioned them for death not captivity — and realized that the rules would have obligated it to treat POWs better than it treated its own soldiers.

It took 11 months from the time of the killings for the Featherston camp to obtain even an English-language version of the Geneva Conventions, which POWs were asked to translate by themselves, Nicolaidi learned.

Prisoners — roughly 200 out of the 800 or so there — grew vegetables and made furniture and concrete, under the direction of James Fletcher, minister of defense construction. The army had argued that New Zealand should try to effect the transfer of the prisoners to Australia, because the camp was "uneconomic." Fletcher argued to the contrary. He planned more factories for the camp, which had been expanded to take up to 2,000 POWs, but none in any large number were sent after the incident.

Fletcher, the patriarch of Fletcher Construction, which has grown to become one of New Zealand's biggest and bluest chip companies, appeared to view the prisoners as a profit source. He "conservatively estimated" that the prisoners' annual production could amount to £100,000 (or roughly NZ$7.1 million in 2006 value).

New Zealand had never accommodated POWs, had not planned to receive any, and had no army personnel trained for that task. Camp guards later were deemed unsuitable due to "lack of training, youth, or physical or mental deficiencies."

Between August 1942 and March 1945, the US brought a total 869 Japanese POWs to New Zealand and 802 of them were repatriated in December 1945. US naval ships landed the POWs at only a few days' notice after rescuing them after naval battles around Guadalcanal. They included combat and non-combat units — the former planned suicide and wouldn't work; the latter wanted to live and were cooperative.

Fate seemed always one step ahead. By the time Wellington asked the US whether it was expected to receive Japanese POWs, 24 were already in the country. By the time several hundred were at Featherston and nearly two years after the first had arrived, New Zealand asked Britain for advice on who was legally responsible for them.

One nation's "incident" is another's "atrocity" and the Featherston disturbance or incident or atrocity — massacre? — provides a lesson in the politics of language. Which word best describes an incident in which guards kill or wound more than half of 240 assembled, unarmed POWs?

Which word would we have used if our nationals had met the same fate in a Japanese POW camp? The question is rhetorical; the answer, obvious.

The war diary of the camp used the words "fracas" and "affray" to describe the POWs' agitation. Then, the prime minister used the word "riot" in his first statement on the matter. Then, a court of inquiry used the word "mutiny." Officials needed to show convincingly that the killings were justifiable self-defense.

New Zealand, which then was a British dominion, deferred to the British government for advice at each stage of the aftermath of the incident. Whitehall officials rewrote much of the court's report. They elevated the word "riot" to "mutiny" out of concern that Japan would retaliate against Allied prisoners if it learned the facts of the shooting.

Though in Tokyo as a journalist I mixed in a circle of people who worked in government and business relations between the two countries, none in this orbit ever mentioned Featherston. It was as though both governments had colluded in their submission to historical amnesia, and their collusion was complete. It still seems that way.

Yet both countries' news media had made intermittent reference to the incident — *Bungei Shunjū* magazine in 1963, *Yomiuri Shimbun* newspaper in 1981; in New Zealand it had been the subject of a play, articles in a literary journal and magazine, radio interviews, and two TV documentaries. The interviews and documentaries were prompted by the occasional visits of survivors of Featherston to New Zealand, which began in 1974.

In the absence of government accounts in the form of documented and verifiable fact sheets, journalistic treatment raised more questions than it answered. *The Press* newspaper said the first prime ministerial announcement about the killings raised "anxious questions." If these were not answered, the newspaper cautioned, rumor would answer "in its own ugly and mischievous fashion."

It took 56 years for a detailed, authoritative account such as *The Featherston Chronicles*, itself a work in the making for seven years, to appear. The profession of history may have reasoned that, in academic or public domain, there would be little return for an effort of labor to record and interpret Featherston. The racial divide or guilt too deep, perhaps such a history can't be written dispassionately without the passage of 50 or more years.

Nicolaidi recalled that a Wellington newspaper editor was unsympathetic to his efforts to research the subject, which he viewed as one that should remain buried. The editor's name was familiar. Years before he had rejected every news and feature article I sent to him from Tokyo. Not only Featherston but all Japan appeared taboo to this discerner of public interest for readers in the capital city. The rejections were exceptional, though, as other editors began to encourage and accept some of my work.

There are footnotes to Featherston. In the way that one lie is told to camouflage another, the secrecy surrounding the killings bore more secrecy. The crash of a US army C-87 Liberator Express transport plane minutes after takeoff from Auckland's Whenuapai airport on 2 August 1943 is an example. Airport hospital and local crematorium staff were sworn to secrecy after they had performed their duties.

A TVNZ *Secret New Zealand* program in 2003 said that the plane was bound for Brisbane. Aboard were 22 Japanese civilians, including ten children, and three Thais. The Japanese were to be exchanged, in Australia, for Allied civilians in Japan. Twelve passengers, including three US crew, were killed. TVNZ posited that the crash, which had occurred on the heels of Featherston, was covered up out of fears that Japan may have retaliated against Allied prisoners if it believed that the cause was sabotage intended to kill Japanese.

The co-pilot survived. He told TVNZ that the crash cause was pilot error due to crew fatigue. Takeoff was at around 2.30 a.m. No one had turned the gyroscope on, he said, and in the dark of a rainy winter's night when the plane banked shortly after takeoff, crew thought it was level.

(The *Dictionary of New Zealand Biography*, in an account of the life of Edna Pearce, a policewoman who had been assigned to take charge of the Japanese women and children detainees, records that eight Japanese, three Thai nationals, and three crew members were killed in the crash, or a total of 14 dead. A Japanese woman had later died of injuries sustained in the crash. The Japanese women and children had been evacuated from Tonga, and were to be exchanged, according to the dictionary, for British and Allied prisoners.)

A year and a half after Featherston, Japanese POWs at an Australian camp at Cowra, New South Wales, staged a breakout. Guards fatally shot 231 escapees and wounded a further 108. Four Australians were killed. Some prisoners had stormed perimeter fences, overcome machine gun posts, and escaped into the countryside. All were caught and the effort was viewed as suicidal.

Some New Zealanders have borrowed the "breakout" part of the Cowra history and applied it to Featherston. The Engineers for Social Responsibility do so in their obituary for Thompson, who belonged to that group. It's as though the engineers, who campaign for peace, can't accept that the Featherston POWs passively resisted orders to work and that the killings were unprovoked.

Cowra has a Japanese War Cemetery and Japanese Garden. They weren't planned at the start. The kindness of Australians who weeded the Japanese graves at a general war cemetery there blossomed into a movement for the establishment of the special cemetery and garden. Those gardening Australians were returned servicemen. One told a researcher that the only opposition to efforts to tidy the Japanese graves had come from people who had never been to war.

Such graves or tombstones will never be possible at Featherston. By accident or mischief, army officers almost certainly "lost" the ashes of the cremated Japanese prisoners. The Geneva Conventions required burial in named and maintained graves. Nicolaidi suggests that the army couldn't bring itself to bury enemy bodies in home soil. It seems only remotely possible that the ashes were returned to Japan aboard the same boat as the surviving prisoners, as no such transport is documented by New Zealand or Switzerland, which represented Japan — and POWs from all fronts — at the time. (Individual files on the prisoners, too, are lost.)

The army in 1965 authorized the destruction of a key file relating to the whereabouts of the ashes, before it could be accessioned by national archives. The "absence of the information is not, I feel, important," wrote a government official. One army memo regarding the lost ashes parenthetically noted that his communication didn't concern cricket — a test match series between England and Australia is called "The Ashes."

Today one of the largest employers in the Wairarapa region, which encompasses Featherston, is a Japanese timber company. Unlike exporters of logs, Juken Nissho adds value by making veneer and plywood and other compound timber products.

———

Some New Zealanders are prisoners of the imagery of war. That isn't a matter for blame, as wars define our history — there have been, on one historian's count, 117 since World War II. But others cling to wartime epithets and slurs as a convenience and comfort and anti-Japanese sentiment lies shallow under still English skin.

Intentionally or unthinkingly, people still abbreviate Japan or Japanese as "Jap.," even in education and media. But then so does the *Concise Oxford Dictionary* (eighth edition, 1990) abbreviate Japanese as "Jap." then note under its definition for "Jap." that the abbreviation is often offensive, as though this is a permissible offence.

A reader wrote to New Zealand's *Listener* magazine in 2004: "Japanese treatment of whales reminds me of their treatment of POWs." Someone known to this reader may have been maltreated in a POW camp and the reader may have studied the issue of whaling. But perhaps neither is the case, given the one-liner, throwaway treatment of two serious subjects. It's likely that the reader doesn't like Japanese people, isn't sure why, but subconsciously recognizes that the POW peg is dated. Pegging prejudice on the whaling issue keeps it current. Some like to be topical in their hatreds.

I grew up in a small rural town among people who hated "the Japanese." Most people couldn't talk about Japan without mentioning World War II. Many still can't. Accounts of Japanese maltreatment of POWs percolated down to school playgrounds, and though the Vietnam War was underway, the enemies depicted in war comics were Japanese and Germans. But anti-Japanese and anti-German sentiment weren't the same.

It was inconceivable that anyone could watch a "Hogan's Heroes"-type TV comedy in which the villains were Japanese, and laugh. I asked an electrician who was working on my house about this. He made a distinction between fanatical Nazis and reasonable Germans. But in Japan's case, he said, we believed that Japanese were fanatics and that Japanese were cruel. I think he made the right connection. In our memory, Japan doesn't benefit from any separate, universally recognizable name for its cabal of wartime leaders, such as Nazi. They were Japanese.

Only about 5 percent of New Zealand's World War II casualties occurred in fighting against Japan, and 95 percent against Germany, according to an official New Zealand war history. Reverse the percentages and we have, I think, a measure of New Zealanders' prejudice toward the two countries. The difference can only be racial.

Probably fewer than 400 New Zealanders were prisoners of Japan, according to the official history. And the great majority of the 1,000 or so New Zealand-resident former POWs and civilian internees who lobbied for cash from Japan for their suffering in captivity were Dutch who were taken prisoner in the Netherlands East Indies, now Indonesia.

A poor postwar Japan had become transparently rich, and holes were being poked in the San Francisco Peace Treaty, which waived war damages claims against it. It was in the lobbyists' financial interest to broadcast the suffering they experienced in captivity. They also must have understood that admission of maltreatment or killing of Japanese in their or other Allied hands would have weakened their case for compensation.

———

A tourist rag says that a sea cave in the Poor Knights Islands is rumored to have harbored a Japanese submarine during World War II, as though boasting of an exotic attraction. Not long ago, such a rumor would have frozen people in fear. The naval coastal lookout points near my home were built out of fear that Japan would invade.

Such fears weren't unreasonable. Japan had attacked Darwin and Sydney and sent midget submarines into Sydney harbor. Britain was no longer a protector, its Singapore outpost lost. But well before militarists planned Japan's Pacific empire, some Japanese were looking southward with envy. J. W. Robertson Scott spoke with them during World War I years. They had emigrated mainly from densely populated Honshū, where it was difficult to improve one's lot as a farmer, to the northerly frontier of Hokkaidō. But land on Hokkaidō hadn't been parceled out fairly, so movement was still on their minds.

At a meeting of "some of the most influential people from the governor (of Hokkaidō) downwards," Scott wrote, one Japanese told him: "The perfect places for Japanese are California, New Zealand and Australia, but the Americans and Australasians won't have us. I do not complain. We do not allow Chinese labor in Japan. But we think we might have had Australia or New Zealand if we had not been secluded from the world by the Tokugawa regime, and so allowed you British to get there first."

SOME PEOPLE

We now make our way back to Niigata and the snow country, Tokyo and Yokohama, and call on some people we've come to know.

CHAPTER 38. THE WAY BACK

At Narita airport as a holder of a permanent residence permit I'm entitled to use the quick line for Japanese. But when I do almost certainly someone will tap my shoulder and point in the direction of the line for foreigners.

On occasion I've sacrificed an hour or more in the non-resident line rather than suffer this indignity of ignorant judgment.

Signs which read "Japanese" and "Foreigner" should read "Resident" and "Non-resident." But in the Edo era residents are only Japanese and the same assumption is made today.

On this arrival the predictable happened but I reserved my protest for the immigration officer.

"It happens every time," I complained. "Your signs are wrong."

"Did someone say something do you?" the officer asked. "Most people understand." Then it occurred to me that such judgment is suffered by ethnic minorities most days of their life, without the understanding of others around them. My circumstance was luxurious.

This would be a short visit to attend to some personal matters. And to go back. I took a bullet train to Niigata.

The *Niigata Nippō* reporter took me to a museum in Tsubame, across the Shinano and Nakanokuchi rivers from Sanjō. There we looked at cutlery. Tsubame once produced 70 percent of the world's knives and forks, an exhibit plaque said.

We can trace the rise and fall of great powers in their table settings. Russia had been a large customer for the finely crafted cutlery. Steak and fish and dessert knives and forks, dessertspoons, and other implements for every imaginable dish conjured an image of a banquet table set in Imperial Russia. After the Bolshevik Revolution new markets were found in the United States.

The reporter suggested we eat out. He chose a traditional restaurant — tatami-mat rooms; exquisitely presented dishes served at low tables by kneeling, no-mistake waitresses in kimono — and invited a young woman of train-stopping beauty to join us. The finest wine would fail to match the clarity of her skin. She radiated the early freshness of plum blossom and after each sentence beamed a searchlight smile.

She was a website designer and worried about her future. Website designers' ranks were increasing and prices for their services — once premium priced like early computers, but now a commodity — were plunging. I thought about the Internet — about Donald Richie not wiring himself to the new world — but briefly. "Not at all," the reporter replied when I asked if his wife minded him inviting this woman to join us. I may have made the invitation possible.

We traded proverbs. He offered *me wa kuchi hodo ni mono o iu* — "the eyes speak more than the tongue." I contributed *jū nin, tō iro* — "ten people, ten colors," as an example of the individualism of Japanese people.

What about *ja no michi wa hebi* — "the path of the snake is for the snake." Did it mean I do my job; you do yours? No, that was *mochiya wa mochiya* — "the rice-cake maker makes rice cakes." The reporter explained the path of the snake: "There may be a shortcut, but it's the type of shortcut that a gangster would take. It's not a path for you." Dictionaries translate this proverb as "A poacher makes the best gamekeeper" or "It takes a thief to catch a thief," so they must read it as "The snake knows the path of snakes," but the reporter's interpretation makes sense to me.

Proverbs I'd thought were English were Chinese, the reporter said, though a universal notion such as *saigetsu hito wo matazu* — "time waits for no one," probably occurs in different cultures and enters the language of each at different times. We talked about world views and *i no naka no kawazu* — "the frog in the well."

He talked about things he wanted to do — make pots, grow herbs. He wanted to pursue these interests now, but his newspaper's pay scale was based on seniority, and only now, in his mid-fifties, did his salary enable him to live comfortably.

He recalled his days as a cub reporter. His editor once gave him a photograph of a flower and told him to write a front-page story about it. The typesetters would come and take copy pages from him as he wrote, which made it hard to finish the piece as he couldn't look back to see what he'd just written.

That night I stayed at the reporter's home. Though from the outside it's an unremarkable two-storied barn of a building, inside it's snug, homely, and naturally floored, lined and furnished in polished woods. A bathroom, separate toilet, and two children's bedrooms, separated by an accordion door, are downstairs, and upstairs are the kitchen and adjoining living area, which, when bedding is brought out from *oshiire* cupboards, doubles as a master bedroom. The two daughters, now adults, had left home some time ago.

The reporter laid out a futon for me alongside a Yamaha drum kit in one of the downstairs rooms. He was a closet jazz drummer. The case of an alto saxophone rested under a baby grand Kaiser piano in a corner of the room. Trio power and pre-amplifiers, and an acoustic guitar gathered dust behind the drums. There was a shelf of records. Wes Montgomery's *Smokin' at the Half Note*, Ron Carter's *Yellow and Green*, and Milt Jackson's *Plenty Plenty Soul* shared space with *The Sound of Music*.

In the morning the reporter's wife, a Japanese language teacher, followed him into the bathroom, sponging up the water he spilled and splashed. She was making way for me. That day I joined her class for foreign students at Niigata University. The students were Chinese. They had already passed their exam and this lesson was in conversation. We conversed with scripts and then without.

We were tested in usage of the particle *ga*, which, among other functions, denotes a subject, but so does *wa* and I still can't always correctly use them. They are used, for example, to distinguish between sentences such as "That is not a problem" — wa and "There is no problem" — ga. And if you introduce yourself as Mr. Watanabe, then wa, but if you say you are Mr. Watanabe in answer to the question, Are you Mr. Watanabe? — then ga. Then we watched a video tape.

A full moon lit a rural setting and autumn insects were in song. A young motorcyclist couldn't find his friend's house. Lost, he came across a temple and asked if he could stay the night. An elderly woman welcomed him inside. A girl, dressed in kimono and fireworks in hand, put her hand on his shoulder and beckoned him outside to play. That night he dreamed of lighting fireworks in the temple precinct. At breakfast he noticed the girl's framed photograph set beside an altar.

The teacher rewound the tape to the point where the man had asked the woman if he could stay the night, then discussed the level of politeness in the grammar of the request.

After the lesson I started to make my way back.

———

Police posters outside Urasa Station gave details of three Aum Shinrikyō cultists wanted in connection with the Tokyo subway gas attack. So, two had been caught. The poster supplied a 24-hour free dial number — 0120-006024. The number is easy to remember. "0060" on a Japanese telephone can be read phonetically as *ōmu,* which is the pronunciation of "Aum," and "24" is for 24 hours.

Two photographs of each of the suspects — two men, ages 32 and 39, and one woman, age 25 — contrasted different hairstyles. What a difference a hairstyle can make.

A reward of ¥6 million ($50,000) was offered for information leading to the conviction of the three, or ¥2 million ($16,700) per individual. I can't say why the reward was offered by a private rather than public fund.

A cluster of temples is accessible from the west exit of the station. Among them is the Fukōji Temple and, within its precinct, Bishamon Hall, named after the deity that protects birds. I walked through the precinct, admiring the oil-stained wood, absorbing the calm of the atmosphere. Then wasps circled my head and I felt unsafe and left.

Women and men would fill Bishamon Hall on the third day after the New Year, undress, let their clothes fall aside and, bodies tight, push as a mass in one direction, then another, Bokushi Suzuki recorded. Women, some naked to the waist, wore only thin cotton. Men wore loincloths.

The seven or so bouts of pushing were followed by a dance, after which a leader would say that a black cloud had descended in front of Bishamon. The crowd would ask what the cloud had come to say, and the leader would respond. "It came down to say that rice would rain." Sake was sprinkled over the heads of the crowd and the cups thrown into their midst. Good fortune visited those who managed to catch a cup.

This was a dance for a bountiful rice harvest. No one had ever been hurt or molested in the pushing and nothing had ever been stolen from the clothing left on the floor, Suzuki reported. The dance, which was never elevated to the status of a festival, brings to mind Donald Richie's account of Tadashi Nakajima and the *Yami Matsuri* — "Festival of Darkness," in *Public People, Private People: Portraits of Some Japanese.*

Richie may have experienced the last such festival at a shrine in Fuchū. He wrote that he was caught amid a mass of pushing bodies as the skin-tight throng entered the shrine, where it remained in a near hypnotic state for much of the night. He felt exhilarated, warm, safe in darkness and in trust. The following year — 1947 — the festival fell victim to prudish authorities, and hundreds of years of a tradition ended.

The pushing ritual at Bishamon Hall has survived, the tourist office in Muika-machi confirmed for me, though in diluted form. It's called *Hadaka Oshiai Matsuri* — "Naked Jostling Festival." Men still wear loincloths but on an all-male night that begins with junior high school students. Modestly attired women are able to participate during daylight hours. It's held 3 March from 6.30 p.m. Rice cakes have been added to the flight of sake containers.

That night at Okabe Hotel, a pleasant establishment in Urasa, the manager asked for my help reading two e-mails from Mexico and checking his reply. In return, after an unnecessary rewrite — I had to change some words to put him at ease — he upgraded my room. He was talking to a bus driver in the morning when I was about to leave, but still noticed and greeted me warmly. The guest from Mexico would arrive in a day or so, all necessary information at hand — directions to the hotel from the station, the room rate, method of payment.

Urasa is the closest station to Kokusai-chō — "International Town." Experience had taught me to regard the word *kokusai* — "international" with some suspicion. I'd seen it in signs on some small buildings along Road 17 but felt no inclination to make inquiries.

The word is added to the name of departments within companies or organizations which are charged with regulating interaction with foreign concerns. Such departments, often wholly domestic in character, perform as gatekeepers. The word is also used to highlight a description of fashions or trends, which may be more Japanese than not.

The "age of internationalism" as in *kokusaika no jidai* is often used to describe threats to what is Japanese or the right to indigenous character. It marks fear more than celebration. In this usage Japan may silently have led some of the world, because doesn't the same fear underlie the concerns of those who protest globalism?

But no ulterior meaning betrays International Town, which is home to the International University of Japan, a postgraduate university, doors opened 25 years ago. I'd seen it signposted when walking, and later regretted not having made the effort to visit it. But I don't have to walk everywhere, so I'd visit it now.

IUJ offers master degrees in business administration, e-business management, international development, international peace studies, and international relations. All programs are taught in English. I arrived unannounced but administration staff graciously took time to brief me. About 250 students from 50 countries were enrolled. Most lived in campus dormitories and a few in apartments in Urasa.

The college occupies a 60-hectare (148-acre) site surrounded by farmland in a landscape which jolts the senses for the survival of trees. Spacious dormitories include apartments for married students. I looked at the modern library, the 24-hour computer and workrooms, and the audiovisual facilities. How times had changed. I remember only a steam-heated library. But that was in 1970s' New Zealand, and it seems that always business and science departments are better funded that those for liberal arts.

I sat down to read a book of resumes compiled for prospective employers. I was curious. Though we don't have to like the young, we need them, as a Kazuo Ishiguro character remarks in *When We Were Orphans*.

One student described himself as a NASDAQ equity trader — "Intra-day trader, remote, New York; direct access level-two interface; real-time technical analysis implementation; intra-minute momentum scalp style; high-volume trading (6,000 + shares / day turnover)." He was buying and selling the same shares in less than 60 seconds, to lock in profits from momentarily rising prices. His computer graphed the movement in prices as the shares were being traded.

He was a "day trader," a species part courageous, part foolish, part dead. Day traders put faith and savings in a seconds-old history called momentum. But it's powered by the past, not a reasoned expectation of the future. Some observers saw in the day traders a parallel with the stock-tipping, shoeshine boys of Manhattan in the late 1920s. The confidence of both foreshadowed a market peak and fall.

I hoped that this student would be able to finance the remainder of his master degree in E-Business. Hobbies? He noted only "surfboard production — shaping, glassing, sanding." Sports? "Big-wave surfing, both paddle- and power-assisted."

One student had "operated and maintained the auxiliary power plant of a ship." He held a bachelor degree in marine engineering and was completing a master degree in international management.

Another recorded work as a soup-kitchen volunteer in Montreal, at a rural bank in Dhaka, and as an intern in Hanoi for the Industrial Development Organization of the UN. Languages: Japanese, English, French, Bengali, Vietnamese. Sport? boxing; Hokkaidō University Boxing Club. Significance? Rudolph Giuliani, formerly major of New York City, had boxed and led. For his bachelor of science degree in geology he had studied the evolution of marine reptiles during the Mesozoic period.

The last one I read was that of a nuclear engineer who for five years had "supervised nuclear power plant personnel to ensure compliance with all operating procedures" and for a year had worked aboard the USS Enterprise — the "world's first and finest nuclear-powered aircraft carrier," according to its home page. I wrestled with the notion of warships maintaining home pages but they, as cities on the water, are home to many.

Takuji Shimano, IUJ's president, told me he had studied in northern Germany — at a university near Kiel he didn't name — some 40 years ago. He said he had liked to explore but had little money. He would put his bicycle in a boxcar and travel cheaply by train. He stressed going out into the world and applying the sciences.

IUJ's mission, Shimano said, was to provide "advanced practical expertise." He said he would like to see an equal number of Japanese and foreign students. Foreign students appeared to outnumber Japanese by at least two to one. But this is an expensive education usually funded by employers for star employees, and the lost decade was extending itself.

The university seemed to lack nothing, and from the spirit within its corridors I felt that it would produce fine leaders. Yet the number of Japanese enrolments was declining. IUJ has its work cut out. It must compete against the perception of American educational superiority. Most graduate students seeking an MBA or other postgraduate degree still brand-shop in the US among Ivy League names in the way that students in Britain's former colonies covet degrees from Oxford or Cambridge universities.

IUJ's founders reasoned that the type of postgraduate education offered in the US should be available at home. It was an embarrassment that it wasn't. But private and public sector employers, which still don't often ask to see an undergraduate's grade record when hiring, have long argued that they can educate their employees best.

Now that flagship companies such as Nissan Motor Co. and Sony Corp. have appointed non-Japanese to revitalize their businesses, that thinking may change. James Abegglen has decried the lack of graduate study facilities and argued for the removal of the "dead hand" of the education ministry from the system. I hope that new Japanese leaders will build on the example of IUJ.

I shared a table with Dr. Kazuhiko Okuda, a professor of political science, at the university cafeteria. He hails from Nagasaki. He spoke of Japan's "duel economy" in which efficient industries are expected to protect and support inefficient ones, such as various food industries. We talked about Japan's perception of its place in the world.

"Actually, a pet theory of mine is that Japan has internationalized and America has insularized," Dr. Okuda said. He tires of hearing the same questions about Japan. So he answers: "Yes, we live in paper houses, and yes, we eat raw fish." He also tires on bullet trains. "I'm not sure why," he said. "It may be the speed." He is right. You never alight from a bullet train feeling rested.

I took a local train to Shiozawa and a taxi to Untoan Temple. The priest recognized me from his kneeling position in the temple office where he was discussing foreign policy and refugees with a townsperson. He invited me to join him.

The prime minister had recently made an impassioned and extraordinary plea to citizens to "please stop not believing what the Japanese government says and stop believing what a foreign government says." He was referring to the incident in May 2002 in which Chinese police had evicted five North Korean defectors from the Japanese consulate in Shenyang.

China claimed that Japanese officials at the consulate had requested the removal of the North Koreans. This made Japan look callous: two of the defectors were women, one a child, and the two men had been seated in the visa section of the consulate for some minutes before their eviction.

Chinese police had dragged the five, whose kicking and screaming appeared choreographed, from the consulate premises and taken them away. The hat of one fell to the ground. A Japanese consular official was caught on camera picking it up and dismissively throwing it outside the compound. His expression was scornful.

In Tokyo, officials tried to claim that Chinese police had acted unilaterally in removing the North Koreans, whose intrusion into the consulate grounds had violated rules of diplomatic relations, the officials said. Many Japanese who watched nightly TV news replays of the scene of the scornful official tossing the hat aside didn't believe this account.

The priest said: "I believe the Chinese government."

His local guest concurred: "So do I."

The *Niigata Nippō* reporter, too, had believed China's account. He said he was disappointed in the performance of so-called elite officials from the foreign and finance ministries.

But who had staged this attempted defection in Shenyang, and why? One of the two women reportedly was pregnant, a condition likely to arouse feelings of outrage in the face of expulsion from a safe haven. Who had informed a TV production crew that at a certain time at the Japanese consulate news would be made?

Someone had schemed the floating of a trial balloon to test a position or measure a reaction. This was the kernel of a larger story.

China, for its part, had missed an opportunity to test Japan's humanitarianism. It should have left the North Korean defectors where they were, stepped back, and watched what happens.

Customers had formed a small queue at the temple counter. *Shōbai! Shōbai!* — "Business! Business!" the priest barked at his elderly assistant, who had absented herself for some minutes. I don't think he's like that. I think he was playing to his audience of two. When she failed to appear, he reluctantly shuffled on his knees across the mats to the cash register, paused to consider the buttons, and managed to press the one that generates a receipt.

The crusades of unification embarked upon in the late 1500s by warlords Oda Nobunaga, Toyotomi Hideyoshi, and Tokugawa Ieyasu, were left in a state unfinished. There was more to do.

In Niigata Prefecture the towns of Koide and Horiuchi and the village of Hirogami are no more. They — and others like them — have been merged into Uonuma City and the Koide Town Office has been renamed Uonuma City Office.

The town of Muikamachi, too, has lost its status as a town. It has become part of Minamiuonuma — South Uonuma — City. The map I used is now old. New maps show these changes, which were part of a national plan to merge around 1,000 villages and towns into cities in the first few years of the new century.

Municipal mergers have occurred in waves since 1888 in the Meiji era, when 71,314 villages were recognized. That number was shrunk to 15,820 the following year, in the largest consolidation, and, in stages, to 8,518 by 1946. There were around 577 villages when I set out on my walk, and 44 or so have since lost that status.

In the postwar years, the number of cities has grown from 205 to 695. Some villages and towns resist Tokyo's guidance — really an instruction — to merge but they lose sweeteners such as subsidies for their recalcitrance.

There's sense in size. A larger administrative unit can support schools of full curricula and Tokyo can more easily implement national policy throughout the regions. It can unify. Citizens are overtaxed — on income, residence, capital gains, gifts, inheritance; when they drive or eat rice or bread or much other food; when they buy imports — yet the public debt is high. If municipal consolidation reduces the indebtedness of the government to the public, it may be worth it.

But it makes little difference when considered from the view from the road. Villages spill over into the towns and the towns meld into the cities, in an omnipresent pattern of rural conurbation.

From Shiozawa I backtracked by local train to Muikamachi. There I boarded the Hokuhoku Line to Tōkamachi, the town which opened its markets only on the tenth day of the month and where Matsue was known to buy her kimonos. They were said to be less expensive there than in Yuzawa.

The train wound its way through a mountain valley clouded in thin mist. Rice paddies were terraced and spinster-neat, and every thumbnail of land put to use on the mountainside as on the flat of the valley. Farmers in straw hats were planting rice and tending vegetables. The train stopped on a siding inside a tunnel and waited for an oncoming train to pass.

I found a soba restaurant and enjoyed a bowl of buckwheat noodles to the background music of "Sixteen Going On Seventeen" from *The Sound of Music*, then tried the Harada Ryokan, which welcomed me. As I emerged that evening from the bath the innkeeper's daughter was practicing an alto saxophone her parents had given her.

Snakes visited me in dreams that night. In the first dream, a snake slithered slowly in a corner of the room. It appeared to be a small, harmless grass snake and though startled I wasn't frightened. I next dreamed of a larger snake, coiled in the same corner of the room. It had the collared neck of a cobra. I was more dumbfounded than frightened as the snake lifted its head and telescoped itself up to my sitting height. Its eyes settled on mine for a few seconds, then it turned its head and moved to the door, upper body still raised. It took the door handle in its mouth, brought the handle down, opened the door and let itself out.

I recounted this dream to a friend, who said: "That snake may have been an omen of good fortune but the motion of letting itself out of your room may mean that the good fortune or wealth that visits you will also leave you."

Tōkamachi had published a list of inns, restaurants and bars at which foreigners were welcome. The World Cup must have prompted this precautionary publication as Croatia had set up a soccer training camp on the outskirts of the town, and I regretted not having kept it as a souvenir. I wanted to ask town officials how many places of lodging and restaurants the town had. I would divide one number by the other, calculate a "welcome" percentage.

A friend called the town office to request a copy of the list. But what should have been a simple matter became complicated. My friend got the run-around and ended up denigrating rural people for their slowness. I think that the town officials understood the intent of the request.

Though the policy of national seclusion — toward Europe at least — ended 150 years ago, it still lives as a reflexive emotion in places such as Koide, Sarugakyō, and Tōkamachi. Suspicion of foreigners still darkens aspects of everyday life. It isn't part of a long-forgotten past. An event of 100 or 200 years ago in a country whose history stretches back some 2,400 or more years isn't old. It is recent, even new.

I visited the Foreign Correspondents' Club of Japan. Blessed with a brilliant location atop the Yurakucho Denki Bldg. in Hibiya, it draws business lunch and dinner crowds whose membership fees subsidize the provision of professional support to journalists. Unlike other press clubs that have fallen prey to public-relations types, this club has always been overseen by journalists, despite their being ever more adept at telling other people how to run their businesses than run their own.

Some correspondents had stuck it out through the lost decade but feared a second decade of dullness. Some foreign newspapers had closed their Tokyo bureaus and fine journalists who one never imagined would be out of work had become teachers or something else.

Surviving reporters tend to specialize in financial markets and are bilingual and able to navigate businesses and the bureaucracy by themselves. The reporter who writes of life is now rare, and unless more food becomes affordable may become extinct. I overheard a businessman praise one journalist for writing a feature article of some depth, as though such practice was now uncommon, replaced by dial-a-quote calls to stock analysts.

There's a camaraderie among journalists that you don't much see among business people. I felt nostalgic to be among people who weren't in each other's company for calculated profit. Nevertheless, doubt had set in about the future of the lowly paid profession.

Apart from article-dumping academics, who seek not pay but publication of their name and views, and the aspiring young who trade pay for experience and exposure, an array of new sources of information and opinion had emerged on the Internet, where established news services and magazines were already giving much of their product away. There were web logs, diaries, the reports of governments, academia and myriad institutions, and more. And most of it was free.

Too, the decision by major American TV networks to "embed" their correspondents with US forces in Iraq had prompted the question, Has journalism died? For the thrill of seeing rolling tanks from the point of view of the tank, some correspondents feared that tenets of objectivity and neutrality had been sacrificed for safety.

Small changes in the policies and practices of businesses here affect lives throughout the world, inevitably so as Japan's economy is the world's second largest. A business press reports on these changes with skill and speed but who will report on the lives behind the businesses?

Encouragingly, a BBC correspondent had recently reported from the city of Nagaoka about joblessness and other effects of a prolonged regional recession. What emerged from the tone of the quoted comments was a distrust of the central government. More journalists working in Tokyo, I think, should visit Japan. I have some story ideas.

Why was Takasaki firebombed after the dropping of the atomic bombs?

Why in Niigata from 1975 to 2003 has the percentage of deaths caused by cancers of various types increased from 21 to 31 percent and the percentage caused by cerebral vascular disease decreased from 30 to 16 percent? "Easy," a friend said. "A Westernized lifestyle has increased the incidence of cancer, and a reduction in salt consumption has reduced the number of brain hemorrhages." But there must be much to learn from the detail of such a sea change.

Why does Saitama Prefecture spend as much as 8 percent of its budget, or $1.2 billion, on police?

But these are questions for others to consider.

JAM

An art exhibition had arrived from London to join Tokyo creations under the theme of a musical jam. Thoughts overlapped themes, so we visit Opera City.

Chapter 39. Opera City

> I'm a virtual rep.
> I'm a Yorkshire terrier breeder, so I click on and talk to other Yorkshire terrier breeders in the Yorkshire terrier breeders' chat room.
> Everything's unparalleled.
> It's a fad that will, like, hopefully last forever, hopefully.
> It's so next-gen mixed with total boredom.
> Why do people insist on putting a dot between the word "dot" and "com" and then say "dot com" when they should say "dot dot com"?

These were comments in sketches by Paul Davis, a graphic designer who had recorded fragments of overheard conversations on scraps of paper. His sketches lampoon by capturing the nonsense that passes for much communication. I studied 100 or so of them, intrigued but also embarrassed by their fidelity.

I was at an exhibition called JAM: Tokyo-London. It had moved to Tokyo's Opera City from London's Barbican Art Gallery. Based on the idea of a musical jam, it featured works of fashion, graphic design, photography, fine art, and music. It promised too much but I was glad I went, and not only for the introduction to Davis' work.

My eyes were drawn to a cube occupied by three figures dressed as mountaineers. From a kneeling position their outstretched arms seemed to plead for food. Fur lining spewed out of their jackets. A child, also in protective clothing, was sitting down. A chocolate bar lay broken over the ground.

Ropes trailed down from the mirrored ceiling. As I moved forward I saw that the ropes were made of paper dolls, thin, joined hand to foot in a chain. They dangled amid shards of broken mirror which formed a twisted ladder dropping downward. Was the sky breaking, heaven or hell opening? Could the broken chocolate save the broken climbers? The words "magazine" and "newspaper" were labeled on the ground beside three sitting dolls.

277

This was a troubling exhibit, where the surreal intersected the real and death held the line. Titled "Final Home," it recalled the harrowing account in Jon Krakaeur's *Into Thin Air* of the ill-fated ascents of Mt. Everest in 1996 in which twelve climbers perished. The exhibit's creator, designer Kōsuke Tsumura, less apocalyptically had subtitled his exhibit "wears for outdoor and urban activities."

Tsumura uses recycled materials. He takes an interest in the homeless, I read, by recycling and designing clothes for them. This was the significance of the separation of the fur lining from its coat — his clothes for the homeless are covered in zippers which allow newspapers to be stuffed inside for insulation.

He had recreated a disaster scene as the stage for his recycled "Final Home" clothing. I wanted to see more of his work, though in this exhibit Tsumura indulges only himself. He should take hot food to the homeless. They can't trade their cardboard for his creations.

In a self-portrait, photographer Yurie Nagashima captured herself as a naked, smoking, pregnant woman holding an index finger up to the camera lens. She had failed if her objective was to disgust. The photograph drew only pity for her and sympathy for the unborn child she was poisoning.

Nagashima had made her debut with a series of nude photographs. One photo of her and her mother, both bare-breasted and sitting behind a kotatsu heater, was oddly erotic for the presence of her mother. Her exhibition bio said she had been critically acclaimed as a "girl photographer in her early work." Since then she had "matured" to become a photographer in "her own right." She continues to "maintain her life-sized view of the everyday environment."

I couldn't easily associate "youth" or the spontaneity of a musical jam with the clothing exhibits, but some apparel provoked thought. Two Japanese designers calling themselves World Design Laboratory presented long, wide, heavily pleated dresses that suggested an armored defense and the fashion of earlier centuries in Europe.

Jessica Ogden's garments were memorable for their appearance on headless and limbless mannequins. But why should a mannequin be made whole or to look attractive? The garments were made from fragments of cloth in a handmade style that suggested both antiquity and modernity.

Visitors converged on photographer Kyōichi Tsuzuki's exhibit titled "The lost dream of love hotels." They seemed bored with this airing of their washing and, after glancing at the large panels in a cursory way, moved on. The word "lost" grated. No dream was "lost" and the hotels still line the back streets behind railway stations and roads off expressway ramps. Photographs of the gaudy hotel interiors showed the beds, mirrors, and fantasy constructions such as space capsules.

"The love hotel, decorated in its unique fashion, has played an important role as a presence on the fringe of contemporary Japanese culture," Tsuzuki's bio said. At center, not fringe, and there is more that is aged than contemporary about the hotels. Tsuzuki self-consciously sanitizes.

Other exhibits showed multicolored flashing lights masquerading as technology, and computer games on giant screens. They didn't convey a sense of the energy and excitement of the pop and street cultures of the two cities. They seemed to be the work of older artists who were guessing at the preoccupations of youth and I felt that youth was somewhere else.

The promoters, too, seemed to be from an older public-relations set, using shell words such as "ongoing" and "proactive." But the opportunity to become acquainted with the irreverent, relevant work of Davis and the apocryphal visions of Tsumura made the exhibit worthwhile for me.

At Opera City most weeks you can enjoy recital and concert performances of music composed throughout the ages — baroque, classical, romantic, and contemporary. Even jazz.

TO THE SNOW COUNTRY

Again, I would go back, to Yokohama and then the snow country. I knew that this journey wasn't over, but for now I decided to rest it amid the tall cedars.

CHAPTER 40. HIGHER GROUND

I took a train to Kannai and, feeling like a prowler, loitered inside Yokohama City Hall, touring floors and reading doorplates. In the Civic Affairs Bureau a subsection was titled "Office for the Promotion of Cooperation Between Men and Women." A rising divorce rate, reflecting increased financial independence for women, had raised an alarm. This was a civic response.

In a day in the life of Kanagawa Prefecture (2004), there are 154 marriages and 52 divorces, which implies a divorce rate of 34 percent. That's high for this country and those divorces are of earlier marriages, so the future divorce rate from current marriages may be higher still.

Some women I know admire Korean, Singaporean, and Swiss men for the military training they must do. It makes them tough and smart, they say. But in their circle compatriot army personnel aren't seen as desirable.

In the library I found a city publication that detailed and discussed US military installations. It's no secret that the US operates air bases at Atsugi, Iwakuni, Kadena, and Yokota, naval bases at Sasebo and Yokosuka, which homeports an aircraft carrier, and an army base at Zama. Tens of thousands of US military personnel live on base — no static figure is useful or believable as the presence is military and mobile.

But the publication showed how deep and suburban is the range of smaller US military installations in Yokohama. These occupy about 535 hectares (1,322 acres) of land. They used to occupy as much as 1,620 hectares (3,988 acres), so about two-thirds of the area has been returned to Japan since 1952, when the Occupation ended.

There are eight facilities — two each for telecommunications, oil storage, and housing, one for warehousing, and the Yokohama north dock for naval repairs. The telecommunications installations occupy nearly half of the requisitioned land, and are managed by the US Naval Air Command at Atsugi and used by the Seventh Fleet, according to the publication.

Yokohama — Past and Present, an English-language history and geography published in 1990 by Yokohama City University, looked worthwhile. Though cleansed — it didn't contain a single unflattering comment — the book was richly detailed, and I thought to acquire it. I telephoned the university's librarian, who said that she had only one copy of the book and that it was out of print. So often valuable books are out of print.

That night I made my way to the Downbeat jazz club.

Jazz flourished in Yokohama, but not because Occupation troops made it their music of choice. Jazz and swing took root here as early as the 1920s, the city's cultural furrows made fertile by immigration and the exoticism — and new music — that ships bring. Mixed marriages may have played some part, as they surely did in New Orleans — black, French, Spanish, Creole — at the turn of the 18th century. The children of such unions learn from an early age to improvise in language and social setting and it's natural that this ability would extend to musical conversations.

Two young women left after I sat down at Downbeat. Two businessmen were the only other customers. Eric Dolphy's *Far Cry* knitted the air.

The club owner's wife invited me to choose from a catalog of recordings, which included 60 or so LP records of Miles Davis, 41 of Charles Mingus, and 19 of Bud Powell. There were others of Kenny Dorham, Kenny Burrell, and Mal Waldron. The owner had begun to soundtrack his life in the 1950s. I asked for Art Pepper's *Meet the Rhythm Section*, which paired the alto saxophonist with the pianist, bassist and drummer of the first Miles Davis quintet.

In *Straight Life*, Pepper describes his mother's attempts to abort him — "My mother starved herself and took everything anybody had ever heard of that would make you miscarry, but to no avail. I was born. She lost." Of his heroin addiction: "That is what I practiced. And that is what I still am. And that is what I will die as — a junkie." He did, at age 56, but not before playing some of the most achingly beautiful music.

Oversized loudspeakers squeezed the small playing area where "standing room only" applied to the musicians. There wasn't room for more than a trio and live performances were staged only once every two months. A grand piano served as a table for leaflets advertising jazz events.

Menu prices showed highest markups for whisky. This is the problem with jazz. The business doesn't celebrate but uses music to create an atmosphere conducive to the consumption of alcohol.

I took a taxi to a Yokohama suburb after missing the last subway train from Kannai. I couldn't have heard jazz if African-Americans weren't playing it, the driver said, in haughty tone. Many Japanese think that. But in racially stereotyping the genre they deny the existence of Japanese jazz. They also miss the point that jazz is an international language, though its followers in a way are like Esperantists — a minority despite or because of the universal possibilities of their practice.

The taxi driver unknowingly belongs to the school of jazz trumpeter Wynton Marsalis — jazz of and by blacks. Whites: don't apply within. Ears only, not eyes, they must be told, and recall Louis Armstrong's advice: "Cats of any color can play jazz."

It was time to write but people whose works I'd referenced — historical, journalistic, literary or musical — seemed not to hurdle their middle years. Alan Booth, E. H. Norman, Jack Kerouac, Uesugi Kenshin, Oscar Wilde — all dead between the ages of 46 and 49. I was spooked. Those were my years. I would wait.

———

Foxes and flying squirrels and black bears and badgers in the forests around the Agatsuma Gorge in Gunma Prefecture about now will be climbing to higher ground. Yamba Dam opponents finally appeared powerless to halt the project.

Their strategy, a leader told me, was to oppose the dam legally in each of the prefectures through which the Tone River downstream of the dam runs and which contribute to financing it, on the basis that the financing represents a misappropriation of prefectural tax revenues.

The healing waters of the Kawarayu spring will merge and rise with the Agatsuma River and dam lake and the water will submerge the burning autumnal reds, oranges, and yellows of the maple and other trees in the gorge. It may not happen by the scheduled dam completion year of 2010 — so massive is this project that it may take five or ten more years — but it will happen. Residents and businesses have been ordered to abandon their homes and buildings by 2007.

The trees ominously bore blight at the time I visited Kawarayu Onsen. I trekked the area to find the new dam lake level in several places sign-marked meters above my head. At night locals, as though already underwater, drank to kill time.

It's too easy to lay the blame on the legacy of Kakuei Tanaka. One man acting alone can't achieve that much. My admiration of Tanaka had made me an accomplice in his promotion of the construction state. He had his willing executioners who dealt death's blow to the environment — the people who accepted his largesse, the people who admired him.

———

I went back.

The earthquake, Japan's deadliest in a decade, struck at 5.56 p.m. on 23 October 2004. It claimed 40 lives and injured 2,860 people. It demolished 2,691 houses, half-demolished 560 "on a large scale," half-demolished a further 5,960, and caused partial damage to 75,530 more dwellings. It damaged 23,276 public facility and other buildings. It caused 442 landslides, and damaged roads and rivers in 6,062 and 219 places. This is the tabulation of the *Niigata Nippō*, which showed its class as a regional newspaper by producing an 88-page documentary and photographic record of the quake.

The Niigata earthquake destroys roads and houses in Nigorimachi on the outskirts of Nagaoka City, 24 October 2004. Photo by Niigata Nippō.

The quake had followed my path. Deaths and injuries were greatest in Nagaoka (6 and 662) and Ojiya (12 and 731), the city I regretted not having explored.

Slabs of mountainside had collapsed and buried segments of road. Falling rocks crushed the car in which a mother, her baby daughter and two-year-old son were traveling. Rescuers found the boy alive four days later. Later he may ask himself why he was saved and make specially good his life.

The rear engine and next carriage of a Niigata-bound bullet train had derailed as the train was traveling at around 200 kilometers (124 miles) per hour as it decelerated in its approach to Nagaoka Station. Operator JR East said that at that speed, the train will travel 2.5 kilometers (1.6 miles) in 1 minute 45 seconds before braking can bring it to a complete halt. No one was hurt.

I'd returned to the snow country via the northern prefecture of Yamagata, taking the Inaho Special Express from Tsuruoka to Niigata and the bullet train to Nagaoka. In a transfer choreographed as smooth as a fire drill for the elderly, bullet train ticket-holders at Nagaoka were guided to buses bound for Echigo-Yuzawa, where the train service resumed. I wasn't expecting the transfer. Everything in Japan always worked. I'd read about the quake but it hadn't registered as real.

A friend in Tsuruoka had been helping battered wives. There was some civic aid for them, she said, but it was hard to make sense of the procedures to get funds released. Some urgency attached to this as a current case involved a woman who had little money and had been secreted to a refuge after her husband had broken her leg.

My friend wanted to get out of the snow country. "It's not as idyllic as you may think," she cautioned. "There are dark elements to life here."

The waitress at the Schi Heil jazz coffee shop in Muikamachi is still there, shaking dried fish shavings into dishes of peanuts. She herself is somewhat shaken. She told me that when the earthquake struck, she rushed for the door, clambered down the stairs, and from a standing position in the middle of the car park below, looked up to see the building sway.

That sounded like everything you're not supposed to do. Wasn't it safer to stay inside under something solid, as outside you were in danger of being hit by shards of glass and bits of buildings?

But you don't chide someone for surviving and instinctively we must want to flee. She was still on edge. People don't recover overnight from the experience of severe earthquakes. She said that CDs and books were tossed to the floor but damage luckily was slight. She brought me coffee.

Yūko, who helped me plan the walk, exchanged earthquakes for hurricanes. She married an American businessman and now lives in Florida. She asked why the movie *Lost in Translation* was about two Americans in Tokyo. She had asked a searching question of our time. Yūko, too, has visited Untoan Temple, and wants to return. When her daughter is older, I think she will.

Echizenya is still casually warm. A photographer was staying there when I visited. He shared a bottle of Hakkaizan sake with me. "I'm so happy we can talk," he said. His current assignment was to photograph statues of Buddhist images at roadside locations in the snow country.

The images don't mark road deaths, the photographer said, adding that some mystery surrounds their origins. They were valued as antiques, and his job was made difficult by theft. He would drive for some hours to locate a particular statue, only to find that it had been stolen. He asked whether Christian symbols attracted thieves or black marketeers. Left at roadside, surely they would.

I asked him what he thought of the late photographer Ken Domon, whose arresting documentary work I'd seen exhibited in Yamagata. "If we are stars, he is the sun," the photographer said.

I have a postcard of a Domon photograph of the Ginza taken in 1937, when Japan was at war with China. The photograph captures more the celebration than the excitement of war. Flags aren't blowing in the wind. They're being waved — both types, the civilian sun against white, and the military sun and its rays against white — by throngs at roadside, and hoisted horizontally from department store windows. Perhaps patriots were anticipating some Imperial procession, but the photograph shows only trams and buses.

———

Next morning the photographer drove me to Untoan in his lived-in caravan of a four-wheel-drive, cluttered with clothes and camera bags. No one responded to his shouts from across the temple fence. Journalists' and photographers' livelihood depends on access, so they shout, put their foot in the door, here as anywhere else. But at this time in the morning an inviolable routine was in progress.

The photographer, perhaps thinking that one temple was as good as another, took me to Kankōji Temple, near Ishiuchi Station. He reminded the head priest of photographs he'd taken of Kankōji and, saying that language wouldn't be a problem, abruptly left me in the sitting room of the priest's house.

After asking my age and place of birth, the priest began to discourse on the spiritual poverty and material wealth of today's Japanese. With perfect teeth and an athlete's physique, he appeared to be in his mid 70s. A tour group arrived and I joined them to listen to a spirited account of the temple's history and manufacture of soybean paste.

The hour now more respectable, I took a local train to Shiozawa and taxi to Untoan. The gatekeeper said he'd been asked not to charge admittance. The photographer's commotion had been understood. The elderly woman appeared and apologized, "We were cleaning."

Why were army officers buried within the temple precinct? They weren't. The fence had been built at a later date for security — here, too, were glue-sniffing youth who made trouble at night — and it had enclosed a number of tombstones which earlier were among all the others.

The apostle Paul had slipped my mind.

The priest devotes some time to the composition of sayings, which he writes in his own swift calligraphic hand, the brush strokes thick and, to my eye, untidy. The ones that don't satisfy him he tosses aside and they litter corners of his office. I framed the saying he gifted me and it's above me as I write — "Feed your heart sorrow and it will grow large. Feed it virtue and it will waste away."

Some temples cater to tourists — domestic and foreign — who seek enlightenment, but on a tight schedule, in the style of the dude ranches in the US west that let visitors experience the cowboy lifestyle for a few days. But Untoan isn't a ranch of the soul and if there is enlightenment, I'll find it by myself and in my own mind.

And at temples such as Untoan and Kōmyōji the priests and townspeople I encountered had the events of the day most on their mind. If you want to take the pulse of politics or discuss social issues here, visit the temples.

I'd kept the taxi waiting outside Untoan but the driver had stopped his meter for my visit. I asked him to charge me. He declined. Time was short. There was a bullet train to catch.

ENGLISH BORROWINGS OF JAPANESE WORDS

Here is a list of Japanese words adopted into the English language, as noted by the *Concise Oxford Dictionary*, eighth edition, 1990.

aikido — a Japanese form of self-defense making use of the attacker's own movements without causing injury.

dojo — a room or hall in which judo and other martial arts are practiced.

geisha — a Japanese hostess trained in entertaining men with dance and song. 2 a Japanese prostitute.

haiku — a Japanese three-part poem of usually 17 syllables.

happi — loose informal Japanese coat.

hara-kiri — ritual suicide by disembowelment with a sword, formerly practiced by samurai to avoid dishonor.

hiragana — the cursive form of Japanese syllabic writing or kana.

hokku — = haiku.

ikebana — the art of Japanese flower arrangement, with formal display according to strict rules.

Jap. — noun and adjective. colloq. often offens. = Japanese. [abbr.]

japan — a hard, usually black varnish "make black and glossy as with japan."

judo — a sport of unarmed combat derived from ju-jitsu.

kabuki — a form of popular traditional Japanese drama with highly stylized song, acted by males only.

kakemono — a vertical Japanese wall-picture, usu. painted or inscribed on paper or silk and mounted on rollers.

kamikaze — a Japanese aircraft loaded with explosives and deliberately crashed by its pilot on its target. 2 the pilot of such an aircraft.

kana — any of various Japanese syllabaries.

kanji — Japanese writing using Chinese characters.

karaoke — a form of entertainment in which people sing popular songs as soloists against a pre-recorded backing.

karate — a Japanese system of unarmed combat using the hands and feet as weapons.

katakana — an angular form or Japanese kana.

kimono — a long loose Japanese robe worn with a sash. 2 a European dressing-gown modeled on this.

koan — a riddle used in Zen Buddhism to demonstrate the inadequacy of logical reasoning.

koto — a Japanese musical instrument with 13 long esp. silk strings.

ninja — a person skilled in ninjutsu.

ninjutsu — one of the Japanese martial arts, characterized by stealthy movement and camouflage.

Nip — slang, offensive, Japanese person. [abbr. of Nipponese]

Nipponese — a Japanese person. adj. Japanese.

noh — traditional Japanese drama with dance and song, evolved from Shinto rites.

obi — a broad sash worn with a Japanese kimono.

origami — the Japanese art of folding paper into decorative shapes and figures.

raku — a kind of Japanese earthenware.

romaji — a system of Romanized spelling used to transliterate Japanese.

ryokan — a traditional Japanese inn.

sake — a Japanese alcoholic drink made from rice.

samisen — long, three-stringed Japanese guitar.

samurai — a member of a military caste in Japan.

sashimi — a Japanese dish of garnished raw fish in thin slices.

satori — Buddhism; sudden enlightenment.

satsuma — a variety of Japanese tangerine originally grown in Japan; cream-colored Japanese pottery.

seppuku — hara-kiri.

shakuhachi — a Japanese bamboo flute.

shiatsu — a kind of therapy of Japanese origin, in which pressure is applied with the fingers to certain parts of the body.

shogun — any of a succession of Japanese hereditary Commanders-in-Chief and virtual rulers before 1868.

sukiyaki — a Japanese dish of sliced meat simmered with vegetables and sauce.

sumo — a style of Japanese wrestling.

sushi — a Japanese dish of balls of cold rice flavored and garnished.

tanka — a Japanese poem in five lines and thirty-one syllables giving a complete picture of an event or mood.

tofu — a curd made from mashed soybeans.

torii — the gateway of a Shinto shrine, with two uprights and two crosspieces.

tsunami — a long high sea wave caused by underwater earthquakes or other disturbances.

zori — a Japanese straw or rubber etc. sandal.

Janglish and Japlish, meaning a blend of Japanese and English, are also noted as words.

Oddly *sayonara*, probably the word most recognized by English speakers, isn't acknowledged to have entered the English language.

BIBLIOGRAPHY

Abegglen, James C. *The Japanese Factory*. Bombay: Asia Publishing House edition, 1959; first edition: The MIT Press, 1958. Published in Japanese as *Nihon no Keiei* by Daimond-sha (Tokyo), 1958; revised translation, also as *Nihon no Keiei*, published by Nihon Keizai Shimbunsha (Tokyo), 2004.

———. *Shin Nihon no Keiei — 21st Century Japanese Management, New Systems, Lasting Values*. Nihon Keizai Shimbunsha, 2004; in English as *21st Century Japanese Management: New Systems, Lasting Values*. Hampshire: Palgrave Macmillan, 2006.

Atkins, E. Taylor. *Blue Nippon*. Durham and London: Duke University Press, 2001.

Axelbank, Albert. *Black Star Over Japan — Rising Forces of Militarism*. New York: Hill and Wang, 1972.

Bird, Isabella L. *Unbeaten Tracks in Japan*. San Francisco: Travelers' Tales, 2000; first published 1880.

Blaker, Richard: *The Needle-Watcher: The Will Adams Story, British Samurai*. Rutland, Vermont, Tokyo: Charles E. Tuttle, 1973; first published 1932.

Booth, Alan. *The Roads to Sata*. New York, Tokyo, London: Kodansha International, 1985.

Bronte, Charlotte. *Jane Eyre*. Connecticut: Eastern Press, 1978. First published 1847.

Brown, J.D. *The Sudden Disappearance of Japan — Journeys Through a Hidden Land*. Santa Barbara, CA: Capra Press, 1994.

Buruma, Ian. *Inventing Japan*. New York: Random House, 2003.

Butow, Robert J.C. *Tojo and the Coming of the War*. Stanford: Stanford University Press, 1961.

Carroll, John. *Trails of Two Cities*. New York, Tokyo, London: Kodansha International, 1994.

Clancy, Tom. *Debt of Honor*. New York: Putnam Adult, 1994.

Crichton, Michael. *Rising Sun*. Ballantine Books, 1992.

Dash, Mike. *Tulipmania, the Story of the World's Most Coveted Flower*. New York: Three Rivers Press, 2001.

Dower, John W. *Embracing Defeat*. New York: W.W. Norton, 1999.

——. *War Without Mercy*. New York: Pantheon Books, 1986.

Durant, Will. *Our Oriental Heritage*. New York: Simon & Schuster, 1935.

Ellington, Duke. *Music Is My Mistress*. New York: Doubleday, 1973.

Emmott, Bill. *Japanophobia — The Myth of the Invincible Japanese*. New York: Times Books, 1992.

Enchi, Fumiko. *The Waiting Years*. Trans. John Bester. Tokyo, New York, London: Kodansha International, 1971; first published 1957.

Fermor, Patrick Leigh. *A Time of Gifts*. New York: New York Review of Books, 2005; first published 1977.

Fielding, Helen: *Bridget Jones' Diary*. Picador edition, 1997.

Frei, Henry. *Guns of February*. Singapore: Singapore University Press, 2004.

——. *Japan's Southward Advance and Australia*. Carlton, Victoria: Melbourne University Press, 1991.

Fukuda, Takeo. *Kaiko Kyūjūnen* — "Memoirs of 90 Years." Tokyo: Iwanami Shoten, 1995.

Fukuzawa, Yukichi. *The Autobiography of Yukichi Fukuzawa*. Trans. Eiichi Kiyōka. New York: Columbia University Press, 1966; first published 1899.

Goralski, Robert. *World War II Almanac 1931–1945 — A Political and Military Record*. London: Hamish Hamilton, 1981.

Havers, Rob. *Reassessing the Japanese Prisoner of War Experience — The Chiangi POW Camp, Singapore, 1942-5*. London and New York: RoutledgeCurzon, 2003.

Hunziker, Steven; Kamimura, Ikuro. *Kakuei Tanaka — A Political Biography of Modern Japan*. Singapore: Times Editions, 1996.

Ishiguro, Kazuo: *The Remains of the Day*. London: Faber and Faber, 2005; new edition.

——. *When Were Orphans*. London: Faber and Faber, 2005; new edition.

Ishihara, Shintarō. *Taiyō no Kisetsu* — "Seasons of the Sun." Tokyo: Shinchōsha, 1957.

——, and Morita, Akio. *No to Ieru Nihon — Shinnichibei Kankei no Hōsaku* — "The Japan That Can Say No — Policy for a New Japan-US Relationship." Tokyo: Kōbunsha, 1989.

Jackson, Shirley. *The Lottery and Other Stories, The Haunting of Hill House, We Have Always Lived in the Castle*. New York: Book-of-the-Month Club, Quality Paperback Books, 1991.

Japan Broadcasting Corporation. *The Unforgettable Fire: Pictures Drawn by Atom Bomb Survivors*. New York: Pantheon, 1981.

Johnson, Chalmers. *Japan: Who Governs?* New York: W.W. Norton, 1995.

Johnstone, Bob. *We Were Burning*. New York: Basic Books, 1999.

Kajima, Morinosuke: *The Diplomacy of Japan 1894-1922*. Tokyo: Kajima Institute of International Peace, 1980.

Kaempfer, Engelbert. *Kaempfer's Japan*. Trans. Beatrice M. Bodart-Bailey. Honolulu: University of Hawaii Press, 1999; first published 1727.

Kawabata, Yasunari. *Snow Country*. Trans. Edward Seidensticker. Tokyo: Charles E. Tuttle, 1957; first published in English 1956.

——. *Thousand Cranes*. Trans. Edward Seidensticker. New York: Vintage Books; first published in English 1958.

——. *Japan, the Beautiful, and Myself*. Trans. Edward Seidensticker. Tokyo: Kodansha International, 1968.

——. *The Sound of the Mountain*. Trans. Edward Seidensticker. New York: Vintage Books, 1996; first published in English 1970.

——. *The Dancing Girl of Izu and Other Stories*. Trans. J. Martin Holman. Washington, D.C.: Counterpoint, 1997.

Keane, Donald. *Dawn to the West — Japanese Literature of the Modern Era*. New York: Columbia University Press, 1998; first published 1984.

——. *The Japanese Discovery of Europe, 1720-1830*. Stanford: Stanford University Press, 1952.

Kerouac, Jack. *On the Road*. New York: Penguin Books, 1976; first published 1955.

Kerr, Alex. *Lost Japan*. Melbourne, Oakland, London, Paris: Lonely Planet Publications, 1996.

——. *Dogs and Demons*. New York: Farrar, Straus and Giroux, 2001.

Kiritani, Elizabeth. *Vanishing Japan*. Tokyo: Charles E. Tuttle, 1995.

Kobayashi, Teruo. *Nihon no Minato no Rekishi* — "The History of Japanese Ports." Tokyo: Seizandō, 1999.

Krakauer, Jon. *Into Thin Air*. Anchor reprint, 1999.

Levy, David. *Beethoven: The Ninth Symphony*. New York: Schirmer Books, 1995.

Mackay, Charles. *Extraordinary Popular Delusions and the Madness of Crowds*. New York: John Wiley & Sons, 1996; first published 1841.

MacLaine, Shirley. *Don't Fall Off the Mountain*. New York: Bantam Books, 1983.

Martin, Bradley K. *Under the Loving Care of the Fatherly Leader — North Korea and the Kim Dynasty*. New York: St Martin's Press, 2004.

Maung, U. Maung. *Burmese Nationalist Movements 1940-1948*. Edinburgh: Kiscadale Publications, 1989.

MacCannell, Dean. *The Tourist*. New York: Schocken Books, 1976.

Mears, Helen. *Mirror for Americans — Japan*. Boston: Houghton Mifflin Company, 1948.

Melly, Jim. *Last Orders, Please — Rod Stewart, The Faces, and the Britain We Forgot*. London: Ebury Press, 2003.

Miller, Henry. *The Air-Conditioned Nightmare*. New York: New Directions Books, 1970; first published 1945.

Miller, Roy Andrew. *The Japanese Language*. Tokyo: Charles E. Tuttle, 1980; first published 1967.

Miyoshi, Masao. *As We Saw Them*. New York, Tokyo, London: Kodansha International, 1994.

Moffett, Sebastian. *Japanese Rules — Why the Japanese Needed Football and How They Got It*. London: Yellow Jersey Press, 2002.

Murakami, Haruki. *Underground*. London: Harvill Press, 2000.

Naitō, Akira and Hozumi, Kazuo. *Edo, the City That Became Tokyo*. Tokyo, New York, London: Kodansha International, 2003.

Neff, Robert. *Japan's Hidden Hot Springs*. Boston, Rutland, Vermont, Tokyo: Tuttle Publishing, 1995.

Nicolaidi, Mike. *The Featherston Chronicles*. Auckland: HarperCollins, 1999.

Norman, E.H. *Origins of the Modern Japanese State*. New York: Random House, 1975.

Orwell, George. *Down and Out in Paris and London*. Penguin edition, 1968; first published 1933.

——. *Inside the Whale and Other Essays*. Penguin edition, 1962.

Pepper, Art and Laurie. *Straight Life*. New York: Schirmer Books, 1979.

Pettinger, Peter. *Bill Evans: How My Heart Sings*. New Haven and London: Yale University Press, 1998.

Plato. *The Republic*. Norwalk, Connecticut: Eastern Press, 1976; first published, in Greek, 1513.

Purchas, Samuel, ed. *Hakluytus Posthumus; or, Purchas His Pilgrimes: Contayning a History of the World, in Sea Voyages & Land-Travells, by Englishmen & Others*. Glasgow: James MacLehose and Sons, 1903-1906; first published 1625.

Reader, Ian. *Religious Violence in Contemporary Japan — The Case of Aum Shinrikyō*. Honolulu: University of Hawaii Press, 2000.

Richie, Donald. *Geisha, Gangster, Neighbor, Nun*. Tokyo, London, New York: Kodansha International, 1987; also as *Different People: Pictures of Some Japanese* (Kodansha America, 1988); and as *Public People, Private People: Portraits of Some Japanese* (Kodansha International; revised edition, 1997).

——. *The Donald Richie Reader — 50 Years of Writing on Japan*. Berkeley: Stone Bridge Press, 2001.

——. *A Hundred Years Of Japanese Film*. New York, Tokyo, Osaka: Kodansha International, 2001.

——. *The Honorable Visitors*. New York, Tokyo, Osaka, London: ICG Muse, 2001.

——. *The Inland Sea*. Berkeley: Stone Bridge Press, 2002; first published, 1971.

Robertson Scott, J. W. *The Foundation of Japan*. New York: D. Appleton and Co., 1922.

Rosenstone, Robert A. *Mirror in the Shrine*. Cambridge, Massachusetts, and London: Harvard University Press, 1988.

Rummel, R.J. *Death by Government*. New Brunswick and London: Transaction Publishers, 1994.

Sabin, Burritt. *A Historical Guide to Yokohama*. Yokohama: Yurindo, 2002.

Satow, Sir Ernest. *A Diplomat in Japan*. New York, Tokyo, Osaka, London: ICG Muse, Inc., 2000; first published 1921.

Seidensticker, Edward. *Kafū the Scribbler — The Life and Writings of Nagai Kafū, 1897–1959*. Stanford: Stanford University Press, 1965.

——. *Low City, High City*. New York: Alfred A. Knopf, 1983.

——. *Tokyo Rising*. New York: Alfred A. Knopf, 1990.

Singer, Kurt. *Mirror, Sword and Jewel*. Tokyo, New York, San Francisco: Kodansha International, 1973.

Smith, Patrick. *Japan — A Reinterpretation*. New York: Vintage Books, 1998.

Steinberg, Michael: *The Symphony — A Listener's Guide*. New York and Oxford: Oxford University Press, 1998; reprint edition.

Suzuki, Bokushi. *Snow Country Tales*. Trans. Jeffrey Hunter and Rose Lesser. Tokyo and New York: Weatherhill, 1986.

Swift, Jonathan. *Gulliver's Travels*. Norwalk, Connecticut: Eastern Press, 1976; first published 1726.

Tachibana, Takashi. *Tanaka Kakuei Kenkyū. Vols. 1 and 2. — "Study of Tanaka Kakuei."* Tokyo: Kōdansha Bunko, 1982.

Theroux, Paul. *The Consul's File*. Boston: Houghton Mifflin, 1972.

——. *Collected Stories*. Penguin edition, 1977.

——. *The Family Arsenal*. Penguin edition, 1977.

——. *The Great Railway Bazaar*. Penguin edition, 1977.

——. *The Old Patagonian Express*. Mariner edition, 1979.

——. *The Mosquito Coast*. Penguin edition, 1982.

——. *The Kingdom by the Sea*. Penguin edition, 1984.

——. *Millroy the Magician*. Penguin edition, 1984.

——. *Sunrise with Seamonsters*. Boston and New York: Houghton Mifflin, 1985.

——. *Riding the Iron Rooster*. Ballantine edition, 1989.

——. *The Happy Isles of Oceania*. Ballantine edition, 1996.

——. *The Pillars of Hercules*. Ballantine edition, 1996.

——. *My Other Life*. Mariner edition, 1996.

——. *Kowloon Tong*. Mariner edition, 1998.

——. "Bottom Feeders" in *The Collected Short Novels*. Penguin edition, 1999.

——. *Picture Palace*. Penguin edition, 1999.

——. *Fresh Air Fiend*. Boston and New York: Houghton Mifflin, 2000.

——. *Sir Vidia's Shadow*. Mariner edition, 2000.

——. *Hotel Honolulu*. Mariner edition, 2002.

Thomas, Lewis. *Late Night Thoughts on Listening to Mahler's Ninth Symphony*. Penguin Books, 1995.

Tuchman, Barbara. *Stilwell and the American Experience in China 1911-45*. New York: Macmillan Publishing, 1970.

Valentino, Benjamin A. *Final Solutions — Mass Killing and Genocide in the Twentieth Century*. Ithaca and London: Cornell University Press, 2004.

Vogel, Ezra F. *Japan as No. 1*. Cambridge, Massachusetts, and London: Harvard University Press, 1979.

Wilde, Oscar. "The Decay of Lying," reprinted in *Letters and Essays*. London: Folio Society, 1993.

Wiley, Peter Booth. *Yankees in the Land of the Gods — Commodore Perry and the Opening of Japan*. New York: Penguin Books, 1991.

Wolff, Christopher. *Johann Sebastian Bach — The Learned Musician*. New York: W. W. Norton, 2000.

Yoshida, Shigeru. *Sekai to Nihon — "Japan and the World."* Tokyo: Chūō Bunko, 1992.

Yoshino, Kōichi. *Fūsen Bakudan — Junkokusan Heiki [Fugō] no Kiroku — "Balloon Bombs — A Record of the Indigenous Weapon 'Fugō.'"* Tokyo: Asahi Shimbunsha, 2000.

General Reference

Gulliver's Travels and Japan: A New Reading. Kyoto: Amherst House, Dōshisha University, 1977. Moonlight Series, No. 4.

Japan — An Illustrated Encyclopedia. Tokyo: Kōdansha, 1993.

Literature of Travel and Exploration — An Encyclopedia. Ed. Jennifer Speake. London and New York: Fitzroy Dearborn, 2003.

New English Bible. Oxford: Oxford University Press, Cambridge University Press, 1970.

Nihongi — Chronicles of Japan from the Earliest Times to A.D. 697. Trans. W.G. Aston. Rutland and Tokyo: Charles E. Tuttle, 1972; first published 1896.

Oxford Companion to Art. Oxford: Oxford University Press, 1970.

Seiki No Isho — "Testaments of the Century." Tokyo: Kōdansha, 1984; first published 1953.

Sugamo Prison Tokyo Japan, APO 500. Eds. Charles F. Smedley, Tommy M. Hight, and Charles W. Patterson. (Privately printed.)

Website References

Chapter 2, "Gulliver Understood," was stimulated by useful material about *Gulliver's Travels* on and via the website www.jaffebros.com.

In Chapter 9, the report of Dr. Takashi Okuma, titled "A Brief History of Japanese Flood Control," which appeared in *World Rivers Review, Vol. 12* (February 1997), was accessed at http://www.irn.org/pubs/wrr/9701/japan.html.

In Chapter 16, data on suicide was accessed at the Tokyo Private Emergency Center website at www.t-pec.co.jp.

In Chapter 20, historical perspective on new religions was gained from the work of Nobutaka Inoue, a professor at Kokugakuin University, which was accessed at http://www2.kokugakuin.ac.jp/ijcc/wp/cpjr/newreligions/inoue.html.

In Chapter 22, perspective on discrimination against Japanese immigrants was gained from Eileen H. Tamura's "Introduction: Asian Americans and Educational History" in *History of Education Quarterly, Vol. 43*, No. 1 (Spring 2003), which was accessed at http://www.historycooperative.org/journals/heq/43.1/tamura.html.

In Chapter 23, the views of Naomoto Okayama were obtained from his speech to the International Society for the Performing Arts Foundation, in Sydney, 14 June 2001, which was accessed at http://www.ispa.org/ideas/okayama.html.

In Chapter 27, Bill Barrette's report "Art and Exchange at Sugamo Prison, 1945–52: Visual Communication in American-occupied Japan," which appeared as JPRI Occasional Paper No. 33 (October 2004), was accessed at http://www.jpri.org/publications.

In Chapter 28, the *Dictionary of New Zealand Biography* entry on Edna Pearce was accessed at http://www.dnzb.govt.nz.

Other

The steal-words listed in Chapter 26 were taken from the 20 February 2005 edition of the *Yomiuri Shimbun*.

INDEX